Management, Change, Strategy and Positive Leadership

Series Editors

Satinder Dhiman
School of Business
Woodbury University
Burbank, CA, USA

Joan Marques
School of Business
Woodbury University
Burbank, CA, USA

More information about this series at http://www.springer.com/series/15772

Joan Marques
Editor

Innovative Leadership in Times of Compelling Changes

Strategies, Reflections and Tools

Springer

Editor
Joan Marques
Woodbury University
Burbank, CA, USA

ISSN 2662-3080 ISSN 2662-3099 (electronic)
Management, Change, Strategy and Positive Leadership
ISBN 978-3-030-67257-7 ISBN 978-3-030-67258-4 (eBook)
https://doi.org/10.1007/978-3-030-67258-4

This Springer imprint is published by the registered company Springer Nature Switzerland AG
The registered company address is: Gewerbestrasse 11, 6330 Cham, Switzerland

Preface

This collective volume was created through a wonderful collaboration of 33 authors, representing six global continents and bringing along a wide range of academic and practical disciplines. This extraordinary work focuses on the need for leaders in personal and professional realms, for-profit and nonprofit, to understand the importance of innovative thinking in order to achieve more responsible progress, safeguard sustainability, and achieve enhanced satisfaction and motivation among stakeholders. This can only happen through an augmented level of design thinking, which will lead to increased innovation, and thus, future-oriented leadership.

Through this book, the widely diverse team of authors presents a multitude of insights and approaches geared toward leading in a more responsible way. They present a set of reflective stances, cautionary points, and roadmaps for leaders who aim to do the right thing. From crisis management to spiritual practices, and from pro-social concepts to social responsibility and sustainability: the common denominator is a collective and concerted effort to developing leadership behaviors and strategies to safeguard generations to come. The profound shift we aim to accomplish with this work is from an understanding that *we* decide what we leave our descendants to one where we understand that we have the earth *in loan* from our progenies, so we should become more respectful and mindful in our planning and decision-making.

Given its emphasis on the unprecedented times we live in, evoking an urgent need for innovative and visionary thinking, this book focuses on three areas, classified into three parts:

1. Leading at a personal level – focused on individuals who want to practice "right livelihood" in any situation they currently reside, whether formally leading or not. The aim will be to increase awareness and reduce ignorance through this section.
2. Leading at a strategic level – focused on those who perform in organizational settings, most likely at the strategic and/or executive level, where decisions are made to affect long-term performance of organizations and their stakeholders.

3. Leading with an innovative mindset – focused on both above-mentioned categories, yet, with the infusion of a visionary approach in actions and decision-making processes.

Part I, titled Personal Leadership to Address Spiritual Challenges and Invoke Design Thinking consists of eight chapters

In Chap. 1, titled, *Awakened Leadership: Leading with Light*, Joan Marques provides a mental and emotional framework to help readers understand how to deal with challenging situations – both – those we can and those we cannot change. After first reflecting on a long-standing concern among members in society when it comes to the short-term, excessive profit focus among leaders, she discusses the concept of wakefulness, briefly analyzes a series of contemporary leadership styles, and subsequently lays out a behavioral roadmap for those interested in adopting a reflective, "awakened" leadership approach.

In Chap. 2, *Mindfulness as a Strategy to Weather Challenges*, Carrie Amani Annabi, considers physiological, sociological, and positive psychological research to help us better understand historic and contemporary studies that feed into business management and leadership disciplines. Her goal is to help readers rationalize and position mindfulness, leading to the understanding that mindfulness is a logical answer for leaders faced with continued challenges.

In Chap. 3, *Inclusive Leadership in an Increasingly Diversified World*, Babar Dharani and Kurt April invite leaders to break free from the fixation on in-groups and out-groups in their work environments. They suggest that exposure to diversity is a foundational step to break free from this fixation. Considering the surge in awareness on diversity management, these authors consider the role of leadership for enhancing diversity and securing inclusion therein to be profound. They explain inclusion as ensuring justice and equity, enabling people to belong to a group while helping them preserve their uniqueness, becoming conscious of one's own privileges, and finding the voice to express our concerns and opinions skillfully when out-grouped.

In Chap. 4, *Leading Reflectively: Treading the Noble Eightfold Path*, Joan Marques presents leadership as a personal choice and discusses – within the scope of Buddhist psychology – the four noble truths, comprising the noble eightfold path, as a useful strategy to identify a set of behaviors that can reduce suffering at the personal and societal level. In each of the elements of the eightfold path, she presents an individual who exerted strong personal leadership, often at the odds of all other opinions, and established a positive change internally as well as for his or her society.

In Chap. 5, *Innovative Leadership: Tools and Techniques to Acquire Innovative and Inspiring Ideas*, M.S. Rao offers innovative tools and techniques to acquire innovative and inspiring ideas. He explains the power of our subconscious mind to acquire creative and inventive ideas and unlock our hidden potential. He thereby differentiates between creativity and innovation and draws a blueprint to achieve creativity and innovation. He also explains and elaborates on innovative leadership, thereby outlining the characteristics of innovative leaders to the likings of Benjamin

Franklin, Thomas Edison, Albert Einstein, Bill Gates, Larry Ellison, Elon Musk, and Mark Zuckerberg.

In Chap. 6, *Transcending Emerging Barriers through Patience,* Varinder Kumar and Satinder Dhiman appraise the benefits of patience as a leadership skill that is fast becoming scarce in today's fast-paced, ever-changing environment. In their assessment of the advantages of patience in leadership practices, these authors point out that patience augurs inner peace and facilitates dealing with sufferings and stressors effectively, helps to pursue long-term goals persistently, and promotes overall well-being and flourishing. They further emphasize that patience acts as a modulating buffer between experience and expression of negative emotions and prevents interpersonal differences spiraling down to expression of anger and hatred.

In Chap. 7, *"The Soft overcomes the Hard": Inspirations for Leadership in the Twenty-First Century from Daoism*, Alicia Hennig and Lena Schiller make a case for gender diversity in leadership by reminding us that women in developed countries are still exposed to discrimination and gender inequality at the workplace in a number of professional fields. As the broad question framing this chapter, they discuss what kind of leadership and management we actually need in regard to work in the twenty-first century and what kind of values should guide our leadership approach accordingly. They subsequently propose an alternative way of leadership based on values and principles derived from Chinese philosophy, in specific Daoism, therein emphasizing the feminine, yin 阴, over the masculine, yang 阳, as this could open up a new way for a more inclusive leadership approach.

In Chap. 8, *Nurturing Empathy*, Svetlana Holt discusses empathy as a critical leadership skill, which can grow only through personal relationships. Listening, she explains, is the centerpiece of empathy and is vital for leaders of all styles. As any skill, it should be trained through consistent practice. She perceives the need to nurture empathy as a critical pathway in today's increasingly immediate, intimate world driven by rapid change, where everyone has to be proficient at identifying opportunities and solving problems.

Part II, titled Leading Innovatively to Address Strategic and Spiritual Challenges consists of seven chapters

In Chap. 9, *Inclusive Leadership in a Creatively Compelling World*, Ginger Grant and Cheryl De Ciantis alert us that the changes we now see, unprecedented in our lifetimes, are calling for extraordinary response and commitment to action. They describe and elaborate on five areas of unprecedented opportunity for leaders to redefine greatness for the coming generations: embracing change as imperative while committing to creating nodes of needed stability; putting people first by prioritizing the value of empathy and getting real about issues of power regarding who gets what and why; commitment to values by "walking the talk"; making it real by ensuring all stakeholders have a place at the table; and re-mything ourselves: using every avenue available to us – from science to the arts – to re-create the narratives that valorize the truths we wish to live as humans within an interconnected web of existence.

In Chap. 10, *Understanding and Reformulating Mental Models*, Babar Dharani and Kurt April explain the use and pitfalls of mental models as a point of attention for leaders. Since mental models are created using prior information, they are susceptible to errors if the information is incomplete, false, miscommunicated, or misinterpreted, or if correct information is ignored. They are also at risk of an oversimplification of reality, stale knowledge, and misapplication of knowledge. Dharani and April point out that leaders have the critical responsibility to facilitate changes to mental models of the followers. They believe that – by limiting stumbling blocks to reforming mental models, and facilitating their evolution through enablers – an optimal degree of flexibility in mental models can be aspired toward to ensure their continued usefulness from a self-leadership perspective.

In Chap. 11, *Nurturing Sustainability as a Future-Oriented Strategy*, Roger Hilton and Diane McCann make the point that leaders must align themselves – both spiritually and emotionally – and focus on delivering sustainable outcomes for the businesses that they lead. They stress that in any business, the commitment of all stakeholders including the Board, employees, and suppliers means an obligation to deliver quality and service excellence to its customers to ensure satisfaction and long-term loyalty while ensuring meeting all necessary compliance and government regulations where applicable. They also explain that consciousness means being able to make choices, not from a reactive mind but an emotionally attuned place that supports the protecting of the planet and ensures all people enjoy peace and prosperity and as well economic survival.

In Chap. 12, *Letting Go as a Liberation*, Pamela Kay Caldwell and Oluseye David Akintunde express concern about the research outcomes pointing out poor leadership in many institutions and systems. They dive into the questions: (a) Why is it, that regardless of many theories, approaches, and styles we have, that we still continue to have to discuss the idea of ineffective leadership and innovative leadership? (b) How as business scholars and professional do we move into a more effective styles of leadership? (c) What do we embrace to have effective and responsible leaders and leadership? These authors explain in their chapter the need for letting go to be liberated.

In Chap. 13, *Leading with a Moral Compass: Virtuous Leadership and Health Management in Turbulent Times: Meeting the Challenges of New Pandemics*, Aikaterini Grimani and George Gotsis focus on some critical insights acquired through the Covid-19 pandemic related to our medical, social, and economic systems. They particularly stress the need to reinvent the healthcare systems to meet the new reality. They underscore that in this era of intense innovation, collaboration, and problem solving, leadership is key to mobilizing people who are facing new demands and must receive motivation and direction on how to deal with adversity while continuing to deliver critical services.

In Chap. 14, *Leadership as Merit Making: The Case of Myanmar and Applications for Western Organizations*, J. Andrew Morris, Aung Chan Aye, David Lingelbach, and Wah Wah Than Oo present the refreshing perspective that Western leadership theory has overemphasized the role of the leader. As a result, they assert, leaders have become overly self-focused and self-interested. These authors suggest that leadership grounded in Buddhist thought can help overcome these problems. Drawing upon our experience as educators in Myanmar (Burma), they build upon the Buddhist concepts of merit and merit-making to present a version of leadership that inspires collaboration and common purpose.

In Chap. 15, *Living the Power Shift in Business and Beyond*, Jo Aschenbrenner aims on expanding awareness about the power shift needed in the world of work. Her vision is to let self-organization for-purpose flourish and ultimately to safeguard mankind's well-being and the sustainment of planet Earth. Aschenbrenner claims that this shift will require new rules – rules in service of freedom – inside of our organizations, as well as intrapersonally, inside the people doing the work. She subsequently presents the new organizational form of the For-Purpose Enterprise and discusses how individuals can calm down their anxious ego and grant purpose more power in business.

Part III, titled Leading with a Future-Oriented Mind consists of seven chapters. In Chap. 16, *Crisis Preparedness as a Sustainability Strategy*, Robert S. Fleming considers how organizational crisis preparedness strategies, developed and implemented in the interest of ensuring organizational resilience in times of crisis, can also contribute to achieving an organization's commitment to sustainability. Fleming considers it important to recognize – aside from global pandemics such as Covid-19 – the more frequent, but less severe and consequential, future crisis situations and events that organizations should anticipate and prepare for in their strategic planning activities. He discusses the role of crisis preparedness within the overall crisis management process and how organizations can prepare to "weather the storm" of future crisis situations and events through informed decision-making and planning.

In Chap. 17, *Imagination and Communication Toward Future Realization*, Manuel Y. Fernandez and Vram Ismailyan focus on how imagination can lead to great innovation, if leaders demonstrate this trait themselves or help foster an environment that will unearth the inner creativity that lives inside everyone. Fernandez and Ismailyan highlight a few methods that allow people to demonstrate their inner creativity through empathy, design thinking, and diversity. They consider the critical message in this chapter to be, the need for leaders to be imaginative when it comes to future trends, to keep themselves informed and to communicate, not only toward learning and understanding facts and trends, but also in making ideas understandable to team members.

In Chap. 18, *Heading for the Future with the Proper Mindset*, Victor Senaji Anyanje and Thomas Anyanje Senaji elaborate on the need for leaders to be imaginative when it comes to future trends, to keep themselves informed and to communicate, not only toward learning and understanding facts and trends, but also in making ideas understandable to team members. Senaji and Senaji stress that leaders have imperiled themselves, their followers, and the society through failure to positively imagine, communicate, and clarify the path to the desired future state or the organizations they lead. They therefore explore imagination, communication, and future realization guided by questions such as, "Why is imagination important?",

"How can communication be improved?", and "How can the execution be unlocked to realize the future?".

In Chap. 19, *Nurturing Creativity in a Culture of Care*, Ginger Grant reminds us that we are in the throes of finding our "new normal". Organizations depend upon capable leadership to guide them through these unprecedented changes. And yet, even some of the best companies are failing to adapt to change and implement their strategic plans successfully, especially in these times of economic turmoil. Grant shares the finding that most senior leaders believe that the next generation of managers is not ready to take over as leaders. She highlights the gap in leadership capabilities among frontline managers and emerging leaders and in particular attributes this gap to lack of training programs or programs of poor quality. She also underscores that these statistics have significant implications for leadership develop programs.

In Chap. 20, *Community-Based Responsible Leadership and Social Value Creation in Social Enterprise Context*, Susanna L. M. Chui and Nazha Gali propose a model of community-based responsible leadership which focuses on moral identification at individual and team levels within the context of social entrepreneurship. They discuss the organizing principles of a community and the relevance of studying responsible leadership within the context of social entrepreneurship. They then conceptualize integrating theories of social identity model of leadership, collective action, and moral identity, a multilevel model of collective responsible leadership that results in social value creation.

In Chap. 21, *Design Thinking in Contemporary Political Leadership: Lessons Learned from Angela Merkel*, Claude Helene Mayer and James L. Kelley explore the phenomenon of design leadership, a conceptual component in design theory, which provides a useful template for leaders in an ever-changing world. By way of illustration, the authors focus on the life and work of the famous German political leader, Angela Merkel, who has become one of the most influential, global, woman leaders in world history. A psychobiographical approach to Merkel's life and leadership is taken to explore design leadership. Findings provide insight into successful global governance in terms of design leadership.

In Chap. 22, *The FuturePerfect Organization: Driven by Quantum-Thinking*, William Guillory explains that a FuturePerfect Organization is comprised of leadership that anticipates to future business paradigms with a high degree of accuracy. The ability to accurately anticipate future business paradigms is called quantum thinking. Guillory affirms that we are in the very active stages of transitioning from the paradigm of Human Potential to Technology Integration. This ability applies equally to predicting future shifts in cultural and societal paradigms. At present, the possibility is a societal/global transformation from a survival-driven consciousness to compatibility. Guillory discusses the model of a FuturePerfect organization for the twenty-first century, including the steps required to successfully implement this transition.

On behalf of all the 33 contributors to these chapters, I hope that this extensive view on leading with future well-being of our planet and those who come after us will assist readers from various walks of life to determine their career choices with a responsible, mindful, and empathetic approach – whenever and wherever possible.

Burbank, CA, USA Joan Marques

Contents

About the Editor

Joan Marques has reinvented herself from a successful media and social entrepreneur in Suriname, South America, to an innovative "edupreneur" (educational entrepreneur) in California, USA. Her entrepreneurial career spans over four decades and includes the creation and successful management of companies in public relations and advertising, import and export, real estate, media productions, and a non-profit, focused on women's advancement. In the USA, she has been a co-founder of the *Business Renaissance Institute* and the *Academy of Spirituality and Professional Excellence* (ASPEX).

Based on her impressive career and ongoing influence, she was awarded the highest state decoration of her home country, Suriname: Commander (Commandeur) in the Honorary Order of the Yellow Star, in 2015. That same year, she was also awarded the Dr. Nelle Becker-Slaton Pathfinder Award from the Association of Pan-African Doctoral Scholars in Los Angeles for her exemplary and groundbreaking professional performance. In 2019, she was awarded the Kankantrie Life Time Achievement Award for her accomplishments in Education from the Suriname American Network Inc. in Miami, FL. In 2016, she was granted the Faculty Scholarly-Creative Award as well as the Faculty Ambassador Award, both awarded by Woodbury University's Faculty Association.

Joan holds a PhD in Social Sciences (focus: *Buddhist Psychology in Management*) from Tilburg University's Oldendorff Graduate School; and an EdD in Organizational Leadership (focus: *Workplace Spirituality*) from Pepperdine University's Graduate School of Education and Psychology. She also holds an MBA from Woodbury University and a BSc in Business Economics from MOC, Suriname. Additionally, she has completed post-doctoral work at Tulane University's Freeman School of Business.Dr. Marques is a frequent speaker and presenter at academic and professional venues. In 2016, she gave a TEDx-Talk at College of the Canyons in California, titled "An Ancient Path Towards a Better Future", in which she analyzed the Noble Eightfold Path, one of the foundational Buddhist practices, within the realm of contemporary business performance. In recent years, she has conducted presentations and workshops on multiple forums, such as at the management, spirituality, and religion research colloquia at the Academy of Management Annual Meetings in 2018 and 2019 on "Phenomenology as a Qualitative Research Method"; a keynote address titled "Ethical Leadership: How Morals Influence Your Communication" at the Center for Communication and Public Relations, in Paramaribo, Suriname; and an interactive workshop with thought leaders and development coaches at the Knowledge and Expertise Center Suriname, titled "On Leadership, Ethics and Social Responsibility". In 2019 and 2020, she also represented her home country Suriname at the annual CALIFEST literary festival in Los Angeles, where she conducted workshops on successful publishing. In 2016, she presented at the Kravis Leadership Institute at Claremont McKenna College on female leadership during the annual Women and Leadership Alliance (WLA) conference, resulting in the collective work "Women's Leadership Journeys: Stories, Research and Novel Perspectives" (Routledge, 2019) in which she contributed the chapter, "Courage: Mapping the Leadership Journey". Dr. Marques further conducts regular presentations at the Academy of Management and at business venues in Los Angeles as well as for professional audiences in Miami and Suriname.Joan's research interests pertain to awakened leadership, Buddhist psychology in management, and workplace spirituality. Her works have been widely published and cited in both academic and popular venues. She has written more than 150 scholarly articles, which were published in prestigious scholarly journals such as *The Journal of Business Ethics, Business and Society*, *International Journal of Organizational Analysis*, *Leadership & Organization Development Journal*, *The International Journal of Management Education*, *Journal of Communication Management*, *Journal of Management Development, Organization Development Journal*, and *Human Resource Development Quarterly*. Dr. Marques has (co)authored and (co) edited more than 30 books, among which, New Horizons in Positive Leadership and Change (Springer 2020) and Social Entrepreneurship and Corporate Social Responsibility (Springer 2020); The Routledge Companion to Inclusive Leadership (2020); Lead with Heart in Mind (Springer 2019); The Routledge Companion to Management and Workplace Spirituality, Engaged Leadership: Transforming Through Future-Oriented Design (with Satinder Dhiman – Springer 2018); Ethical Leadership, Progress with a Moral Compass (Routledge 2017); Leadership, Finding Balance Between Acceptance and Ambition (Routledge 2016); Leadership Today: Practices for Personal and Professional Performance (with Satinder Dhiman – Springer 2016); Business and Buddhism (Routledge 2015); and Leadership and Mindful Behavior: Action, Wakefulness, and Business (Palgrave MacMillan 2014).Joan currently serves as Dean at Woodbury University's School of Business, in Burbank, California, where she works on infusing and nurturing the concept of "Business with a Conscience" into internal and external stakeholders. She is also a Full Professor of Management and teaches business courses related to leadership, ethics, creativity, social entrepreneurship, and organizational behavior in graduate and undergraduate programs.Dr. Marques is a member of the executive committee of the Management, Spirituality, and Religion interest group of the Academy of Management, where she serves as the officer for Membership and Community Building. As such, she conducted workshops on qualitative research methods to global cohorts of doctoral students in 2018 and 2019.

Notes on Contributors

Oluseye David Akintunde, from Oyo State, Nigeria, has many years of experience in education. Back in his home country, he taught Civics Education at several colleges, including Oritamefa Baptist Model School, Total Garden, Nigeria. He decided to further his education and experience global travel, which brought him to China, where he obtained two master's level degrees: Master of Law (International Relations) from Jilin University and an MBA from Changchun University of Science and Technology. He is currently a Management Science and Engineering Doctoral Student at the School of Finance and Economics of Jiangsu University in China.

Carrie Amani Annabi, PhD, is a Senior Lecturer (Associate Professor) at Royal College of Surgeons in Ireland (RCSI) Institute of Leadership. She has a demonstrated history of working in the higher education and industry, with rich and versatile skills in negotiation, business planning, operations management, analytical skills, and creating effective learning and development strategies. Her research is focused on business/logistics and supply chain and change management and healthcare education. She has authored several peer-reviewed publications and white papers. In addition to holding a PhD and three master's degrees, she has also acquired contract law and litigation experience within the UK court/legal system.

Victor Senaji Anyanje is an advocate of the High Court of Kenya and a commissioner for Oaths specializing in telecommunications, commercial, and family law. He holds a Master of Law in Information Communication Technology from the Open University of Tanzania and the United Kingdom Telecommunications Academy; Certification in International Space and Cyber Law; Institute du Troit de l'Espace des Telecommunications, International Humanitarian Law; ICIL, International Strategic Aspects for Internet Governance and Innovations and Broadband Internet and Future Networks from the International Telecommunication Union; Switzerland, a Bachelor of Laws from the Catholic University of Eastern Africa; Kenya and a post-graduate diploma from the Kenya School of Law. He is also engaged in assignments in academia and has been previously retained as a part-time lecturer at the Africa Nazarene University teaching evidence law and human rights law. He also volunteers in children's matters across a wide spectrum ranging NGOs and private clients including through awareness creation, capacity building, and legal representation. On the ancillary, he is a writer and an English editor.

Kurt April, PhD, MSc, MBA, is the Allan Gray Chair, an Endowed Professorship, and Director of the Allan Gray Centre for Values-Based Leadership, specializing in leadership, diversity, and inclusion at the University of Cape Town's Graduate School of Business (South Africa, 1998–present), Adjunct Faculty at Saïd Business School, University of Oxford (UK, 2001–present), and is an Orchestrator and Faculty member of Duke Corporate Education, Duke University (USA, 2008–present).

Jo Aschenbrenner, PhD, has 20 years of experience as a lawyer and coach, and is a former Freshfields lawyer. She is currently a partner of Encode.org (Holacracy Practice), a business coach and entrepreneur, and a syndicate lawyer at the Bucerius Law School. She has made it her professional mission to transform the conventional power structures inside organizations. As a business coach, she encourages people to embark upon careers filled with purpose. For further information, check her LinkedIn profile or her website www.for-purpose.de.

Aung Chan Aye is an assistant lecturer of Management at Monywa University of Economics, Myanmar. He holds Bachelor of Commerce, Master of Commerce degrees from Monywa University of Economics, Myanmar, and a Master of Business Administration degree from Panyapiwat Institute of Management (PIM), Thailand. He has worked as a tutor at the Department of Management Studies of Sagaing Co-operative University and as a tutor in the Department of Management Studies, Monywa University of Economics. He has had two articles published in an academic journal, *TNI Journal of Business Administration and Languages*.

Pamela Kay Caldwell, DM, is a business professor at Jilin University Lambton College, Changchun, China, Jilin Province. She is also the owner of the KAM Group, as well as a speaker, author, and certified life and integrative health coach. She has created a framework for navigating transitions that she has coined, "My Greatest Me: Becoming, Being, Sustaining". She uses this concept in her coaching practice. She wrote about this concept in her soon to be released book, "I Know What the World is Missing…My Greatest Me!". She discusses in the book how she has used this framework while navigating her wellness journey and life as an expat. The work further discusses how individuals and organizations can use this framework to navigate transitions as well.

Susanna L. M. Chui, PhD, is an assistant professor of the Department Management at the Hang Seng University of Hong Kong. Susanna has completed her PhD in Leadership at the Durham University Business School (UK). Her publications cover research areas in leadership, social entrepreneurship, and social impact measurement. Her research experience extends to examining social impact measurement, CSR, stakeholder management, and human resources issues. Her teaching encompasses leadership, social entrepreneurship, corporate social responsibility (CSR), business ethics, and organization behavior.

Cheryl De Ciantis, PhD, is co-founder of Kairios, an independent human development research and practice group. She is co-author of the Kairios Values Perspectives theory and survey; and of *What's Important: Understanding and Working with Values Perspectives* (2014). Cheryl served as Senior Faculty and Director of the European Campus of the Center for Creative Leadership in Brussels and has consulted extensively in public, private, and educational institutions and across business sectors as a coach and designer/facilitator of in-depth experiential creative/reflective development methodologies. An artist and writer, Cheryl obtained her Doctorate in Mythological Studies and Depth Psychology from Pacifica Graduate Institute. Cheryl's most recent book, *The Return of Hephaistos: Reconstructing the Fragmented Mythos of the Makers* (2019), explores the mythic intersection of art and technology, and the powerful archetype that emanates from the core of current societal attitudes toward both. Cheryl lives with her work and life partner, Dr. Kenton Hyatt, in Tucson, Arizona.

Babar Dharani, PhD, is a senior lecturer of the Allan Gray Centre (AGC) for values-based leadership at the University of Cape Town Graduate School of Business, South Africa. He became a member of the Institute of Chartered Accountants in England and Wales (ICAEW) in 2004 and became a fellow of the ICAEW in 2015. His career started at Deloitte in London, and he excelled in the diamond industry in his capacity as CFO in Dubai. His interest in finance and organizational psychology is founded on the belief that managing finance departments require technical knowledge and also insights into organizational psychology. He believes that this complementary interest supported his career and laid foundations for his personalized approach to research.

Satinder Dhiman, PhD, EdD, has delivered pioneer contributions to the field of transformational leadership, workplace spirituality, workplace well-being, sustainability, and fulfillment in the personal and professional arena. He holds a PhD in Social Sciences from Tilburg University, Netherlands; an EdD in Organizational Leadership from Pepperdine University, Los Angeles; an MBA from West Coast University, Los Angeles; and a master's degree in commerce from Punjab University, Chandigarh, India, having earned the Gold Medal. He has also completed advanced executive leadership programs at Harvard, Stanford, and Wharton, and has done over 50 conference presentations and more than 50 invited keynotes, plenary sessions, distinguished key guest lectures, and creative workshops – nationally and internationally; published over 60 peer-reviewed journal articles and book chapters; authored, coauthored, coedited, and translated over 30 management, leadership, spirituality, and accounting related books and research monographs. He currently serves as associate dean, chair, and director of the MBA program as well as as professor of Management at Woodbury University, Burbank, California.

Manuel Y. Fernandez is an Investment Control Manager at Capital Group. He is an innovative thinker that enjoys challenging the status quo in efforts to find better and more efficient methods to accomplish outcomes so that associates can provide the greatest value to organizations. Through the thoughtful utilization and combination of practices such as design thinking, business analysis, project management, and agile product development, he has successfully led teams to achieve various organization goals. Manny holds an MBA from Woodbury University and has developed digital products for critical middle office teams that help ensure compliance and facilitate the execution of trades at a financial firm that manages over $2 trillion in assets. In his free time, he enjoys spending time with his twin daughters.

Robert S. Fleming, PhD, is a professor of management and past dean of the Rohrer College of Business at Rowan University. He has an affiliate appointment as a professor of crisis and emergency management. The focus of his research, teaching, and consulting has been on enhancing organizational effectiveness. He is frequently called upon by print, radio, and television media sources as a subject matter expert on an array of issues related to business continuity, emergency preparedness, and crisis management. He has over 40 years of operational and administrative crisis management experience, including serving in roles at the local, regional, state, and national levels. His books include *Effective Fire and Emergency Services Administration*, *Survival Skills for the Fire Chief*, and *Emergency Incident Media Coverage*.

Nazha Gali, PhD, is currently a Postdoctoral Research Fellow at the Institute for Research on Innovation and Science. She completed her PhD in 2018 in Management, Entrepreneurship from Durham University Business School, UK. She has worked on diverse research projects in entrepreneurship, social entrepreneurship, corporate social responsibility, corporate governance, team leadership emergence, and disruptiveness of research. She is an expert in mixed research methods and econometric analysis. She has published in peer-reviewed academic journals and presented her work at international conferences. She has taught several undergraduate courses such as introduction to management, human resource management, entrepreneurship, and leadership as well as graduate courses such as sustainability entrepreneurship and organizational behavior. Lastly, several of her students have won international awards at international conferences.

George Gotsis, PhD, is a professor of Philosophy and History of Economics at the Department of History and Philosophy of Science, National and Kapodistrian University of Athens, Greece. He holds two PhD degrees in Political Science from Panteion University of Social and Political Sciences, Greece, and in Economics from National and Kapodistrian University of Athens, Greece, respectively. He teaches history of economic thought, principles of economics, organizational behavior and leadership, ethics and human resource management, and ethics and philosophy of HRM in business organizations. His main research interests comprise, among others, diversity management ethics, emerging leadership theories, workplace spirituality, religion in business, and organizational politics.

Ginger Grant, PhD, is an associate dean, Applied Research at Humber College Institute of Technology and Advanced Learning. As an innovation researcher and academic entrepreneur and activist, Ginger's passion is creativity in business – the design, development, and implementation of narrative game plans that transform corporate culture and drive employee engagement and high-performance teams for competitive advantage. She has held senior leadership positions and consulted in a variety of fields including engineering, telecommunications, education, transportation, government, law, software development, gaming, and the creative industries. She is a sought-after international speaker on corporate culture, high-performance teams, and creativity/innovation and has given several TED talks.

Aikaterini Grimani, PhD, is a research fellow at Behavioral Science Group of Warwick Business School, University of Warwick, UK, and a member of the National Institute for Health Research (NIHR) Policy Research Unit (PRU) in Behavioral Science. She holds a PhD degree from the Department of History and Philosophy of Science, National and Kapodistrian University of Athens. She has obtained a BA in sociology, an MSc in Healthcare Management, and an MSc in Cognitive Science. Her main research interests include employee relations, organizational behavior, health and safety at the workplace, worker well-being, inclusive workplaces, and leadership. She has 13 scientific publications in refereed journals, 3 chapter books, and 1 book.

William Guillory, PhD, is CEO of Innovations International and Executive Director of the Center for Creativity and Inquiry. He is a respected scientist as well as an authority on diversity, empowerment, leadership, creativity and innovation, and quantum thinking. His most recent cutting-edge program explores the subject of "work-life quality" from a powerful new perspective. Dr. Guillory has presented over 4,000 seminars throughout corporate America, Great Britain, Europe, Mexico, and Canada. He has facilitated seminars for over 300 corporations including the senior leadership of American Airlines, Amoco, Avon, Daimler-Chrysler, Dow Chemical, Eastman Kodak, Electronic Data Systems, Hewlett Packard, Kellogg USA, Lockheed-Martin, Merck, Proctor & Gamble, Sempra Energy, and more.

Alicia Hennig, PhD, is an associate professor of Business Ethics at Southeast University, Nanjing, China. She is an interdisciplinary cross-cultural researcher working on Chinese philosophy and its application in business and management.

Roger Hilton, PhD, is currently CEO of Lean Sigma Institute, an education management consultancy. He previously has experience across a range of manufacturing and service industries in quality and risk management. He has lectured at graduate levels and undertaken research into sustainable continuous improvement. Roger is a Doctor of Business Administration, Master of Econometrics and Applied Statistics, and a Chartered Fellow of the RSS (UK). Roger has coached executives in personal change, facilitated improvement projects and has championed the deployment of continuous improvement. Roger believes a necessary condition for continuous improvement is for everyone to understand their subconscious behaviours and patterns.

Svetlana Holt, EdD., has been teaching management, leadership, organizational behavior, and strategy undergraduate and graduate courses at Woodbury University School of Business since 2004. She has broad experience in corporate training for performance improvement, quality control, small business administration, database management, student support, and new curricula design and evaluation. She is a registered practitioner for Yale's Mayer-Salovey-Caruso emotional intelligence model of organizational development. Her research and publications topics include empathy in leadership, leadership in multicultural settings, emotional intelligence as it relates to organizational performance, international marketing and entrepreneurship, leading the millennial generation, and academic achievement in higher education.

Vram Ismailyan is senior vice president of eReceivables focused on Technology, Media, and Telecommunication at Wells Fargo bank. For over 13 years, he has been a noteworthy leader in the payments and payments technology space. He is also trained in payroll and workers' compensation fundamentals. He was a TED Talks presenter at the 2018 Merchant Advisory Group on card payment cost optimization and cybersecurity. He has consistently been honored by Wells Fargo as a top performer over the last decade for his leadership contributions. He is a Cum Laude graduate with a BS degree in Business Management from Woodbury University and currently resides in Glendale, CA.

James L. Kelley has over a decade's experience in the publishing worlds of psychiatry, history, theology, and vocational studies. As a researcher, he has published books and articles in various fields since 2009, when *A Realism of Glory* (Rollinsford, NH: Orthodox Research Institute) appeared. Since then, his translations, essays, and monographs have been published in the USA, Canada, France, Romania, and Greece. He has taught at East Central University (Ada, OK) and the University of Oklahoma (Norman, OK).

Varinder Kumar is working as an associate professor in Commerce in the Post Graduate Department of Commerce, Government College, Kapurthala (North India). He has authored more than 20 books on business communication, soft skills, human values, and professional ethics, which are prescribed in course syllabi at different Indian universities. His areas of interest include spirituality at workplace, transformational leadership, and creativity.

David Lingelbach, PhD, MS, MIT, is an associate professor of entrepreneurship at the University of Baltimore's Merrick School of Business. His research interests include oligarch studies and entrepreneurship in resource-constrained, uncertain environments. He has authored or co-authored ten articles in journals including *Journal of Management Inquiry*, *Venture Capital: An International Journal of Entrepreneurial Finance*, *International Journal of Entrepreneurship and Innovation*, and *Asia Pacific Business Review*. He is co-author of the textbook, *Entrepreneurship in Africa: Context and Perspectives* (2020). He founded UB's innovative Entrepreneurship Fellows Program in 2011. He has been awarded a Fulbright grant to Myanmar in 2018–19, selected as a Fulbright Specialist in Colombia, and nominated for an Andrew Carnegie Fellowship.

Joan Marques, PhD, EdD, serves as a dean and professor of Management at Woodbury University's School of Business. She holds a PhD from Tilburg University and an EdD from Pepperdine University's Graduate School of Education and Psychology. She teaches, presents, and writes on workplace spirituality, ethical leadership, Buddhist psychology in management, and leadership awareness. She has been widely published in scholarly as well as practitioner-based journals and has authored/co-authored and edited more than 31 books on management and leadership topics. Her most recent single-authored book is *Lead with Heart in Mind* (Springer, 2019).

Claude-Hélène Mayer, Dr habil., PhD, PhD, is a professor in Industrial and Organisational Psychology at the Department of Industrial Psychology and People Management at the University of Johannesburg; an adjunct professor at the European University Viadrina in Frankfurt (Oder), Germany; and a senior research associate at Rhodes University, Grahamstown, South Africa. She holds PhDs in Psychology, Management, and Cultural Anthropology as well as a Habilitation (European University Viadrina, Germany) in Psychology with focus on work, organizational, and cultural psychology. Her research areas are transcultural mental health and well-being, sense of coherence, shame, transcultural conflict management and mediation, women in leadership, constellation work, coaching, and psychobiography.

Diane McCann director of Beyond the Ordinary, has run seminars internationally, specifically for men, women or couples for over 30 years. Diane trained in many fields, including iridology, kinesiology, energetic medicine and many more. A pioneer, she brought to Australia many leading lights in their field (Robert Kiyosaki, Deepak Chopra, Dr Darren Weissman). She promoted many new innovative workshops and modalities in Australia. She helped develop the first curriculum for the Australian Institute of Rebirthing and took that modality into Yatala Prison; none of the men she worked with reoffended. She had a private practice for over 50 years. Her passion is to raise the consciousness of those she works with, leading to peace on the planet, which is her vision.

J. Andrew Morris received his PhD from the University of South Carolina in organizational behavior and international business. He is a professor of Management at the California State University Channel Islands' Martin V. Smith School of Business and Economics. Andrew has published numerous articles and cases in such journals as the *Academy of Management Review*, *Human Relations*, and the *Journal of Management Education*. His current research interests include emotions in the workplace and leader humility. He was awarded a Fulbright grant to Myanmar 2019–2020.

Wah Wah Than Oo, BCom (Hons), MCom, PhD, is an associate professor in the Department of Management Studies at the Monywa University of Economics, Sagaing Region, Myanmar. She is also a faculty member of the MBA Programme of Monywa University of Economics. She has authored several articles in various research journals. Her research interests include organizational commitment and customer service. Currently, she provides management training to local businesses and government and non-government organizations.

M. S. Rao, PhD, is the founder of MSR Leadership Consultants, India. He is an International Leadership Guru with 39 years of experience and the author of 48 books including the award-winning *See the Light in You*. He is a C-suite advisor and a sought-after keynote speaker globally. He brings a strategic eye and long-range vision given his multifaceted professional experience including military, teaching, training, research, consultancy, and philosophy. He is passionate about serving and making a difference in the lives of others. He trains a new generation of leaders through leadership education and publications.

Lena Schiller is Co-Director, House of Leadership. As an entrepreneur, author, and lecturer, she has been working for more than 10 years on the future of work and the impact and co-creation possibilities of the digital transformation of the economy and society. After studying political science, American studies, and Italian studies as well as a few years in the Danish corporate world, she has been active in the German start-up scene since 2009. She was co-founder and managing director of the "betahaus Hamburg" and built a frequented bridge between creative start-ups and the corporate world. She accompanied organizations in the implementation of intrapreneurship projects and wrote the book *New Business Order* (Hanser 2014). At the Goethe Business School, she is responsible for the Digital Transformation Division and the Female Leadership Program.

Thomas Anyanje Senaji is a professor of Strategy and Knowledge Management and a researcher in strategy, leadership, organizations behavior and change. He holds a PhD, MBA, BSc (Electrical Engineering) and is currently the deputy vice chancellor in charge of Academics and Research at The East African University, Kenya. He previously served as associate professor and PhD program leader at Kenya Methodist University. He is an international consultant in Information and Communications Technologies (ICT) and Broadband communication. He has published extensively in journals, book chapters, and several consultancy reports. Prof. Senaji is a founding member of the Africa Academy of management where he serves in the membership committee and a member of the Academy of Management. He has over 30 years' experience in academia, business management, and telecommunications/ICT spans over business and academia. He previously worked at Kenya Institute of Mass Communication, Telkom Kenya Limited, Alcatel East Africa, and Jamii Telcom Limited. He is a professional engineer, member of the Institution of Engineers of Kenya, and member of the Academy of Management. He is also a choral music composer, arranger, and conductor.

Part I
Personal Leadership to Address Spiritual Challenges and Invoke Design Thinking

Chapter 1
Awakened Leadership: Leading with Light

Joan Marques

Abstract This chapter provides a mental and emotional framework to help readers understand how to deal with challenging situations, both, those we can and those we cannot change. It reflects first on the long-standing concern among members in society when it comes to the behaviors of leaders. The short-term, excessive profit focus at the expense of the well-being of living stakeholders is at the core of this concern. This chapter subsequently introduces us to the need for and the concept of wakefulness, briefly analyzes a series of contemporary leadership styles, and subsequently lays out a behavioral road map for those interested in adopting a reflective, "awakened" leadership approach, built on value-based, ethical, trust-driven, visionary, respectful, passionate, committed, compassionate, kind, forgiving, courageous, loving, attentive, inspired, authentic, connected, multidimensional, fulfilled, initiative-oriented, and change-focused qualities.

Keywords Wakefulness · Awakened leadership · Awareness · Change · Reflection

Introduction

There is an emerging awareness in society about a problem area which future leaders will have to correct. This problem area pertains to an increasing degree of inefficiency in business practices and processes, which can become very costly in a progressively globalizing corporate environment. Current and future leaders will have to be able to tackle this problem on multiple fronts simultaneously. A little over a decade ago, Hannah and Zatzick (2008) captured the societal shock of the first decade in this century, the manifestation of massive unethical practices in corporations, by asserting, "In the past few years corporate America has witnessed [...] the largest dollar level of fraud, accounting manipulations and unethical behavior in corporate history" (p. 361). Around the same time, Davis (2009) added the finishing

J. Marques (✉)
Woodbury University, Burbank, CA, USA
e-mail: joan.marques@woodbury.edu

J. Marques (ed.), *Innovative Leadership in Times of Compelling Changes*, Management, Change, Strategy and Positive Leadership, https://doi.org/10.1007/978-3-030-67258-4_1

gloom to the already dismal picture, stressing, "Like a loose thread that manages to unweave an entire sweater, the mortgage crisis evolved into a credit crisis and ultimately into an economic crisis that is rivaling the Great Depression of the 1930s" (p. 27). Marshall et al. (2013) attributed the lingering problem of corporate greed to "dark leadership," grounded in a blend of Machiavellianism (interpersonal manipulation), psychopathy (remorseless lack of concern for others), and narcissism (excessive concern with admiration, status, and prestige). Focusing on the road ahead, Burnes (2009) illuminated, "we are now entering a new era where ethical and socially-responsible behavior is becoming more important than profit maximization and self-interest" (p. 359).

Indeed, the reputation of business has been tarnished for the longest time by an excessive short-term focus, leading up to the challenges of the past two decades. It has dawned on researchers and practitioners alike that changes need to be applied to the twentieth-century management, if only to adhere to the expanded environment of business today with global constituents playing a much more amplified role than ever before. Maak and Pless (2009) accentuate that responsible leadership today is "a social-relational and ethical phenomenon, which occurs in social processes of interaction" (p. 99). Maak and Pless elucidate that leadership literature of the past has mostly focused on the relationship between leaders and followers in the organization, but that the requirements are different today and that contemporary leaders have to interact with stakeholders in and outside the organization. They speak of a global, interconnected world, with a "global, complex, uncertain, and interconnected business environment" (p. 99). They consider traits and attributes such as vision, trust, ethical conduct, and integrity to be important for leaders in contemporary times.

Leadership and Wakefulness

Even though many people in private and professional sectors agree that we need a mental, moral, and spiritual awakening in our leadership practices, "wakefulness" has yet to be widely established as a leadership style. Yet, once fully understood and evaluated on its many advantages for leaders, their followers, and their organizations, it will get there. Let us look at the concept of wakefulness as a leadership skill, examine some of the rewards for leaders and their organizations of applying awakened leadership, and consider some of the disadvantages of not applying awakened leadership.

Wakefulness, although practiced by various leaders, has thus far not been formally identified as a specific leadership trait. Yet if you look deeper, you may find that some leaders are applying wakefulness, sometimes partially and sometimes fully. Awakened leaders maintain a high level of alertness in every regard: toward themselves and their driving motives in various matters, toward the people and organizations they lead, toward the environment in which their organizations operate, and toward the entire universe. In more popular terms, an awakened leader could be described as a "situational-plus" leader. A situational leader is one who modifies his or her leadership style on the basis of both the situation and the people he or she works with. Such leaders evaluate these two factors and then determine the leadership style that will work best under the circumstances. Awakened leadership goes far beyond situational leadership, however. The wakeful leader also pays close attention to his or her personal values, the organization's mission, and the well-being of all stakeholders. This means that an awakened leader remains aware of internal moral considerations, environmental issues, societal issues, and the interests of customers, suppliers, and other constituents before determining his or her leadership style.

Four Approaches

The wakeful aspect of leading is initially difficult to understand but is easy to apply once mastered. The awakened leader first decides whether to take a task or a relationship orientation to the issue at hand (i.e., he or she chooses between the two main areas of leading) and then determines which of four approaches to leadership—laissez-faire, empathetic, autocratic, or democratic (which together form the acronym LEAD)—will work best.

The laissez-faire approach works best in organizations that have a strong sense of self-direction—such as law firms, consultancies, and high-tech companies—and in which every worker is highly skilled and manages his or her own circle of clients.

The empathetic approach works best in organizations that are fairly small and primarily people oriented. Many nonprofit organizations fit into this category.

The autocratic approach is not the most popular style, but there are organizations in which it works. For example, it is useful when a crisis occurs and the leader is expected to give directions instead of calling a meeting and finding out what everyone suggests. The armed forces, because they often have to act on the spur of the moment and in crisis situations, are receptive to this leadership style.

The democratic approach, in which meetings are usually held to share information about emerging issues and to contemplate possible solutions, lends itself especially well to the academic environment. But determining whether to take a people or a process approach and subsequently deepening one's choice by reviewing the four styles is just half the work of implementing awakened leadership.

The next step for the leader is to evaluate, and if possible develop, a set of traits that will support a wakeful approach. Emotional intelligence and authenticity are the major requirements here. Emotional intelligence is important because the awakened leader needs to know where he or she comes from, to be in touch with his or her values and morals, and to be attuned to co-workers' values and morals. Authenticity is important because people are finally starting to realize that it is unnatural to park one's soul at the door when entering the workplace. Bringing your entire self into the workplace, without fear of being ridiculed or backstabbed, and using your entire self for the betterment of yourself and your organization are the keys to authenticity.

Face the Music

There are numerous consequences of not being wakeful. Leaders who refrain from a wakeful approach in today's increasingly interdependent business world will find themselves becoming outsiders in the global village. The continuous intermingling of cultures leaves no room for holding onto a single leadership style. Even when a leader operates in just one city, county, or state, he or she will find the need to apply an awakened approach because workforces are becoming more multiethnic and multicultural and display an increasing diversity of ages and skills.

Organizations in which leaders employ a single style—even if this style has worked well in the past—will find themselves at a disadvantage compared with competitors who move faster because they have mastered the multidimensional approach of wakefulness. Organizations with wakeful leaders are more open to change and therefore encourage organizational learning, both inside and outside the work environments. These organizations encourage workers to continuously question current processes in the workplace and to suggest improved methods. They focus on encouraging continuous education among their workers, realizing that even though some workers may exit once they have obtained an increased level of skills and knowledge, workers who feel valued and encouraged are less likely to leave a nurturing environment. This decreases turnover and enhances the organization's quality of output, which in turn positively affects the bottom line.

Words of Wisdom

I asked a number of leaders that I considered wakeful in their approaches, what advice they had for leaders who are aspiring to become more wakeful, and they suggested the following:

- See your responsibility in a much broader way. Too many business executives are overly occupied with a narrow vision and do not consider the full responsibilities their companies have to the societies in which they operate. It is important that today's leaders consider their responsibilities beyond the bottom line.
- Walk your talk. Pay more than lip service to your relationships with your employees. Mission statements should be more than just plaques on walls or desks. One leader said, "If you take good care of your people, they will take good care of you and your mission."
- Be more in touch with all levels of your company. Encourage a team spirit and an elevated sense of meaning. This will lead to greater employee satisfaction and, ultimately, increased productivity.
- Promote a corporate culture that addresses humanity as a whole. Focus on all stakeholders (workers, shareholders, customers, suppliers, and society) rather than just the stockholders.

- Continue to develop the qualities of awakened leadership. By doing so you will convert leadership from a duty to a highly gratifying experience.

Awakened Leadership: A Behavioral Road Map

Before getting into more details, it may be interesting to present some foundational information. The name for the leader described in this chapter is, "the awakened leader." This name was derived from Buddha's (approximately 563 BCE) post-enlightenment answer to the question of a passerby whether he was a god, a magician, a wizard, or anything else, upon which Buddha simply stated, "I'm awake" (Kornfield, 1999).

Awakened leaders are those who lead from the heart and soul. They are the corporate, community, and household leaders, official or unofficial, who refuse to put on different hats when it comes to their personality. They do not believe in parking their souls at the door. Awakened leaders practice a holistic and authentic approach in every environment and at every time (Marques, 2009).

As you may have gathered thus far, awakened leadership could be labeled as one of several "new-age" leadership styles, born out of frustration with the self-centered, greed-based, mindless leadership actions of past decades, or it can be considered an entire way of being.

Regardless of how you decide to look at it, it remains a highly useful way of dealing with the responsibility of leadership in any setting, whether private or professional; small, mid-sized, or large scaled; or whether pertaining to the self or others.

So, what is so useful about it? The main reason is this: Awakened leadership is reflective. When you reflect on things, you consider them from multiple angles and think deeper about them than a superficial thought or two. Your job, position, work relationships, the industry you are involved in, the very purpose of your performance, your private or social connections, the things you say, the things you do, and those you refrain from saying and doing, reflecting on all these can help you understand yourself better and make you more mindful from here onward.

One of the greatest favors you can do yourself is understanding why you do what you do and who is affected by your actions. Especially when you are about to make major decisions, such as laying off a number of employees, discontinuing or starting a new production or service line, engaging in a new relationship, or terminating an old one, it may be helpful if you write down the perceived impact. When considering important steps, we often underestimate the number of stakeholders whose lives will be influenced by these steps. Take a few minutes and start writing. The group of affected parties is usually five times higher than what your initial thoughts may have wanted you to believe.

Awakened leadership is the opposite of sleepwalking leadership. First: what is sleepwalking leadership? It is the trend of making decisions without considering that:

- Everything changes, and nothing is today as it was yesterday, so you cannot continue to make the same decisions you made yesterday hoping they will have the same outcomes.
- "Reality," as you see it, is not the same as how others see it. Your reality is shaped by a number of influencing factors, such as your upbringing, culture, character, generation, education, values, and more. You can therefore not consider that others will always understand and appreciate your perspectives.

Traditional patterns or habits are the most common ways of driving you into the autopilot state, thus, sleepwalking mode: you follow these patterns or apply these habits without thinking and, definitely, without reflecting if they still make sense in your life as it is today. Mindlessly submitting to recurring patterns or habits makes us followers, not leaders.

Focusing too much on the details can make you lose sight of the bigger purpose of something. Some people can get so lost in the details that these become the main goal of their performance, causing them to entirely lose track of the larger scheme of things.

Mindless leadership has maneuvered us into a global ecological crisis, and every plan, step, decision, or action you undertake from now on—individually or collectively—will either be instrumental to a positive turnaround or will further augment the problems we, the human species, have created in past decades.

With the above stipulated, awakened leadership can easily be understood, through the following behavioral road map. Awakened leadership is the continued awareness in your thoughts, actions, and communications that:

- You have to make your decisions by reflecting on your lessons learned from past experiences, but even more by reflection on your wishes for the future and the possible effects these decisions will have on that.
- You should consider the perspectives of others, and keep an open mind to potentially different ideas, which as they may enrich your understanding, insight, and, consequently, the directions you will choose going forward.
- You should question, even doubt, established patterns and procedures, as many of them were created when times, expectations, circumstances, goals, and mindsets were entirely different. If you find that the old patterns and procedures still suffice, you can continue with them, but if you find that there is room for improvement or drastic change, you should implement that.
- You should keep in mind that, while details are important to safeguard quality in everything, you also have to keep the big picture in mind, so that you can focus on what really matters in the long run.
- You should make mindfulness your new habit. Your mind is a wonderful instrument, but it has the tendency to lead you astray at every opportunity it gets. This is the time to step up in awareness and regain control over the directions your mind moves into.

Restore your priorities in the right order, and realize the impermanence of everything, including yourself. If you can keep yourself mindful of the fact that you want to leave this world a better place than you encountered it, you have set an important step on the path to awakened leadership.

Case in Point: Marc Benioff and Salesforce

A good example of the kind of leader today's generation of workers seem to call for is Marc Benioff, founder and CEO of Salesforce, an Internet company with about 28,000 employees, that ranked no. 1 on Fortune's 2017 Future 50 leaders list of companies with a market value above $20 billion that are exceptional and should be followed. Innovation and creativity seem to be the fluid that streams through Benioff's veins. Salesforce's product line is not so much revolutionary in our times, as is its entire approach to business. Benioff's company is known for three business trends that are now established in daily performance or have been adopted by many business people: (1) a technology model now known as the cloud, (2) the subscription business model, and (3) the 1-1-1 model, the latter being Salesforce's philanthropic commitment to give away 1% each of equity, products, and employee hours.

One of the main reasons to conclude that Benioff must be doing something good is the fact that his strategies have been widely copied by more than 3000 current business leaders. It seems that leading business assessment authorities such as Wall Street have their eyes on Salesforce as an auspicious trendsetter, not merely through its own growth but also through well-considered acquisitions. In the past decade alone, Salesforce has acquired 55 companies, which manifested innovativeness or market pioneering. Yet, what makes Salesforce—and Benioff—so special is their approach to giving: social causes such as funding of schools, hospitals, and other well-being-focused entities receive millions of dollars in support from Salesforce.

In 2018 Benioff was the sole billionaire supporter of a San Francisco ballot measure addressing homelessness ("Prop C"), which turned into a national "Battle of the Big-Tech Titans." Prop C, which ultimately passed with 60% of votes, aims to raise an additional $250–$300 million in corporate taxes annually—making it the largest tax increase in city history—for a fund dedicated to solving the homeless crisis in San Francisco. The companies with the highest revenues will have to pay the most to support this effort. What made Prop C such a hot topic was the fact that it started as a grassroots voter initiative, but became an elite political battleground as soon as it became a twitter debate between billionaires.

Over a year in the making, the proposed tax was the result of a collaboration between various local organizations that focus on helping the homeless. However, it erupted into a tech elite political battleground when billionaires like Marc Benioff (Salesforce) and Jack Dorsey (Twitter and Square) started a tweet debate about it. Several other billionaires expressed their opposition against Prop C, claiming that they did not consider it the proper way to help the homeless community. Even the San Francisco mayor at the time, London Breed, opposed the proposition and listed a number of reasons why he felt Prop C should not be supported. One of those reasons was that there had already been $300 million spent on homeless programs and that businesses might leave San Francisco with such a high tax to pay for homeless support (Au-Yeung, 2018).

Considering the Prop C homeless tax in hindsight, Benioff stated that he had priests, rabbis, and imams helping him, but no other CEOs. It was only after Prop C won the popular vote that other business leaders finally started dripping in with their support pledges. Benioff holds the opinion that many of these late CEO supporters have decided to make a support pledge after their employees expressed disappointment in these leaders' callous ignorance of the homelessness problem (Ghaffary, 2018).

As for the way Salesforce is conducting its business practice, the entire product and service package the company offers is geared toward ease, affordability, and timeliness. By putting its products online, the company ensures that customers always have access to the latest version of the software they use without frustration, delay, or extra expenses. Benioff performs with the understanding that business success should not only be focused on shareholders but that all stakeholders should benefit. Employees are encouraged to use the "Ohana" (family) floor that is included in each Salesforce building. The Ohana floor is a community space where all employees are welcome to share in the family atmosphere (Lashinsky, 2017).

Benioff is very much invested in Salesforce, but does not plan to keep the company at all costs. He admits that doing a good job as a leader takes about 95% of one's time and that there is more to life than working all the time. So far, however, he stays at the helm and continues to set revolutionary, yet humane trends in his leadership and corporate performance.

Awakened Leaders in Reflection

Based on the findings from over a dozen interviews with corporate and academic leaders that exhibit and nurture awakened qualities, a number of useful reflections emerged: many awakened leaders have made their share of mistakes and have experienced some pretty humbling situations before they reached the stage of wakefulness. As part of the interview process, the participants engaged in thorough self-reflection about their leadership performance and came to the conclusion that trial and error was exactly what makes them such bright persons today: they explained that they had been sleepwalking through life and that something drastic happened in their life, which woke them up. Overall they agreed that it is exactly because of their blunders in the past that awakened leaders are now such reliable, honest, fair, and flexible persons to work with (Marques, 2009).

More specifically, the following attention points emerged.

Morals and values: Awakened leaders may have been confronted with issues that caused them to question their morals and reconsider them. As one of the participants put it, "Sometimes we have to be challenged by the opposite of our beliefs before we learn to respect other perspectives." Due to confrontations with intensely mind-boggling circumstances in life, awakened leaders have learned to understand different perspectives, which, in turn, made them reevaluate their own morals and values in order to conclude whether they still made sense or whether they needed to be modified. This, then, is how they obtained moral intelligence, which, according to Lennick and Kiel (2006), "is the mental capacity to determine how universal human principles should be applied to personal values, goals, and actions" (p. 13).

Ethics: Work-related ethics in particular surface in everyone's life. They can be small or big issues, but they lead to the insight that ethics, like morals and values, are subjective perspectives, which are heavily culture bound. In the case of ethical considerations, it is important to realize that pluralism is a real factor to consider, because ethics are very personal and oftentimes our considerations of what is ethical and what is not are shaped by our upbringing, education, religion, culture, and numerous other shaping factors (Marques, 2017). Awakened leaders are not spared from ethical dilemmas. And sometimes it is one such dilemma that causes a leader to become wakeful. It can be a case of a co-worker who got fired due to unethical behavior; but it can also be the making of a decision, whereby ethical considerations drove the leader toward choosing for the less advantageous alternative for the sake of ethicality. But seeing what loss of ethics can do to people usually strengthens the leader in his or her ethical standpoints.

Integrity, honesty, and trust: In an analysis of Csorba's book *Trust*, *Business Line* (2006) cites, "There are three things that make leaders trustworthy. One, a track record of credibility and reliability. Two, not making 'bad decisions willfully or consciously'. And three, acting and leading with wisdom and integrity" (p. 1). We all know how bad it feels when we get confronted with people who do not hold their side of a bargain and damage our trust with that. Awakened leaders, on their way to becoming who they are, have also experienced their share of dealing with these people. And it taught them an important lesson: to keep their word when they give it, in order to avoid being perceived as untrustworthy. They know too well what it feels like to get disappointed by others' deceitful behavior. And they learn from it.

Vision: Either through reading, listening, or immediate experience, awakened leaders have learned the importance of having a vision and communicating it properly. Marques (2017) stresses that leaders should overcome the urge to simply convey their visions and then leave: they should establish rotating employee teams that keep in communication with one another. Awakened leaders have seen too many organizations floating around, either without a long-term perspective or with one that is obsolete, because it is a hundred years old. They see mergers and acquisitions from gigantic companies go sour due to lack of vision and insufficient consideration of a strategy after the fusion. And they learn from that.

Respect: In his review of the most important strengths of leaders and workers in billion-dollar—or blueprint—companies, Thomson asserts, "they must have complete trust in and respect for one another" (Thomson, 2006, p. 22). In private as well as in professional situations, awakened leaders have learned the value of showing respect. They may have made their own share of mistakes in this regard as well.

After all they, too, were once rebellious teenagers and know-it-all youngsters who did not feel that anyone could teach them anything. But they woke up: oftentimes through pain and shame. Yet, they learned from it.

Passion: An interesting reflection presented by several of the participants to this study was that awakened leaders rarely become leaders in the work environment where they started at an early age. The participants considered this a positive fact, which they clarified by asserting that we all need exposure to multiple environments in order to learn the differences and determine what we really want. They clarified that, due to their encounters with people from various walks of life, awakened leaders learned to distinguish the different types of characters one needs to work with: from passionate ones to ever-dissatisfied ones. This is how awakened leaders determined whom they should adopt as role models. James (2012) adds another insightful dimension by alerting us that pursuing our passion will bring a sense of purpose, thus happiness, while pursuing our idea of what pays most may bring riches, but will also rob us from our innermost sense of happiness and contentment.

Commitment: In their elaborations of this theme, the participants to the study clarified that awakened leaders matured through their encounters with people who were committed to their goals and those who just performed for a paycheck. The participants concluded that awakened leaders, on their way to maturity, considered these extremes and all the shades in between and realized that commitment is a great asset, as long as it does not turn into obsession. It is also critical to keep in mind that employees will perform better and be more committed if they have a committed leader they trust and have a good relationship with (Marques, 2017).

Compassion: In their review of a leader's road map to renewal, McKee et al. (2006) affirm, "The first element of renewal is mindfulness, or living in a state of full, conscious awareness of one's whole self, other people, and the context in which leaders live and work" (p. 1). McKee et al. (2006) continue, "The second element, hope, enables leaders to believe their vision of the future is attainable, and to move toward their goals while inspiring others to reach for their dreams as well" (p. 1). Vision was described earlier as one of the important trial and error points through which leaders ultimately become wakeful. Finally, focusing on the attribute under review here, compassion, McKee et al. (2006) avow, "When leaders experience the third critical element for renewal, compassion, leaders understand people's wants and needs and feel motivated to act on their concern. The real solution lies in renewal, which is a function of leaders' individual capacity for mindfulness, hope and compassion" (p. 1). The participants to the study presented in this chapter agreed that awakened leaders encountered great compassion as well as a total lack thereof in both work and private environments. They concurred that awakened leaders have learned the upside and downside of both extremes. Excessively compassionate people run the risk to fall prey to ruthless abusers and may run into situations where all their time and energy gets absorbed by other people's problems. Those who are entirely deprived of compassion are usually disliked and will not be supported when they need their followers to do so.

Kindness: Zoghbi-Manrique-de-Lara and Viera-Armas (2019) associate kindness as one of four factors that comprise compassionate behavior in leaders, along with empathic concern, common humanity, and mindfulness. In the here conducted study, the participants felt that, whether it was through personal experience or the observation of arrogance applied toward someone close, awakened leaders acknowledge the value of kindness. In their opinion this, too, has been a lesson, which awakened leaders learned through life. A few of the participants added that the awareness about the value of kindness could very well emerge from a positive experience: the leader could have encountered a person who was very kind to him or her, an act that may have been crucial at the moment when it was delivered. This experience of kindness may have opened the leader's eyes for the value of being kind to others in return. Yet, stressed another participant, kindness does not mean giving in to everything. It means bringing your point across with appropriate respect to others and their perspectives.

Forgiveness: It was a common opinion of the participants to the study here reviewed that awakened leaders have encountered forgiveness in their lives: from parents, siblings, children, spouses, friends, or colleagues. The participants explained that, once a person receives forgiveness from others, he or she will understand how good it feels, what a humbling experience it is, and how it will make an individual with good intentions strive to be much better than before. All participants agreed that awakened leaders have learned the lesson of forgiveness well and have consequently mastered the art of applying it in every setting where they operate.

Courage: Rijamampianina (2018) posits that courage has been evoked as an essential component of character in effective leaders, as it lays the foundation for other virtues and values to emerge and develop. Courage is definitely one of the important aspects of awakened leadership. Without having learned this lesson, awakened leaders would probably not be leaders. As one of the participants emphasized, "Living takes courage. And leading takes courage." From the various statements of the participants, it could be concluded that awakened leaders have learned that nothing will happen without someone being courageous to set a first step. So, they learned that they might as well be that person. One participant clarified that courage does not always pay off in terms of material or financial turnout, yet it always leads to enrichment of experiences and insights. So, awakened leaders value that.

Love: This lesson may be the most precious one of all. In general, all participants agreed that love is the ultimate caring concern an individual develops through life, on his or her way toward awakened leadership. They also agreed that it has everything to do with empathy, understanding, and acceptance. A few participants noted that, in awakened leadership, it is not only important for the leader to love what he or she does, but also to make his or her workforce feel appreciated. Love, in this perspective, has everything to do with learning that diversity is a good thing and that people from different backgrounds and cultures ultimately bring about greater insights. This was also stressed by several of the participants to the study on awakened leadership. These participants emphasized that love in a leader-follower relationship also has everything to do with knowing what the right actions are. They underscored that it has everything to do with realizing that the differences among people were not implemented without reason, but that there was a purpose for these differences. Awakened leaders have learned to love people from all walks of life equally, and to respect them equally, even if they do not always understand them. Yet, in such cases, these leaders will seek to understand their people, even if it takes time. Thus, these leaders have learned the essence of love.

Deep listening: On our way through life, we learn that there is a difference between hearing and listening and between listening and listening. The participants to the study here described concurred that awakened leaders have learned that people greatly appreciate it when you listen to them with more than just your ears. These leaders may have learned this because they were once (or more than once) also granted the art of being listened to with more than ears alone. So, these leaders have learned to focus on their counterpart in a dialogue and listen deeply. And this has been valuable toward their awakening.

Inspired and inspiring: Through the various interviews for this study, it became clear that awakened leaders are those that have obtained inspiration from various sources. No one develops special skills without inspiration. This inspiration, as one participant put it, can come from other human beings, but also from other living entities such as animals or plants or nature in its entirety. Awakened leaders have learned from the sources of inspiration they encountered through life. One of the most important overarching lessons they adopted from being inspired is that it is crucial to have a source of inspiration. So, now that they became awake, they do their utmost to also become a source of inspiration to others. This can be seen in their way of communicating with others: the time they take to listen, to encourage, to provide guidelines, and to be available when needed. Inspired leaders know first and foremost the essence of being available.

Authenticity: It was the participants' opinion that awakened leaders practice authenticity in the sense of being genuine and not in the sense of what they think others would want to see or hear. Although worded slightly differently by the various interviewees, they all seemed to agree that awakened leaders have concluded that it is too much hassle to put on different hats under different circumstances and to play different roles in front of different audiences. One of the leadership thinkers and practitioners interviewed for this chapter stated that, if you always tell the truth, you do not have to remember. Awakened leaders are aware of that and live like that. They refrain from adopting different attitudes and behaviors, because they know that there are far more important things in life than putting up "fronts." And that is the power of authenticity: honesty, and straightforwardness, which translates to others as simplicity, or the way of being uncomplicated. And what is more rewarding than being valued for your simplicity? No one has to worry about your hidden intentions: everyone knows where they stand with you. That is what awakened leaders are about.

Connection with one's being, one's spirit: "Leaders who have the presence of mind to simply 'be' know in their hearts that correct action flows naturally from being fully awake" (Marques, 2010). It was repeatedly emphasized by the participants in this study that awakened leaders are good listeners, because they know that sometimes all people need is an ear, for they already know the answers to their problems. Awakened leaders, according to the thinkers that contributed to this study, apply the strategy of listening because they have learned through self-reflection. They know that it is not more than fair toward oneself to take some time off through the day for contemplation, and for turning to the source of wealth and knowledge within, in search for answers. Awakened leaders have learned that, by doing so frequently, the connection with their core becomes easier and can be done more swiftly if they do it often enough. So, awakened leaders turn inward regularly for answers. It should be stressed here that the process of turning inward has nothing to do with religion, as was also clarified by the participants in this study. The variety of environments from which these participants derived should already be an indicator that awakened leaders can be found among all groups: among people from various religions and among people who do not practice any religion.

Multidimensional: A multidimensional approach is almost inevitable in today's multi-continental, and multiethnic work environment. The study participants agreed that awakened leaders apply their leadership styles to the situational, follower, and environmental needs they encounter. The participants further asserted that, aside from their multidimensional leadership style, awakened leaders have learned to see things in different dimensions. Therefore, they make their decisions as such. A few of the participants elaborated that awakened leaders carry the conviction that if you allow yourself to be driven by the right causes, the rewards will follow. At least half of the participants affirmed that awakened leaders are therefore never primarily money-driven. They know that the bottom line will ultimately be served in much more rewarding ways if the people and the relationships are maintained. The majority of participants concluded that awakened leaders are relationship oriented, firstly because they like developing relationships and because they know the mutual value of maintaining them and secondly because they know how important good relationships are for the advancement of their organization.

Fulfillment: The participants felt that awakened leaders have learned that there is no gratification in material and financial affluence without fulfillment. They reflect on that experience toward themselves as well as those they surround themselves with. They strive, in the first place, for everyone to have a sense of fulfillment with what they do. And, as stated earlier, they know that financial and material rewards will follow once a person is doing the thing he or she gets a sense of fulfillment from. So, according to the sources for this study, fulfillment is very high on the agenda of an awakened leader.

Initiative: The study participants asserted that awakened leaders have learned that nothing comes from waiting for others to do it for you. So, they take initiatives. And with that, they are aware that not all initiatives work out, but they are still willing to go for it. Some of the participants stressed that awakened leaders perceive failed initiatives as life lessons toward better ones. So they go for what they believe in, even if it takes a while. They develop creativeness to get there. And they usually get there. They also realize that there are many people who may stand behind an idea, but who lack the willpower or courage to take the initiative to realize it. So, the awakened leader steps forward and creates a structure, a platform. And then he or she finds others to join in.

Change: All participants agreed that awakened leaders have learned, through many experiences, that one cannot survive in today's world without being amenable to change, because changes are continuously brought upon us. It was the participants' opinion that awakened leaders have also learned that the most effective way to deal with change is to be just one step ahead and reinvent oneself on a regular basis. How? By keeping track of developments in one's interest areas, by adopting a pro-learning mindset, and by refusing to let setbacks prevail. To quote one of the participants, "[Awakened leaders] know that setbacks always occur in everyone's life, but that it are the losers who dwell on them, while the winners look for the lessons to be learned from these setbacks and the opportunities hidden within or behind them."

Chapter Takeaways

- Wakefulness, although practiced by various leaders, has thus far not been formally identified as a specific leadership trait.
- An awakened leader could be described as a "situational-plus" leader. A situational leader is one who modifies his or her leadership style on the basis of both the situation and the people he or she works with.
- The awakened leader first decides whether to take a task or a relationship orientation to the issue at hand (i.e., he or she chooses between the two main areas of leading) and then determines which of four approaches to leadership—laissez-faire, empathetic, autocratic, or democratic (which together form the acronym LEAD)—will work best.
- Leaders who refrain from a wakeful approach in today's increasingly interdependent business world will find themselves becoming outsiders in the global village.
- Organizations in which leaders employ a single style—even if this style has worked well in the past— will find themselves at a disadvantage compared with competitors who move faster because they have mastered the multidimensional approach of wakefulness.
- Wakeful leaders suggest to (1) consider your responsibilities in a much broader way, (2) walk your talk, (3) be more in touch with all levels of your company, (4) promote a corporate culture that addresses humanity as a whole, and (5) continue to develop the qualities of awakened leadership.

- Awakened leadership is reflective. When you reflect on things, you consider them from multiple angles and think deeper about them than a superficial thought or two.
- Awakened leadership can easily be understood, through the following behavioral road map.
  - Make your decisions by reflecting on your lessons learned from past experiences.
  - Consider the perspectives of others, and keep an open mind to potentially different ideas.
  - Question, even doubt, established patterns and procedures.
  - Details are important to safeguard quality in everything, but you also have to keep the big picture in mind.
  - Make mindful leadership your new habit.
  - Restore your priorities in the right order.
- Several interviewed awakened leaders reflected on a series of qualities and behaviors that have served them well, such as being value-based, ethical, trust-driven, visionary, respectful, passionate, committed, compassionate, kind, forgiving, courageous, loving, attentive, inspired, authentic, connected, multidimensional, fulfilled, initiative-oriented, and change-focused qualities.

Reflective Questions

1. The chapter describes an awakened leader as a "situational-plus" leader. Engage in some research to find out what situational leadership entails and explain.
2. The chapter encourages those interested in wakeful leadership to doubt established patterns and procedures. Why is that?
3. Which of the reflective qualities of awakened leaders come easy to you, and why?
4. Which of the qualities could be challenging for you, and why?
5. Do you think becoming an awakened leader is attainable for you? Why or why not?

References

Au-Yeung, A. (2018). San Francisco voters approve tax ballot measure to help homeless, tech billionaire Marc Benioff wins big. *Forbes.Com*, p. 4.

Burnes, B. (2009). Reflections: Ethics and organizational change – Time for a return to Lewinian values. *Journal of Change Management, 9*(4), 359–381.

Businessline. (2006). Leadership is being, not doing. *Businessline*, p. 1.

Davis, G. (2009). The rise and fall of finance and the end of the society of organizations. *Academy of Management Perspectives, 23*(3), 27–44.

Ghaffary, S. (2018, November 14). Marc Benioff says he had rabbis and imams supporting the Prop C homelessness tax—But not tech CEOs. *Recode.* Retrieved from https://www.recode.net/2018/11/14/18093170/marc-benioff-homeless-tax-prop-c-tech-ceos

Hannah, D., & Zatzick, C. (2008). An examination of leader portrayals in the US Business Press following the landmark scandals of the early 21st century. *Journal of Business Ethics, 79*(4), 361–377.

James, G. (2012, April 9). What is success? Here's a better definition. *Inc*. Retrieved from http://www.inc.com/geoffrey-james/what-is-success-better-definition.html

Kornfield, J. (1999). *Teachings of the Buddha*. Barnes & Noble Books.

Lashinsky, A. (2017). Benioff in bloom. *Fortune, 176*(6), 64–72.

Lennick, D., & Kiel, F. (2006). Moral intelligence for successful leadership. *Leader to Leader, 40*, 13.

Maak, T., & Pless, N. (2009). Business leaders as citizens of the world. Advancing humanism on a global scale. *Journal of Business Ethics, 88*(3), 537–550.

Marques, J. (2009). Awakened leaders: Born or made? *Leadership and Organization Development Journal, 31*(4), 307–323.

Marques, J. (2010). Awakened leaders: Who are they and why do we need them? *Development and Learning in Organizations: An International Journal, 24*(2), 7–10.

Marques, J. (2017). *Ethical leadership: Progress with a moral compass*. Routledge.

Marshall, A., Baden, D., & Guidi, M. (2013). Can an ethical revival of prudence within prudential regulation tackle corporate psychopathy? *Journal of Business Ethics, 117*(3), 559–568.

McKee, A., Johnstone, F., & Massimilian, R. (2006, May/June). Mindfulness, hope and compassion: A leader's road map to renewal. *Ivey Business Journal*, 1–5.

Rijamampianina, R. (2018). Leaders and decision making: A study of the drivers of courage. *Problems and Perspectives in Management, 16*(1), 320–329.

Thomson, D. G. (2006). Inside-outside leadership for exponential growth. *Leader to Leader, 40*, 22.

Zoghbi-Manrique-de-Lara, P., & Viera-Armas, M. (2019). Does ethical leadership motivate followers to participate in delivering compassion? *Journal of Business Ethics, 154*(1), 195.

Chapter 2
Mindfulness as a Strategy to Weather Challenges

Carrie Amani Annabi

Abstract This chapter considers physiological, sociological, and positive psychological research to help readers better understand historic and contemporary studies that also feed into business management and leadership disciplines. The backstory to these evolutionary theories will help readers rationalize and position Mindfulness, which is still a fairy nascent area for academic enquiry, undoubtedly involves a more multidisciplinary approach. The author hopes that by appreciating extant literature in ancillary but disparate areas, readers will be able to see that Mindfulness is a logical answer for leaders faced with coping with endless challenges and understand why the movement is currently led by written accounts in books and not by academic publications at this stage.

Keywords Mindfulness · Oxytocin · Leadership · Positive psychology · Culture

Physiological Issues

The recent pandemic has interrupted normal life for the majority and removed typical everyday opportunities for oxytocin stimuli. The more characteristic cocreators of the hormone would rely on such things as smiling and simple physical contact (including social hugs and non-sexualized contact). Social distancing, mask wearing, and reduced social interaction have minimized opportunities for oxytocin-boosting situations. It is fortuitous that oxytocin, or the feel-good hormone, can be recreated through Mindfulness.

Oxytocin is a peptide hormone comprising of nine amino acids and has crucial importance to physiological responses given its impact on the brain. Oxytocin impacts physiologic integrity and enhanced sociality. This matters because oxytocin

C. A. Annabi (✉)
RCSI University of Health and Medical Sciences, Dubai, United Arab Emirates
e-mail: carrieannabi@rcsi.ie

J. Marques (ed.), *Innovative Leadership in Times of Compelling Changes*, Management, Change, Strategy and Positive Leadership, https://doi.org/10.1007/978-3-030-67258-4_2

governs more general social behavior and physical interaction as well as sexual contact (Campbell, 2010). Changes in oxytocin levels impact social functioning (Hoffman et al., 2012). An increase in oxytocin levels is more readily associated with physical stimulation (e.g., massage of somatosensory organs), but research also indicated that this feel-good hormone can also be heightened by alternative sensory stimuli (Donadon et al., 2018). Ito et al. (2019) proposed that oxytocin levels can be increased by psychologic stimulation such as Mindfulness meditation.

Feeling alone and being alone are well-known risk factors for disease and poor health and accelerated mortality. Social isolation plays a role in reduced levels of oxytocin (Magen, 2018). Rokach (2014) addressed the duality of leadership and loneliness and found that leaders often suffer from feelings of stress, isolation, and loneliness. These stressors are antecedents for health and social issues. Silard and Wright (2020) provided a critique of leadership styles and suggested that there is a "dark side" to "popular leadership theories, especially with respect to the lack of development of high-quality relationships—and the resultant loneliness of both leaders and follower" (p. 1).

Ringleb and Rock (2008) were among the first proponents of neuroleadership, which is an interdisciplinary research area which combines brain science and psychology to better inform effective leadership skills that supports emotional regulation. Neuroleadership delivers a scientific substantiation of the way that leadership behavior promotes trust and impacts the brain's oxytocin production (Pittman, 2020). Early research on employee trust being associated with positive corporate growth (Zak & Knack, 2001) has now being built upon to confirm that trust requires sufficiency of oxytocin (Zak et al., 2007; Zak, 2017, 2018). Mindfulness interventions have been shown to increase oxytocin (Donadon et al., 2018; Ito et al., 2019) and well-being (Lindsay et al., 2019).

Positive Psychology and Sociology

The simplest concept of Mindfulness refers to consciousness of what is happening within the present moment. It is fostered by a diverse range of practices which are designed to help you as an individual set aside biased personal constructs which would normally govern your innate response. Mindfulness replaces these automatically triggered responses with responses which are less automatic.

Mindfulness is intrinsic to positive psychology. Positive psychology focuses on well-being as opposed to dis-ease, which is a lack of the feeling of ease. I use the hyphen deliberately to underscore the notion that ease is about optimum functioning, whereas, *disease* often results from long-term dis-ease. Positive psychology and sociology both examine whether there is a common human nature and, if so, what properties exist therein.

Several authors have chronicled governing principles of subconscious and unconscious behavior, and some of these scholars and their research will be briefly presented in order to inform your thinking about the well-known sociological theories that have been created to explain automatic human responses.

Mindfulness as a Sociological Construct

Charles Wright Mills (1959) studied social stratification and intellectual craftsmanship in his book entitled *The Sociological Imagination*, where he recognized that "it is difficult to avoid going beyond one's immediate subject, because the reality of any one stratum is, in large part, its relations to the rest" (1959, p. 2).

Mills (1963) further focused on a biographical understanding of the interconnectivity between public and private space through his writings on *Power, Politics, and People,* which were an articulation of the confusion of his private life. Subsequent authors have connected his biography with "spaces of selfhood" to comprehend his image of sociology.

Brewer (2005) offered the following description which best illustrates why reflexive journeys and Mindfulness provide significance in relation to your lived experiences. This also could equally apply to a variant of an intersectionality debate (which will also be touched upon in this chapter).

> Mills famously staked sociology's claim to be the study of the intersection between private troubles and public issues since this located the discipline as the study of individuals within their social structural context. The intersection was presented as one of constant flow, as people's private troubles became public issues and as public issues caused people private troubles, exemplifying the mutual embeddedness of individuals and society. (Brewer, 2005, p. 662)

In applying Mills (1959, 1963) to your own Mindfulness voyage, you will undoubtedly think of components or compartments of your life that include work where, perhaps, the issues you face are individual private struggles and include concerns about your interaction with others. These troubles impact upon social interaction and personal awareness, thereby making the context of your troubles directly relational to your lived experiences and resultant action. Mills opined that issues are more aligned to external material problems which go beyond the range of individual troubles and that organizations, institutions, or society impact upon issues and become public matters. Mills provides an interesting argument that may release people from taking constructive steps within personal Mindfulness because it places the emphasis and responsibility on societal changes. On the other hand, Mindfulness recognizes that individual steps, whether in isolation or as part of a larger collective movement, will make a fundamental change to personal interactions.

Does Culture Matter?

The word culture has many connotations. Indeed, the words *culture* and *civilization* were accorded 160 different meanings in the seminal work by Kroeber and Kluckhohn (1952). One brief narrative from their book stated that:

> Culture consists of patterns, explicit and implicit, of and for behavior acquired and transmitted by symbols, constituting the distinctive achievement of human groups, including

> their embodiments in artefacts; the essential core of culture consists of traditional (i.e. historically derived and selected) ideas and especially their attached values; culture systems may, on the one hand, be considered as products of action, on the other as conditioning elements of further action. (p. 181)

It is not my intention to disaggregate or define the various forms of culture, but rather to draw attention to the ambiguity which prevails in interpretations. For example, is the creation of culture inherent in life and relationships simply because people prefer to be constituted by culture as a safety net to guard against taking a position outside of it? (see Social Identity Theory). Cultural production constitutes a perpetually enacted performance of, often mutually contradictory, discourses which are time and place bound meanings and related practices. These discussions do not always recognize the fluidity of cultural production nor consider the nuance of Mindfulness where living in the moment can provide isolated but conjoined behavioral patterns.

Kroeber and Kluckhohn (1952) suggested that culture in the future would be expanded to incorporate the interrelationship forged by cultural systems and inconsistency and the individual. This is an excellent understanding of how discrepancy and discrete Mindfulness can still work while using wider sociological concepts for mapping interrelations. Therefore, instead of using contemporary rendition of culture, I want to introduce you to Bourdieu as a way of charting an understanding of relationships.

Charting an Understanding of Relationships

Bourdieu (1990) contended that individuals were governed by dispositions which provide an individualized framework for a predisposition toward the way one thinks or feels and are not merely an unconscious practice. Dispositions are preconscious habits which direct both the physical and psychological image of and to the world. For example, dispositions incorporate the way one eats or moves, self-posture, and speech patterns. Bourdieu believed that the body itself incorporates the preconscious historic patterns into an individualized physicality of presence guided by unconscious thought. The accumulative dispositions are habitus, which in turn epitomizes ways of thinking that subconsciously cue an individual to behave in a particular way. Habitus is the individual's response to, and the interplay with, the world they inhabit which has been moderated by disposition. Using Bourdieu as a mechanism for self-reflection on personal leadership strategy still has currency (see Evans, 2018).

Looking Inside Out or Outside In

Cooley's (1972) theory of the looking-glass self believed that our self-view comes from the self-contemplation of impressions of how others perceive us teamed with our personal qualities. Identity and the logical construction of self is demarcated by the sameness of differences between the self and others. Therefore, the creation of an individual identity is often aggregated with the simultaneous creation of a social identity, which is developed via social interaction, and the consequent validation process that this offers.

Social Identity

Social identification is the personal understanding of oneself in relation to a larger group of people. Tajfel (1981, p. 255) defined social identity as "that part of the individual's self-concept which derives from his or her knowledge of membership to a social group (or groups) together with the value and the emotional significance attached to it." Tajfel and Turner (1979, 1986) advocated the theory that an individual's concept of self was the composite of several social identities. Social identity theory (SIT) (Tajfel, 1978, 1981; Tajfel & Turner, 1986) encompasses constructs related to both personal and group behavior and can scaffold perceptions of selectivity as SIT theorizes that people assign themselves to social categories (e.g., tough boss or approachable leader), which may lead them to respond favorably to stimuli (e.g., hardline policy adherence like maintaining strict working hours or advocating corporate social responsible issues) that in turn cause the individual to recognize their social category distinctiveness (Tajfel, 1978, 1981).

However, an individual often belongs to a variety of groups which makes it difficult to categorize the intersecting identities. There is potential to have an intersection between identities, so that the totality of one group membership or partial elements of other group memberships are considered: It is feasible to have partial memberships while also having self-belief of out-group status. This means that simultaneous identification becomes impossible without considering intersectionality.

Intersectionality

Intersectionality is most often used as a feminist term and is attributed to Crenshaw (1989) who emphasized the "multidimensionality of marginalized subjects' lived experiences" (p. 139). Intersectionality theory developed as a critique of race and gender studies and as a means of exploring the oppression of women of color within society. However, the analysis has been applied to a range of social categories, including social identities where it is difficult to create one specific identity as either fully independent or dominant. Intersectionality discards a "single-axis framework" and instead adopts a multi-frame analysis to analyze the multiple ways in which race and gender interact (Crenshaw, 1991, p. 1244).

Intersectionality as a Metaphor

However, Crenshaw herself was quoted as saying that intersectionality was just a metaphor (see Guidroz & Berger, 2009). A metaphor "requires a process of adjusting the linguistically encoded concept to derive an ad hoc concept whose denotation is broader than that of the lexical concept" (Carston & Wearing, 2011, p. 283). I believe that Crenshaw was saying that intersectionality was a continuum of approximate definitions, given that it can be used in such a wide array of circumstances to cover many themes. In its widest construct, intersectionality considers the interconnected nature of social categorizations such as race, class, and gender, regarded as creating overlapping and interdependent systems of discrimination or disadvantage and offers a theoretical approach that brings together many diverse themes, based on such a premise. This was emphasized by Guy-Sheftall (1995, p. 8) who noted that intersectionality "is currently the reigning metaphor for complex identities insofar as they are constituted by race, ethnicity, class, and sexual orientation together with gender." Intersectionality is a one-size-fits-many terminologies that have multiple connotations, not unlike the array of uses for the word *culture* (see Kroeber & Kluckhohn, 1952).

Identity Politics

The seminal work by Crenshaw (1991, p. 2299) on intersectionality determines that intersectional analysis of identity-based groups is "in fact coalitions, or at least potential coalitions waiting to be formed." Crenshaw's view of identities as coalitions provides a fracture between coalitional and identity-based groups. Coalitions are places of dissimilarity where consensus has been reached to agree to ignore or mute the differences, while identity-based groups are places of similarity. Carastathis (2013) was able to align these concepts to political identity groups but did not distill her writing from the collective to an individual inference. Carastathis (2013, p. 492) reasoned that "we are foreclosing a potential coalition with all those who share the repressed or excluded identities—not to mention betraying the possibility of a coalition among all parts of ourselves" because people are typically obliged to suppress elements of their identities in order to construct a personality that is able to be considered in singularity. However, this still acknowledged that intersectionality was about collectivism and individuals finding coalition—not individuals maintaining a separate uniqueness.

Carastathis (2013) saw that in the quarter century since the formal inception of intersectionality as a term, the concept itself had become an institutionalized intellectual project, and she argued that identity is still a vestige for creating an organizing dialogue, providing identities are seen more as coalitions. She mentioned that:

> Identity politics is often contrasted with coalitional politics in that the former is viewed as a kind of separatism based on sameness while the latter depends on alliances built

> across differences. Yet this distinction between identity and coalition focuses exclusively on differences between groups, failing to consider differences within groups, which an intersectional critique of identity categories illuminates. (p. 941)

Pulling the Stands of Sociological Implications Together

Social identification underpins the antecedents of SIT and that this supports identity politics. Tajfel (1969) espoused the view that the values and practices of in-group identity are characterized as being unique. The normalization of groups being unique, as opposed to individual being unique, lies contrary to the literature which indicates that intersectionality is a metaphor and not a classification (Crenshaw, 1991; Guy-Sheftall, 1995). This provides the bedrock for questioning whether SIT is an appropriate lens from which to review individuals whose identities put them beyond simple group taxonomy particularly as Mindfulness explores the individualist concept of possessing an authentic private self which is counterintuitive to the collectivist constructs presented within sociology. This has importance for those who follow authentic leadership styles because, as we will see later in this chapter, authenticity suggests individualism as opposed to generic labeling.

So far, this chapter has highlighted that most people fall somewhere on the individualist-collectivist spectrum. Even within a very collectivist culture, you will find people who are more individualist. Individualistic self-expressions and styles may seem anathema to collectivism. Inversely, the collectivism requires social agreement and many people struggle with estrangement from collective concepts. Because academic research often relies on quantitative studies for perceived credibility, many academic journals have steered away from looking at smaller sample, qualitative research relating to identity and the personification of triggers which create isolation. As a rule, individuals themselves do not always attribute this separation to class, gender, race, or sexuality. Researchers need to make more sense of the narrative of the individuals rather than get absorbed by the problems of umbrella classificatory competition. Grace (1998, p. 206) attested the success of critical social theory is that it "must be grounded in the self-understandings of the actors" (p. 206). You are the main actor in your life.

Authentic Leadership

Authentic leadership is a relatively new leadership trait construct (Baron, 2016) with connections to the positive psychology movement (Luthans & Avolio, 2003). The classification of authentic leadership was defined by Luthans and Avolio (2003, p. 243) as an approach which melds together dimensions from positive psychology and organizational development "which results in both greater self-awareness and self-regulated positive behaviors on the part of leaders and associates, fostering positive self-development."

Recent research showed that Mindfulness could be a predictor of authentic leadership, in the perceptions of both leaders and their followers (Nübold et al., 2020). In addition, a mindful leader was positively evident to the followers through the way authentic leadership was manifest.

This provides a useful academic platform from which to discuss Mindfulness and its implications for leadership theory and leader development. Leading people, as opposed to just managing others, results in healthier interactions and increased employee performance. Authentic leadership inculcates self-awareness, which allows leaders to appreciate the differences between self and others. Mindfulness provides tools which allow you to become more comfortable with being uncomfortable. Welcoming challenges, including ideas that challenge core beliefs, is consistent with authentic leadership, as evidenced by the 16-item Authentic Leadership Inventory scale developed by Neider and Schriesheim (2011). Additionally, demonstrating vulnerability forges stronger connections and releases the trust hormone oxytocin while also allowing space for open and honest discussions (Zak, 2018).

This runs contrary to gender-biased extant theory and empirical research which had been skewed toward a "belief that leaders need to be agentic in order to be effective and that men are more agentic than women which yields a male advantage in leadership evaluations" (Schaumberg & Flynn, 2017, p. 1859). Although this belief system is frequently pedalled within literature, the authors challenged those sexist hypotheses. The found that self-reliance was depicted by followers as a central to how well a leader was perceived and that female leaders with self-reliance were equally positively perceived as men. Baykal (2018) linked resilience and self-confidence to authentic leadership. Kaplan et al. (2017) illustrated that resilience could be learned through Mindfulness and identified it as a means of negating the impact of stress and burnout.

Weathering Challenges

The following section of this chapter will touch upon the importance of recognizing why Mindfulness is a necessary solution for your automatic responses and how it underpins an alternative approach to your personal successful leadership style.

Where conformity to collectivism runs contrary to the values of an individual, then Mindfulness has been demonstrated as an effective approach to promote feelings of self-awareness, self-reliance, and self-confidence. Mindfulness is essential for your ultimate public journey toward authentic leadership because, irrespective of your culture or industry sector, mindful leadership allows leaders to look inside and develop mechanisms to guide their attention and intentions. Looking inside is highly personal and must start with a private journey.

Examples of the types of practices which support Mindfulness are explored in other chapters. These include a simple focus on your breathing and run through a continuum of immersive opportunities that ask you to observe and connect with your direct environment. This allows you to become aware of the outcomes of even the most routine daily activities. Mindfulness also embraces judgment-free listening opportunities to train your mind to assess situations without resorting to the stimuli of preconceptions led by your past experiences. Exercises in Mindfulness allow you to become immersed in the moment and find appreciation for your current experience and, ultimately, can incorporate meditative practices to help still your mind. Each of these opportunities can help you navigate daily challenges and effectively lead and support followers in a non-challenging way that fosters innovation.

The effects of Mindfulness are as germane for leaders and they are for their followers and benefit organizations (Decuypere et al., 2020). Lazarus and Folkman (1984, p. 141) defined coping as "constantly changing cognitive and behavioral efforts to manage specific external and/or internal demands that are appraised as taxing or exceeding the resources of the person."

The necessity to cope well is not just important for your leadership style but also for your well-being (Wasylkiw et al., 2015) and the well-being of your followers (Pinck & Sonnentag, 2018). Gibbons (2010) found that handling situations on an avoidance basis was a prognosticator of adverse well-being for the individual. Followers found the laissez-faire style of leadership as a stressor because it increased their own uncertainty with task (Skogstad et al., 2014). Mindfulness was reported as an important tool to optimize leadership quality (Lange et al., 2018).

Mindfulness is viewed as an antidote for emotional exhaustion (Reb et al., 2017) and a remedy for burnout. It also increases innovation (see Sutcliffe et al., 2016) which is imperative for dynamic organizations to thrive. Research on the effectiveness of Mindfulness in organizations is embryonic. However, Decuypere et al. (2020) reported that emergent studies are currently looking at Mindfulness in relation to friendly failure management, work-avoidance rationale, and understanding operational processes. Reviewing operational processes is particularly significant because the lean management ethos has long since been lambasted for its attention to systems and ignoration of human-centric approaches. Despite an implicit acknowledgment that Mindfulness is gender-neutral, there is still a nod within some academic writing that mindful masculinities must be tacitly explored in order to make it an acceptable masculine construct (e.g., Davis & Moody, 2018; Smallen, 2019). This is something which must be challenged as Mindfulness is human centric and is equally useful as a nonbinary leadership approach.

Understanding the Nature and Environment of Academic Research with Reference to Mindfulness

It is important to understand how emergent themes for research evolve in relation to academic publications. Mindfulness is still an emergent area for academic research within business and management disciplines, even though spirituality, as a categorization, has been around for much longer. Well-being practices have often been seen more as a feminine construct. Scholars such as Smallen (2019, p. 134) suggest that Mindfulness as a theory has been "reworked in strongly masculine settings to promote neo-liberal hegemonic masculine goals under a symbolic veneer of spirituality and mental health."

Professor McKinnon, a prominent academic in his field, wrote a polemic paper that challenged the principle and practice of journal ranking for types of business research. McKinnon (2013) saw academic research as a "retreat into ivory towers" (p. 6) and that "academics concentrate their efforts on publishing in the select group of more highly ranked journals and neglect lower-rated publications" (p. 7). He criticized senior university management (in the UK) for their slavish focus on 3* and 4* business and management publications and the emphasis that this focus has on the quality of individual research outputs. It should also be noted that 3-star and 4-star academic journals prefer quantitative research. Given the subject matter and the focus on the individual, most research on Mindfulness is qualitative.

Furthermore, research on gender indicated that women have a predilection for producing qualitative research (e.g., Ashmos Plowman & Smith, 2011; Leuschner, 2015), and this has led to a paucity of women being taken seriously in some academic disciplines (e.g., Haslanger, 2008; Leuschner, 2015; Krämer et al., 2016). The selection criteria for professorial roles and senior management in universities invariably demand research outputs from journals whose acceptance criteria demand quantitative paradigms, thereby providing an inequality for qualitative researchers. This equally has ongoing implications for research because most academic business and management destination publications seek quantitative research.

Ashmos Plowman and Smith (2011) found that gender plays a significant role in research method selection. They reviewed the methodology of men and women over a 20-year period from four prominent management journals from North American journals. The findings were that women were underrepresented in published quantitative studies, with the trend remaining constant over the 20 years reviewed. Gender was never discussed within any of the methodology sections as an influence on research methods.

Another notable point is that the vast majority of the 3 and 4 star journals favor research into single silo-like disciplines. These are very few credible destination journals for either multidisciplinary or interdisciplinary writing which, in turn, stifles the fusion of concepts which results in fewer avenues for academic journal publication. This chapter started by highlighting that the research that would be reviewed herein would emanate from physiological, sociological, and positive psychological. This was synthesized with business management research in order to highlight the veracity of Mindfulness as a valid approach in leadership.

While there is undoubtedly academic research on Mindfulness, there is still a paucity of dedicated journals to this topic currently. This knowledge gap has created space for this book. Addressing Mindfulness is crucial because we must move forward, toward fluidity in both theory and practice to establish normative nonbinary gender and leadership constructs that incorporate and enshrine this great discipline.

Chapter Takeaways

- Mindfulness is not a standalone topic, but rather it incorporates several strands of past research areas such as physiology, sociology, positive psychology, and leadership.
- Oxytocin, the feel-good hormone, which is more commonly associated with physical contact, can also be created through Mindfulness.
- Mindfulness is strongly associated with authentic leadership.
- Academic literature is nascent on Mindfulness. This is mostly because academic journals favor single-silo research areas, whereas Mindfulness can be seen to straddle multidisciplinary and interdisciplinary themes.
- Despite a strong acknowledgment on the efficacy of Mindfulness and an implicit acknowledgment that Mindfulness is gender-neutral, some academic writers have tried to masculinize the theoretical construct of Mindfulness to promote its neoliberal acceptability.

Reflective Questions

1. Name as many research areas listed in the chapter areas as you can and provide a brief explanation of how each one connects with Mindfulness.
2. Explain how Mindfulness can be described as neuroleadership.
3. What are the main deterrents that currently prevent Mindfulness from entering mainstream academic literature?
4. How does Mindfulness connect with the concept of authentic leadership?
5. How does Mindfulness normalize nonbinary gender and leadership theories and practices?

References

Ashmos Plowman, D., & Smith, A. D. (2011). The gendering of organizational research methods: Evidence of gender patterns in qualitative research. *Qualitative Research in Organizations and Management: An International Journal, 6*(1), 64–82.

Baron, L. (2016). Authentic leadership and mindfulness development through action learning. *Journal of Managerial Psychology, 31*(1), 296–311.

Baykal, E. (2018). Promoting resilience through positive leadership during turmoil. *International Journal of Management and Administration, 2*(3), 34–48.

Bourdieu, P. (1990). Structures, habitus, practices. In *The logic of practice* (pp. 52–65). Polity Press.

Brewer, J. D. (2005). The public and private in C. Wright Mills's life and work. *Sociology, 39*(4), 661–677.

Campbell, A. (2010). Oxytocin and human social behavior. *Personality and Social Psychology Review, 14*(3), 281–295.

Carastathis, A. (2013). Identity categories as potential coalitions. *Signs: Journal of Women in Culture and Society, 38*(4), 941–965.
Carston, R., & Wearing, C. (2011). Metaphor, hyperbole and simile: A pragmatic approach. *Language and Cognition, 3*(2), 283–312.
Cooley, C. H. (1972). The looking glass self. J. In J. Manis & A. Meltzer (Eds.), *Symbolic interaction* (pp. 231–233). Allyn & Bacon.
Crenshaw, K. (1989). Demarginalizing the intersection of race and sex: A black feminist critique of antidiscrimination doctrine, feminist theory and antiracist politics. *University of Chicago Legal Forum, 1989*(1), 139–167.
Crenshaw, K. (1991). Mapping the margins: Intersectionality, identity politics, and violence against women of color. *Stanford Law Review, 43*(6), 1241–1299.
Davis, T., & Moody, B. (2018). Practices for promoting mindful masculinities. *New Directions for Student Services, 2018*(164), 95–104.
Decuypere, A., Audenaert, M., & Decramer, A. (2020). Leader mindfulness: Well-being throughout the organization. In *The Palgrave handbook of workplace well-being* (pp. 1–28). Palgrave Macmillan.
Donadon, M. F., Martin-Santos, R., & Osório, F. L. (2018). The associations between oxytocin and trauma in humans: A systematic review. *Frontiers in Pharmacology, 9*, 154.
Evans, D. (2018). Inside out leadership: Leadership strategies when resistance is high. *Education Today*, pp. 6–9.
Gibbons, C. (2010). Stress, Coping and Burn-Out in Nursing Students. *International Journal of Nursing Students, 47*(10), 1299–1309.
Grace, G. (1998). Critical policy scholarship: Reflections on the integrity of knowledge and research. In G. Shacklock & J. Smyth (Eds.), *Being reflexive in critical educational and social research* (p. 202). Falmer Press.
Guidroz, K., & Berger, M. T. (2009). A conversation with founding scholars of intersectionality: Kimberlé Crenshaw, Nira Yuval-Davis, and Michelle Fine. In *The intersectional approach: Transforming the academy through race, class, and gender* (pp. 61–78). University of North Carolina Press.
Guy-Sheftall, B. (1995). *Words of fire: An anthology of African-American feminist thought*. The New Press.
Haslanger, S. (2008). Changing the ideology and culture of philosophy: Not by reason (alone). *Hypatia, 23*(2), 210–223.
Hoffman, E. R., Brownley, K. A., Hamer, R. M., & Bulik, C. M. (2012). Plasma, salivary, and urinary oxytocin in anorexia nervosa: A pilot study. *Eating Behaviors, 13*(3), 256–259.
Ito, E., Shima, R., & Yoshioka, T. (2019). A novel role of oxytocin: Oxytocin-induced well-being in humans. *Biophysics and Physicobiology, 16*, 132–139. https://doi.org/10.2142/biophysico.16.0_132
Kaplan, J. B., Bergman, A. L., Christopher, M., Bowen, S., & Hunsinger, M. (2017). Role of resilience in mindfulness training for first responders. *Mindfulness, 8*(5), 1373–1380.
Krämer, N. C., Karacora, B., Lucas, G., Dehghani, M., Rüther, G., & Gratch, J. (2016). Closing the gender gap in STEM with friendly male instructors? On the effects of rapport behavior and gender of a virtual agent in an instructional interaction. *Computers & Education, 99*, 1–13.
Kroeber, A. L., & Kluckhohn, C. (1952). *Culture: A critical review of concepts and definitions* (Papers of the Peabody Museum of Archaeology & Ethnology, Harvard University). The Museum.
Lange, S., Bormann, K. C., & Rowold, J. (2018). Mindful leadership: Mindfulness as a new antecedent of destructive and transformational leadership behavior. *Gruppe. Interaktion. Organisation. Zeitschrift für Angewandte Organisationspsychologie (GIO), 49*(2), 139–147.
Lazarus, R. S., & Folkman, S. (1984). *Stress, appraisal, and coping*. Springer.
Leuschner, A. (2015). Social exclusion in academia through biases in methodological quality evaluation: On the situation of women in science and philosophy. *Studies in History and Philosophy of Science Part A, 54*, 56–63.

Lindsay, E. K., Young, S., Brown, K. W., Smyth, J. M., & Creswell, J. D. (2019). Mindfulness training reduces loneliness and increases social contact in a randomized controlled trial. *Proceedings of the National Academy of Sciences, 116*(9), 3488–3493.

Luthans, F., & Avolio, B. J. (2003). Authentic leadership development. In K. S. Cameron, J. E. Dutton, & R. E. Quinn (Eds.), *Positive organizational scholarship* (pp. 241–258). Berrett-Koehler.

Magen, J. (2018, February). This is why loneliness is bad for your health. In *World Economic Forum*.

McKinnon, A. C. (2013). Starry-eyed: Journal rankings and the future of logistics research. *International Journal of Physical Distribution & Logistics Management, 43*(1), 6–17.

Mills, C. W. (1959). The promise. In *The sociological imagination* (pp. 3–24). Oxford University Press.

Mills, C. W. (1963). *Power, politics, and people: The collected essays of C. Wright Mills*. Oxford University Press, USA.

Neider, L. L., & Schriesheim, C. A. (2011). The authentic leadership inventory (ALI): Development and empirical tests. *The Leadership Quarterly, 22*(6), 1146–1164.

Nübold, A., Van Quaquebeke, N., & Hülsheger, U. R. (2020). Be(com)ing real: A multi-source and an intervention study on mindfulness and authentic leadership. *Journal of Business and Psychology, 35*(4), 469–488.

Pinck, A. S., & Sonnentag, S. (2018). Leader mindfulness and employee well-being: The mediating role of transformational leadership. *Mindfulness, 9*(3), 884–896.

Pittman, A. (2020). Leadership rebooted: Cultivating trust with the brain in mind. *Human Service Organizations: Management, Leadership & Governance, 44*(2), 127–143.

Reb, J., Narayanan, J., Chaturvedi, S., & Ekkirala, S. (2017). The mediating role of emotional exhaustion in the relationship of mindfulness with turnover intentions and job performance. *Mindfulness 8*(3), 707–716.

Rokach, A. (2014). Leadership and loneliness. *International Journal of Leadership and Change, 2*(1), 6.

Schaumberg, R. L., & Flynn, F. J. (2017). Self-reliance: A gender perspective on its relationship to communality and leadership evaluations. *Academy of Management Journal, 60*(5), 1859–1881.

Silard, A., & Wright, S. (2020). The price of wearing (or not wearing) the crown: The effects of loneliness on leaders and followers. *Leadership, 16*, 389–410.

Skogstad, A., Hetland, J., Glasø, L., & Einarsen, S. (2014). Is avoidant leadership a root cause of subordinate stress? Longitudinal relationships between laissez-faire leadership and role ambiguity. *Work & Stress, 28*(4), 323–341.

Smallen, D. (2019). Mindful masculinity: Positive psychology, McMindfulness and gender. *Feminist Review, 122*(1), 134–150.

Sutcliffe, K. M., Vogus, T. J., & Dane, E. (2016). Mindfulness in organizations: a cross-level review. *Annual Review of Organizational Psychology. Organizational Behavior*. 3, 55–81.

Tajfel, H. (1969). Cognitive aspects of prejudice. *Journal of Social Issues*, 25, 79–97.

Tajfel, H. (1978). Intergroup behavior. In *Introducing social psychology* (pp. 401–466). Penguin Books.

Tajfel, H. (1981). *Human groups and social categories: Studies in social psychology*. CUP Archive.

Tajfel, H., & Turner, J. C. (1979). An integrative theory of intergroup conflict. *The Social Psychology of Intergroup Relations, 33*(47), 74.

Tajfel, H., & Turner, J. (1986). The social identity theory of intergroup behaviour. In S. Worchel & W. G. Austin (Eds.), *Psychology of intergroup relations*. Nelson Hall.

Wasylkiw, L., Holton, J., Azar, R., & Cook, W. (2015). The impact of mindfulness on leadership effectiveness in a health care setting: A pilot study. *Journal of Health Organization and Management, 29*(7), 893–911.

Zak, P. J. (2017). The neuroscience of trust. *Harvard Business Review, 95*(1), 84–90.

Zak, P. J. (2018). How oxytocin can make your job more meaningful. *Greater Good Magazine*. Online https://greatergood.berkeley.edu/article/item/how_oxytocin_can_make_your_job_more_meaningful

Zak, P. J., & Knack, S. (2001). Trust and growth. *The Economic Journal, 111*(470), 295–321.
Zak, P. J., Stanton, A. A., & Ahmadi, S. (2007). Oxytocin increases generosity in humans. *PLoS One, 2*, e1128. https://doi.org/10.1371/journal.pone.0001128

Chapter 3
Inclusive Leadership in an Increasingly Diversified World

Babar Dharani and Kurt April

Abstract An instinctive in-grouping and out-grouping of people by our psyche is a form of an adaptive 'fixation' that can lead to immense suffering for those excluded. Exposure to diversity is a foundational step to break free from this fixation, which has been supported by social movements pioneered by iconic leaders and is now vastly regulated through legislation, moral inclinations, as well as an acute recognition of the benefits of diversity to groups and organizations. Therefore, the role of leadership in enhancing diversity is proven and profound. However, the needs have now shifted to enhancing inclusion. While a concise definition of 'inclusive leadership' is under debate and overlaps yet differentiates itself from other forms of leadership, it is embedded in ensuring justice and equity, enabling people to belong to a group while helping them preserve their uniqueness, becoming conscious of one's own privileges, as well as finding the voice to express our concerns and opinions skilfully when out-grouped. Inclusive leadership emanates at all levels in an organization, from top management to managerial levels, as well as at an employee level—from those belonging to privileged groups to those being out-grouped/marginalized. Collective leadership initiatives from all levels can allow for enhanced inclusivity.

Keywords Group dynamics · Exclusion · Diversity · Inclusion · Inclusive leadership

Introduction

Theories of group dynamics (Friedkin & Johnsen, 2011; Lewin, 1947) highlight that when we interact with others, we tend to marginalize and out-group some people and include and in-group others (Tajfel et al., 1971), or revert to purposeful social distancing (April et al., 2013). In-grouping leads to inclusion, while

B. Dharani (✉) · K. April
University of Cape Town, Cape Town, South Africa

J. Marques (ed.), *Innovative Leadership in Times of Compelling Changes*, Management, Change, Strategy and Positive Leadership, https://doi.org/10.1007/978-3-030-67258-4_3

out-grouping bears the risk of exclusion of others. These largely subconscious decisions are based on a variety of reasons to collectively either differentiate individuals from others or allow for similarities to resonate between them. The fundamentals of who forms a part of one's in-group and who does not are founded in human biology and can be explained through evolutionary theories (Boyd & Richerson, 2009). Social distancing concerns an individual's feelings towards other individuals or groups (providing essential clues to human attitudes) and affects levels of intimacy, or intensity of rejection, between the members of widely represented culture groups—sometimes referred to as social approval (Payne et al., 1974)—used as a measurement of spatial distance (Park & Rothbart, 1982) or social proximity (Ogunlade, 1980), used as an explanation for social decisions (Akerlof, 1997), and is also often used as a tool in the study of intergroup conflict (Pettigrew, 1960).

Fundamentals of Inclusion

Charles Darwin's (1859) theory of natural selection through evolution focused on the adaptation of species to the environment as they grow and reproduce, such that only those attributes of the species that are best suited to their surroundings survive over generations. One such attribute is our ability to form an identity and in-group with those similar to us, e.g. in the field of ethnography, zoologist Konrad Lorenz's concept of 'imprinting' (cited by Vicedo, 2009) explored a form of learning in which an animal gains its sense of identification. In Lorenz's popular experiment with geese, instead of the mother goose, Lorenz was present during the 'sensitive time' after the hatching of the eggs. This made the hatchlings 'imprint' Lorenz as their self-identifiers. As such, these baby birds followed Lorenz around as they would their mothers in nature.

Similar to imprinting in animals, imprinting is explored in human psychology as attachment theory (Bowlby, 1958). Attachment theory suggests that after birth and during our infancy, we form our initial foundations of self-identity based on our primary caregivers. Since these people ensured our survival as an infant through the provision of physiological, safety, and belonging needs (Maslow, 1943) such as the provision of food, security, and appropriate temperature and emotional connections, this infantile attachment develops our identity in the image of our caregivers and regards people similar to the caregivers to be trustworthy—our in-group. Such behaviour is 'fit' for survival, therefore, it is passed on over generations and present in nearly all mammalian species. To verify self-identity based on visual characteristics, the doll experiment (Clark & Clark, 1950) tested children of ages three to seven by presenting them with four identical dolls of different shades of skin colours to check the accuracy of their self-identification. It was noted that even at such an early age, children could accurately identify which doll represented them.

Allport's contact hypothesis confirmed that young children show a preference for playing with children whom they regard to be similar to their identity. In his hypothesis, children preferred those of the same skin colour or those who simply happen to be wearing similar clothes (Allport & Kramer, 1946). Thus, the reason for inclusion in our in-group stems from our own self-identity, and exclusion of others stems from 'othering' (Brons, 2015) those who are seen to be different from us in aspects that form our identity.

Freud (1921) theorized the concept of transference, where all interactions in our life, subsequent to our first interactions after birth, are founded on feelings, desires, and expectations of that initial interaction that is redirected and applied to another person. Hence, our interactions are never 'pure', but always marred with transference from past interactions, prone to prejudging people. As we grow, we develop a variety of categorizations of humans and subconsciously attribute similar expectations from all within that category (socially known as pigeonholing). Generalized expectations of groups of people develop as mental models, and societal consensus of these leads to stereotyping and prejudice against certain groups of people and the social orientations of groups of people. A cognitive response to such overgeneralization by our psyche leads to discriminatory behaviour.

Current Inclusion Concerns

Exclusion forms the basis for pigeonholing, stereotyping, prejudice, marginalization, and discrimination against groups of people. Another test from the doll experiment in 1950 (Clark & Clark, 1950) asked African American children to choose a doll they preferred. The children preferred the white doll and assigned positive characteristics to it, highlighting the lack of positive connotations associated with the doll they referred to as representative of themselves. Jane Elliott's famous arbitrary, blue eyes-brown eyes experiment with white children in Riceville, Iowa, in 1968, a day after the assassination of Rev. Dr. Martin Luther King Jr., surprised many as it highlighted how quickly and easily prejudice could be learned. Most worryingly about the Elliot classroom experiment was the almost immediate negative effects, such short periods of discrimination had on the reading and mathematical abilities of the children, who were doing much better in the period before the experiment was conducted—and we can only imagine such impacts over a lifetime of prejudice and discrimination from childhood and into adulthood. The Clarks concluded that prejudice, discrimination, and segregation created feelings of inferiority among African American children and damaged their self-esteem. Thus, the implications of exclusion are far-reaching in respect of fairness, justice, as well as emotional and psychological well-being.

To avoid these negative implications against certain groups of people, legislation has been introduced in many countries to protect them from continued exclusion and marginalization. For example, South Africa's recent history of white supremacy enforced by the apartheid government has resulted in a constitution that is regarded as one of the most well-drafted in the world in respect of promoting equality. *The constitutional right to equality in South Africa (section 9 of the Constitution, 1996)* protects against discrimination based on race, gender, sex, pregnancy, marital status, ethnic or social origin, colour, sexual orientation, age, disability, religion, conscience, belief, culture, language, and birth, thus recognizing the susceptibility for exclusion based on these identifiers. Affirmative action has encouraged diversity and greater levels of intergroup contact, increasing levels of proximity to out-groups have allowed opportunities for citizens' adaptive fixation to fade, and the moral compass to slowly shift over generations such that inequalities imposed through exclusion in the country's history are now viewed as cringeworthy. They reinforce a dedication to correct injustices of the past by ensuring diversity in social and work settings going forward.

While diversity often refers to the degree of diverse personnel in an organization and their varied strands of difference such as ascribed gender and non-binary, race and ethnicity, physical abilities, age, nationality, language, religion, heritage, value systems, roles and functions, thought processes, psychological profiles, life experiences, sexual orientation, family status, talent, skills, beliefs, education, and perspectives, among others, inclusion entails: '… the right to access and active participation and achieving equity through engagement in all aspects of daily life' (Hyde, 2014, p. 5) or '… about creating empowering environments of difference, where people can be themselves, comfortably contributing their full selves and all the ways in which they differ from others, and respecting others without making it difficult for others to be their full selves' (April, 2007). As such, inclusion requires in-grouping those who are 'othered'. A host of additional benefits arise when diversity in an organization progresses to inclusion. Inclusion is proven to positively affect an organization's performance by tapping into a greater pool of talent for hiring, ensuring higher levels of employee engagement, a broader range of employees having their ideas developed and prototyped, improving customer understanding and service to a broader customer base, providing opportunities to enter into niche markets, and enhancing flexibility and capability to respond and adapt to change, all of which allow for greater accessibility to customer segments and capital markets through showcasing of such organizational attributes and potentials (April & Blass, 2010).

However, diversity can fall short of optimally reaping all of these benefits in the absence of inclusion. For example, while diversity leads to: '… opportunities for creativity through different perspectives, [it may exist] at the cost of group members finding it difficult to identify with the work group due to its diversity' (Randel et al., 2018, p. 200) in the absence of inclusion. Inclusion allows for harvesting optimal benefits of diversity in an organization; it improves employee performance and retention through happiness at work (Fisher, 2010) and allows for diverse problem-solving through varied perspectives, all of which are vital in today's globalized economy that is fast-changing, presenting a potential source of sustained competitive advantage for an organization as it can be challanging and relatively slow to replicate by its competitors (Achor, 2010; Barney, 1991).

Due to increased recognition of the usefulness of diversity, globalization, legislation, and acceptance of the suffering associated with marginalization, there is increased diversity in our surroundings. Exposure to diverse people from a young age for many of the new generations has rendered several reasons for 'othering' as redundant in their psychological frame of mind. However, this does not halt the psychological processes of 'othering'. Since identities are based on intersectionality (Crenshaw, 1991), where many social categories and attributes that form one's identity mesh together in an intersectional way to form a person's identity, recent research reveals a gradual move away from grouping people based on differences classified under protected classes. For example, during our research into reasons for out-grouping, one of our interviewees shared:

> To get a deeper impression of what they [children interviewed] consider relevant attributes for [othering—identifying children that are different], I asked them to mention 'other kids' in their groups that are different from the rest. The examples they provided suggest that in their eyes, the relevant attributes are related to the skills and behaviors of others, rather than their physical properties. For example, one kid was mentioned because of her beautiful handwriting. Another one was mentioned because she tends to be rude. In contrast, skin colour seemed to be totally irrelevant, as it did not appear on their list of 'different' children. (P202)

Comparing this more modern response to the 1950s doll experiment (Clark & Clark, 1950), it is evident that attributes prompting exclusion are changing and hopefully will continue to do so. While racism, sexism, ageism, and discrimination against other protected classes are not entirely eliminated and total inclusion continues to remain a dream, legal protection, education regarding matters of exclusion which promotes empathy, and shifts in morality have assisted. Instead, expressions of exclusion have moved from dehumanization, where excluded groups were considered sub-humans, to other forms of pressures. These include deculturalization, defeminization, and having to overcompensate to fight preconceived ideas—these are all still experienced by minority groups to be fully accepted by dominant groups. For example, evidence of minority cultures facing deculturalization for integration is explicit in lack of traditional (non-Western) attire in certain settings to behaviours such as straightening of hair by African women of Bantu or other origins that typically have curly hair. Additionally, women experience pressures of defeminization, whereby women adopt typical masculine behaviours to gain recognition or appreciation in male-dominated environments while simultaneously experiencing pressures for fulfilling the traditional roles associated with womanhood and having to battle the glass ceiling they encounter in commercial settings or when supposedly 'accepted' in corporate boardrooms, set up in glass cliff scenarios.

Inclusive Leadership

Having addressed the biological nature of humans towards 'othering', it is intriguing how leaders can contribute to inclusivity when its foundations are embedded in our instincts. Many historic leaders have contributed to this shift from exacerbated examples of exclusion in our history, pioneering the concept of equality, to lead to significant progress towards acceptance of diversity. For example, Martin Luther King Jr., Mother Teresa, Mahatma Gandhi, Rosa Parks, and Nelson Mandela are all hailed as heroes for their immense resilience and self-sacrifice for their contributions to the cause of fighting discrimination and promoting equality, which emanated as a 'dream' and has slowly progressed towards becoming reality (King, 1999). One known role model that pioneered such social movements is Elizabeth Cady Stanton, a well-educated and chief philosopher of women's rights and suffrage movements who in the mid-nineteenth century formulated the agenda for women's rights that ultimately guided the struggle well into the twentieth century. Similarly, Rosa Parks who refused to adhere to the legal obligation to forgo her seat on a bus to a white person fundamentally had an acute sense of justice, a strong belief of being equal to the dominant group, and bravery to act on her beliefs. Numerous such heroes broke through the barriers of institutionalized exclusion through activism.

Activism was the dominant remedy to correct exclusion that was legislated. However, institutionalized discrimination and the moral compass have changed, and with that, both the leadership demands and the remedies against exclusion have shifted. They now incorporate a host of varied solutions for enhancing inclusion from a combined effort from a variety of people in different leadership positionings. In light of the changing nature of inclusion demands, and the need for continued effort to advance towards the realization of the dream, the novel requirements from leaders at all levels for continuous efforts towards inclusion are discussed below:

Top Leadership

Diversity in an organization refers to the fair representation of varied groups of people that are present in the organization. The expectations are set with reference to the diversity that socially surrounds the organization—the society in which the organization operates. Top leaders of institutions have easier access to levers of power and networks and can direct the path to equality. Based on national diversity, many countries have adopted employment equity and affirmative action policies, which aim to protect marginalized groups in societies and encourage a degree of their presence in organizations. Such legislation affirms diversity in organizations through regulations and regards a lack of diversity as evidence of institutionalized discrimination against protected groups. The legislation may establish quotas, and, in its compliance, human resources departments in organizations may ensure hiring accordingly to avoid legal implications such as fines while preventing reputational damage to the organization. As the first step to inclusive leadership, it is important to take account of the level of diversity in the organization by measuring it (April & Blass, 2010) and ensuring adherence to regulations pertaining to it.

While such legislation gives diversity a governmental seal of approval, it does not necessarily promote heightened consciousness about it in an organization. How well matters of diversity are addressed in an organization's policies and procedures, and encouraged and emphasized in the workplace, are subject to those in top leadership positions in organizations to move it to the centre of the organization's consciousness, rather than letting it fester in its shadow—the unacknowledged, dark side of an organizational psyche that is instinctive, irrational, and prone to psychological projections (Corlett & Pearson, 2003). After ensuring a diverse employee base, it is also the extent of fair representation of diverse people in the organization that indicates how well it is grounded in an organization's consciousness. A lack of fair representation is evident in many scenarios, such as different hierarchical levels in an organization represented by different groups of people (e.g. presence of men in the boardroom and women in support and administrative roles), physical segregation or physical distancing of diverse employees (such as formations of groups and cliques that are visually evident), or task distancing where the distribution of work is along the lines of group divisions, even if segregation is not visually evident (e.g. a racial group dominant in managerial positions and another racial group in subordinate positions in an open plan office environment), to name a few (April et al., in press). Hence, fair and transparent appraisal systems of performance and promotions are key elements for fair representation of out-groups throughout the organization.

Transformational leadership is necessary to trigger-start diversity and fair representation. Such leadership requires an unshakably strong pro-diversity stance, as Abraham Lincoln had which led the world to change its stance on slavery. In respect of inclusive leadership, it also overlaps with empowering and servant leadership styles. While a concise definition of inclusive leadership is being debated, it is the general consensus that leadership styles that are conducive for managing all employees' emotions and concerns are vital fundamentals of inclusive leadership. So, not only do people in top leadership positions have the power to introduce and incorporate policies that ensure diversity, and place emphasis on such policies to support fair representation across the organization, inclusion may also require empowering out-groups through the flexibility of norms to specially cater for out-groups and take actions to accommodate for them (e.g. the physical office environment may require to be changed to cater for employees with disabilities, such as those in wheelchairs).

Featured Case in Point: Dimexon Diamonds Ltd

A row of parked scooters, and some approaching, greeted me one morning during my first visit to India. Solo riders, or two on some, the scooters mildly screeched as they parked. Disembarking the scooters one by one, the ladies smiled and chin wagged with one another while fixing their outfits for any creases that the scooter ride may have subjected on their colourful clothes. I had never seen such unique colours anywhere else before, and I doubt that they have identifying names in English. Unsurprisingly, the scene tickled my senses well before the sight of a single diamond at the polishing facility I was visiting. The purr of the scooter engines mingled with delicate noises of the sonorous bells dangling from the women's ankle jewellery—'paayal'. The grey tar of the road layered with dirt on the edges formed hues of dull, brown-grey that sharply contrasted with the ample folded, eye-catching, bright fabrics which the women wore. The subtle smell of burning gasoline of the scooters was frequently whisked away by the refreshing fragrance of fresh jasmine that each woman wore in her hair. Small, but bright bunches of white flowers, on a background of jet-black hair, accompanied with their melodious 'paayal', and the shimmering of their shiny embroidery sparkling in the gentle morning sun, as if 'Surya', the Hindu sun goddess, was selectively showering blessings on them as they happily walked into the compound. I joined the women to enter the well-manicured lawns of the factory, which resembled a pampered, elite estate, dotted with houses, but which were factories where the women worked. Each factory resembling a house focused on a process in the conversion of pebble-like rough diamonds into excellent cut, polished diamonds for worldwide distribution.

I soon discovered that the blessings of financial independence to women were delivered through employment at Dimexon Diamonds Ltd by its founder and Chairman, Mr. Pankaj Mehta. Dimexon – the 50-year-old-plus business was the only manufacturer of diamonds that employs women, with well over 90% of its workforce being women. Oppression and subordination of women is a worldwide phenomenon. India's customs, be it ancient ones such as 'sati' (where a widow sacrificed herself by sitting atop her deceased husband's funeral pyre), or those lasting till date, such as the financially burdensome dowries (payment by the women's family to a man for marriage) are evidence of it. It is intriguing that in such a hostile environment against women, their potential was recognized, and they were given employment opportunities by this entrepreneur. A role other than that of a home-maker has allowed them financial and physical freedom, as they scoot around the city, and to and from work, with their friends and colleagues.

Talking to Mr. Mehta, his strong stance for the inclusion of women and his regard for their contribution to his success are evident. The decision to employ women was initially seeded on business acumen, where operationally, smaller hands were better suited for the turntables for polishing small diamonds, which remains Dimexon's niche business, and a stronger sense of integrity in women entailed less leakage of this precious commodity. Also, a lack of alternative employment opportunities in the city had ensured high retention rates. This decision to employ women soon became a prime source of competitive advantage for the business. Clearly, a symbiotic relationship thrived, where the business flourished due to women, and women flourished in the city of Coimbatore due to Dimexon—a prime example of a win-win scenario of inclusion.

The business and social case are evident, but it was the psychological set-point that allowed Mr. Mehta to acknowledge the potential of women beyond the traditional role as a homemaker which bore the seeds that allowed both parties to flourish. Questioning the status quo, challenging it, and changing it requires a collision with long-standing cultural norms, and a strong, brave leadership stance. A clear hint of the foundations of such a psychological stance is evident from one of Mr. Mehta's corporate social responsibility projects, where a College funded by him is named after his mother. It can be presumed that respect and acknowledgment of women exhibited by Mr. Mehta were founded in his childhood home, which over the years allowed his business, as well as his community, to reap the benefits.

While the benefit from inclusion led to Dimexon's success, the company's continued care for women at work was evident in how happy the women at the factory looked, the hygiene of the canteen catering for them, a fully vegetarian menu well aligned to the cultural and religious values, the supply of sanitary pads, as well as numerous posters with contact details of the Human Resource Management personnel responsible for attending to any issues of sexual harassment. The environment was transparent about the empowerment of women and the provision of a safe haven for them. The benefits of caring for female employees, yet again, were not limited to the women. The Human Resources Department revealed how women employed, over the years, have encouraged their daughters to seek employment at Dimexon upon completing school; thus, enabling the company to retain its source of competitive advantage over generations, and reap the immense benefits of employee loyalty that stretched across generations—inter-generational employee loyalty.

Additionally, the fair progression of women in this global organization has entailed that they have progressed up the ladder; for example, to hold finance manager positions in Dubai and Antwerp offices, several senior sales positions, as well as being a part of the senior leadership team in Hong Kong for the global company. 50 years on, Mr. Metha's attitude to women in the workplace has been transformative for the organization and the city, and a continuous effort to the cause is evident as female representation on the board is explicitly discussed and sought. At the end of my visit and subsequent work for the organization for 6 years, I can't help but consider the surroundings of the factory as rough diamonds, and Dimexon as the polished diamond in the city.

Managerial Leadership

Encouraging diversity, efforts to recruit diversely and fairly promote individuals, even those that do not form part of the dominant culture of the organization, are only the first steps in tapping into all employees' potential for contribution to the organization. The next level is their inclusion, which requires inclusive leadership to take a more hands-on management of diversity in groups and a more personalized leadership towards those 'othered'. Managerial roles are differentiated from the top leadership in their proximity to the other employees at work on a regular basis. Management of group dynamics is relevant to all groups in an organization, stretching from junior groups to the board. As such, even in the case of top leadership, they play the dual role of leadership in their capacity as top management for the organization, as well as a managerial role for the board and senior leadership team.

Managerial leadership for inclusion, due to their frequency of interactions and proximity to subordinates, can influence the work environment differently to top leadership to ensure that it is conducive for inclusion. Scholars have theorized the climate for inclusion as a construct and tested its empirical evidence in contribution to matters of diversity and inclusion. The climate for inclusion is concluded as: '…

an important starting point… to minimize divisive conflict and to do so by minimizing structural inequalities, norms for assimilation, and exclusionary decision-making processes' (Nishii, 2013, p. 1769).

Diversity and fair representation can fall short of inclusion where minorities have penetrated the in-group in an organizational culture by the adoption of the dominant cultural practices and behaviours, such as through deculturalization or defeminization, thus dampening the varied contribution that diversity has the potential for. These adaptations of out-groups form the repressed energies that fall short in their potential contribution to organizational strategy, direction, and culture, as their uniqueness is suppressed by the dominant culture and their loud, relatively homogenous voices (compared to what an out-group member can provide) in group settings.

Social identification theory conceptualizes the need for individuals to be a part of the group, hence fulfilling belonging needs (Maslow, 1943), and yet be seen as an individual. Individual group members wish to belong to the group and contribute while remaining authentic to the aspects that caused them to be different from the dominant culture of the organization. These needs are argued to exist simultaneously (Randel et al., 2018). While these may seem to be contradictory, the push and pull factors of both the needs entail that a balance is needed within each individual's psyche—between the degree of in-grouping and individuality. Hence, the core requirement for inclusive and deft leadership in respect of group dynamics is a requirement for leaders to signal the inclusion of group members while allowing them to maintain their sense of individuality and uniqueness.

As such, inclusive leadership at a managerial level requires a different 'type of animal' than executive leadership. While top leadership must ensure diversity, promote it to the centre of the organization's consciousness, establish fair appraisal and promotion systems, even encourage the human resources department to provide diversity and inclusion training and facilitation, etc., the role of a managerial leader is more embedded in group dynamics, person engagement, and fundamentally around communications, as one of our research participants stated:

> I realised the need to more carefully listen to people and not just assume I understood their needs, expectations, and points of view. It made me aware of the importance to develop a set of tools with which to deal with diversity, recognising that self-improvement was a large part of understanding others. Initially, it was very difficult to interact with all the different cultures, but as I started to listen more and as I started to realise to deal with differences in a non-emotional way… communication and understanding became easier. (P55)

Entering into dialogue regarding inclusion is a critical first step in what Carl Jung called 'mysterium coniunctionis' (coming together of the different points of views to honour diverse positions and transcend the group to emerge a variety of perspectives to a united position) (Jung, 1921). In addition to active listening, diplomatic and clear communication, and promoting dialogue, sharing of 'air time' fairly during group meetings, facilitation of meetings to turn up the volume of the unheard voices, showing appreciation of varied perspectives, and encouraging shared decision-making are found to positively contribute to group members' perceptions of inclusion which, in turn, contribute to the group through their unique perspectives which adds variety to the thought and decision process of the group (April et. al., in press).

Due to the proximity of such leaders to group members, their aptitude for managing interpersonal interactions as well as conflict, which requires a variety of skills, is seen as a quality suitable for inclusive leaders. Additionally, their exhibitions of the inclusiveness of out-group members outside of group scenarios are also vital. They need to act as a role model for inclusion outside of group scenarios to allow it to be replicated by group members in group situations. Such behaviour is more likely to be exhibited by those who are pro-diversity, exhibit humility and emotional maturity, and possess cognitive complexity (Randel et al., 2018).

Empowered Individuals

Since our subconscious largely dictates in-groups and out-groups, the effect of encountering people we instinctively out-group is one of having to manage our anxiety levels arising from the encounter which our psyche regards as a threat (Baumeister et al., 1998). In addition to the personal threat of such an encounter, in groups, the dominant or privileged group introduced to a minority as a potential new group member also evokes anxiety stemming from preconceptions and prejudice about the other group which the outsider represents. Unless addressed through the facilitated release of this negative group energy, it can progress to expressions, ranging from subtle micro-aggressions to overwhelming dehumanization of the group member seen as an outsider. The continued inclusion of out-group members, without the release of this anxiety, can repress the sentiments of the dominant group feeling anxious and fearing to become a minority themselves, leading to a deep-seated fear of losing their privilege that can result in high-tension conflict (Smit, 2014).

However, the dynamics of exclusion are changing from predominantly protected groups feeling out-grouped to a host of reasons for feeling excluded. Firstly, as protected groups are increasingly introduced to organizational settings, the reasons for exclusion shift. For example, women introduced to a workplace are likely to feel out-grouped due to being female in a male-dominated corporate environment. However, as more women join the workforce, the reasons for exclusion may not remain restricted to gender, but progress to alternative reasons for feeling out-grouped, for example, women talking about motherhood in the workplace may alienate those who are not a mother, and those who come from rural areas may be alienated by more urbanized women—because our identities are not restricted to one category, but act in an intersectional way (Crenshaw, 1991). Such intersectionality can greatly alter privilege and access, e.g. white males may be a privileged group, but add in the category of being homosexual and the privilege changes significantly (Christensen & Jensen, 2014).

As such, people are experiencing a host of reasons for being excluded, including language (globalization creates an interactive melting pot of dialects), conversations (which vary immensely based on socio-economic backgrounds, e.g. one group may talk about their next travel destination while others struggle to make ends meet), appearance (where body size and length, as well as conventional norms of beauty, provide distinct advantages), education (where one's school and university alma maters can lead to access, hierarchy, and clique formation), and where training/discipline backgrounds provide social and economic status, to name a few (April et al., in press). As such, despite a group's historic privileges, an increasing number of individuals are facing evolving scenarios of exclusion.

A prime benefit of these increased variations of exclusion, and an increasing number of people who have experienced it, is that the consciousness of privilege is increasingly being recognized by members of dominant groups—with a heightened sense of privileged identification than those who are out-grouped—hopefully with the necessary, accompanying sensitivity towards others. While organizationally, less powerful groups may not immediately be granted increased power and authority (such as top leadership or those in managerial positions) for addressing matters of inclusion, they can still be 'inclusive leaders' in their own right that act within employee groups. Such in-group leadership stems from diversity and inclusion training, high emotional intelligence, other-awareness, and conscientiousness—more frequently observed by those who have 'out-of-box experiences', e.g. overseas secondments, emigration/relocations, or interdepartmental transfers. They have the potential to be in-group champions of inclusion and can trigger acknowledgement and recognition of privilege and power dynamics for the entire group should they take on the leadership role.

Inclusive leaders need to be seen to be building organizations that acknowledge bias and privilege and empower everyone towards identifying, recognizing, and compassionately calling out occurrences of exclusion. Such leaders must themselves solicit input from people and say 'thank you' when others point out their bias(es). If they do get it wrong occasionally, they need to quickly apologize. The rule is to not 'perfect' the outcome, but rather to make 'progress' toward the outcome, which takes time. Additionally, inclusive leaders must structure decision-making with clear criteria and set transparent, objective standards in advance, for evaluating individuals' performances. During meetings, contributions from everyone need to be noted, and success also needs to be accurately attributed.

Disempowered Individuals

Leadership is frequently associated with power; thus, it is counterintuitive to fathom the idea that leadership can arise from those stripped of power in society. It was Plato who intuited that true leadership emerges from demerited and challenging experiences and environments, e.g. as stated earlier, Martin Luther King Jr., Mahatma Gandhi, and Nelson Mandela all rose from the depths of dehumanization and actively led social movements towards inclusion—providing moral compasses for others, choosing to serve, and ended up leading as a result. By being a voice for the marginalized and downtrodden, they have left a challenge for leaders across the globe to be the best for the world, and not only the best in the world, through non-traditional means.

First, an awareness of the protected group's rights, stemming from either legislation or organization policies, is vital to allow those who are protected to feel empowered (Santoso & Kulathunga, 2016). Such empowerment can be leveraged by out-group members to avoid oppression and demand and enhance equal treatment. Bullying and oppression is a common concern for out-group members. Examples of these are instances where out-group members, due to repression of their voices and privileges, or traditional roles associated with their group, are subject to delegation of tasks beyond the scope of the individual, namely, an expectation of women to serve refreshments or take notes in meetings or younger employees expected to perform menial tasks even where their employment grade does not require them to. Awareness of one's job profile and channels of reporting can support those feeling marginalized to avoid oppression. However, the expectation from those facing such scenarios is that they must take a leadership position in voicing the concerns of the oppressed group.

The negative psychological effects of feeling excluded, oppressed, marginalized, and discriminated against are intense, vast, and varied—ranging from discomfort to anxiety, from anger to depression, all of which can result in mild to severe negative psychological consequences of learnt helplessness to victimization mentality, developing poor self-esteem, and even paranoia (April et al., in press). A major leadership role from those feeling alienated is one of hermetic transformation of the group (Corlett & Pearson, 2003). Its prominence lies in the fact that the dominant group has had their privileges 'embedded' in their lives for extended periods; thus, they take it for granted and are largely ignorant of the fact that others may not experience similar privileges in life. By voicing personal experiences, awareness of the experiences of out-groups can resonate with the morality of inclusion and penetrate the dominant group that can lead out-group members to be acknowledged for the challenges they face.

However, opportunities to share experiences and attempting to increase the volume of the repressed voices are highly subject to the level of empowerment perceived by the out-group members. Historical or ancestral disempowerment, the native culture of the out-group members, and personality traits dictate an out-group member's ability to lead the group towards a path of inclusion. For example, a core self-evaluation personality trait of external locus of control (Judge & Bono, 2001; Rotter, 1966), where control is perceived to exist in the hands of powerful others, or on fate/luck, can pose a hindrance in taking initiatives for inclusion. Such a personality regards occurrences in one's life to lie outside the control of the individual and is frequently associated with learnt helplessness and hopelessness (Seligman, 1972). Similarly, a victimization mentality does not encourage an individual to take a leadership role towards inclusion. While leadership potential from out-group members towards inclusion is a vital ingredient towards inclusive group dynamics, empowerment of out-group members is required to allow for such leadership to be seeded. As such, the role of executive leadership, managerial leadership, and leadership from empowered individuals is a necessary facilitator for inclusive leadership from out-group members.

Since the voices of those oppressed play an important role in this leadership, psychological traits that allow one to find one's voice (such as self-esteem, empowerment to allow for risk-taking associated with being heard) and communication skills (such as diplomacy, directness, clarity of expression, and judgement calls regarding confronting expressions of exclusion) are critical skillsets for this leadership.

Chapter Takeaways

As a result of overwhelming suffering from exclusion, the world has embarked upon a journey towards inclusivity. This has entailed legislative changes, moral shifts, and an understanding of the benefits of inclusion in a globalized world. However, 'othering' people is instinctive, and inclusion requires leadership—the demands of which are ever-changing. First, the basis of exclusion is changing from protected classes to a variety of reasons for feeling alienated. Second, the legislative stance on diversity is empowering those susceptible to discrimination. In such an environment, inclusive leadership has shifted from being dominated by activism to incorporate inclusive leadership at all levels within organizations. Executive leadership is primarily responsible for ensuring justice and equity, leaders at a managerial level can help group dynamics such as assisting to preserve uniqueness yet enabling those alienated to belong to the group, and fellow employees can lead the cause by becoming conscious of their own privileges, while disempowered individuals can contribute greatly by a hermetic transformation of group dynamics by sharing concerns and voicing their opinions skilfully when out-grouped.

Reflection Questions

1. Identify people/groups that are excluded by any group you belong to (e.g. your group of friends, a group of colleagues, your family, or your organization) and query why they are out-grouped?
2. What can assist (or has assisted) to contain and manage triggers of exclusion of these people?
3. How would the inclusion of these people/groups benefit the stakeholders? (i.e. how would your friends, family, colleagues, or organization benefit from the inclusion of these people/groups?)
4. Identify leadership characteristics that you would like to develop within yourself, and examine if these qualities promote inclusion.
5. In light of the changes in demands of inclusion over time, how do you foresee them changing further in the future?

References

Achor, S. (2010). *The happiness advantage: The seven principles of positive psychology that fuel success and performance at work*. Ebury Publishing.

Akerlof, G. A. (1997). Social distance and social decisions. *Econometrica, 65*(5), 1005–1027. https://doi.org/10.2307/2171877

Allport, G. W., & Kramer, B. M. (1946). Some roots of prejudice. *The Journal of Psychology, 22*(1), 9–39. https://doi.org/10.1080/00223980.1946.9917293

April, K. A. (2007). Ways of looking at reality. In K. April & M. Shockley (Eds.), *Diversity: New realities in a changing world* (pp. 9–13). Palgrave Macmillan.

April, K. A., & Blass, E. (2010). Measuring diversity practice and developing inclusion. *Dimensions, 1*(1), 59–66. https://doi.org/10.4102/sajbm.v45i2.122

April, K., Dharani, B., & April, A. (in press) *Lived experiences of exclusion: The psychological and behavioural effects*. Bingley: Emerald Publishing.

April, K., Loubser, J., Özbilgin, M., & Al-Ariss, A. (2013). Managing diversity in higher education: Understanding and tackling ethnic stratification in social comfort. *South African Journal of Higher Education, 27*(5), 1164–1180.

Barney, J. (1991). Firm resources and sustained competitive advantage. *Journal of Management, 17*(1), 99–120. https://doi.org/10.1177/014920639101700108

Baumeister, R., Dale, K., & Sommer, K. (1998). Freudian defense mechanisms and empirical findings in modern social psychology: Reaction formation, projection, displacement, undoing, isolation, sublimation, and denial. *Journal of Personality, 66*(6), 1081–1124. https://doi.org/10.1111/1467-6494.00043

Bowlby, J. (1958). The nature of the child's tie to his mother. *International Journal of Psychoanalysis, 39*, 350–371.

Boyd, R., & Richerson, P. J. (2009). Culture and the evolution of human cooperation. *Philosophical Transactions of the Royal Society B: Biological Sciences, 364*(1533), 3281–3288. https://doi.org/10.1098/rstb.2009.0134

Brons, L. (2015). Othering, an analysis. *Transcience: A Journal of Global Studies, 6*(1), 69–90. https://doi.org/10.17613/M6V968

Christensen, A., & Jensen, S. Q. (2014). Combining hegemonic masculinity and intersectionality. *NORMA: International Journal for Masculinity Studies, 9*(1), 60–75. https://doi.org/10.1080/18902138.2014.892289

Clark, K. B., & Clark, M. P. (1950). Emotional factors in racial identification and preference in negro children. *The Journal of Negro Education, 19*(3), 341–350. https://doi.org/10.2307/2966491

Corlett, J., & Pearson, C. (2003). *Mapping the organizational psyche: A Jungian theory of organizational dynamics and change*. Centre of Application of Psychological Type.

Crenshaw, K. (1991). Mapping the margins: Intersectionality, identity politics, and violence against women of color. *Stanford Law Review, 43*(6), 1241–1299. https://doi.org/10.2307/1229039

Darwin, C. (1859). *On the origin of species*. John Murray.

Fisher, C. D. (2010). Happiness at work. *International Journal of Management Reviews, 12*(4), 384–412. https://doi.org/10.1111/j.1468-2370.2009.00270.x

Freud, S. (1921). Group psychology and the analysis of the ego. In *The standard edition of the complete psychological works of Sigmund Freud: Vol. XVIII* (pp. 65–144). Hogarth Press. https://doi.org/10.1037/e417472005-429

Friedkin, N. E., & Johnsen, E. C. (2011). *Social influence network theory: A sociological examination of small group dynamics*. Cambridge University Press.

Hyde, M. (2014). *Understanding diversity, inclusion and engagement*. Oxford University Press.

Judge, T. A., & Bono, J. E. (2001). Relationship of core self-evaluations traits—Self-esteem, generalized self-efficacy, locus of control, and emotional stability—With job satisfaction and job performance: A meta-analysis. *Journal of Applied Psychology, 86*(1), 80–92. https://doi.org/10.1037/0021-9010.86.1.80

Jung, C. G. (1921). *"Psychological types". Collected works of C.G. Jung*. Princeton University Press.

King, M. (1999). Mahatma Gandhi and Martin Luther King Jr.: The power of nonviolent action. In *Cultures of peace series*. UNESCO Publishing.
Lewin, K. (1947). Frontiers in group dynamics. *Human Relations, 1*(1), 5–41. https://doi.org/10.1177/001872674700100103
Maslow, A. H. (1943). A theory of human motivation. *Psychological Review, 50*(4), 370–396. https://doi.org/10.1037/h0054346
Nishii, L. H. (2013). The benefits of climate for inclusion for gender-diverse groups. *Academy of Management Journal, 56*(6), 1754–1774. https://doi.org/10.5465/amj.2009.0823
Ogunlade, J. O. (1980). Social distance among the Yoruba of Nigeria. *Social Behaviour and Personality, 8*(1), 121–124. https://doi.org/10.2224/sbp.1980.8.1.121
Park, B., & Rothbart, M. (1982). Perception of out-group homogeneity and levels of social categorization: Memory for the subordinate attributes of in-group and out-group members. *Journal of Personality and Social Psychology, 42*(6), 1051–1068. https://doi.org/10.1037/0022-3514.42.6.1051
Payne, M. C., York, C. M., & Fagan, J. (1974). Changes in measured social distance over time. *Sociometry, 37*(1), 131–136. https://doi.org/10.2307/2786473
Pettigrew, T. F. (1960). Social distance attitudes of South African students. *Social Forces, 38*(3), 246–253. https://doi.org/10.2307/2574088
Randel, A. E., Galvin, B. M., Shore, L. M., Ehrhart, K. H., Chung, B. G., Dean, M. A., & Kedharnath, U. (2018). Inclusive leadership: Realizing positive outcomes through belongingness and being valued for uniqueness. *Human Resource Management Review, 28*(2), 190–203. https://doi.org/10.1016/j.hrmr.2017.07.002
Rotter, J. B. (1966). Generalized expectancies for internal versus external control of reinforcement. *Psychological Monographs: General and Applied, 80*(1), 1–30. https://doi.org/10.1017/CBO9781107415324.004
Santoso, D. S., & Kulathunga, H. E. R. (2016). Examining happiness: Towards better understanding of performance improvement. *Procedia Engineering, 164*, 354–361. https://doi.org/10.1016/j.proeng.2016.11.630
Seligman, M. E. P. (1972). Learned helplessness. *Annual Review of Medicine, 23*(1), 407–412. https://doi.org/10.1146/annurev.me.23.020172.002203
Smit, H. (2014). *The depth facilitator's handbook: Transforming group dynamics*. Moonshine Media.
Tajfel, H., Billig, M. G., Bundy, R. P., & Flament, C. I. (1971). Social categorization and intergroup behavior. *European Journal of Social Psychology, 1*(2), 149–178.
Vicedo, M. (2009). The father of ethology and the foster mother of ducks: Konrad Lorenz as expert on motherhood. *Isis, 100*(2), 263–291. https://doi.org/10.1086/599553

Chapter 4
Leading Reflectively: Treading the Noble Eightfold Path

Joan Marques

Abstract This chapter presents leadership as a personal choice and discusses, within the scope of Buddhist psychology, the Four Noble Truths, comprising the Noble Eightfold Path, as a useful strategy to identify a set of behaviors that can reduce suffering at the personal and societal level. In each of the elements of the eightfold path, this chapter presents an individual who exerted strong personal leadership, often at the odds of all other opinions, and established a positive change, internally, as well as for his or her society. The eight individuals used as cases in point in this chapter derive from a wide range of backgrounds, ethnicities, and cultures, therewith demonstrating that reflection in leadership transcends boundaries and has the capacity to elevate entire communities toward greater awareness and improved performance.

Keywords Personal leadership · Buddhist psychology · Four Noble Truths · Noble Eightfold Path · Awareness

Introduction

Leadership is often described as a phenomenon that requires followers and a situation. Yet, without leading yourself in any situation, it will be hard to convince others to follow you. This chapter therefore maintains that leadership starts with a personal assessment of qualities and skills needed to lead yourself in the most proper way.

When we compare the qualities that were critical for leaders in the twentieth century with the ones that matter today, we distinguish a world of difference. Thanks to many unprecedented experiences, today's workforce members have arrived at some major insights. One of the most important ones is that individuals with sheer

J. Marques (✉)
Woodbury University, Burbank, CA, USA
e-mail: joan.marques@woodbury.edu

J. Marques (ed.), *Innovative Leadership in Times of Compelling Changes*, Management, Change, Strategy and Positive Leadership, https://doi.org/10.1007/978-3-030-67258-4_4

profit focus and with self-serving agendas, void of concern for the well-being of those they deal with, can no longer be considered suitable leaders. We have seen numerous companies sink into nothingness due to greed and excessive focus of their leaders.

Employees in today's workplaces have become very vocal on their ideas about leadership. Over the past decades we have moved into a Knowledge Revolution, which requires an entirely different construction in workplace dynamics than before. Values such as integrity, communication, and flexibility (Robles, 2012) have gained immense popularity among the working class. The entire concept of "wealth" has changed: no longer is it seen as an accrual of material or monetary assets. Instead, the wealth of knowledge and understanding has risen to the forefront (Gilder, 1990). Even if we cannot see this trend clearly in all work environments, it remains a fact that the exchange of intellectual output is rapidly surpassing the exchange of goods and services in importance (Rifkin, 2000).

How Buddhism Fits In

Increasingly, people realize that Buddhist practices do not necessarily have to infringe with their religious views and values. Buddhism can very well be considered a way of living. Buddhism is the summarized reference to the teachings of the Buddha. A Buddha is a person who attained Bodhi, which means wisdom in meaningful, morally responsible thinking and behaving. "Buddha" therefore means "enlightened one." The first person to be generally known as "Buddha," and also the one credited as the founder of Buddhism, was Siddhartha Gautama, the son of an Indian tribal leader. While Siddhartha enjoyed the privileges of his life at a young age, his confrontation with sickness, old age, and death as a young adult made him realize that life was neither perfect nor eternal. He promptly left his privileged life behind and set out to seek wisdom, which he obtained in his mid-30s after much wandering and many struggles. When Siddhartha engaged in insight meditation, also known as "Vipassana," he gained insight in the fact that everything is interdependent and everything is impermanent: nothing lasts. The fact that he referred to himself as "awake" afterward got him the name "Buddha." Over the next 45 years, the Buddha listened to many people and shared many insights, with the Four Noble Truths, including the Noble Eightfold Path, as some of the key concepts.

The Four Noble Truths reflect life at its core. In the most basic terms, they are as follows:

1. Suffering exists.
2. Suffering has a cause.
3. Suffering can be ended.
4. There is a path to end suffering, which is the Noble Eightfold Path.

The first three Noble Truths are intended to enhance our understanding about the need and purpose of the Noble Eightfold Path. This "path" comprises eight interrelated practices: (1) right view, (2) right intention, (3) right speech, (4) right action, (5) right livelihood, (6) right effort, (7) right mindfulness, and (8) right concentration. The practices should not be seen as a sequence with any specific order, but rather as a set of practices that are incomplete without each other.

It may be useful to elaborate slightly on each of the above concepts to help us obtain a better understanding of them.

The First Noble Truth tells us that suffering exists. Suffering should be seen in a much broader context here than a specific pain or ailment. The context that the Buddha used was that life in general brings many forms of suffering along: birth, aging, illness, death, sad and disheartening experiences, the loss of something or someone precious, the inability to get something or someone we want, and more. Even if we would say that many of these moments can be seen as highlights, there is still always an element of suffering involved.

The Second Noble Truth implies that suffering has a cause. Some of these causes are external and cannot be avoided, such as death of a loved one, the loss of a job, or a home. Yet, there are other causes of suffering that we can address internally. Sometimes we suffer because we are envious of someone else's performance and mirror that to our own. Comparing is a strong cause of suffering. Yet, it is avoidable. If you can train yourself to stop comparing, the cause of that suffering is gone.

The Third Noble Truth, which affirms that suffering can be ended, is an important one. You have the ability to free yourself from much of your suffering, but you have to understand that it might require a step up in awareness. You will have to engage in critical thinking, thus, take a critical look at your life and your desires, and analyze whether you really want them to cause you suffering. In doing so, you may have to drill deep inside and question the reasons why you want what you want. Very often, your desires have been dictated by expectations outside yourself. It may be that your parents, peers, or even your community expected you to evolve in a certain way and embark upon a particular career such as an attorney at law, a medical doctor, or an economist, and you simply never questioned if this was also what you would wanted.

The Fourth Noble Truth is the most comprehensive one, and also the most challenging one, but at the same time, the real action-oriented and helpful one. It is also known as the Noble Eightfold Path, and it is considered one of the most important teachings of the Buddha. The eightfold path consists of eight actions that should be implemented simultaneously to end suffering. So, not an eight-step action plan, but a collective union of interrelated behaviors that help in thinking and acting right. Thich Nhat Hanh (1998), a revered Buddhist monk, does a great job of explaining the eight elements on the Path. He perceives *right view* as a deep understanding of the Four Noble Truths, *right thought* (also referred to as right intention) as a means to improve right view, *right speech* as a manifestation of right thought, and *right action* as a consequence of right view, right thought, and right speech, as well as the path toward *right livelihood*. Thich further evaluates *right effort* to be the energy that helps us walk on the Noble Eightfold Path. He states, "Our practice should be intelligent, based on Right Understanding of the teaching. It is not because we practice hard that we can say we are practicing Right Diligence" (p. 99). Thich considers *right mindfulness* to be the heart of the Buddha's teachings. He clarifies, "When we are mindful, our thinking is Right Thinking, our speech is Right Speech, and so on. Right Mindfulness is the energy that brings us back to the present moment" (p. 64). Finally explaining *right concentration*, Thich affirms, "The practice of Right Concentration is to cultivate a mind that is one-pointed" (p. 105).

Buddhism's focus on consciousness aims to peel off the layer of ignorance and mindless acceptance of the status quo, in which we have been conditioned through modern society; elevate us from the ignorance of going through our daily motions as if we were sleepwalking; and rise to expanded awareness. Thich stresses that, when our ignorance has been transformed, our consciousness becomes wisdom.

In the next section, the eight elements of the Noble Eightfold Paths will be discussed, each with an example of contemporary leadership.

Right View

If you want to live right, you cannot implement just one or a few parts of the Noble Eightfold Path and ignore some other parts. In other words, you cannot work on having a right view, but then ignore what would be the right intention. You cannot practice right speech and then promptly engage in mindlessness. Yes, it is a challenge in today's fast-paced world to practice all elements of the Noble Eightfold Path, but it is the only way that you will be able to cross-check for yourself if you are on the right path: when all eight elements are in place, you know you are doing the right thing (O'Brien, 2017). Right view has been described as "seeing a thing in its true nature, without name and label" (Rahula, 1974).

There is an old story about the right view and how you obtain and behold it. It is about an old man who taught a younger one that there are two wolves in each of us. The wolves continuously fight each other. One wolf signifies your jealousy, meanness, spite, anger, negativity, and hate. The other wolf is your generosity, tolerance, understanding, peace, and harmony. The wolf that wins is the one that you feed. That wolf will also determine your view. Will your view be driven by the first set of emotions or by the second set? If you think about it, this means that your view determines your attitude. It influences the choices you make, the way you see things, and the way you act upon them.

Case in point: Ayah Bdeir and littleBits. A person that seems to have the ability to practice right view is Ayah Bdeir, a Lebanese Canadian, who founded littleBits, an open-source system of small, preassembled, modular circuits that snap together with magnets. Ayah was born in Montreal, Canada, in 1982, and raised in Beirut, Lebanon. Her late father was an entrepreneur and her mother a banker. Ayah received firsthand motivation to attend college from her mother, who pursued her own degree while her daughters were in school. Today, she can proudly refer to herself as an engineer and interactive artist and, more precisely, as the founder and CEO of littleBits. Ayah has earned countless awards for her work, including acquisition into the MoMA (Museum of Modern Art) permanent collection (Henry, 2017). littleBits' mission is to put the power of electronics in the hands of everyone and to break down complex technologies so that anyone can build, prototype, and invent. Because of the magnets, it is easy to know which sides snap together and which reject one another, so even children can become very creative with littleBits, even if they do not have any engineering experience. By developing and making littleBits accessible to everyone (it is open source, remember), Ayah sees it as her mission to democratize hardware. Indeed, she has been widely praised for her great ideas and even more for the visionary, generous approach of sharing the outcomes of her creative insights to anyone who might be interested.

Ayah Bdeir's approach appeals to many, most likely because of the greater purpose behind its existence: littleBits aims to bring progress to as wide a group of people all over the world and is secure enough in its mission to share the "recipe" of its product with anyone interested. On top of that, littleBits crosses boundaries by bringing engineering and art together. For those reasons, littleBits has experienced rapid growth, raising $44.2 million in Series B funding in 2015, thus bringing its total capital raised to nearly $60 million within 2 years after creation. The company sells its electronic building blocks for students and hobbyists in 130 countries and works with more than 3500 schools (Henry, 2017).

Right Intention

Right intention is sometimes also referred to as "right thinking" or "right thought," and the context is the same: you have to focus consciously and refrain from making decisions that are based on questionable motives. Because right view and right intention depend so much on your mental state, they are often classified as the wisdom aspects in the eightfold path. Right intention is wonderful, but it can be rather challenging, because there will always be factors that steer you in different ways, causing you to overlook or forget your real motives (See: Why "right intention" is important in Buddhism).

Thich Nhat Hanh has developed four simple activities that are very helpful in case you wonder if you still maintain right intention:

1. Always question what you see, hear, or read. Things can seem one way, but if you think deeper on them, you may realize that there are completely different interpretations possible and that your first thought may have been hasty and incorrect.
2. Take a pause regularly to ask yourself what you are doing and why. This will encourage you to take some distance from your actions and face the reasons behind them. It is a powerful way to practice critical thinking, and it can help you release behaviors and practices that you were just implementing mindlessly, but that no longer make sense.

3. Spend some time on a regular basis to consider your habits. It is easy to give in to your habits without even questioning them. Especially the bad habits seem to stick their head up when you least need them, and they can taint valuable courses of action. So, be alert of your behaviors and responses, and, just as in point two, try to find out what drives them.
4. Keep an awakened mind that always considers the well-being of others. Buddhists call this "Bodhicitta." Boddhicitta pertains to the intention to do well onto others and help them become happier, more fulfilled beings.

Case in point: Raj Panjabi's Passion About Saving Lives. Converting right intention into right action is what matters most in bringing about actual change. Raj Panjabi, a young man of Indian heritage born in Liberia, understood this need when he co-founded Last Mile Health, a nonprofit organization that focuses on saving lives in some of the world's most isolated communities. In his early years, Raj and his family moved to the USA, where he earned a medical degree and a Master's degree in Public Health. He returned to Liberia in 2005 as a medical student and founded Last Mile Health in 2007, along with a team of five Liberian civil war survivors and American health workers. Raj and his team started their organization because they felt passionate about the fact that no one should die because they live far from the nearest doctor, clinic, or hospital (Last Mile Health, 2020).

So, how does Last Mile Health try to save lives in remote areas? It partners with governments to develop networks of community health workers (CHWs). CHWs usually have a middle or high school education and work in their own villages, where they are trained by nurses and medical assistants, and receive medicines, which they distribute among their neighbors. CHWs also learn to refer ill people in their communities to local clinics for treatment. Of course, the CHWs, nurses, and medical assistants need to be paid, so Last Mile Health always welcomes financial assistance. In 2017, Raj and his organization received a prize from TED of $1 million to launch a Community Health Academy, a project that will redesign the education of CHWs and leaders for the digital age.

Right Speech

In these times of massive communications in many diverse ways, and an abundance of social media, it is critical that we fully understand the importance of right speech. Engaging in right speech means that you deliberately refrain from saying things that have negative effects on others. It also means that you remain cautious about spreading news of which you are unsure or of which the contents can be devastating to some. Practicing right speech means that you attempt to resolve division and disharmony and try to promote or restore unison and harmony. Right speech also means that you are telling the truth to your best of abilities, not creating divisiveness by telling different people different things, refraining from cruelty in your speech, and withholding yourself from exaggerating facts, only to make them seem more interesting.

In line with Buddha's teaching, Thomas Bruner suggests for us to ask ourselves the following questions to ensure we are engaging in right speech:

- Is it true? Just because we think, feel, or believe something does not make it true. Right speech is asking if what we are about to say is accurate, factual, or objectively verifiable.
- Is it helpful? We often speak for our own benefit. Right speech is asking ourselves whether what we will say is helpful, useful, or beneficial to others.
- Is it timely? We usually speak when we want to speak. Right speech asks whether now is the proper or appropriate time to say what we have to say.
- Is it kind? Sometimes we speak out of anger and frustration. Right speech means we speak with good intent, goodwill, and compassion for others, even – or especially – when we are angry or frustrated (Bruner, 2017).

Case in point: Paul Polman's Bold Stance Toward Shareholders. In 2009, Paul Polman became the new CEO of Unilever, a global consumer product and food corporation. The business world was still very much in the clutches of the global financial crisis, and Polman did what very few CEOs dare to do, especially new ones: he notified Unilever's shareholders that they should stop expecting quarterly annual and earnings guidance reports for the stock market. He stressed that the company was now going to take a longer view and whoever was not happy about that could take their money and invest it somewhere else (Boynton, 2015).

Shortly after making this bold statement, Unilever's share price declined by 8%, because a fear emerged that there was bad news on the horizon in a company that had not done too well in recent history. But Polman, who was the first Unilever CEO in a long time to come in from the external environment rather than internally rising through the ranks, did not stop there. He started disinviting some shareholders, which is quite unheard in business circles, and caused quite an upheaval in the company (Boynton, 2015). Polman, a major advocate for value-creation and sustainable approaches, openly resented shareholders that are only out to get their money multiplied without really caring for the nature and progress of the business they have invested it in.

During his tenure at Unilever, Paul Polman saw his main responsibility to a large group of stakeholders, including consumers from all parts of the world and climate change activists. He took it as his leadership task to double Unilever's revenue while at the same time halving its environmental footprint. To that end, the company established the Unilever Sustainable Living Plan (Sustainable Living, 2020). He was aware that a change toward massive adoption of a sustainable mindset would be a herculean task that would not happen overnight. He was also aware that there would be many opponents and skeptics that would try to impede any effort toward doing the right thing. And indeed, he experienced opposition from companies that benefitted from keeping things as they were, such as the carbon-based industry. Yet, he considered every opposition an opportunity for future collaboration (Boynton, 2015).

Paul Polman, who stepped down as chief executive officer of Unilever in 2019, particularly criticized Milton Friedman's teachings about the purpose of business to be self-serving and make profit and do so without any further regard for the environment. Polman continues to believe in serving: in helping those that cannot help themselves. In order to expand the circle of awareness, Polman engaged in a lot of networks, many of them consisting of young people and social entrepreneurs. This is how he encountered creative ideas and positive engagement, as well as hope that the world is getting closer to an overall awareness that we have to change our thought patterns toward more sustainable living (Boynton, 2015).

Polman's efforts have been noticed by attentive and sustainability conscious sources. In 2017, he was recognized as one of the inaugural "Heroes of Conscious Capitalism" at the annual CEO Summit along with 27 other business leaders. He was recognized for his contribution toward realizing a world in which business is both practiced and recognized as a force for good.

Right Action

Right action starts, interestingly enough, with the discontinuation of the action of harming ourselves and others. Right action requires a careful examination of our behavior. It encompasses the protection of life and the preservation of well-being of all living creatures in the broadest sense possible. In Buddhist circles, right action consists of three main considerations: no killing, no stealing, and no sexual misconduct. Looking deeper into this, it really means no killing (of any living being), no stealing, no insulting, no lying, no cheating, no backbiting, no harsh words, no manipulating, no mean-spirited thoughts or behavior, and not engaging in any type of misconduct.

Because we are continuously caught in all sorts of situations, it is not always easy to engage in right action, especially when we consider that right action is, in many cases, a personal judgment. Let us zoom into the subject of killing as an example. Killing is an extremely broad topic, because it does not only pertain to one person killing another. Killing also entails the practice of killing for pleasure, which often happens when we hunt or fish, and many people become uncomfortable when we address that aspect of killing. Yet, if we consider that all life is precious, not just our own, and not just the lives of humans, then this mindset makes a lot of sense! Right action is more critical in our times, because our collective wrong actions have led to massive problems such as global warming and the extinction and destruction of many innocent lives due to inconsiderate practices.

Humanity, as a whole, has progressed in many ways, but all too often this progress happened at the expense of other beings. Today, the imbalance in income is greater than ever, which means that some pay for the prosperity of others. Human beings and animals in many parts of the world are victimized on a daily basis by those who have become accustomed to extracting and killing what they consider resources for their business or leisure. The immense destruction of natural resources in our few global rainforests without proper replenishment, for instance, has demanded its toll, and since we are not living on an island, we will all ultimately suffer the negative effects of these mindless actions.

Case in point: Jeremiah Kimbugwe's Health Conscious Initiative. A splendid example of a young leader living "right action" is Jeremiah Kimbugwe, who is only 27 years old at the time of writing this chapter (Jeremiah Kimbugwe, 2020), but is already involved in several constructive projects in his home country, Uganda. Jeremiah, who holds a degree in Social Development, focuses on bringing about healthy changes and works with Sovhen Uganda, a registered national nongovernmental organization that operates in the slums of Kampala City and other remote areas in Uganda. His aim is to lead positive transformation among the youth with the intention of bringing about a peaceful, united, and healthy world.

One of the projects Jeremiah oversees is a sanitary napkin-making project, which is a solution to dangerous and unsanitary circumstances for young women in his home country. The sanitary napkins are made from local materials and are environmentally friendly, as a way to protect and conserve nature. With this project, Jeremiah focuses on girls' education and income generation, because the availability of sanitary pads improves female school attendance, combats high dropout rates, and provides employment opportunities for local women. Jeremiah is aware that keeping girls in school is crucial for the future strength of the country. The jobs Jeremiah's organization creates not only generate income but also focus on training the women to be entrepreneurs themselves (Jeremiah Kimbugwe, 2017).

Another project that Jeremiah is passionate about is a community-based health center, created to combat the high spread of malaria in his community. Each of these projects aims at producing affordable items while at the same time creating employment opportunities for the young mothers and helping the young girls to stay in school. A third effort that Jeremiah is involved in is a business development project run by volunteers and aimed at providing business training to young people (Jeremiah Kimbugwe, 2017). Several of the trainees from this program have since started up businesses or improved on the ventures they had before. Jeremiah sees this as a sign of development in his career and an inspiration to continue advocating for entrepreneurship in the communities he serves. With small steps, humility, and a strong belief in his peers, Jeremiah believes that he is starting to build stronger, more stable communities (Jeremiah Kimbugwe, 2017).

Right Livelihood

Right livelihood is about the way in which we earn our living. It requires for us to ask ourselves a number of reflective questions, such as: Is my job constructive and not harmful to others? Am I not, directly or indirectly, participating in the production, sales, or promotion of tools that can be used to kill or destroy? Is there any element of slave trade, oppression, or abuse of others? Am I not contributing to the production of items that can be detrimental to others? Is my job entailing dishonest and unfair practices that prey on others' good intentions and beliefs?

These types of questions can help us discover whether our work entails wrong livelihood and whether we should consider a change of job or even a change of career. It makes sense that the reflections we engage in to determine right livelihood have a lot to do with other parts of the eightfold path as well. Right livelihood fits right along right speech and right action, as part of the "moral conduct" section of the eightfold path, which is connected to the earlier mentioned precepts of not killing, not stealing, not misusing sex, not lying, and not abusing intoxicants (O'Brien, 2018b). Zen master Thich Nhat Hanh suggests that, in practicing right livelihood, we will have to find a way to earn a living without undermining our ideals of love and compassion. Our daily work should be a worthy expression of your deepest self rather than a source of suffering for ourselves and others (Thich Nhat Hanh, 1998).

All that said, however, it may become clear how difficult it really is to be completely sure that you do not engage in wrong livelihood. You may try to do everything right, but purchase items that come from a person or company that exploits others. You may think that you are selling decent products, but you cannot be completely sure that your suppliers truly acquired their products through right livelihood as well. The global business environment of today, in which we deal with stakeholders from many nations and backgrounds, has made this even more complicated than it was before. Sometimes you can also be a supplier of something pure, such as grain, which could be used by one of your customers to brew alcoholic beverages. So, it is complicated, especially if we realize that everything is interconnected, and all we do ultimately leads to the effects we experience around us, the good and the bad ones. This means, that, willingly or not, we contribute to good and bad consequences, and our right livelihood can be converted into wrong livelihood by others at any point in the production or service chain (O'Brien, 2018b).

We should also be mindful of other effects of our livelihood onto ourselves. If you work so hard and much that your health suffers from it, you are not engaging in right livelihood, regardless of the ethical magnitude of what you are doing. The demands and desires that we pick up from society may influence us to such an extent that we basically abuse our right livelihood in order to make more money, thus increase our wealth, to an extend that is far beyond what we really need. There is nothing wrong with making money, but if it happens at the expense of your health or the health of those around you, that is not right. At that point, the emphasis of your livelihood has shifted from what you do to what you get, and you should regroup your thoughts. The art is to do the right thing, not only in your practices toward others but also toward yourself (Sockolov, 2016). In sum, there are three areas in which you should consider right livelihood: (1) in the type of work you do, (2) in the circumstances at your workplace and how these affect you, and (3) in the amount of work you do to gain your earnings and how that affects you and those around you (Sockolov, 2016).

Case in point: Andy Moon's Dream to Bring Energy to the Deprived. Andy Moon has focused his passion in the area of developing solar energy projects in developing countries. By doing so, he devotes his professional skills to both the environment and international development. Andy is a Stanford University graduate, who started his career at McKinsey & Company's Sustainability and Nonprofit practices in New York, but would spend his summers in Cambodia and the Philippines, which undoubtedly influenced his awareness of the needs in developing nations. His interest in public health grew through his volunteer involvement in the innovative nonprofit "Possible," for which he served as a fundraiser and energy advisor. Possible has a partnership with the government of Nepal to find ways to deliver high-quality, low-cost health care to areas in rural Nepal.

In 2009 Andy became a project developer at SunEdison, which focused on building mega-scale power plants in the USA, Canada, and Europe. Through this job, Andy learned the ropes of the solar energy industry. Meanwhile, in 2011, Andy learned from the main physician at Possible that electricity was the greatest challenge for their hospital, because diesel transport for conventional energy generation was costly and sporadic, resulting in just a few hours of electricity being available each day. This severely impeded the efforts to provide high-quality health care, and it was obstructing Possible's efforts to expand health-care services through hospital expansion (SunFarmer, 2020).

In 2013, Andy started SunFarmer, a nonprofit social enterprise that incubates and launches locally run solar businesses in developing countries. He founded SunFarmer with a co-worker, Jason Gray, supported by a grant of $2 million, received from a SunEdison foundation (Pipia, 2016). In order to make a solid and responsible start with their venture in Nepal, their inaugural performance ground, Andy and Jason partnered with Avishek Malla, a highly respected Nepali entrepreneur and solar engineer. In this team setting, they installed the first solar energy installation. The three men then launched SunFarmer Nepal, a Nepali solar energy company dedicated to installing and maintaining world-class solar installations in Nepal (Sunfarmer, 2020).

In his blog, Andy described a common error that start-ups make, which his company also fell prey to: wanting to do too many things at the same time. Thanks to some good advice from seasoned solar entrepreneurs, however, Andy and his team came to realize that their product, solar for farmers, was already very challenging at its core. Any additional focus aside from that would only lead to diminished success. He came across several examples of solar entrepreneurs in other developing nations, who tried the approach of multiple product lines, in hopes to accelerate growth, only to find that there was no growth at all.

Finally taking the lessons to heart, Andy and his SunFarmer's team engaged in a new product development process, identifying a customer segment on which they could focus fully. Their research paid off: they found their target community in the mid-hills region of Nepal where high-value vegetable crops are grown without access to electricity for irrigation in the fields, and with little chance on conventional electricity access, due to the extremely high costs of building an electric grid in such a remote area.

SunFarmer has now installed solar at more than 200 hospitals, schools, businesses, and farms in ten districts of Nepal. Through these energy projects, schools and health clinics were able to receive much-needed power, while disaster victims could be served with appropriate relief. The goal of SunFarmer is to provide power to 4000 hospitals, schools, and water projects around the world by 2020.

In 2017 Andy relinquished the CEO position at SunFarmer, yet, he remains actively involved as a board member and advisor.

Right Effort

Right effort is sometimes also listed as "right diligence." Effort is a commendable practice, but we can direct it to constructive or destructive activities. People who work in the weapon or drug-abuse industry undeniably invest effort in their job, but, unfortunately, this is not right effort, due to the suffering this effort causes. Right effort is a very personal task, just like all other elements of the path: it also pertains to the act of contemplating about the roots of our suffering and then engaging in the effort to release those roots.

Right effort, along with right mindfulness and right concentration, comprises the mental discipline section of the Noble Eightfold Path (O'Brien, 2018a). At its very core, right effort entails that we should try to adopt and develop wholesome qualities and behaviors and release unwholesome ones.

Also, right effort does not mean "hard" effort, as you should enjoy what you are trying to do. If your effort become laborious, you are probably not doing it right, according to Zen master Thich Nhat Hanh. At the same time, it is still effort, which means that there may be hindrances that can impede you from achieving your goals. A Sutta of the Pali Canon enumerates five aspects that can obstruct right effort. They are (1) sensual desire; (2) ill will; (3) sluggishness, indolence, or lethargy; (4) impatience and anxiety; and (5) ambiguity or skepticism.

Case in point: Maria Mayanja and Her Efforts to Make Nonbiodegradable Waste Useful. A promising trend of our times is that more and more young entrepreneurs take on roles that combine economic advancement with social well-being. In Rwanda, a young woman by the name of Maria Mayanja co-founded Angaza Ltd., a company that upcycles nonbiodegradable waste into fashion accessories such as bags, wallets, and gadget covers, creating green jobs along the way (Conscious Company Magazine, 2016). As they help restore the environment, these young people also work on the awareness levels of upcoming youth in their country by engaging students in fun, hands-on activities such as tree planting, competitions, and upcycling to engender a more conscious generation of Africans rooted in sustainable practices.

Angaza was founded in 2012 and considers its industry to be in "ethical fashion." With this laudable initiative, Maria expressed her passion for environmental conservation and her drive to help people understand it better in a more simplistic way. On the company's website, Angaza is explained as the Swahili words for "to illuminate" or "to shed light" (Angaza, 2018). Through the Angaza project, Maria and her partners aim to take a lead in environmental solutions in Rwanda, hoping to shed light on newer concepts and doing so through innovative creations and community engagement. And of course it is not only about the products, but about the entire social advancement that lies behind this initiative: education for youngsters to do the sustainably responsible thing, offering green jobs to employable citizens, and doing the environment a huge favor by making people more aware of the need to dispose of nondegradable materials. Angaza uses nonbiodegradable waste, such as vinyl advertising banners and jute rice bags and converts them into one-of-a-kind accessories, such as purses, wallets, and various types of bags. The producers line these products with a special fabric, which is called Kitenge in East Africa or Ankara in West Africa. Yet, due to the nature of the products they work with, each item is unique and has no second one like it on the market. This has high appeal to fashionistas.

On Maria Mayanja's LinkedIn page, she states that she ended her employment at Angaza and Impact Hub Kigali in November 2016. At the time of writing this chapter, she served as the student recruitment and marketing officer for Carnegie Mellon University Africa. The current managing director is Monica Umwari.

Right Mindfulness

In Sanskrit, they use the word "smriti" for mindfulness, and it means, literally, "to remember." Remembering here means returning to the present moment when we realize that our mind has a tendency to wander. Thanks to our mindfulness, we may be able to truly appreciate what we see, and where there is responding life involved (a person or pet), we may indicate our gratitude for their presence, so that they, too, may become mindful of the moment. The appreciation that is part of such mindfulness can ease the suffering of our usual mindlessness and encourage us to go a step further, so that we concentrate on the other, understand him or her better, and transform our own suffering and theirs into joy (Marques, 2015).

We can achieve mindfulness in several ways. A frequently practiced way is meditation. One of the most well-known forms of meditation is Vipassana, or insight meditation, which is the meditation practice in which Siddhartha Gautama, generally referred to as "the Buddha," engaged when he became enlightened. Vipassana is now used in various schools of Buddhism to promote attention, awareness, and mindfulness. Vipassana has grown into a global movement and is even more westernized than, for instance, Zen, because it does not require traditional techniques. There are Vipassana meditation centers in all parts of the world. Because it can be practiced in a nonreligious way, it is attractive to Buddhists and non-Buddhists alike

(Marques, 2015). Vipassana literally means "special seeing" or insight. Since it is a mindfulness technique, Vipassana draws attention to your breath and to every object of consciousness. Business people and academicians, but also prison inmates, seem to experience major transformations when they engage in this meditation practice.

Case in point: William Kamkwamba: The Boy Who Harnessed the Wind. A young person who used mindfulness to drive his actions is William Kamkwamba, a young innovator, engineer, and author, who was born in Kasungu, Malawi, in 1987. He grew up in poverty, to the extent that he had to drop out of school during a famine, which affected the entire village. His family could no longer afford the $80 annual tuition for school (Wulff, 2011), but William was desperate to continue his education and discovered the village library as a source for ongoing self-education. Through his readings he became aware of his love for electronics. Then, William read a book titled "Using Energy," carefully studied the illustrations in the book, and decided to create a makeshift windmill in 2006 with the aim of alleviating the needs in his community. He first made a miniature version with a cheap dynamo, and once he found that it worked, he used blue gum trees, bicycle parts, and other materials from a scrapyard to create a functioning windmill that powered several electrical appliances in his family's house. In the months that he perused the scrapyard across the road from his previous school, many youngsters made fun of him, and even his mother started questioning his sanity. But William knew what he was doing and incessantly continued his digging and storing of bottle caps, bicycle and tractor parts, and flipflop rubbers. Once he demonstrated his ability, he had the entire village in awe! He soon wired his entire house, and neighbors would ask if they could charge their cell phones at the home of the Kamkwambas (Wulff, 2011). Generating his own electricity source was a huge accomplishment in a village where only the homes of the very affluent, only two percent of the local population, had their own electricity (Wulff, 2011).

The local newspaper learned about William's accomplishment and wrote an article about him. A Ted director learned about the young man and invited him to a global Ted event in 2007 in Tanzania. The Ted audience embraced him, and the director went back home with William to see the windmill with his own eyes. He was so impressed by the meticulousness of William's work that he pledged then and there that he would do anything in his power to get this boy to finish high school and get a college education. The *Wall Street Journal* also wrote about his efforts, and William got the long-desired opportunity to go to college. Many media outlets interviewed him, and he served as a guest speaker at several global events. Engineering professors referred to him as a "Natural" since he had been able to build such a complicated device with no tools other than a few nails.

The news spread like wildfire as William continued his efforts: he built a solar-powered water pump to supply drinking water in his village and two other windmills. In 2013 *Time Magazine* named William one of 30 People Under 30 Changing the World. Meanwhile, William had written a book about his story, titled, *The Boy Who Harnessed the Wind* (Kamkwamba & Mealer, 2010). With the book being selected by public library systems to cover entire communities, and being donated to many youngsters through gift funds, William soon had a bestseller on his hand! *The Boy Who Harnessed the Wind* managed to remain on the *New York Times* bestseller list for a full 5 weeks! In 2014, William Kamkwamba graduated from Dartmouth College in Hanover, New Hampshire.

Thanks to his great effort, his mindful practice, but definitely also his awe-inspiring and pleasant mannerisms, Kamkwamba now has a whole team of experts to turn to. Yet, his fame has not changed his sober outlook on life. While life in abundant societies has been pleasant, he has not forgotten where he came from and that he and his family once lived on four spoons of porridge a day to survive a terrible famine. He has created a nonprofit called "Moving Windmills," which now sponsors the local soccer team in a deliberate effort to keep youngsters from drug use and loitering. He helps put his sisters through school by paying their tuition out of his own pocket. He continues to work in his village and continues to examine areas of need that he can alleviate with his skills. He has built a deep-water well with a solar-powered pump that his entire village can access. Thanks to this project, women in the village are now spared a 2-hour walk to a public well. William also just opened a maize-grinding mill, which will guarantee a steady income for his family. He is also rebuilding the local primary school, to give all children in the village a chance to get an education. In addition, he has started an evening adult literacy program to also bring education to older members of the community (Kamkwamba & Mealer, 2010).

Right Concentration

Right concentration has everything to do with focusing on what is important. Sometimes it is important to focus on one particular thing, such as our breathing when we engage in Vipassana meditation (explained in previous chapter). At other times it is important to concentrate more actively on a set of activities. An example is driving: when we drive, we focus on our driving, but also on the lights, other vehicles on the road, people crossing the streets, our speed, the condition of the road, the direction in which we are going, possibly on the rain, and so on.

We have to concentrate in order to be mentally present, and when we do that, we experience each moment to the fullest. When we focus fully on each moment instead of constantly thinking about the past and the future, we may discover beautiful details in the here and now, that would have escaped us if we were not concentrating. Right concentration can therefore offer us greater happiness in the current moment, as we are more focused on what matters now. Also, right concentration can help us realize better than anything else, that everything is temporary. Our feelings of aggravation or anger, and our feelings of euphoria: they eventually subside. Thanks to our concentration, we can thus learn to see them in their right scope: as fleeting senses, which we can release if we want to (Thich Nhat Hanh, 1998).

Case in point: Kendall Ciesemier's Compassion for Kids. When Kendall Ciesemier was only 11 years old, she watched an Oprah Winfrey show that highlighted aids orphans in Africa. Having had her share of health struggles in life, Kendall could vividly envision the despair that so many of these orphans were going through, having to take care of their younger siblings, yet with no security for their own future. At the same time, she was awestruck by the dogged hope these young children, many of her age or younger, displayed in their struggle for life. This became a decisive moment in Ciesemier's life (Ciesemier, 2013).

Born in Wheaton, Illinois, in 1993, Kendall struggled with a rare liver disease called biliary atresia, a rare liver defect where the bile duct – which is supposed to be present between the liver and the small intestine – is either blocked or is absent. The health problem caused Kendall to undergo two liver transplants at a time when other youngsters were only concerned or excited about their next technological gimmick or their next social media posting. She got the first half of her liver from her father, and the other from a donor, but had to remain hospitalized all summer to ensure that her body would not reject the new liver (Ciesemier, 2013).

Seeing a program about the aids orphans in Africa drew Kendall to start searching for other children in the world who were struggling, yet did not have the means to make any progress. Her first gift was a $360 donation to a then 8-year-old girl from Mauritania without parents, who could finally dare to dream of a future by enrolling in school thanks to Kendall's support. Establishing this connection with another youngster who also experienced major challenges in life gave Kendall a strong sense of purpose, and she decided that her path would be to do whatever she could to help other kids in need. She started raising money, from family, friends, but also other children who learned about Kendall's efforts and wanted to help. In the summer of 2004, Kendall had raised the sum of $15,000 and could sponsor an entire village in Zambia, named Musele (Ciesemier, 2013).

In 2005, when Kendall was barely 12 years old, she received assistance in converting her project Kids Caring 4 Kids (KC4K) into a 501(c)3 not-for-profit organization. Her purpose with this organization was to inspire kids in the USA to care for and support those in need. Kendall's main focus was to awaken empathy within kids, living under more fortunate circumstances, for those who experienced far greater challenges and less opportunities, such as the aids orphans in Africa. In order to spread the word, Kendall took to schools, youth groups, and service organizations and invited them to get involved. Since she started her not-for-profit organization, Kendall has been able to sponsor eight projects in four African countries. Among those projects are building a dormitory and two orphan centers and providing 400 specially built bikes, school supplies, medical care, indoor plumbing, healthy meals, and boreholes to increase the quality of life for these African kids. Her dedicated work caught the attention of major celebrities in the US society, such as Oprah Winfrey and former President Clinton. Kendall keeps inspiring youngsters till today to continue giving by way of finding a purpose, since it is so rewarding to help a person in need. Kendall Ciesemier has received multiple awards for her philanthropic work. Prudential and the National Association of Secondary School Principals have named her one of America's top ten youth volunteers. She has also been listed as one of the 20 Amazing Young Women of Glamour magazine and won the Woman of the Year Reader's Choice Award (Horsfield, 2018).

Today, Kendall Ciesemier is described as an activist, a journalist, a writer, and a social entrepreneur (Harrison, 2018). She has successfully completed her education at Georgetown University, has managed to juggle her hectic study schedule with managing KC4K, and meanwhile also co-founded OWN IT, a women's leadership initiative to empower college-aged women to engage with women leaders (Harrison, 2018). At the time of writing this chapter, Kendall was a producer at digital news company Mic, where her focus ranges from criminal justice reform, racial justice, the #MeToo movement, and more (Harrison, 2018).

Living and Leading with the Eightfold Path: A Personal Leadership Choice

Leadership is, ultimately, a very personal thing that requires continuous reflection. You can read as many theories and hear as many stories as you want, but in the end, you will make the decision in regard to the path you will tread, the way you will treat others, and how you will carry yourself through different circumstances.

Keeping the Noble Eightfold Path in mind is always a good idea. And, as stated throughout this chapter, the eight treads of this path are interrelated. Right intentions emerge from right views and incite right efforts and right actions. A point of caution is in place here: just as the right interpretation of all elements of the path is interrelated and supportive of one another, just so are malicious implementations and interpretations interrelated and mutually supportive. In other words, you can get trapped by wrong intentions, wrong views, wrong efforts, wrong actions, and so on and maybe even believe they are right, because the human psyche is a miraculous thing: we stand on different sides of reality, and what some of us may consider right, others may consider dead wrong.

Because it is all so personal, your only true guide will be… you! Try to engage in insight meditation, even if it initially seems hard to do. We are living in dazzling times, where even 5 quiet minutes seem like forever, so engaging in 20 or 30 minutes of meditation may seem like an impossible chore. But practice makes perfect, and if you allow yourself to follow your breathing, and decide not to get upset if you catch your mind wandering, you may ultimately get the hang of leading reflectively – all by yourself.

Chapter Takeaways

- Today's workforce members have arrived at some major insights. One of the most important ones is that individuals with sheer profit focus and with self-serving agendas, void of concern for the well-being of those they deal with, can no longer be considered suitable leaders.
- Buddhism can very well be considered a way of living. The Four Noble Truths, including the Noble Eightfold Path, are some of Buddhism's key concepts.
  - The Four Noble Truths reflect life at its core. In the most basic terms they are as follows: (1) suffering exists, (2) suffering has a cause, (3) suffering can be ended, and (4) there is a path to end suffering, which is the Noble Eightfold Path.
  - The Noble Eightfold Path. This "path" comprises eight interrelated practices.
- Right view means to do away with negativity, mean-spiritedness, spitefulness, and prejudice.
- Right intention compels you to focus consciously and refrain from making decisions that are based on questionable motives.
- Right speech means that you deliberately refrain from saying things that have negative effects on others.
- Right action starts with the discontinuation of the action of harming ourselves and others. It requires a careful examination of our behavior. Right action encompasses the protection of life and the preservation of well-being of all living creatures in the broadest sense possible.
- Right livelihood is about the way in which we earn our living. It requires for us to ask ourselves a number of reflective questions that can help us to discover whether our work entails wrong livelihood and whether we should consider a change of job or even a change of career.
- Right effort requires that we carefully distinguish our actions, thoughts, and intentions, so that our effort remains constructive.
- Right mindfulness enables us to also engage in right view, right intention, right speech, right action, right livelihood, right effort, and right concentration. In Sanskrit, they use the word "smriti" for mindfulness, and it means, literally, "to remember."
- Right concentration has everything to do with focusing on what is important. We have to concentrate in order to be mentally present, and when we do that, we experience each moment to the fullest.

Chapter-End Reflection Questions

1. Reflect on leadership in the twentieth century versus today. What, according to your findings, are the main differences?

2. This chapter reflects on Buddhist psychology as a foundational strategy toward proper leadership. Can you consider another creed, religion, or philosophy that also instills proper leadership values? Please explain your selection and briefly elaborate on the values.
3. Reflect on the Four Noble Truths: what type of suffering do you consider most present in your life at the moment, and how do you plan to exert proper leadership toward discontinuing this form of suffering?
4. Consider the cases in point presented in this chapter: which of the cases did you consider most compelling? Why?
5. Consider the individuals discussed in the eight cases in point in this chapter: what did they have in common?

References

Angaza. (2018). *Our story: Beautiful is different.* Retrieved from https://angazarwanda.com/story-en

Boynton, A. (2015, July 20). Unilever's Paul Polman: CEOs can't be "slaves" to shareholders. *Forbes*. Retrieved from https://www.forbes.com/sites/andyboynton/2015/07/20/unilevers-paul-polman-ceos-cant-be-slaves-to-shareholders/#53da9874561e

Bruner, T. (2017, July 24). *Leadership and right speech.* Retrieved from http://brunerstrategies.com/2017/07/24/leadership-right-speech/

Ciesemier, K. (2013). MyName is Kendall: This is MyStory…. *MyNameMyStory*. Retrieved from http://mynamemystory.org/kendall-ciesemier.html

Conscious Company Magazine. (2016, June 1). 17 young social entrepreneurs who are making the world a better place. *EcoWatch.* Retrieved from https://www.ecowatch.com/17-young-social-entrepreneurs-who-are-making-the-world-a-better-place-1891147411.html

Gilder, G. (1990). *Microcosm: The quantum revolution in economics and technology*. Simon and Schuster.

Harrison, C. (2018, November 7). New York Film Academy (NYFA) documentary alum Kendall Ciesemier talks activism, social causes. *New York Film Academy*. Retrieved from https://www.nyfa.edu/film-school-blog/nyfa-alum-kendall-ciesemier-talks-activism/

Henry, Z. (2017, February 7). This Startup Founder Offers Up the Perfect Response to Trump's Travel Ban: Ayah Bdeir, the founder and CEO of LittleBits, wants to counter the perception of Arabic as "the other". *Inc*. Retrieved from https://www.inc.com/zoe-henry/how-littlebits-founder-ayah-bdeir-pushing-back-against-trump-immigration-ban.html

Horsfield, P. (2018). Kendall Ciesemier. *The Extraordinary.org*. Retrieved from https://www.theextraordinary.org/kendall-ciesemier

Jeremiah Kimbugwe. (2017). Jeremiah Kimbugwe. *The Huffington Post.* Retrieved from https://www.huffingtonpost.com/author/kimbugwe-jeremiah

Jeremiah Kimbugwe. (2020). Retrieved from https://www.oneyoungworld.com/profile-main/19872

Kamkwamba, W., & Mealer, B. (2010). *The boy who harnessed the wind: Creating currents of electricity and hope*. William Morrow.

Last Mile Health. (2020). *What we do*. Retrieved from http://lastmilehealth.org/what-we-do/

Marques, J. (2015). *Business and Buddhism*. Routledge.

O'Brien, B. (2017, September 1). Right view—The Buddhist eightfold path. *ThoughtCo.* Retrieved from https://www.thoughtco.com/right-view-450073

O'Brien, B. (2018a, April 15). Right effort in Buddhism: Part of the eightfold path. *ThoughtCo.* Retrieved from https://www.thoughtco.com/right-effort-450065

O'Brien, B. (2018b, June 22). Right livelihood: The ethics of earning a living. *ThoughtCo*. Retrieved from https://www.thoughtco.com/right-livelihood-the-ethics-of-earning-a-living-450071

Pipia, A. (2016, March 23). These 24 Americans are changing the world—And they're all under 40. *BusinessInsider*. Retrieved from https://www.businessinsider.com/23-americans-who-are-changing-the-world-2016-3#andy-moon-sunfarmer-1

Rahula, W. (1974). *What the Buddha taught* (p. 49). Grove Press.

Rifkin, J. (2000). *The age of access*. Penguin Putnam.

Robles, M. M. (2012). Executive perceptions of the top 10 soft skills needed in today's workplace. *Business Communication Quarterly, 75*(4), 453.

Sockolov, M. (2016, November 21). Right livelihood in Buddhism. *Mindfulness*. Retrieved from https://oneminddharma.com/livelihood/

SunFarmer. (2020). *Our story*. Retrieved from http://www.sunfarmer.org/our-story/

Sustainable Living. (2020). *Unilever website*. Retrieved from https://www.unilever.com/sustainable-living/

Thich Nhat Hanh. (1998). *The heart of the Buddha's teaching: Transforming suffering into peace, joy, and liberation*. Broadway Books.

Why "right intention" is important in Buddhism: Wisdom and the eightfold. *ThoughtCo*. Retrieved from https://www.thoughtco.com/right-intention-450069

Wulff, J. (2011, September-October). The power of one. *Dartmouth Alumni Magazine*. Retrieved from https://dartmouthalumnimagazine.com/articles/power-one

Chapter 5
Innovative Leadership: Tools and Techniques to Acquire Innovative and Inspiring Ideas

M. S. Rao

Abstract The purpose of this chapter is to offer innovative tools and techniques to acquire innovative and inspiring ideas. It explains the power of your subconscious mind to acquire creative and inventive ideas and unlock your hidden potential. It differentiates between creativity and innovation and draws a blueprint to achieve creativity and innovation. It explains and elaborates on innovative leadership. It outlines the characteristics of innovative leaders. It illustrates with inspiring examples of innovative international leaders including Benjamin Franklin, Thomas Edison, Albert Einstein, Bill Gates, Larry Ellison, Elon Musk, and Mark Zuckerberg. It explains that failure is an integral part of innovation. It implores to acquire every piece of information to achieve innovation. It emphasizes the importance of synthesis to generate more ideas. It reminds us that all seeds that you sow will not germinate and bear fruits. It concludes to strive from a theoretical and practical perspective to acquire innovative and inspiring ideas to achieve extraordinary success in your life.

Keywords Creativity · Innovation · Entrepreneurship · Entrepreneurial leadership · Inspirational leadership · Organizational development and Leadership development

Introduction

> If I have 300 ideas in a year and just one turns out to work, I am satisfied.—Alfred Nobel.

During my leadership development training programs, participants ask me several questions such as how do I get ideas to author my books and how can they fast-track their career and how can they resolve their problems creatively. In this chapter, we discuss innovation, innovative leadership, and how to acquire innovative and

M. S. Rao (✉)
MSR Leadership Consultants, New Delhi, India

J. Marques (ed.), *Innovative Leadership in Times of Compelling Changes*, Management, Change, Strategy and Positive Leadership, https://doi.org/10.1007/978-3-030-67258-4_5

inspiring ideas to resolve personal, professional, and social problems to achieve peace, happiness, and success in your life.

The Miracle of Your Subconscious Mind

When you want to acquire innovative and inspiring ideas, you must develop a positive mindset that creativity can be cultivated and innovation can be nurtured. You must take the support of your subconscious mind to achieve creativity. Most people do not realize the significance of the subconscious mind. Joseph Murphy unveiled the importance of the subconscious mind as follows: "All you have to do is unite, mentally and emotionally with the good you wish to embody. The creative powers of your subconscious will respond accordingly." Napoleon Hill remarked, "The possibilities of creative effort connected with the subconscious mind are stupendous and imponderable. They inspire one with awe." And Andrew Wyeth quoted, "I dream a lot. I do more painting when I'm not painting. It's in the subconscious." That is the power of your subconscious mind to enhance your creativity!

Creativity Versus Innovation

People often confuse between creativity and innovation. There is a huge difference between them. Creativity is to create something new while innovation is to add value to the existing one. Creativity is to create new ideas that are mostly intellectual and theoretical, while innovation is the practical application of ideas to resolve problems or to add value to the existing ones. Watts Humprey rightly remarked, "Innovation is the process of turning ideas into manufacturable and marketable form." And Lynne C. Levesque remarked, "To be creative you have to contribute something different from what you've done before. Your results need not be original to the world; few results truly meet that criterion. Most results are built on the work of others."

How to Spark Innovation?

Henry Ford had uncanny creative ability toward problem-solving. He was successful in bringing innovation in automobiles. When people fight, creativity sparks. The research has shown that conflict over ideas is good, especially for groups and organizations that do creative work. However, it should be constructive and intellectual rather than personal. Constructive conflict is referred to as a task or intellectual conflict. It happens when people argue over ideas rather than individuals. If the conflict gets personal, it is essential to use humor and get the discussion back to the intellectual mode.

In hierarchical establishments, there is less chance for innovation because there will be people who block innovation. Hence, innovative leaders encourage lean and flat organizations to promote innovation in their employees. People working in an organization have a preconceived mindset. To enhance innovation, it is essential to include people outside the organization to generate fresh ideas. Sometimes the scarcity of resources forces people to adopt the innovation. Telling people "what to do" and rather than "how to do" promotes creativity among the people. It is essential to spend regularly at least 20 minutes a day to build innovation skills. Over a period of time, the insight capacity increases, and new ideas evolve.

What Is Innovative Leadership?

If you ask an Indian child what does alphabet "A" stand for? The child immediately says, "A for Apple." If you ask the same question to an American child, the response would be, "A for Apple and innovation." That is the impression the Apple Computers has created in America. Innovation is almost synonymous with Apple Computers. It has created new products and services by following the road less traveled. It took many years for Apple to build its brand for innovation under the visionary leadership of Steve Jobs.

When we look at Benjamin Franklin, he was a great innovator who championed innovation. Innovation in pictorial advertisements in newspapers, championing infotainment through ballads, an invention of the lightning rod, a bifocal lens, and a gas stove made him stand out as an innovative leader much long ago. Eminent people including Albert Einstein, Bill Gates, Larry Ellison, Elon Musk, and Mark Zuckerberg can be called innovative leaders who stand out from the pack with their unconventional ideas and approaches. In this context, let us discuss innovative leadership.

There are three kinds of people—the first kind of people focuses on individuals, the second on issues, and the third on ideas. The third kind is the innovative leaders who emphasize ideas rather than brood over issues and spend time unnecessarily on individuals. These leaders can also be called "eureka leaders."

Innovative leadership is all about encouraging people who have new ideas and insights and helping them to experiment and explore the same to minimize failures. It also involves respecting their failures and handholding them to try and test their ideas. It calls for extraordinary gut feeling and intuition on the part of these leaders. Innovative leadership should not be confused with creative leadership as creative leadership involves creating new ideas and insights. However, innovative leadership involves the implementation and commercialization of ideas.

Innovation is like a "eureka moment." In addition to adding value by implementing and commercialization, it also places all capabilities and competencies in unconventional ways. It brings either radical or incremental improvements in products, processes, or services. Innovation replaces the existing outdated tools and techniques and methods and strategies by unconventional approaches and ideas. It could be in the area of any activity. For instance, innovation could be about human resources or marketing or operations or outsmarting the competition. As everyone aspires to outsmart others, the companies endeavor to outsmart other companies, and it calls for innovative leadership.

Innovation is the engine for growth and expansion for any enterprise. It is the ideas and insights that fuel innovation. Innovation does not come on a platter. You must dig deep within and explore and experiment immensely with passion and perseverance. Innovation is also about reinvention as per the changing times and technologies. Innovation happens with mistakes. You must display a "never say die attitude," and you must persevere with a passion to make innovation happen. Innovation does not happen overnight. It needs continuous efforts and energies. Warren Bennis explained, "Innovation—any new idea—by definition will not be accepted at first. It takes repeated attempts, endless demonstrations, monotonous rehearsals before innovation can be accepted and internalized by an organization. This requires courageous patience."

Innovators believe in observation and experimentation. They are basically thinkers with a tendency to question, associate, and imagine. They learn a lot by networking, sharing, and listening from others. Innovative leaders care for their people for *what* they know rather *how* much they know. They care for their people, knowledge, and experience they bring in across the table and share the same with others.

Innovative leadership is essential irrespective of the verticals and sectors because it helps either cut down costs or promote new products, features, and activities.

Hallmarks of Innovative Leaders

Innovative leaders are of a different breed. They are rarely found. They are knowledge workers who go by the road less traveled. These leaders constantly search for new ideas and encourage people to come up with new ideas and insights and new business proposals that improve the performance and image of the organization. These leaders explore and experiment. They have curiosity and are passionate about delivering something different and unique. They enjoy adding value to existing products and services. Here are some hallmarks of innovative leaders. They are mentally flexible and passionate about their work. They are highly focused and always aim to hit bull's-eye. They treat failure as an integral part of the learning process. They move forward with renewed energy and enthusiasm as every failure is a learning experience. They are future-oriented and forward-looking and are unmindful of short-term setbacks. They shed inhibitions and wed technology. They have "never say die" attitudes like Thomas Edison and Colonel Sanders. They are agents of change. They do not innovate for the sake of innovation. They have an insatiable appetite for discovery and learning. They acquire firms that believe in innovation since it offers synergy. Besides, it helps in minimizing the failure rates in innovations. They go by their heart rather than the head. They believe in substance rather in style. They roll up their sleeves. They have a strong vision and have the ability to articulate their vision through pictures to their followers. For instance, Steve Jobs presented his ideas and inventions through his presentations effectively. They respect failures and empathize with failed people. They collaborate rather than compete with others. They keep their communication channels open for all. They reward innovative people. They see the invisible. They are out-of-the-box thinkers. Innovative leaders appear to be quirks or jerks. However, they are people with a unique mindset. They build effective teams who have a passion for excellence and innovation. Above all, they constantly probe for unconventional ways of doing things.

The Role of Innovative Leaders to Encourage Innovation

Innovative leaders must adopt the following strategies and techniques to encourage innovation in their organizations.

- Create a conducive organizational culture and climate for creativity and innovation.
- Tolerate ambiguity and uncertainty.
- Support and empathize. Provide all necessary inputs and resources for the people.
- Tolerate the actions of jerks and eccentrics.
- Promote team spirit and provide an intellectual challenge. Ask people to work in teams as teams provide more food for thought and discussion.
- Encourage people to be innovative both by words and deeds.
- Do not tell them how to do it. Just tell them what to do. They will evolve their own methodologies to execute the tasks.
- Respect failures. But do not encourage.
- Encourage job rotation. Job rotation is all about the rotation of existing talent across the business units, verticals, and departments to know what is really happening in other places. It helps in cross-functional knowledge and gets to know the root of challenges and furthers innovation. It helps in widening the mental horizons of the people. It is especially essential for the people who aspire and intend to assume leadership roles and responsibilities within the organizations.
- Encourage upward communication and down-to-top leadership in getting ideas from people. Talk to the lower cadre people who are the source of ideas.
- Encourage discussion and sharing knowledge and information. It is essential to respect failures as sometimes "fear of failure" may be a stumbling block to innovation.
- Provide motivational incentives for innovation depending on the needs of the people.
- Make things transparent as far as possible to encourage innovation.
- Encourage mavericks that enjoy innovation.

- Promote research and development.

A Blueprint to Acquire Innovative and Inspiring Ideas

When you want to grow in a specific career in your life or area or industry, you must build a team of like-minded people and discuss with them regularly. For instance, Einstein discussed with his friends and colleagues to get innovative ideas. In this way, you acquire new triggers to explore and experiment. Jot down the different approaches and ideas in a journal. Go to an isolated place and reflect on them. Discuss those ideas in public forums, meetings, and associations to generate more ideas. When you speak you get more ideas. When you discuss you get more ideas. When you write you get more ideas. Usually, people ask you questions at the end of the seminars and meetings. Show your enthusiasm to respond to them and research the questions raised by them. The best thing is to write in a journal and reflect on them during your leisure time. Feed those ideas into your subconscious mind. Before you go to sleep, throw the complicated ideas and issues to your subconscious mind by giving clear and constructive instructions that you are getting them resolved effortlessly. You will be amazed to find solutions on the next day morning. You will find the complicated issues getting simpler and clearer in the next day morning.

Believe in the art of synthesis. When you want to innovate new things, interconnect your existing knowledge and integrate mentally with new ones and explore by trial and error method. It leads to further breakthroughs. Arthur C. Clarke explained, "New ideas pass through three periods: 1) It can't be done; 2) It probably can be done, but it's not worth doing; 3) I knew it was a good idea all along!"

Identify your bad habits to break them. Cognitive psychologist Anthony McCaffrey[1] explains, "There's a pattern that, during the inventive process, people notice something that was overlooked and then they use that overlooked feature to build a new solution." He adds, "We're basically geared towards noticing the common things because that's most helpful in our daily experience. We don't want to have to figure out how to get a drink of water each time. But if you want to be innovative then your habits are your enemy and you have to fight against doing the common or habitual and know how to get to the obscure things."

Innovative Tools and Techniques to Acquire Innovative and Inspiring Ideas

Here are some tools and techniques to acquire innovative and inspiring ideas:

[1] http://www.inc.com/jessica-stillman/want-to-be-more-inventive-think-like-a-fifth-grader.html

- Be curious. Have an open mind to explore and experiment. Albert Einstein remarked, "I know quite certainly that I myself have no special talent. Curiosity, obsession, and dogged endurance, combined with self-criticism, have brought me to my ideas."
- Create a document by name, "Ideas Box," to write down your ideas whenever they pop up in your mind. Read them during your leisure time to explore.
- Do meditation to keep your mind free from clutter and think from a fresh perspective.
- Follow the road less traveled to avoid getting caught in the rat race. Do not do what others do. Think differently and act differently to stand out from others.
- Get out of your comfort zone. Break the routines that obstruct your creativity. James Bertrand rightly remarked, "Once we rid ourselves of traditional thinking, we can get on with creating the future." If you are not failing in your life means you are not doing anything worthwhile in your life.
- Avoid preconceived notions. Break the rules and enjoy the playfulness of your mind. Remember, your mind is a child at heart. Mencius (Meng-Tse) rightly remarked, "Great is the human who has not lost his childlike heart."
- Find out your biological clock to capture your ideas. Some people are morning people, some people are evening people, and some people are evening people. That means some people can leverage their hidden potential during the morning while some in the evening or night depending on their biological clocks. Identifying such an appropriate time is essential to create your ideas and leverage your potential fully.
- Capture your dreams, if possible. It leads to your creativity. Unfortunately, most people fail to remember their dreams.
- Read books in your area of interest. Reading helps widen your mental horizons. It provides peace of mind. It helps broaden your thinking and generate more ideas.
- Do not imitate others because what worked for others may not work for you. Draw your own blueprint to explore regularly. Be a trendsetter, not a trend follower.
- Use your time judiciously before you sleep and after you wake up to execute your tasks effectively.
- Stop dreaming and start daydreaming because most inventors are daydreamers. Carl Jung rightly quoted, "Without the playing with fantasy no creative work has ever yet come to birth. The debt we owe to the play of imagination is incalculable."
- Take a break. Go for traveling to see different places. Traveling teaches toleration and enhances exploration. When you go to different places, you encounter new experiences culminating with new ideas.

Albert Einstein rightly said, "Imagination is more important than knowledge. For knowledge is limited to all we know and understand, while imagination embraces the entire world, and all there ever will be to know and understand." When you have imagination, you can create more knowledge. Imagination is infinite while knowledge is finite. Hence, strive to increase your imagination to create more ideas.

Neil Gaiman once remarked, "You get ideas from daydreaming. You get ideas from being bored. You get ideas all the time. The only difference between writers and other people is we notice when we're doing it." Hence, observe your surroundings and the people around you to acquire ideas. At times, it is difficult to assert when and how you get your ideas. For instance, I acquire ideas when I go for a walk. I have the habit of carrying paper and pen whenever I go for a walk to capture the ideas that flash in my mind. Whenever I go outside, I have the habit of carrying a book and journal to capture the ideas that pop up my mind. Hence, it is obvious that ideas may flash at any time but you must be prepared to capture them immediately. Mere thinking does not help. It is essential to ink your ideas. Remember, a short pencil is better than a long memory.

Olivia Fox Cabane and Judah Pollack[2] unveil in their book, *The Net and the Butterfly: The Art and Practice of Breakthrough Thinking* as follows: The human brain thrives on a wide range of ideas and experiences, especially those it isn't expecting to encounter. Talk to people doing the same thing as you are. Bell Labs, the famed research center to which we owe the transistor, the calculator, laser technology, UNIX, and many of today's most essential technologies, famously encouraged its newest junior members to knock on the door of Nobel Prize winners and ask questions of "the guy who wrote the book."

Acquire Every Piece of Related Information

When you want to create or invent new things, every piece of information may not be useful to you. But do not start with a negative approach that entire information will go waste. Keep certain topics at the forefront of your mind and feed them into your subconscious mind before you go to sleep. They give tremendous results the next day morning.

I coined a new leadership style—"Soft Leadership." It took almost 5 years to create it. I wrote research papers and authored books on it. Some of the research papers are award-winning and are frequently downloaded and appreciated globally. For instance, my award-winning research paper titled "Soft leadership: a new direction to leadership" was among the most frequently downloaded research paper in Industrial and Commercial Training, Emerald UK. Because of my consistent contributions and persistent efforts, I came to be known as the father of "Soft Leadership" globally. It has become possible because I worked on my Ph.D. topic—Soft Skills and synthesized it with leadership—and collected every piece of related information regularly into my files and notebooks. I started writing research papers, authoring books, and discussing with participants during my leadership development training programs. During my research journey, there was criticism on my new

[2] https://www.fastcompany.com/3068331/the-science-of-work/your-brain-has-a-shuffle-button-heres-how-to-use-it

leadership perspective, and I worked seriously and sincerely to overcome them by doing intensive research. Additionally, I have the habit of taking feedback regularly and noting them regularly in my journals since my childhood. It worked wonders in my life. So far, I have done 10 years of research on this topic. I am still doing more research on "Soft Leadership" to create more tools and techniques to turn around global organizations, achieve organizational excellence and effectiveness, and promote global peace and prosperity. I am optimistic that this new leadership perspective will be relevant to future organizations and generations.

Innovation in Global Organizations

Organizations including Apple and Google are the top innovators globally. They emphasized innovation and left deep imprints through innovative leadership. The turbulent times call for innovation. Hence, it is the responsibility of the CEOs to drive innovation by donning the hat as innovative leaders. Innovation is the key to survival and success. It is the mantra for success in the twenty-first century. It calls for innovative leadership to beat competition and complexity arising out of rapidly changing technologies. Hence, innovative leadership is essential for cutting across the sectors to achieve all-round progress and prosperity.

Summary

To summarize, collect as much appropriate information as possible and write them in your journal regularly. Encourage your brain to make new connections in your area of interest. Remember, when you sow seeds, all seeds will not germinate and bear fruits. Some bear fruits while some do not bear fruits. It is not possible to achieve success completely. Hence, absorb more ideas to enable you to achieve the desired success.

I aspired to become one of the bestselling authors in the world. Hence, I have authored 50 books on various genres (i.e., Rao 2012, 2013, 2017, 2020), and some succeeded including the award-winning book *See the Light in You.* If I had authored only a few books, the success rate would have diminished. Hence, you must sow more than what you need to bear the fruits in life. During your journey of innovation, do not be afraid of failures. Edwin H. Land rightly remarked, "The essential part of creativity is not being afraid to fail." In fact, failures are an integral part of innovation. But learn from failures by taking feedback to improve your success rate. To conclude, strive from a theoretical and practical perspective to acquire innovative and inspiring ideas to achieve extraordinary success in your life.

All achievements, all earned riches, have their beginning in an idea.—Napoleon Hill.

Chapter Takeaways

- Offers innovative tools and techniques to acquire innovative and inspiring ideas.
- Explains the power of your subconscious mind to acquire creative and inventive ideas and unlock your hidden potential.
- Differentiates between creativity and innovation and draws a blueprint to achieve creativity and innovation.
- Elaborates innovative leadership.
- Outlines the characteristics of innovative leaders.
- Implores to acquire every piece of information to achieve innovation.
- Emphasizes the importance of synthesis to generate more ideas.

Reflection Questions

1. How to unlock the power of your subconscious mind to spark inspiring ideas?
2. What is the difference between creativity and innovation?
3. Can you name some of the innovative leaders globally?
4. What are the strategies the innovative leaders adopt?
5. What are the tools and techniques to acquire innovative and inspiring ideas?

References

Soft Leadership: A New Direction to Leadership by Professor M.S. Rao *Waterside Productions* (2020). Retrieved from https://www.amazon.com/Soft-Leadership-New-Direction/dp/1949003523

See the Light in You: Acquire Spiritual Powers to Achieve Mindfulness, Wellness, Happiness, and Success by Professor M.S. Rao *Waterside Productions* (2020). Retrieved from https://www.amazon.com/See-Light-You-Spiritual-Mindfulness/dp/1949003132

Soft leadership: a new direction to leadership by M.S. Rao, *Industrial and Commercial Training* (12 April 2013). Retrieved from https://www.emerald.com/insight/content/doi/10.1108/00197851311320559/full/html

Your Brain Has A "Shuffle" Button–Here's How To Use It by Judah Pollack and Olivia Fox Cabane Fast Company (2017). Retrieved from https://www.fastcompany.com/3068331/the-science-of-work/your-brain-has-a-shuffle-button-heres-how-to-use-it

Want to Be More Inventive? Think Like a Fifth Grader by Jessica Stillman *Inc.* (2012). Retrieved from http://www.inc.com/jessica-stillman/want-to-be-more-inventive-think-like-a-fifth-grader.html

Chapter 6
Transcending Emerging Barriers Through Patience

Varinder Kumar and Satinder Dhiman

Abstract This chapter aims to appraise the benefits of patience as a leadership skill that is fast becoming scarce in today's fast-paced, ever-changing environment. Research shows that patience augurs inner peace and facilitates dealing with sufferings and stressors effectively, helps to pursue long-term goals persistently, and promotes overall well-being and flourishing. Psychologically speaking, patience acts as a modulating buffer between experience and expression of negative emotions and prevents interpersonal differences spiraling down to expression of anger and hatred. This chapter chronicles the contribution of different moral philosophers and spiritual writers besides reviewing some pertinent leadership literature pertaining to patience. It discusses various behavioral barriers in the smooth functioning of the organization that may be overcome with patience.

Keywords Patience · Perseverance and growth · Patience as moral virtue · Patience and leadership · Barriers to patience

Introduction

Patience builds inner peace and facilitates dealing with sufferings and stressors in an effective way (Deng et al., 2019; Wallace & Shapiro, 2006); helps to pursue long-run goals persistently (Fowler & Kam, 2006), generates harmony (Ji, 2009); and promotes overall happiness, human flourishing, and well-being (Elliott, 2014; Schnitker, 2012; Schnitker & Emmons, 2007). In situation of interpersonal relations, it fosters smooth and soothing interpersonal interaction (Fowler & Kam,

V. Kumar
NJSA Govt College, Kapurthala, India

S. Dhiman (✉)
Woodbury University, Burbank, CA, USA
e-mail: Satinder.Dhiman@woodbury.edu

J. Marques (ed.), *Innovative Leadership in Times of Compelling Changes*, Management, Change, Strategy and Positive Leadership, https://doi.org/10.1007/978-3-030-67258-4_6

2006) by acting as a buffer between experience and expression of negative emotions and prevents interpersonal differences spiraling down to expression of anger and hatred. Consequently, different moral philosophers and spiritual writers have emphasized patience as a unique virtue that tests the worth of a person in testing times. On the contrary, impatience breeds anxiety, fear, resentment, discouragement, and failure. Daily hassles, anxiety, and frustration resulting from being impatient have negative impact on physical health and happiness even with greater magnitude than major life events, whereas patience is positively correlated with subjective well-being (Schnitker & Emmons, 2007). However, scant attention has been paid to it in psychology and management literature except this trait has assumed recent attention in empirical investigation in psychology (Schnitker, 2012, p. 263) or has been described as one of six perfections along with generosity, ethical discipline, enthusiastic effort, concentration, and wisdom that a leader should possess to have distinct ability to affect others in profound ways (Lama & Muyzenberg, 2008, p. 36–38). This chapter attempts to evaluate the advantages of patience as a leadership skill that is becoming alien in today's fast-pace, ever-changing environment.

Meaning and Manifestation of Patience

The *Merriam-Webster Dictionary* (n.d.) defines patience as "the ability to remain calm and not become annoyed when dealing with difficult situation or person, and the ability to give attention to something for a long time without becoming bored or losing interest." Buddhist authors are of the view that the word patience is derived from the Sanskrit term Kshanti translated into Chinese as Chanti or Chandi (Deng et al., 2019 p. 224). However, the Sanskrit word Kshanti not only encompasses patience but also forbearance and forgiveness in its scope. Kshanti is renunciation of anger and other negative emotions and maintains an attitude of forgiveness. Patience is self-control, restraint, and remaining calm despite experiencing undesirable situations like pains, frustrations, setbacks, and sufferings. This is quite in contrast to impulsiveness, impatience, and nurturing anger and resentment against some person.

Patience is "the propensity of a person to wait calmly [without complaint] in the face of frustration, adversity and suffering" (Schnitker, 2012, p. 263). In the context of Buddhist literature, patience is "strength to face the challenges and difficulties of life without losing composure and inner tranquility" (Deng et al., 2019, p. 224). To Gampopa (1998) patience is "not being disturbed, not retaliating and a peaceful state of mind in the face of all manner of suffering, from annoyance to physical and emotional pain."

Thus patience as deduced from the above means:

- Remaining tolerant under provocation.
- Exercising self-restraint.

- Maintaining calm and inner pose despite undergoing pains, frustrations, setbacks, and sufferings.
- Sufferance and endurance as Tibetan proverb states "Without someone to make you angry, how can you practice patience?"
- Renunciation of anger and other negative emotions and maintaining an attitude of forgiveness.
- "Freedom within the domain where necessity rules" (Harned, 1997, p. 101)
- Favoring choice of larger-later reward over smaller-sooner gratifications.

However patience does not mean servility, sneaking servility towards superiors and supercilious arrogance towards inferiors as we notice in case of hypocrisy, calm endurance of oppression or injustice due to ignorance or folly, lack of courage, greed, laziness, blanket impassivity and resignation towards evil, failure to get angry at the right person at the right time as Aristotle advocates, and being dormant. In these cases, maintaining patience is compulsion than choice.

Patience in Religious Perspective

"Spiritualists need great patience as they meditate continuously with blink possibility of illumination, in spite of persistent efforts. This patience acts as antidote to ego and helps to perpetuate one's pursuit for cherished goal. Without it, one becomes a bull in china shop, blithely destroying future happiness [as well as chances of illumination]" (Kalam & Tiwari, 2015, p. 17). To spiritualists, meditation is reaction-free consciousness or equanimity attained through patience and forgiveness. Consequently, different religions have advocated patience in their texts.

Eastern religions such as Hinduism, Buddhism, Jainism, and Taoism advocate practicing patience for ethical and spiritual elevation. In Hinduism, patience has been described as *titiksha* – the capacity to endure all sorrow and sufferings without struggling for redress or for revenge, being always free from anxiety, or lament over them: सहनं सर्वदुः खानामऽप्रतकिारपूर्वकम् | चन्तिावलािपरहतिं सा ततिक्षिा नगिद्यते॥ (*Vivekachudamani*, sloka 24). Elaborating further Swami Chinmayananda (2013) describes it as "the faculty of mind which it maintains when intellectually it is governed by a tempo and a conviction which is complete and self-ordained, divine and noble" (p. 44) to accommodate cheerfully all the vicissitudes and ignore any obstacle that may come. This *titiksha* has been described as one of six disciplines within the fourfold qualifications of spiritual seeker (other being discrimination between real and the unreal, detachment from enjoyment of fruits of actions, and burning aspiration for liberation (*Vivekachudamani,* sloka 19). There are incidences in epics *Ramayana* and *Mahabharata* where patience of king and royal prince has been extolled. Tamil text *Tirukkural* suggests patience for ethical living and long-term happiness. *Bhagavad Gita* advocates *titiksha* for realizing nectar of immortality by enduring all relatives of mundane existence which cause heat and cold, pleasure and pain, etc. and remaining steadfast in one's pursuit (B.G. 2.14 and 2.15).

Only a mind that is not disturbed by these inevitable pinpricks of life is fit to pursue the highest spiritual goal.

In Taoism, Lao Tzu teaches patience along with simplicity and compassion to allow things to unfold in their natural way: "If you take muddy water and still it, it gradually becomes clear. If you bring something to rest in order to move it, it gradually comes alive" (Henricks, 1993, ch 15). Jainism advocates equanimity, self-control (*shramana*), and renunciation of anger and passions and maintenance of an attitude of forgiveness for one's spiritual development. In Buddhism, patience has been described as one of the six *paramitas* (perfection) for bodhisattva practices (Rinpoche, 1992) and to practice pure ethics (Gyatso, 1992, p. 107). Dalai Lama (1997) describes patience as almost mediator between anger and compassion. To him, opposing forces of anger and hatred can be overcome through patience and tolerance and transformed to love and compassion.

> In a traditional Zen story, a student asked a Zen master, "Is there a concept of Grace in Buddhism?"
>
> The master replied, "Yes, there is a concept of Grace in Buddhism. It is called patience!"
>
> Then he added, "All things come to those who work humbly and wait."

Jewish religion describes features of God as patient, compassionate and gracious, slow to anger, loving humanity, forgiving wickedness (Exodus 34:6–7), and conceptualizes as virtue for humans to develop in themselves as "patience is better than pride" (Ecclesiastes 7:8). Christianity advocates patience: "Be completely humble and gentle, be patient, bearing with one another in love" (Ephesions 4:2). Saint Augustine (1952) describes patience as "companion of wisdom." To John Calvin (1990) patience is feeling the providence and sovereignty of God. Islamic scriptures hold patience as fundamental virtue as reflected in *Ash-Shura* of Koran, "But indeed if any shows patience and forgives that would truly be an exercise of courageous will and resolution in the conduct of affairs" (42:43). Islam advocates *Sabr* that literally means endurance or perseverance and persistence, remaining spiritually steadfast despite facing opposition or setbacks. It mentions 99 names of God, and *As-Sabr*, patience, being the last name. There are different precepts in Koran that advocate patience: "Seek God/Allah's help with patient perseverance and prayer. It is indeed hard except for those who are humble" (2:45); "O you who believe! Seek help with patient perseverance and prayer, for God is with those who patiently persevere" (2:153); "O you who believe! Persevere in patience and constancy. Vie in such perseverance, strengthen each other, and be pious, that you may prosper" (3:200); "No one will be granted such goodness except those who exercise patience and self-restraint, none but persons of the greatest good fortune" (41:35); and "Be patient, for your patience is with the help of Allah" (16:127).

Patience and Stoicism

> *The only thing that isn't worthless: to live this life out truthfully and rightly. And be patient with those who don't.* – Marcus Aurelius.

The above quote sums up the stoic approach to life and leadership: Act truthfully and rightly and be patient with those who do not. Patience accords the understanding about what is in our control and what is not. Our own behavior is in our control. In our interactions with others in and outside the workplace, we should always act righteously and fairly. However, we have no control regarding how others are going to act. Getting upset about what is not in our control only adds to our stress and anxiety. Stoicism's final injunction is: *Bear and forbear.*

This attitude of forbearance is essentially a dynamic principle that fosters all-around peace of mind and happiness. According to Stoics, the principle – that we can achieve happiness or *eudemonia* by limiting our thoughts and actions to things under our control ("up to us") and accepting equanimously what are not ("not up to us") – encompasses all the wisdom needed to achieve happiness. The well-known "Serenity Prayer" generally attributed to Reinhold Niebuhr is thoroughly "Stoic":

> *God, grant me the serenity to accept the things I cannot change,*
> *The courage to change the things I can,*
> *And wisdom to know the difference.*

It echoes Epictetus's observation that some things are under our control and some things are not. Wisdom lies in minding those things that are under our control and treating what we cannot control or change with patience, equanimity, and calm indifference.

It is important to remember that patience is an important virtue for self-leadership – something that leaders should practice themselves. We cannot expect others to be patient towards us. That will be against the stoic dichotomy of control – expecting to control what is *not* up to us.

Patience and Leadership

Leaders have to exercise tolerance and patience in different situations or in handling difficult persons. In the present fast-changing environment with accelerated pace of living and with greater dependence upon technology, this skill is becoming alien among people. Present-day customer wants speedy and spontaneous service without losing time, and business cannot afford losing customers and referral opportunities. If company people do not exercise patience in such situations, negative emotions accelerate and relations get destroyed. Leaders have to demonstrate patience in such type of difficult situations by taking fair and firm actions.

One's style of leadership is usually the product of one's self or personality, surrounding of circle of close associates, and the situation. Situation may be routine or peaceful or of crisis. If the leader has cultivated profound peaceful state of mind with patience, s/he is more likely to respond with "calm, collected and concentrated mind" (Dalai Lama and Muyzenberg, 2008) undisturbed by reactive thoughts and negative emotions. The opposite of such state of mind lacking patience is least-effective and hyper-reactive mind as witnessed in abusive supervision (Bies, 2001; Tepper, 2000) with fits of anger thrown at subordinates destroying the peace of organization. Therefore, Dalai Lama and Muyzenberg (2008) advocate patience as one of six perfections that a leader should possess as trait (other being generosity, ethical discipline, enthusiastic effort, concentration, and wisdom) that has a definite ability to affect others in a profound way especially in provocative circumstances, hostility, criticism, and disappointment (p 37). However, patience does not mean inaction, but control over anger and reactive behavior and flow of one's energy in positive manner.

In the context of leadership, Abdul Kalam witnessed patience in spiritual leader Pramukh Maharaj of Akshardham, Gandhinagar, who defeated the nefarious designs of the terrorists in 2002 by not reacting to provocation designed to elicit a backlash, but encouraged his followers to pray for restoring peace in the state of Gujrat. Abdul Kalam narrates that Pramukh Swamiji showed magnanimity by avoiding blame game or imputing motives. "There was not even a hint of anger in his eyes. …When I would later meet Nelson Mandela, I once again saw this power of tolerance, patience and forgiveness" (Kalam & Tiwari, 2015, p. 15). In corporate world, leaders thrived because of resilience and their ability to view setbacks as learning experiences and challenges as opportunities to excel (Sonnenfeld & Ward, 2017).

In politics, we find Mahatma Gandhi and Nelson Mandela practicing patience. Gandhi channelized his spirituality, self-control, and self-elevation for emancipating Indian masses from social evils and liberating the country from British Raj by unifying Indians besides bringing their social transformation and inner awakening among them. He pursued his mission through nonviolent means without losing hope and practicing patience. Gandhi believed that the only test of truth is action based on the refusal to do harm – *ahiṁsā* through deeds, speech, and thought. We have been told by experts that anger instigates almost 80 percent of the violence that we experience either in our personal lives or as a society or nation. Anger leads to conflict and conflict to violence. Learning how to use the powerful energy of anger intelligently and effectively is the foundation of Gandhi's philosophy of nonviolence. Nelson Mandela, spending 27 years in imprisonment, "never lost hope that this great transformation [of freeing his countrymen from apartheid] would occur" (Mandela, p. 384).

Growth Takes Patience and Perseverance

The following story about the moso bamboo tree widely attributable to motivational speaker Zig Ziglar (who attributes it to his friend, Joel Weldon) splendidly illustrates the virtues of patience and perseverance in nature:

> The moso is a bamboo plant that grows in China and the far east. After the moso is planted, no visible growth occurs for up to five years – even under ideal conditions!
>
> Then, as if by magic, it suddenly begins growing at the rate of nearly two and one half feet per day, reaching a full height of ninety feet within six weeks.
>
> But it's not magic. The moso's rapid growth is due to the miles of roots it develops during those first five years, five years of getting ready. (Cited in Cavanaugh, 2004, p. 35).

One is also reminded of the famous lines by Henry Wadsworth Longfellow that ring true today as it was when he wrote them in 1847:

> The heights by great men reached and keptWere not attained by sudden flight,But they, while their companions slept,Toiled ever upward through the night.
>
> ~Henry Wadsworth Longfellow (1847), *The Ladder of St. Augustine*, stanza 10.

Patience and the Zen of Learning

An old Chinese parable (Cited in Watts, 1975, p. 127) tells how the two fastest horses began with a race with the sun behind them in the *east* and at the end of the day inevitably found themselves facing the sun in the *west*. A Zen proverb says, those in a hurry do not arrive. This principle says that in matters of true learning, he who goes slow goes far. Hence, the currency of such expressions as "Haste makes waste" or "Speed is useless if you are going in the wrong direction." The trick is to haste slowly, i.e., to take time to absorb and assimilate information and to shun short cuts. Patience is the key here.

> The following tale (Cited in Fields et al., 1984, p. 124) illustrates this principle as follows:
>
> "What do you wish from me?" the master asked.
>
> "I wish to be your student and become the finest karateka in the land," the boy replied. "How long must I study?"
>
> "Ten years at least," the master answered.
>
> "Ten years is a long time," said the boy. "What if I studied twice as hard as all your other students?"
>
> "Twenty years," replied the master.
>
> "Twenty years! What if I practiced day and night with all my effort?"
>
> "Thirty years," was the master's reply.
>
> "How is it that each time I say I will work harder, you tell me that it will take longer?" the boy asked.
>
> "The answer is clear. A pupil in such a hurry learns slowly."

Barriers in Organizations

As organization behavior tourist, we witness the following barriers in the smooth functioning of the organization that need to be overcome with patience:

Mistrust

Mistrust among people at workplace acts as barrier in the organization, whereas trust accelerates the speed and lower organizational cost of working (Covey, 2006). With growing number of corporate scams and scandals such as Enron, WorldCom, Taco, and Satyam, honesty, truthfulness, and integrity of corporate leaders have gained focus of attention (Clapp-Smith et al., 2009; Dirks & Ferrin, 2001), and trust on leadership is questioned. In business dealings people do not like to follow and deal with people who are "duplicitous, deceitful and dishonest" (Covey, 2006, p. 9). To overcome this barrier of mistrust, leaders have to practice integrity, honesty, and trustworthiness (Brown & Trevino, 2006) by practicing ethical leadership. In the absence of charisma, people hesitate to trust them despite their ethical behavior. Therefore, such a situation demands patience on their part to win the heart of their people.

Stereotypes and Prejudice

Stereotypes ("fixed and distorted generalizations made about all members of a particular group" (Loden & Rosener, 1991, p. 58)), prejudices (harboring negative judgment about a particular group (Morrison, 1992, pp. 34–35)), and conclusions (drawn without adequate knowledge or evidence) all act as barriers in smooth and flawless functioning of the organization as it results in either the systematic inclusion or exclusion of a particular group based upon characteristics such as gender, ethnic background, and nationality. To overcome these though, affirmative action laws (commonly used in the United States and known as *quota systems* in other countries) provide access to equal opportunities, yet they address little to deal with underlying prejudices and stereotypes (Fiske & Taylor, 1991; Morrison, 1992; Smith & Stewart, 1983). To overcome these stereotypes and prejudice, one needs to understand others' merits and that requires patience. Nelson Mandela (1994) after going through sacrifices and sufferings talks about liberating not only oppressed but also oppressors from the prisons of hatred, prejudice, and narrow-mindedness:

> I knew as well as I knew anything that the oppressor must be liberated just as surely as the oppressed. A man who takes away another man's freedom is a prisoner of hatred, he is locked behind the bars of prejudice and narrow-mindedness. I am not truly free if I am taking away someone else's freedom, just as surely as I am not free when my freedom is taken from me. The oppressed and the oppressor alike are robbed of their humanity. (p. 385)

Harassment, Discrimination, Injustice, and Toxic Environment

Workplace harassment has attracted attention for study since the 1980s because it acts as a barrier in the functioning of organization. Scornful and vindictive attitudes, indifference, and utterance of carping words by bosses or colleagues destroy the inner well-being of an employee and consequently adversely affect his or her level of engagement, performance, and quality of life. As a result, the organization suffers diminishing team spirit and loss of morale; its workforce is deprived of organizational learning and creativity. Both the individual and the organization fail to perform to their peak levels and ultimately settle at below optimum (Adams, 1992; Baron & Neuman, 1996; Chappell & Di Martino, 2000; Leymann, 1990). Another harmful practice that acts as barrier in the organization is discrimination faced by certain organizational members (Fernandez, 1993/1991). This discrimination may be on the basis of casteism, communalism, gender, regionalism, or other categories. The victims experience injustice perpetuated by others. If the leader or powerful group of the organization does not behave in an ethical manner, the power is likely to fall into the hands of cliques, coteries, and cauci that exert power over others and siphon resources. They eulogize their insignificant acts and seek back-patting and patronization from persons in power, typically remaining mute about misdeeds and rationalizing them in cunning and manipulative ways. As a result, others experience unfettered and undeterred discrimination and injustice that harm the growth of the organization.

Another unethical practice that acts as barrier is allowing the development of a toxic environment where certain members of the organization have to work under unfavorable conditions. These include manipulation through fear, setting unrealistic targets, defamation and debasement, putting others in untenable positions, and creating conditions of discomfort for others. When dominating groups exert power in unethical ways through the formation of cliques and coteries, they deliberately discriminate against person(s) of other groups by framing rules that set unfavorable and unmanageable targets for them. They do not hesitate to withdraw their comforts to deprive them of meaning at work. As a result, the person(s) being victimized first resists through agitation and, if not sufficiently addressed, becomes alienated from the organization. This toxic environment leads the person from a state of frustration to depression.

Patience is needed to tolerate harassment, discrimination, injustice, and toxic environment without depletion of one's inner resources. Reaction in such situation in violent manner becomes counterproductive as it further deteriorates the situation to bring reform in positive direction.

Envy in the Workplace

Envy in the workplace is an inevitable and unavoidable phenomenon. The feelings of distress and discontent because of another's talent, level of learning, skills, resources, and attainments, are commonly experienced. Whether admitted or not, often because of fear of incorrectness, envy is the most pervasive and powerful of all the disruptive emotions at workplace. Dogan and Vecchio (2001), who specialize in studying envy in the workplace, report that 77% of employees surveyed have witnessed jealousy around the office within the past month. The undercurrent of jealousy is often manifested through the use of foul language, demonstration of negative attitudes, belittling of others through disrespectful gestures, and displaying overall arrogance. The reasons for such jealousy include competition for limited resources, vying for important assignments, gaps in talent and skills, and continuous comparisons between rewards and efforts. Patience helps to overcome envy within oneself as it helps to wait and watch for positive results and favorable circumstances that may take their time.

Lack of Harmony

Lack of harmony causes negative consequences like conflicts (considered the other side of the same coin with harmony on one side; Leung & Brew, 2009) that result in unnecessary bickering with emotional scars and adverse effects on resonance among members and group cohesiveness and consequently affect the smooth functioning of the organization. This harmony is not confined to prevention and resolution of conflict and forcing wrapped-up phenomenon with superficial harmony (Huang, 1999/2016), but fostering positive intragroup relationship (Seashore, 1954) to social integration (O'Reilly et al., 1989) to genuine quality relationship in the form of high degree of mutually communal sharing and connectedness. This requires high degree of involvement, cohesion, and collaboration among members (in contrast to competitive behavior as well as interpersonal conflicts); respect, trust, support, and concern for the welfare of others (Eddleston & Kellermanns, 2007); and sense of responsibility for the organization as well as society. Patience helps to build up the harmony in such cases as it enables to tolerate the differences with grace, to understand others' perspective, and to demonstrate genuine respect. To cultivate harmony with the surrounding environment, one's inner harmony with the surrounding environment is essential as the outer conflicts are the manifestation of the inner conflicts of man (Horowitz, 1957). Patience not only fosters harmony within oneself but also with others by enabling to feel "comfortable with oneself as well as with others" (Balsekar, 2003).

Mismanagement of Diversity and Backlash

Diversity of workforce plays a significant role in the expansion of business at global level as it provides unique competitive advantage (Griggs, 1995; Jackson, 1991) because diverse groups produce higher-quality ideas and are more likely to make high-quality decisions (McGrath, 1984; McLeod & Lobel, 1992) and make greater number of innovations (Bantel & Jackson, 1989; Cox & Black, 1991). However, if the diverse members do not share the same goals, the group's creativity will suffer and performance shall be negatively affected (Williams & O'Reilly, 1998). It can result into social categorization-based stereotypes and biases (Tajfel & Turner, 1986) causing problems to organizational entry, career advancement due to discrimination and reverse discrimination, and social integration of underrepresented groups. Therefore if diversity is not properly managed, it acts as barrier. Because of mismanagement of diversity, negative reactions to the attainment of power by people of certain religions or regions may result as a form of backlash (Chemaers et al., 1995). When certain group members within the organization are perceived as attempting to acquire power through either individual or collective means, such reactions usually happen. This type of backlash may be in the form of strikes or organized resentment. Typically, it occurs before power has actually been obtained by other groups as it is a reaction to the threat of loss of power by the minority group. Sometimes these organizations are accused of providing special treatment to certain group members. To effectively engage the heads and hearts of diverse groups, leadership needs patience to explore the best among its people and to overcome negative reaction through slow and steady ways.

Benefits of Patience

Patience offers the following advantages in personal and professional life:

Patience and Positive Emotions

To Anderson (2003), positive emotions like unconditional love, compassion, etc. enhance health as these push aside the negative emotions. For instance, generosity stemming from altruism gives rise to love for humanity and casts out the fear and anxiety emerging from self-centeredness. To him three negative emotions – sadness/depression (depressive emotions), fear/anxiety, and anger/hostility (aggressive emotions) – increase susceptibility to disease and worsen health outcomes. On the other hand, altruism and forgiving act as protective factor against morbidity and mortality. Similarly, Daniel Goleman (2003, p 33) states that negative feelings like anger, anxiety, and depression if strong and prolonged can "increase vulnerability to disease, worsen the symptoms, or hinder recovery. On the other hand, more positive states like equanimity and optimism seem to have salutary effect on health." Positive emotions broaden and build an individual's personal resources like physical, intellectual, and social (Fredickson & Levenson, 1998; Fredickson, 2000/2004) as they produce unusual, flexible, creative, and receptive pattern of thought (Isen et al., 1987; Isen & Daubman, 1984) and increase brain's dopamine levels. Positive emotions can overcome the cardiovascular reactivity (Fredickson & Levenson, 1998) and depressive tendencies and can undo negative emotions. Positive emotions broaden people's momentary thought-action repertoires (Fredickson, 2000) and enlarge the cognitive context (Isen et al., 1987). Positive emotions also increase one's social resources as the persons feel connected with their surrounding members.

Persons acting out of tolerance and patience prevent negative emotions like fear, anxiety, anger, hostility, etc. to take place as these emotions increase susceptibility to diseases and worsen health outcomes (Anderson, 2003; Goleman, 2003). On the other hand, more positive states like equanimity and optimism seem to have salutary effect on health of the members. Leaders demonstrating patience can prevent negative emotions to spread among members.

Fostering Creativity

Creative scientists need patience to observe and record the phenomenon to avoid superficial findings out of quick reactions. The creative scientists and poets have to watch and listen to the events and phenomenon patiently, unfolding with new meaning that may alternate between "passionate involvement and sardonic detachment" (Csikszenmihalyi, 1996, p. 243). George Sylvester Viereck (1929) describes Einstein's "infinite patience" as he never resented questions but loved to explain the complex problems to even a 10-year-old son of his friend. Regarding emergence of creative idea, Noble laureate of physics Hans Bethe (1996) comments, "Two things are required. One is a brain. And second is the willingness to spend long times in thinking, with a definite possibility that you come out with nothing" (Csikszenmihalyi, 1996, p. 61). To the creative poet Mark Strand (1996), "Poetry is about slowing down.... reading the same thing again and again, really savoring it, living inside the poem. There's no rush to find out what happens in a poem" (p. 240).

Patience and Teamwork

Teamwork and engagement of people is the major pillar of the functioning of the modern organization as the performance of organization depends upon group members' cooperation for the common goals. However, people differ in their level of contribution to the group goal. Experimental studies demonstrate that patience as reflected in delay discounting is positively correlated with the people's level of engagement and other group-beneficial behavior (Curry et al., 2008). Patient people in general are more cooperative and less competitive and consequently achieve higher level of synergy than groups of impatient individuals (Espin et al., 2019). Moreover, patient people being more aware and grateful for the contribution of others and are likely to reciprocate other members' cooperation, and that strengthens the team spirit.

Celebrating Diversity

Patience plays its unique role in celebrating diversity and transforming business as more profitable and efficient when diverse labor forces from different disciplines and cultural and ethical background contribute to business. Celebrating diversity means engaging the heads, hearts, and spirit of different members of the workforce for realizing organization's objectives, tolerating differences as these coexist despite our disagreement or discomfort, and valuing other people, and conflicting opinions for their differences (Dhiman et al., 2019). Celebrating diversity is extension of healthy spirituality that leads us to celebrate our differences and view diversity as different manifestations of the underlying unity that permeates every phenomenon.

Patience is also needed to transform the organization as learning organization that helps to celebrate diversity by tapping people's commitment and capabilities to learn at all levels, by creating new and expansive patterns of thinking, setting collective aspiration free, and facilitating people to learn as whole together which Peter Senge (1990) advocates. Patience is needed to pursue dialogues, to become open to one's assumption, to build shared vision, and to develop new capacities of a team which are part of learning organization.

Patience and Happiness

Patience leads to both hedonic and eudaimonic happiness. Hedonic view of happiness attempts to define happiness as good life and pleasant feelings (Kahneman et al., 1999; Ryan & Deci, 2001; Ryff & Singer, 2000/2008) with focus on pleasures. Eudaimonic view based upon Aristotle's interpretation of happiness indicates happiness in self-realization, understanding meaning of experiences and meaning of one's life, fulfillment of inner potentials, and living according to one's own domino-one's talent and deeply held values (Seligman, 2002/2011; Sheldon & Elliot, 1999; Warr, 2007). Accordingly, happiness does not lie in living relaxed and lazy life that leads to losing track of time and forgetting personal problems, but making challenges in effective way to pursue inner growth and life, the life of self-actualization (Maslow, 1968) and fully functioning person (Rogers, 1961). The sources of happiness are not only successful economic pursuits and feeling of emotional satisfaction in interactions with surrounding members but also finding the meaning in the work and existence to deep state of human flourishing – deep contentment and calm that one develops around oneself.

Patience contributes to hedonic well-being as it acts as buffer in emotions, allows coping with adverse situation, and facilitates resonance and positive interaction and achievement of goals and long-term outcomes (Galston, 1988). It also leads to eudaimonic happiness, as it facilitates realization of human potentials, helps to meet challenges of life in an effective way, and provides insights to realize meaning in one's life (Frankl, 1959). Using 3-Factor Patience scale study, Schnitker (2012) measures three types of patience – interpersonal, life hardship, and daily hassles – which differentially relate to well-being and personality. Patience facilitates pursuit of goal and satisfaction in the face of obstacles. Training programs designed to enhance patience lead to increased patience along with decreased depression and increased positive effect. As patience decreases the daily hassles and frustrations that have a negative impact on physical health and well-being, it maximizes human functioning and is positively correlated with subjective well-being, positive copying, and virtuous living and thriving (Schnitker & Emmons, 2007).

Empathy

Empathy, the ability "to comprehend another's feelings and to re-experience themselves" (Salovey & Mayer, 1990), has been emphasized in leadership (Goleman, 1995; Yukl, 1998; George, 2000), psychotherapy, and clientage for bringing about change and learning and in personal bonds (Plutchik, 1987, p. 43). Practicing patience hypothetically leads to empathy with emotional appreciation of another's feelings and understanding others' subjective experiences. The most common barriers in empathy include impulsive behavior, concern with oneself, lack of time to listen to others, and lack of sensitivity. Patience helps to overcome these barriers by allowing a person to invest time in listening others, eliciting others' perspective, showing them respect and concern, and engaging with them.

Cultivating Patience with Mindfulness

"Patience is positively correlated with mindfulness because patient individuals are more mindful and absorbed in everyday tasks, so they devote less attentional resources to temporal cues "(Schnitker & Emmons, 2007, p. 198). Hashmei et al.'s research study (Hashemi & Moustafa, 2018) explores the mediating role of patience on the relationship between mindfulness and suicide ideation, indicating positive relationship between mindfulness and patience ($r = 0.32$, $p < 0.001$). The study claims that mindfulness affects patients' suicidal thoughts negatively through patience.

If patience is positively correlated with mindfulness, patience can be cultivated through deliberate practice of mindfulness. Different spiritual texts have recommended patience for spiritual elevation and peace of mind. Meditation contributes to cultivation of patience as the purpose of meditation is "not to shut down the mind or anaesthetize it, but rather to make it free, lucid and balanced" (Ricard, 2010). Mindfulness is one of the techniques of meditation practiced by Hindus, Buddhist, Zen, Christians, and Sufis with purpose of cultivating awareness of the continuously changing body-mind mechanism with endless ideas, feelings, perceptions, sensations, memories, fantasies, moods, etc. to develop affectionate and compassionate attention of the present moment. It has been described as the process of bringing a certain quality of attention to moment-to-moment experience (Kabat-Zinn, 1990), remembering to bring attention to present moment experience in an open and nonjudgmental manner (Huxter, 2007), and keeping one's consciousness alive to the present reality (Hanh, 1975). Mindfulness requires being highly concentrated, focused, poised, and calm to become aware of oneself and the surrounding world as well as one's purpose (Houlder & Houlder, 2002). Boyatzis and McKee (2005) describe it as the capacity to be fully aware of all that one experiences *inside the self* – body, mind, heart, and spirit – and to pay full attention to what is happening *around us,* people, the natural world, our surroundings, and events (Boyatzis & McKee, 2005). Mindfulness in the context of daily life means being aware of the moment-to-moment act and its impact upon oneself and others, paying affectionate and compassionate attention, overcoming egoistic and body-centered point of view, understanding surrounding environment with open eyes and caring attitude, and realizing the impermanence of different phenomena to end the sufferings of others. This helps to cultivate patience on a daily basis.

In his book *Mindful Leader: Ten Principles for Bringing Out the Best in Ourselves and Others,* Carroll opines that the regular practice of mindfulness meditation can help develop ten innate leadership talents needed to revitalize our workplace: simplicity, poise, respect, courage, confidence, enthusiasm, patience, awareness, skillfulness, and humility. Developing these innate talents through mindfulness, the author believes, can lead to cultivating courage, establishing authenticity, building trust, eliminating toxicity, pursuing organizational goals mindfully, and leading with wisdom and gentleness. (Carroll, 2007).

Kabat-Zinn (1990, pp. 33–40) describes the following attitudinal qualities that serve as a foundation of mindfulness practice, which include the key virtue of patience: nonjudging, patience, beginner's mind, trust, non-striving, acceptance, and letting go. Letting go is the way of letting things be, of accepting things as they are. *The wisdom of patience involves an understanding and acceptance of the fact that things can only unfold in their own time.* These psychological habits are essential building blocks of every mindfulness practice. Kabat-Zinn has carefully presented the most succinct summary of the practice starting with most fundamental aspect of remaining as a nonjudgmental witness of our experience. Once this aspect is grasped properly, one can appreciate the value of other virtues such as patience, non-striving (in the sense of non-forcing), acceptance, and its expression in letting go and letting things be.

Concluding Thoughts

This chapter considered the benefits of patience as a leadership skill that is fast becoming scarce in today's fast-pace, ever-changing environment. This chapter reviewed how different moral and spiritual traditions viewed the virtue of patience and presented some pertinent leadership literature pertaining to patience. It discussed various behavioral barriers in the smooth functioning of the organization and presented some strategies to transcend those barriers with patience. It illustrated the importance of patience through some teaching stories. All good things take time. According to Garfield (cited in Baughman, 1958, p. 64), "If nature wants a pumpkin tree, it takes three months; if it wants an oak tree, a hundred years." Learning to work hard humbly and wait patiently seems to be a great recipe of success both in personal and professional life. All things come to those who work and wait.

Chapter Takeaways

- Patience as a moral virtue has been extolled in all major wisdom, spiritual, and contemplative traditions of the world. It helps us go through the arrows and slings of life with the perspective that "this too shall pass."
- As a leadership skill, patience is fast becoming scarce in today's fast-pace, ever-changing environment. When cultivated properly, patience can overcome several organizational barriers such as mistrust, envy, conflict, lack of harmony, and mismanagement of diversity.
- Research shows that patience augurs inner peace and facilitates dealing with sufferings and stressors effectively, helps to pursue long-term goals persistently, and promotes overall well-being and flourishing.
- Psychologically speaking, patience acts as a buffer between experience and expression of negative emotions and prevents interpersonal differences spiraling down to expression of anger and hatred.
- Patience bestows several organizational advantages such as fostering creativity and teamwork and garnering positive emotions such as empathy, compassion, and harmony. Patience garners an understanding that good things take time and facilitates the acceptance of the fact that things can only unfold in their own time.

Reflection/Questions

1. How does patience help in transcending various behavioral and psychological barriers in organizations?

2. What positive benefits accrue to individuals and organization by exercising patience in personal and professional realms?
3. Can patience be developed or is it something inborn? Discuss briefly with some examples.
4. How can organizational training and learning different perspectives and understanding divergent views foster the development of patience?
5. What role does patience play specifically in fostering learning?

References

Adams, A. (1992). *Bullying at work: How to confront and overcome it*. Virago.

Anderson. (2003). *Emotional longevity*. Viking.

Augustine, S. (1952). *On patience* (L. Meagher, Trans.), Washington, DC: Catholic University of America Press. (Original work published 418).

Balsekar, R. (2003). *Peace and harmony in daily living: Facing life moment to moment, being anchored in tranquility*. Yogi Impressions.

Bantel, K. A., & Jackson, S. E. (1989). Top management and innovations in banking: Does the composition of the top team make a difference? *Strategic Management Journal, 10*, 107–124.

Baron, R. A., & Neuman, J. H. (1996). Workplace violence and workplace aggression: Evidence on their relative frequency and potential causes. *Aggressive Behavior, 22*, 161–173.

Baughman, M. D. (1958). *Teacher's Treasury of stories for every occasion*. Prentice Hall.

Bethe, H. (1996). As quoted in Csikszenmihalyi, M. (1996). *Creativity: Flow and the psychology of discovery and invention.* : Harper & Row.

Bies, R. (2001). Interactional (in)justice: The sacred and profane. In J. Greenberg & R. Cropanzano (Eds.), *Advances in organizational behavior* (pp. 89–118). Stanford University Press.

Boyatzis, R., & McKee, A. (2005). *Resonant leadership: Renewing yourself and connecting with others mindfulness, hope, and compassion*. Harvard Business School Press.

Brown, M. E., & Trevino, L. K. (2006). Ethical leadership: A review and future directions. *The Leadership Quarterly, 17*, 595–616.

Calvin, J. (1990). *Institutes of Christian religion* (H. Beveridge, Trans.) Grand Rapids, MI: W.B. Eerdmans Publishing Co. (Original work published 1536).

Carroll, M. (2007). *The mindful leader: Ten principles for bringing out the best in ourselves and others*. Trumpeter.

Cavanaugh, B. (2004). *The Sower's seeds: One hundred and twenty inspiring stories for preaching, teaching and public speaking*. Paulist Press.

Chappell, D., & Di Martino, V. (2000). *Violence at work*. International Labour Office.

Chemaers, M., Oskamp, S., & Constazo, M. (1995). *Diversity in organizations: New perspective for a changing workplace*. Sage Publication.

Chinmayananda, S. (2013). *Vivekacudamani: Commentary by Swami Chinmayananda-an intellectual exploration into the infinite and the eternal*. Central Chinmaya Mission Trust.

Clapp-Smith, R., Vogelgesang, G. R., & Avey, J. B. (2009). Authentic leadership and positive psychological capital: The mediating role of Trust at the Group Level of analysis. *Journal of Leadership & Organizational Studies, 15*(3), 227–240.

Covey, S. M. R. (with Merrill, R. R.). (2006). *The speed of trust: The one thing that changes everything*. New York: Free Press.

Cox, T., & Black, S. (1991). Managing cultural diversity: Implications for organizational competitiveness. *Academy of Management Executive, 5*, 45–56.

Csikszenmihalyi, M. (1996). *Creativity: Flow and the psychology of discovery and invention*. Harper & Row.

Curry, O. S., Price, M. E., & Price, J. G. (2008). Patience is a virtue: Cooperative people have lower discount rates. *Personality and Individual Differences, 44*, 778–783.
Deng, J., Li, T., Wang, J., & Zhang, R. (2019). Optimistically accepted suffering boosts happiness: Associations between Buddhism patience, selflessness, and subjective authentic-durable happiness. *Journal of Happiness Studies, 21*, 223–240.
Dhiman, S. K., Modi, S., & Kumar, V. (2019). Celebrating diversity through spirituality in the workplace: Transforming organizations holistically. *The Journal of Values-Based Leadership, 12*(1), 1–19.
Dirks, K. T., & Ferrin, D. L. (2001). The role of trust in organizational settings. *Organization Science, 12*, 450–467.
Dogan, K., & Vecchio, R. P. (2001). Managing envy and jealousy in the workplace. *Compensation and Benefit Review, 33*(2), 57–64.
Eddleston, K., & Kellermanns, F. W. (2007). Destructive and productive family relationships: A stewardship theory perspective. *Journal of Business Venturing, 22*(4), 545–565.
Elliott, M. (2014). Thai Buddhism and well-being: An application of stress process theory, mental health. *Religion & Culture, 17*(9), 923–936. https://doi.org/10.1080/13674676.2014.951920
Espin, A. M., Correa, M., & Ruiz-Vallaverde, A. (2019). Patience predicts cooperative synergy: The roles of in-group bias and reciprocity. *Journal of Behavioral and Experimental Economics, 83*, 101465.
Fernandez, J. P. (1993). *The diversity advantage: How American business can outperform Japanese and European companies in the global marketplace*. Lexington.
Fields, R., Taylor, P., Weyler, R., & Ingrasci, R. (Eds.). (1984). *Chop Wood carry water: A guide to finding spiritual fulfillment in everyday life*. Jeremy P. Tarcher.
Fiske, S. T., & Taylor, S. E. (1991). *Social Cognition* (2nd ed.). McGraw-Hill.
Fowler, J. H., & Kam, C. D. (2006). Patience as a political virtue: Delayed gratification and turnout. *Political Behavior, 28*, 113–128. https://doi.org/10.1007/s11109-006-9004-7
Frankl, V. E. (1959). *Man's search for meaning: An introduction to Logotherapy*. Random House.
Fredickson, B. L. (2000). Cultivating positive emotions to optimize health and well-being. *Prevention & Treatment, 3*, Article 0001a.
Fredickson, B. L., & Levenson, R. W. (1998). Positive emotion speed recover from the cardiovascular sequelae of negative emotions. *Cognition and Emotion, 12*, 191–220.
Galston, W. A. (1988). Liberal virtues. *American Political Science Review, 82*(4), 1277–1290.
Gampopa. (1998). *The Jewel Ornament of Liberation.* Translated by Khenpo Konchog Gyaltsen Rinpoche. Edited by Ani K. Trinlay Choedron. Ithaca: Snow Lion Publications.
George, J. M. (2000). Emotions and leadership: The role of emotional intelligence. *Human Relations, 53*(8), 1027–1055.
Goleman, D. (1995). *Emotional intelligence*. Bantam Books.
Goleman, D. (2003). *Healing emotions: Conversations with the Dalai Lama on mindfulness, emotions and health*. Shambhala.
Griggs, L. B. (1995). Valuing diversity: Where from...where to? In L. B. Griggs & L. Louw (Eds.), *Valuing diversity: New tools for a new reality* (pp. 1–14). McGraw-Hill.
Gyatso, G. K. (1992). *Buddhism in the Tibetan tradition: A guide*. Tharpa Publication.
Hanh, T. N. (1975). *The miracle of mindfulness: A manual on mindfulness*. Beacon Press.
Harned, D. B. (1997). *Patience: How we wait upon the world.* Cowley Publications.
Hashemi, R., & Moustafa, A. A. (2018). Rahmati, Kankat, L., Valikhani, a., mindfulness and suicide ideation in Iranian cardiovascular patients: Testing the mediating role of patience. *Psychological Reports, 121*(6), 1037–1052. https://doi.org/10.1177/0033294117746990
Henricks, R. G. (1993). (Trans.) *Tao Te Ching*. New York: Modern Library.
Horowitz, I. (1957). Bertrand Russell on war and peace. *Science & Society, 21*(1), 30–51.
Houlder, D., & Houlder, K. (2002). *Mindfulness and money: The Buddhist path of abundance*. Broadway.
Huang, L. L. (1999). *Interpersonal harmony and conflict: Indigenous theory and research* (In Chinese). Taipei: Laurel.

Huxter, M. J. (2007). Mindfulness as therapy from a Buddhist perspective. In D. A. Einstein (Ed.), *Innovations and advances in cognitive behaviour therapy* (pp. 43–55). Australian Academic Press.

Isen, A. M., & Daubman, K. A. (1984). The influence of affect on categorization. *Journal of Personality and Social Psychology, 47*, 1206–1217.

Isen, A. M., Daubman, K. A., & Nowicki, G. P. (1987). Positive affect facilitates creative problem solving. *Journal of Personality and Social Psychology, 52*, 1122–1131.

Jackson, B. E. (1991). Team composition in organizational settings: Issues in managing an increasingly diverse workforce. In S. Worchel, W. Wood, & J. Simpson (Eds.), *Group process and productivity* (pp. 138–173). Sage.

Ji, Q. (2009). *Jie Zhuang anthology*. Shanghai Ancient Press.

Kabat-Zinn, J. (1990). *Full catastrophic living: Using the wisdom of your body and mind to face stress, anxiety and depression*. Guildford Press.

Kahneman, D., Diener, E., & Schwarz, N. (1999). *Well-being: The foundations of hedonic psychology*. Russell Sage Foundation.

Kalam, A.P.J. Abdul with Arun Tiwari (2015). Transcendence: My spiritual experiences with Pramukh Swamiji. : Harper Element.

Lama, D. (1997). Tr. Jinpa, Thupten. *Healing anger: The power of patience from a Buddhist perspective*. : Snow Lions.

Lama, D., & Muyzenberg, V. D. (2008). *The leader's way: Business, Buddhism and happiness in an interconnected world*. Nicholas Brealey Publishing.

Leung, K., & Brew, F. P. (2009). A cultural analysis of harmony and conflict: Toward an integrative model of conflict styles. In R. S. Wyer, C. Y. Chiu, & Y. Y. Hong (Eds.), *Understanding culture: Theory, research and application* (pp. 411–428). Psychology Press.

Leymann, H. (1990). *The Mobbing Encyclopedia*. Retrieved from www.leymann.se

Loden, M., & Rosener, J. B. (1991). *Workforce America! Managing employee diversity as a vital resource*. Business One Irwin.

Longfellow, H. W. (1847). *The Ladder of St.. Augustine*. https://www.poetryfoundation.org/poems/44636/the-ladder-of-st-augustine.

Mandela, N. (1994). *Long walk to freedom: The autobiography of Nelson Mandela*. Little, Brown and Company.

Maslow, A. H. (1968). *Toward a psychology of being* (2nd ed.). Van Nostrand.

McGrath, J. E. (1984). *Groups: Interaction and performance*. Prentice-Hall.

McLeod, P. L., & Lobel, S. A. (1992). The effect of ethnic diversity on idea generation in small groups. *Academy of Management Annual Meeting Best Papers Proceedings*, pp. 227–231.

Merriam-Webster. (n.d.). Dictionary. In Merriam-Webster.com *dictionary*. Retrieved October 12, 2020, from. https://www.merriam-webster.com/dictionary/dictionary

Morrison, S. (1992). *The new leaders: Guidelines on leadership diversity in America*. Jossey-Bass.

O'Reilly, C., Caldwell, D., & Barnett, W. (1989). Work group demography, social integration, and turnover. *Administrative Science Quarterly, 34*(1), 21–37. https://doi.org/10.2307/2392984

Plutchik, R. (1987). Evolutionary bases of empathy. In N. Eisenberg & J. Strayer (Eds.), *Empathy and its development* (pp. 38–46). Cambridge Univ. Press.

Ricard, M. (2010). (Tr. Kohn, Sherab Chodzin). *The Art of Meditation*. London: Atlantic Books.

Rinpoche, K. K. (1992). *Dharma paths* (N. Burkhar & C. Radha, Trans.; L.M. Roth, Ed.). Ithaca, NY: Snow Lion Publishers.

Rogers, C. (1961). *On becoming a person: A Therapist's view of psychotherapy*. Constable.

Ryan, R. M., & Deci, E. L. (2001). On happiness and human potential: A review of research on hedonic and eudaimonic well-being. *Annual Review of Psychology, 52*, 141–166.

Ryff, C. D., & Singer, B. (2000). Interpersonal flourishing: A positive health agenda for the new millennium. *Personality and Social Psychology Review, 4*, 30–44.

Salovey, P., & Mayer, J. D. (1990). Emotional Intelligence. *Imagination, Cognition and Personality, 9*(3), 185–211. https://doi.org/10.2190/DUGG-P24E-52WK-6CDG

Schnitker, S. A. (2012). An examination of patience and well-being. *The Journal of Positive Psychology, 7*(4), 263–280. https://doi.org/10.1080/17439760.2012.697185
Schnitker, S. A., & Emmons, R. A. (2007). Patience as a virtue: Religious and psychological perspectives. *Research in the Social Scientific Study of Religion, 18*, 177–207.
Seashore, S. E. (1954). *Group cohesiveness in the industrial work group*. University of Michigan, Survey Research.
Seligman, M. E. P. (2002). *Authentic happiness: Using the new positive psychology to realize your potential for lasting fulfillment*. Free Press.
Senge, P. (1990). *The fifth discipline, the art and practice of the learning organization*. Doubleday.
Sheldon, K. M., & Elliot, A. (1999). Goal striving, need satisfaction and longitudinal well-being: The self-concordance model. *Journal of Personality and Social Psychology, 76*(3), 482–497.
Smith, A., & Stewart, A. J. (1983). Approaches to studying racism and sexism in Black women' lives. *Journal of Social Issues, 39*(3), 1–15.
Sonnenfeld, J., & Ward, A. (2017). Firing back: How great leaders rebound after career disasters: Managing big professional setback. In D. Goleman, J. A. Sonnenefeld, & S. Achor (Eds.), *Resilience (HBR Emotional Intelligence Series)* (pp. 69–108).
Strand, M. (1996). As quoted in Csikszenmihalyi, M. (1996). Creativity: Flow and the psychology of discovery and invention. : Harper & Row.
Tajfel, H., & Turner, J. C. (1986). The social identity theory of intergroup behavior. In S. Worchel & W. Austin (Eds.), *Psychology of intergroup relations* (pp. 7–24). Nelson-Hall.
Tepper, B. J. (2000). Consequences of abusive supervision. *Academy of Management Journal, 43*(2), 178–190.
Viereck, G. S. (1929). What Life Means to Einstein: An interview by George Sylvester Viereck. In *The Sunday Evening Post* (Oct 26, 1929).
Wallace, B. A., & Shapiro, S. L. (2006). Mental balance and well-being: Building bridges between Buddhist and Western psychology. *American Psychologist, 61*(7), 690–701.
Warr, P. (2007). *Work, happiness and unhappiness*. University of Sheffield.
Watts, A. (1975). *Tao: The watercourse way*. Pantheon Books.
Williams, K. Y., & O'Reilly, U. A. (1998). Demography and diversity in organizations: A review of 40 years of research. *Research in Organizational Behavior, 20*, 77–140.
Yukl, G. A. (1998). *Leadership in organizations*. Upper Saddle River, NJ: Prentice-Hall.

Chapter 7
"The Soft Overcomes the Hard": Inspirations for Leadership in the Twenty-First Century from Daoism

Alicia Hennig and Lena Schiller

Abstract Recent newspaper articles keep reminding us that women in developed countries are still exposed to discrimination and gender inequality at the workplace in a number of professional fields. Yet, global consultancies stress the "business case" for gender diversity and more specifically gender parity. Hence gender diversity through increased gender parity should be a strategic business imperative (Sanders et al., 2011). At the same time, a number of academic publications also underline the "business case" for more gender equality, for example, by highlighting women's leadership style being better aligned with what is perceived as "good leadership" today (Eagly, 2007; Weyer 2007; Esser et al., 2018). Yet, the broader question framing this chapter is what kind of leadership and management do we actually need with regard to work in the twenty-first century. And, more importantly, what kind of values should be guiding our leadership approach accordingly. This chapter proposes an alternative way of leadership based on values and principles derived from Chinese philosophy, in specific Daoism. These Daoist values and behavioral principles emphasize the feminine, yin 阴, over the masculine, yang 阳, which could open up a new way for a more inclusive leadership approach.

Keywords Barriers to leadership · Leadership styles · Chinese philosophy · Daoism · *Yin-yang* logic

---

A. Hennig (✉)
Southeast University, Nanjing, People's Republic of China
e-mail: alicia@newvirtues.com

L. Schiller
House of Leadership, Frankfurt am Main, Germany

J. Marques (ed.), *Innovative Leadership in Times of Compelling Changes*, Management, Change, Strategy and Positive Leadership, https://doi.org/10.1007/978-3-030-67258-4_7

Introduction

Recent newspaper articles for example in *The New York Times* and *The Guardian* keep reminding us that women in developed countries are exposed to discrimination and gender inequality at the workplace until today in a number of professional fields like science (Pickett, 2019), technology (Hicks, 2018), literature (Dempster, 2016), or surgery (Donato-Brown, 2019) among others. Yet, global consultancies stress gender diversity and more specifically gender parity, as these could positively affect financial performance (Chief Executive Women, 2019; McKinsey, 2017), innovation revenue (Lorenzo et al., 2018), and even value creation (Hunt et al., 2018). Accordingly, gender diversity through increased gender parity should be a strategic business imperative (Sanders et al., 2011). Moreover, increasing gender diversity and gender parity are also imperative for a functioning and further growing economy (Giesa & Schiller Clausen, 2014). However, in a study by Bain & Company (Sanders et al., 2011), only 55 percent of male employees vs. 76 percent of female employees believed in the "business case" for gender parity. Here, the so-called double bind (Eagly, 2007; Eagly & Carli, 2003; Esser et al., 2018) – conflicting expectations about women's characteristics and abilities in the workplace on the one hand, such as being caring, non-confrontational, and non-assertive and leadership requirements including assertiveness, aggressiveness, and directness on the other hand – is standing in the way of having more women in higher management, as often they are not perceived as being equally qualified for leadership. In addition, due to a "double standard" applied to women's performance, they are required to demonstrate extra confidence and ability compared to men in order to receive the same recognition (Eagly & Carli, 2003; Walker & Aritz, 2015). This phenomenon of women being stuck in the – often male-dominated – corporate hierarchy and not being able to reach leadership positions is called "glass ceiling," which "indicates a plateau for women at levels below top management" (Goodman et al., 2003, p. 476; Weyer, 2007; Carli & Eagly, 2016).

More recent studies by consultancies on women in the workplace declare a slow progress globally regarding gender parity especially at higher management levels across developed countries (McKinsey, 2017), with the USA apparently stalling (McKinsey, 2018). At the same time, a number of academic publications underline the "business case" for more gender equality, for example, by highlighting women's leadership style being better aligned with what is perceived as "good leadership" today (Eagly, 2007; Esser et al., 2018; Weyer, 2007), reducing turnover rates of women and thereby organizational brain drain (Goodman et al., 2003), improving organizational effectiveness by expanding the talent pool (Powell & Butterfield, 2015), and being perceived as a fair employer (ibid.), as well as the link between gender diversity, for example, on board and C-suite level, and financial performance (Eagly, 2007).

Yet, aside the question of how to enable more women to become leaders, the broader question framing this chapter is what kind of leadership and management do we actually need with regard to work in the twenty-first century and what kind of values should be guiding our leadership approach accordingly.

This chapter proposes an alternative way of leadership based on values and principles derived from Chinese philosophy, in specific Daoism. These Daoist values and behavioral principles emphasize the feminine, *yin* 阴, over the masculine, *yang* 阳, which could open up a new way for a more inclusive leadership approach. The theoretical contribution of this chapter is twofold. It adds to the broader field of feminist organizational theory and to the discussion of how to sustain the organization in the future, as Daoist values and principles could present a more balanced approach to organization and leadership more generally.

The remainder of this chapter is structured as follows: First, we will look into barriers to leadership faced by women, second, we will look at different leadership styles, and third, we will discuss the question of "ideal" leadership. In the fourth part, we will look into Chinese philosophy and Daoism including the concept of *yin-yang*. This provides the foundation for the introduction of a new leadership approach derived from Daoist values in the fifth and last part. This chapter closes with a conclusion and concrete insights formulated as "key takeaways."

Women's Multiple Barriers to Leadership

Diehl and Dzubinski (2016) conducted a more comprehensive macro-, meso-, and micro-level analysis of leadership barriers affecting women based on qualitative research. In total, they identified 27 barriers distributed across the societal (macro), organizational (meso), and individual (micro) level. On the *societal level*, six barriers were identified which range from women's voices being controlled; their choices being culturally constrained, over gender stereotypes and gender unconsciousness to specific leadership perceptions; and generally higher levels of scrutiny perceived compared to men (ibid.). On the *individual level*, another five barriers emerged such as constraints regarding communication style, conscious unconsciousness of gender (bias), assuming personal responsibility for organizational problems, a self-imposed psychological glass ceiling, and conflicts in balancing private and professional life (ibid.). On the *organizational level*, however, most of these barriers (16 of 27) are to be found. These include a general devaluation of women's more communal leadership style and lack of full recognition of their abilities due to a masculine organizational culture and norms (cf. Walker & Aritz, 2015); a systemic lack within the organization regarding mentoring, sponsorship, and support, that is, development, of women (cf. Gipson et al., 2017); the glass cliff phenomenon (selecting women predominantly for high-risk leadership roles with the likelihood to fail, cf. Glass & Cook, 2016; Gipson et al., 2017); procedural insufficiencies expressed in unequal remuneration and unequal performance standards (cf. Chamorro-Premuzic, 2019); exclusion practices such as no access to informal networks and male gatekeeping; and, worse, discrimination and even workplace harassment. Two more barriers according to Diehl and Dzubinski (2016) inhibiting the advancement of women in organizations are the "Queen Bee Effect" (cf. Faniko et al., 2017) and tokenism.

The comprehensive observation and analysis by Diehl and Dzubinski (2016) essentially captures previous discussions regarding barriers to leadership faced by women that are now systematically linked to the macro, meso, and micro level. This brings to the fore the full scope of barriers in an organizational context and additional reinforcing mechanisms from both macro and micro level.

Differences in Leadership Styles

In light of the barriers mentioned, the question is what actually characterizes the "female" way of leadership for which women are apparently not adequately recognized and appreciated. These are outlined in Table 7.1 and contrasted with characteristics of the "typical" male way of leadership.

Yet, we need to bear in mind that the discussion of gender and leadership is more complex. The information outlined in the table is based on publications drawing on empirical studies. These are reflections of characteristics observed in men and women, respectively, whereas "men" and "women" linguistically speaking are nouns representing biological categories (Eagly et al., 2004). However, next to our biological sex, which is predominantly perceived in dichotomous categories of either man/male or woman/female (Eagly et al., 2004), there is also gender. Gender according to Butler (2004, p. 1) "is a kind of a doing, an incessant activity performed," expressed in what we call "masculine" or "feminine." The latter two are not necessarily tied and in line with the corresponding biological sex but describe "the cultural part of what it is to be a man or a woman" and hence are "describing culturally variable characteristics" (Archer & Lloyd, 2002, p. 17; cf. Paechter, 2006). This is further supported by Butler (2004), claiming that attribution of "feminine" to females or women happens on a normative basis. Accordingly, being a woman does not necessarily entail "feminine" behavior or character traits. Similarly, designations like "masculine" and "masculinity" only capture those ways of behavior and character traits found in dominant male groups, which are also referred to as "hegemonic" in contrast to other, "subordinated" masculinities (Paechter, 2006). Hence, these labels of "feminine" and "masculine" only capture the sociocultural characteristics of the most dominant group within the respective biological sexes. Yet, with regard to empirical studies, it is difficult to determine with certainty to what extent the behavioral characteristics observed need to be attributed to biological sex or predominantly to gender (Xu, 2003), that is, the question whether these characteristics are "female" or "feminine."

That women do not necessarily behave in gender stereotypical ways is also apparent in organizations. For example, women in leading positions are not bound to follow a leadership approach based on characteristics typically observed in other women and thus attributed to gender. Women could also take up a less communal and more masculine style (Appelbaum & Shapiro, 1993) or behave like a "Queen

Table 7.1 Behavioral characteristics observed in men and women in leadership positions

Behavioral characteristics observed in men being in leadership positions	Reference	Behavioral characteristics observed in women being in leadership positions	Reference
Self-regarding/advancing their own career, less focus on others/ individualistic/ independent/self-interested/self-promoting	Alimo-Metcalfe, 2010; Appelbaum & Shapiro, 1993; Chamorro-Premuzic, 2019; Esser et al., 2018; Lipman-Blumen, 1992; Post, 2015	Other-regarding/fair and objective	Chamorro-Premuzic, 2019; Esser et al., 2018; Post, 2015
Unemotional/rational/ analytical	Sharma, 1990	More empathy (emotional and social competence)	Chamorro-Premuzic, 2019; Esser et al., 2018; Post, 2015
Accumulation of personal power	Eagly & Carli, 2003; Esser et al., 2018; Lipman-Blumen, 1992	Better empower and mentor subordinates	Chamorro-Premuzic, 2019; Eagly & Carli, 2003; Eagly, 2007; Lipman-Blumen, 1992
Competitive, aggressive, determined, taking risks	Alimo-Metcalfe, 2010; Appelbaum & Shapiro, 1993; Esser et al., 2018; Lipman-Blumen, 1992	More relational, building/maintaining relations	Alimo-Metcalfe, 2010; Esser et al., 2018; Post, 2015
Assertion of authority (also by way of a dominant/bold/loud communication style)	Alimo-Metcalfe, 2010; Chamorro-Premuzic, 2019; Eagly & Carli, 2003; Esser et al., 2018;	More collaborative/ teamwork	Lipman-Blumen, 1992; Post, 2015
Command-and-control	Alimo-Metcalfe, 2010; Eagly & Carli, 2003; Esser et al., 2018; Lipman-Blumen, 1992	More participative, cooperative	Alimo-Metcalfe, 2010; Esser et al., 2018; Post, 2015
Avoiding to solve problems until they become acute	Eagly, 2007	More creative and flexible problem-solving	Chamorro-Premuzic, 2019; Esser et al., 2018
Absent/uninvolved in critical times	Eagly, 2007	Able to drive positive change in teams	Chamorro-Premuzic, 2019; Alimo-Metcalfe, 2010
		Higher level of self-control	Chamorro-Premuzic, 2019
		Persistence/endurance	Esser et al., 2018

(continued)

Table 7.1 (continued)

Behavioral characteristics observed in men being in leadership positions	Reference	Behavioral characteristics observed in women being in leadership positions	Reference
Leadership style only weakly related to effectiveness, sometimes even hindering effectiveness	Eagly, 2007	Leadership style linked to effectiveness	Eagly, 2007; Post, 2015
Transactional leader	Alimo-Metcalfe, 2010; Appelbaum & Shapiro, 1993	Transformational leader	Alimo-Metcalfe, 2010; Chamorro-Premuzic, 2019

Bee," that is, women denying gender discrimination, having a nonsupportive attitude toward other women (Diehl & Dzubinski, 2016; Faniko et al., 2017). Moreover, Adams (2015) reminds us "gender differences are not always the same as the population gender differences" (p. 11). Accordingly, studies on women in leadership and board positions may not adequately reflect characteristics in the female population as such.

Apparently, since "femininity" and "feminine" are sociocultural constructs, also 'feminine leadership" must be seen as a construct. As Due Billing and Alvesson (2000) argue, "the idea of feminine leadership should be seen as a regulative ideal, a normative construct, rather than an empirical phenomenon" (p. 149). However, this gives us the opportunity to view "feminine leadership" as an alternative to the dominant, "masculine" way of leadership, as it is actually not limited to women only. Thus, it could equally serve as an alternative way of leading for men not identifying with the dominant paradigm of their own gender.

Is There an "Ideal" Way of Leadership?

Generally, it needs to be stressed that the "ideal" way of leadership must be defined in relation to context (Post, 2015), that is, whether it needs to be more "masculine" or "feminine." There is no 'ideal' way of leadership in the sense of one "best practice" (Appelbaum & Shapiro, 1993). Leaders, whether women or men, need to have a diverse competency profile incorporating both 'masculine' and 'feminine' competencies. In this regard, Lippa (2001) stresses "extreme femininity in females or extreme masculinity in males is not necessarily desirable" (p. 178). Hence, in the organization of the future, both men and women need to learn to become more versatile with regard to their respective behavioral style, drawing from a broad set of characteristics and thereby leaving behind gender stereotypes.

There have been already attempts to making leadership styles more mixed or diverse. For example, Appelbaum and Shapiro (1993) highlight the right mixture of qualities, comprising good listening abilities with regard to both hard facts and emotional undertones, being able to lead discussions, mastering the stretch between being authoritarian and democratic, as well as between expressing and controlling emotions, among others. Gartzia and Baniandrés (2019) underline the combination of agentic ("masculine") and communal ("feminine") qualities. There has been also a clear link established between women's qualities and transformational leadership (Alimo-Metcalfe, 2010; Eagly & Carli, 2003), which is perceived as a new way of leadership for a more complex world (Rosener, 2011). Yet, there are concrete approaches especially highlighting female characteristics, such as "connective leadership" (Lipman-Blumen, 1992) or "relational leadership" (Uhl-Bien, 2011; cf. Enderstein, 2018). However, to our knowledge there has not been any attempt to approach gender and leadership from a non-Western perspective, that is, Chinese philosophy, advocating this approach as an alternative to the currently prevailing "masculine" style or other mixed styles. For a better understanding of a non-Western alternative, we will now turn to Chinese philosophy and relevant concepts therein.

Chinese Philosophy, Daoism, and *Yin-Yang* Logic

Next to Confucianism, Daoism is another prominent and influential philosophical school in Chinese philosophy (Hansen, 2007). It came into existence at roughly the same time as Confucianism with its most prominent work, the *Dao De Jing* 道德经 dating back to the fourth century BCE (Kohn, 2009). At its core, Daoism is concerned with harmony between heaven, earth, and the human being, which is achieved by following *dao* 道. *Dao* is primarily interpreted as the way (Cheung & Chan, 2005), the "natural way of things," which inspired the underlying concepts of the Daoist philosophy (Miller, 2006). Generally, whatever we find in Chinese philosophy is ultimately a reflection of what can be observed in reality and with specific regard to Daoism: in nature. The three most prevalent "concepts" in Daoism are dualism, the logic of reversion, and the idea of cycles. All these are to be found in nature and represented by the *yin-yang* 阴阳 symbol. Although *yin-yang* is an epistemology shared by "all philosophies in China" (Li, 2014, p. 31), Daoism most heavily draws on that and made *yin-yang* its "core logic."

Yin-yang are alternating, complementary categories and in large present a "complex network of classifications" (Moeller, 2004, p. 106), structuring the Chinese perception of reality. They are symbolic and generic, only pointing to a contrast between and in relation of two appearances (Yang, 2006). Together, they form an integrated and dynamic whole.

Originally, these categories were derived from natural observations, as *yin* represents the dark (originally recurring to the shady side of a hill), carrying the symbol of the moon, and *yang* means bright (originally recurring to the sunny side of a hill), carrying the symbol of the sun (Ames, 2003). Accordingly, the two categories establish a cyclical or alternating dualism, as bright/day and dark/night are changing phases. This leads to the "logic of reversion" or "conquest cycle" (LaFargue, 1992):

whatever is *yin* can turn into *yang* and vice versa, same as day is turning into night and night into day. The *yin-yang* pair first appeared in the *Yijing*, the *Book of Changes* (one of the earliest books in Chinese history dating back to ninth century BCE), in the context of change (Rutt, 2002). In a major Daoist work, the *Dao De Jing* (*DDJ*), however, this logic of alternating contrasts is applied to human beings (Cheng, 2003). It emphasizes the mutual complementarity of *yin-yang* but articulates a clear preference for the female and the feminine (Xu, 2003; cf. Chap. 28, Waley, 1958). This preference indicates a reversion movement, a "return" from high (strong/masculine) to low (weak/feminine) (Ma, 2009).

This chapter draws on the *yin-yang* logic inherent in Daoism to develop a leadership style based on non-Western, alternative values and principles. The *DDJ* as a starting point is most suitable in this context for two reasons. First, Chinese philosophy by that time was predominantly political philosophy with the objective to convince the ruler of a certain way of government (Bell, 2011). Accordingly, its ideas and concepts are based in a context of leadership and guiding values. Second, it draws on "traditional feminine images such as the female, mother, valley, and water to symbolize the Dao and advocating humility, yieldingness, and receptivity feminine characteristics attributed to women by the patriarchal culture" (Xu, 2003, p. 49). Yet, precisely by drawing on these images and "recommending feminine ways to the male sage as the way to govern the empire, however, the *DDJ* both implicitly and explicitly breaks down traditional norms and conceptions of Man and Woman" (ibid., p. 50). However, we need to bear in mind that the *DDJ* is not advocating a "feminist" perspective; rather, the ideal promulgated therein coincides with what Chinese traditional culture considers being "feminine" (ibid.).

A significant change in leadership style seems to be advised especially in light of an expected increased use of artificial intelligence in the workplace, which will create new demands with regard to qualities and personality of the leader, as well as her leadership style. Thus, breaking down traditional norms appears to be vital in developing a viable alternative leadership style utilizable by both women and men, as gender stereotypes and dichotomies are not conducive for either men or women (Diehl & Dzubinski, 2016; Gartzia & Baniandrés, 2019; Xu, 2003).

Moreover, breaking down traditional gender-based norms is also ethically important, as it focuses on what is "truly human" (Xu, 2003, p. 63), our very essence as human beings, rather than increasing the chasm between men and women. Focusing on our human qualities and what makes as human is especially relevant in the context of rising automation and artificial intelligence, as this is indispensable to differentiate ourselves from machines in the future (cf. Chamorro-Premuzic, 2019).

Daoism and Leadership

In this section, we will take up concrete references from the *DDJ* to explain the "feminine," which is for example expressed in values like softness and weakness that are both related to characteristics the *DDJ* also attributes to water.

The Dao De Jing *and the Feminine (Female)*

In the *DDJ*, *yin* and *yang* are only used once explicitly in Chap. 42 (p. 195, Waley, 1958) in the more literal meaning of bright and dark. Yet, the *DDJ* makes use of another term indicating the "female": *pin* 牝. This term is used in Chap. 6 (the "valley spirit" as the "mysterious female" from which "Heaven and Earth sprang," p. 149, Waley, 1958), in Chap. 55 ("the union of male and female," p.209, Waley, 1958), and Chap. 61 ("the female by quiescence conquers the male," p. 217, Waley, 1958). Accordingly, the female "dark" valley spirit plays an important role as from it Heaven and Earth emerge; the female and male belong together as constituting *yin* and *yang*, respectively, but the female is considered the more powerful.

Softness and Weakness

The following three chapters are illustrating the Daoist logic of reversion (also called "conquest cycle" by LaFargue, 1992, p. 13), namely, that the soft/female eventually overcomes the hard/male, which is exemplified by quotes from Chap. 36 (p. 187) and 43 (p. 197), respectively (Waley, 1958): *It is thus that the soft overcomes the hard, And the weak, the strong. What is of all things most yielding can overwhelm that which is of all things most hard.*

Also, that the soft and weak is preferred over the hard and supposedly strong is illustrated in Chap. 76 (p. 236, Waley, 1958):

> *When he is born, man is soft and weak; in death he becomes stiff and hard. The ten thousand creatures and all plants and trees while they are alive are supple and soft, but when they are dead they become brittle and dry. Truly, what is stiff and hard is a 'companion of death'; what is soft and weak is a 'companion of life'. Therefore 'the weapon that is too hard will be broken, the tree that has the hardest wood will be cut down'. Truly, the hard and mighty are cast down; the soft and weak set on high.*

According to the specific logic inherent in Daoism, softness and weakness represent flexibility and vitality and therefore are seen as long-lasting. This is represented by the female as in *yin* or *pin*. On the other hand, the male *yang* is associated with strength and hardness (Fang, 2011). Yet, in the context of *yin-yang* logic as applied in the *DDJ*, the male *yang* is construed as the negative, the status to be avoided in the long term, as hardness is linked with becoming dry, brittle and firm, losing its flexibility and hence vitality and longevity (cf. Chap. 30, 76, Waley, 1958).

The Water Metaphor

Water is mentioned in a number of chapters; thus it presents an indispensable element of Daoist thought (Moeller, 2004; Chan, 1969; Waley, 1958) and is generally an important element in Chinese history and philosophy (Allan, 1997; Ball, 2016).

The values of softness and weakness are so-called "wateristic" characteristics (Lee et al., 2008). According to Waley (1958) water takes the "low ground," following the logic of "To be perfect is to invite diminution; to climb is to invite a fall" (p. 56), in line with the *yin-yang* logic of reversion. Thereby, water serves as a metaphor to illustrate exemplary behavior throughout the *DDJ*. Water generally has a "beneficiary role" and has three important qualities according to Ma (2012). First, it always lies in the lower position, but since being soft and flexible, it can move to all directions. Hence, it can nourish and embrace everything: "The highest good is like that of water. The goodness of water is that it benefits the ten thousand creatures; yet itself does not scramble, but is content with the places that all men disdain. It is this that makes water so near to the Way" (cf. Chap. 8, p. 151, Waley, 1958). Second, since being in the lower position it does not "compete" (cf. Chapters 8 and 61, Waley, 1958). And lastly, because it is associated with soft, flexible, low, weak, and powerless, it eventually conquers the strong and powerful due to the *yin-yang* logic of reversion: "Nothing under heaven is softer or more yielding than water; but when it attacks things hard and resistant there is not one of them that can prevail" (cf. Chap. 78, p. 236, Waley, 1958). Here, the water metaphor serves to illustrate and underline the actual strength of softness and weakness.

From the water metaphor and the "wateristic" characteristics softness and weakness, some more guidance can be derived with regard to exemplary behavior. From a complete analysis of the *DDJ* from the perspective of virtue ethics, Hennig (2017) derives virtues such as humbleness, modesty, kindness, supportiveness, and generosity among others. Furthermore, LaFargue (1992) identified a number of themes related to water in his own translation of the *DDJ* such as a particular excellence consisting in avoiding boasting (cf. Chaps. 1, 2 and 3), excess (cf. Chaps. 4 and 21), desire (cf. Chap. 20), and competition (cf. Chap. 4) while at the same time cultivating a good character by nurturing qualities such as being selfless (cf. Chap. 10), calm (cf. Chap. 23), unpretentious (cf. Chap. 40), and intuitive (cf. Chap. 41) and especially "femininity" (cf. Chap. 17). This "feminine way" is also linked to keeping a "low profile," that is, not appearing impressive but leading with subtle influence and power (cf. Chaps. 54, 56, and 57).

Constructing a Leadership Style Inspired by Daoism

Apparently, the female *yin* values are more positively connoted in Daoism than the supposedly stronger male *yang* values. From the sections above, a more comprehensive picture of Daoist values as presented in the *DDJ* emerges.

For the sake of a modern interpretation in a contemporary context, the values derived from the Daoist female characteristics are separated into more strategic values such as flexibility, adaptability, and avoiding competition and ethical values such as humbleness (including modesty); selflessness, which is also linked to kindness (including supportiveness); moderation (including avoiding excess and desires); and authenticity through being unpretentious and intuitive over superficially knowledgeable. Originally these all served the purpose of longevity and long-term vitality. Taken together these values nowadays are constitutive for an alternative leadership style, a so-called soft style'.

Here, two examples shall be given to illustrate how the two value sets inherent in the "soft style" approach to leadership could play out in business. Rising implementation of automation and artificial intelligence (AI) will significantly impact the entire organization in terms of hierarchical structures and the organization of work as such. In addition, technological change more broadly also impacts the human being and her demands and needs. Thus, transformation of the organization will not be only driven merely by technological change but also by human beings and her needs and demands affected by technological change, leading to new ideas regarding the organization of work in the future (Giesa & Schiller Clausen, 2014). Under these conditions, a "soft style" approach to leadership could be leading the way.

First, if hierarchies are breaking away and the boundaries of roles are becoming more fluent – such as in Drucker's management outlook and vision of work in the twenty-first century (Drucker & Wartzmann, 2010) – adopting a leadership style based on strategic values like flexibility and adaptability and ethical values like humbleness, kindness, and moderation is vital to equally "fulfill" the role of the employee as well as that of the leader. Here, especially the water-like ethical values promote an atmosphere of cooperation as opposed to competition, superiority, and thus latent aggressiveness. Moreover, as stressed by Chamorro-Premuzic (2019), competent people engage in more self-criticism and self-doubt, which is reflected by Daoist humbleness and modesty. Hence, in the context of good leadership he advocates "humble leadership" (pp. 70) as the opposite of charisma, which he links to overconfidence, as in his opinion charisma diverts from actual competence.

In this context it is also important to understand the difference between leadership and management as highlighted by Esser et al. (2018). While leaders are supposed to be visionary, inspiring, and motivating, thereby driving creativity, innovation, and change, managers on the other hand have more administrative tasks such as taking responsibility for reliable and efficient operations. This understanding of the function(s) of management is linked with a more scientific, Tayloristic approach to business, which in the twenty-first century seems to be less and less appropriate (Niedenführ & Hennig, 2020). Thus, in light of a necessary departure from scientific management, the role of leaders in organizations becomes more important. Leaders are supposed to focus on people and promoting their potential, whereas managers focus on structures and systems (Esser et al., 2018; Giesa & Schiller Clausen, 2014). Yet, the "soft style" is breaking with the typical leader-follower relation, as it is based on "leading from behind," that is, being supportive but always in the background (Hennig, 2017; cf. Chap. 66, Waley, 1958).

Second, adopting the *yin-yang* logic can lead to new ways of self-development and self-management altogether. Together with the more strategic water-like characteristics of flexibility and adaptability derived from Daoist softness, it can also improve our resilience for example. By relieving us from thinking in typical Western binary and exclusive categories of either/or, it allows us to become more flexible, being able to better tolerate paradox and contradictions, as eventually these are all part of a larger whole (cf. Li, 2014; Moore, 1967; Peng et al., 2015). Accordingly, this flexibility also increases our ability to better manage uncertain, contradictory, or even chaotic situations. With regard to resilience the *yin-yang* logic of reversion helps us to avoid hasty judgments of good or bad, as according to this logic, something that looks negative at first glance may ultimately turn into something rather positive (cf. Jullien, 2004; Wong, 2014). Thus, it can help us to better endure seemingly negative situations.

In conclusion, these values and behavioral characteristics derived from the *DDJ* could promote specific characteristics or attitudes, which enable a supportive, cooperative, nonaggressive leadership style (see Gerstner, 2011; Lin et al., 2013). This style apparently is also very much in line with what other researchers have stated with regard to the "female" way of leadership as observed empirically (Alimo-Metcalfe, 2010; Chamorro-Premuzic, 2019; Eagly, 2007; Eagly & Carli, 2003; Esser et al., 2018; Lipman-Blumen, 1992; Post, 2015); see Fig. 7.1 (below).

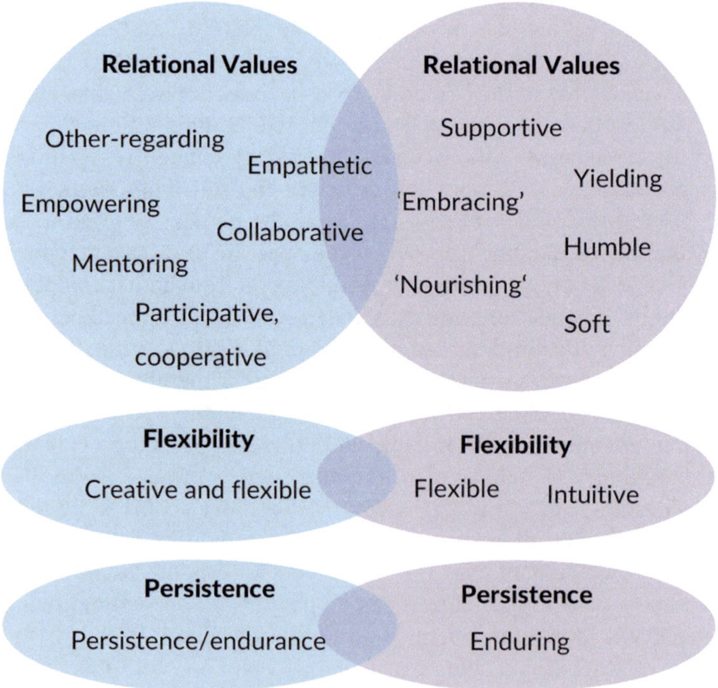

Fig 7.1 (developed by the author), Behavioral characteristics observed in women being in leadership positions (left) and their overlap with Daoist values (right)

In light of a high number of disengagement of employees globally (about 70 percent), which can be also attributed to bad leadership (Chamorro-Premuzic, 2019), it is about time to develop and implement a leadership style that is both timely and beyond gender (stereotypes) to sustain the organization in light of future challenges such as automation and AI.

Key Takeaways

This chapter concludes with five key takeaways from the discussion of more diverse approaches to leadership.

First, it has been sufficiently confirmed that emulating masculine behavior is not necessarily beneficial for women either. Thus, in order to innovate leadership, the organizational culture needs to be revised (Diehl & Dzubinski, 2016), and less gendered ways of leadership need to be introduced and implemented.

Second, aspects of the Daoist "soft style" approach based on *yin-yang* are reflected in empirical observations, as well as in Western "feminine" approaches to leadership such as "connective leadership" or "relational leadership." This indicates a strong connection to already present ideas and feasibility regarding the potential implementation of a "soft style" leadership approach due to a shared common basis.

Third, in contrast to other Western approaches that advocate a "feminine" and a "mixed style" approach in leadership, the Daoist approach, however, overcomes the feminine-masculine dichotomy still present in Western conceptions of leadership.

Fourth, the Daoist "soft style" approach transcends gender dichotomy by dissolving the two gender categories through making formerly gendered values available to everyone (Xu, 2003; Ma, 2009), that is, by turning the female physical weakness and softness upside down and promulgating these as values to be adopted by men for successful leadership. Moreover, in Daoism the "feminine" is not construed in relation to the "masculine" (Ma, 2009; cf. Paechter, 2006, who claims "femininity" is construed as merely being the other of masculinity).

Fifth, this transcendence of gender dichotomy may make this particular leadership style also more accessible to men who do not subscribe to hegemonic masculine values of competition and aggressiveness but rather seek a cooperative style that is rather gender-neutral. In this regard, it is important to bear in mind that gender is actually not only a women's issue, as in fact it impacts men, women, and organizations.

As the organization of the future will be exposed to significant changes induced through automation and AI, the change in work as such being more centered on knowledge (Drucker & Wartzmann, 2010) but also by a generation of employees having different needs and demands, we will need new ways of management and organization to sustain the organization in the future. For example, we will need to reduce hierarchical silo structures and create more agile and flexible ways of organization (ibid.; cf. Sanders et al., 2015) and a different set of values in line with these new developments, emphasizing our human essence and emotions (cf. Chamorro-Premuzic, 2019). In this context, also a different leadership style will be essential for a successful transformation of the organization.

Reflection Questions

1. To what extent do you yourself identify with the gender-related behavioral characteristics provided in Table 7.1?
2. Based on the literature about female leadership introduced here, what characterizes female leadership?
3. Based on women's barriers to leadership discussed in part one of this chapter, what barriers can you identify in your professional environment?
4. What could be problematic about work environments that are significantly dominated by a single gender?
5. Would you consider the *yin-yang* approach to leadership introduced here as an option worth to be implemented? What could be upsides and downsides in practice?

References

Adams, R. B. (2015). Women on boards: The superheroes of tomorrow? *The Leadership Quarterly, 27*(3), 371–386.

Alimo-Metcalfe, B. (2010). An investigation of female and male constructs of leadership and empowerment. *Gender in Management: An International Journal, 25*(8), 640–648.

Allan, S. (1997). *Way of water and sprouts of virtue*. New York, NY: State University of New York (SUNY) Press.

Ames, R. T. (2003). *Yin* and *Yang*. In A. S. Cua (Ed.), *Encyclopedia, of Chinese philosophy* (pp. 846–847). Routledge.

Appelbaum, S. H., & Shapiro, B. T. (1993). Why can't men Lead like women? *Leadership & Organization Development Journal, 14*(7), 28–34.

Archer, J., & Lloyd, B. B. (2002). *Sex and gender* (2nd ed.). Cambridge University Press.

Ball, P. (2016). *The water kingdom: A secret history of China*. London: Penguin Random House.

Bell, D. A. (2011). Introduction. In X. Yan (Auth.), A. D. Bell, & S. Zhe (Eds.), E. Ryden (Transl.), *Ancient Chinese thought, modern Chinese power* (pp. 1–20). : Princeton University Press.

Butler, J. (2004). *Undoing gender*. Routledge.

Carli , L. L., & Eagly, A. (2016),Women face a labyrinth: an examination of metaphors for women leaders. *Gender in Management: An International Journal, 31*(8), 514–527.

Chan, W.-T. (1969). *A source book in Chinese philosophy*. Princeton, NJ: Princeton University Press.

Chamorro-Premuzic, T. (2019). *Why do so many incompetent men become leaders?* Harvard Business Review Press.

Cheng, C.-Y. (2003). *Dao* (*Tao*): The way. In A. S. Cua (Ed.), *Encyclopedia of Chinese philosophy* (pp. 202–206). New York/London, UK: Routledge.

Cheung, C., & Chan, A. (2005). Philosophical foundations of eminent Hong Kong Chinese CEOs' leadership. *Journal of Business Ethics, 60*, 47–62.

Chief Executive Women. (2019). Better together: Increasing male engagement in gender equality efforts in Australia. *Bain and Company*. Retrieved from https://cew.org.au/topics/ better-together/. Accessed 1 July 2020.

Dempster, L. (2016). If you doubted there was gender bias in literature, this study proves you wrong. *The Guardian*. Retrieved from https://www.theguardian.com/books/2016/jun/10/if-you-doubted-there-was-gender-bias-in-literature-this-study-proves-you-wrong. Accessed 1 July 2020.

Diehl, A. B., & Dzubinski, L. M. (2016). Making the invisible visible: A cross-sector analysis of gender-based leadership barriers. *Human Resource Development Quarterly, 27*(2), 181–206.

Donato-Brown, D. (2019). The sexism in surgery is shocking 1 from 'banter' to discrimination. *The Guardian*. Retrieved from https://www.theguardian.com/commentisfree/2019/jan/08/sexism-surgery-shocking-colleagues-patients-diversity. Accessed 1 July 2020.

Drucker, P. F., & Wartzmann, R. (Eds.). (2010). *The Drucker lectures: Essential lessons on management, society and economy*. McGraw-Hill.

Due Billing, Y., & Alvesson, M. (2000). Questioning the notion of feminine leadership: A critical perspective on the gender labelling of leadership. *Gender, Work and Organization, 7*(3), 144–157.

Eagly, A. (2007). Female leadership advantage and disadvantage: Resolving the contradictions. *Psychology of Women Quarterly, 31*, 1–12.

Eagly, A., & Carli, L. L. (2003). The female leadership advantage: An evaluation of the evidence. *The Leadership Quarterly, 14*, 807–834.

Eagly, A. H., Beall, A. E., & Sternberg, R. J. (2004). Introduction. In A. H. Eagly, A. E. Beall, & R. J. Sternberg (Eds.), *The psychology of gender* (2nd ed., pp. 1–8). The Guilford Press.

Enderstein, A.-M. (2018). (Not) just a girl: Reworking femininity through women's leadership in Europe. *European Journal of Women's Studies, 25*(3), 325–340.

Esser, A., Kahrens, M., Mouzughi, Y., & Eomois, E. (2018). A female leadership competency framework from the perspective of male leaders. *Gender in Management: An International Journal, 33*(2), 138–166.

Fang, T. (2011). Yin Yang: A new perspective on culture. *Management and Organization Review, 8*(1), 25–50.

Faniko, K., Ellemers, N., Derks, B., & Lorenzi-Cioldi, F. (2017). Nothing changes, really: Why women who break through the glass ceiling end up reinforcing it. *Personality and Social Psychology Bulletin, 43*(5), 638–665.

Gartzia, L., & Baniandrés, J. (2019). How feminine is the female advantage? Incremental validity of gender traits T over leader sex on employees' responses. *Journal of Business Research, 9*, 125–139.

Gerstner, A. (2011). Leadership and organizational patterns in the Daodejing. *Journal of Management Development, 30(7/8)*, 675–684.

Giesa, C., & Schiller Clausen, L. (2014). *New Business Order: Wie Start-ups Wirtschaft und Gesellschaft verändern*. Carl Hanser Verlag.

Gipson, A. N., Pfaff, D. L., Mendelsohn, D. B., Catenacci, L. T., & Burke, W. W. (2017). Women and leadership: Selection, development, leadership style, and performance. *The Journal of Applied Behavioral Science, 53*(1), 32–65.

Glass, C., & Cook, A. (2016). Leading at the top: Understanding women's challenges above the glass ceiling. *The Leadership Quarterly, 27*(1), 51–63.

Goodman, J. S., Fields, T. L., & Bloom, T. C. (2003). Cracks in the glass ceiling: In what kinds of organizations do women make it to the top? *Group & Organization Management, 28*(4), 475–501.

Hansen, C. (2007). Daoism. *Stanford encyclopedia of philosophy*. Retrieved from http://plato.stanford.edu/entries/daoism/. Accessed 1 July 2020.

Hennig, A. (2017). Applying Laozi's Dao De Jing in business. *Philosophy of Management, 16*, 19–33.

Hicks, M. (2018). Why tech's gender problem is nothing new. *The Guardian*. Retrieved from https://www.theguardian.com/technology/2018/oct/11/tech-gender-problem-amazon-facebook-bias-women. Accessed 1 July 2020.

Hunt, V., Prince, S., Dixon-Fyle, S., & Yee, L. (2018). Delivering through diversity. *McKinsey & Company*. Retrieved from https://www.mckinsey.com/~/media/mckinsey/business%20functions/organization/our%20insights/delivering%20through%20diversity/delivering-through-diversity_full-report.ashx. Accessed 15 June 2019.

Jullien, F. (2004). *A treatise on efficacy: Between Western and Chinese thinking*. University of Hawai'i Press.

Kohn, L. (2009). *Introducing Daoism*. Routledge.

LaFargue, M. (1992). *The Tao of the Tao Te Ching*. New York: State University of New York (SUNY) Press.

Lee, Y.-T., Han, A.-G., Byron, T. K., & Fan, H.-X. (2008). Daoist leadership: Theory and application. In C.-C. Chen & Y. T. Lee (Eds.), *Leadership and management in China: Philosophies, theories and practices* (pp. 8–107). Cambridge University Press.

Li, P. P. (2014). Toward the geocentric framework of intuition: The Yin-Yang balancing between the eastern and Western perspectives on intuition. In M. Sinclair (Ed.), *Handbook of research methods on intuition* (pp. 28–41). Edgar Elgar.

Lin, L.-H., & Ho, Y.-L., & Lin, W.-H.E. (2013). Confucian and Taoist work values: an exploratory study of the Chinese transformational leadership behavior. *Journal of Business Ethics, 113*, 91–103.

Lipman-Blumen, J. (1992). Connective leadership: Female leadership styles in the 21st-century workplace. *Sociological Perspectives, 35*(1), 183–203.

Lippa, R. A. (2001). On deconstructing and reconstructing masculinity–femininity. *Journal of Research in Personality, 35*, 168–207.

Lorenzo, R., Voigt, N., Tsusaka, M., Krentz, M., & Abouzahr, K. (2018). How diverse leadership teams boost innovation. *Boston Consulting Group*. Retrieved from https://www.bcg.com/de-de/publications/2018/how-diverse-leadership-teams-boost-innovation.aspx. Accessed 15 June 2019.

Ma, L. (2009). Character of the feminine in Lévinas and the *Daodejing* «道德经». *Journal of Chinese Philosophy, 36*(2), 261–276.

Ma, L. (2012). Lévinas and the *Daodejing* on the feminine: Intercultural reflections. *Journal of Chinese Philosophy, 39*(supplement), 152–170.

McKinsey & Company. (2017). Women Matter: Time to accelerate. Retrieved from https://www.mckinsey.com/featured-insights/gender-equality/women-matter-ten-years-of-insights-on-gender-diversity/de-de. Accessed 15 June 2019.

McKinsey & Company. (2018). Women in the Workplace. Retrieved from https://www.mckinsey.com/featured-insights/gender-equality/women-in-the-workplace-2018. Accessed 15 June 2019.

Miller, J. (2006). Daoism and nature. In R. Gottlieb (Ed.), *Handbook of religion and ecology* (pp. 220–235). Oxford University Press.

Moeller, H. G. (2004). *Daoism explained: From the dream of the butterfly to the fishnet allegory*. Open Court Publishing.

Moore, C. A. (1967). Introduction: The humanistic Chinese mind. In C. A. Moore (Ed.), *The Chinese mind: Essentials of Chinese philosophy and culture* (pp. 1–10). University of Hawaii.

Niedenführ, M., & Hennig, A. (2020). Confucianism and ethics in management. In C. Neesham & S. Segal (Eds.), *Handbook of philosophy of management* (pp. 1–13). Springer.

Paechter, C. (2006). Masculine femininities/feminine masculinities: Power, identities and gender. *Gender and Education, 18*(3), 253–263.

Peng, M. W., Li, Y., & Tian, L. (2015). Tian-ren-he-yi strategy: An Eastern perspective. *Asia Pacific Journal of Management, 33*, 695–722.

Pickett, M. (2019). I want what my male colleague has, and that will cost a few million dollars'. *The New York Times*. Retrieved from https://www.nytimes.com/2019/04/18/magazine/ salk-institute-discrimination-science.html. Accessed 15 June 2019.

Post, C. (2015). When is female leadership an advantage? Coordination requirements, team cohesion, and team interaction norms. *Journal of Organizational Behavior, 36*, 1153–1175.

Powell, G. N., & Butterfield, A. D. (2015). The glass ceiling: What have we learned 20 years on? *Journal of Organizational Effectiveness: People and Performance, 2*(4), 306–326.

Rosener, J. (2011). Ways women lead. In P. H. Werhane & M. Painter-Moorland (Eds.), *Leadership, gender and organization* (pp. 19–29). Springer.

Rutt, R. (2002). *The book of changes (Zhouyi)*. Routledge.

Sanders, M., Hrdlicka, J., Hellicar, M., Cottrell, D., & Knox, J. (2011). What stops women from reaching the top? Confronting the tough issues. *Bain and Company*. Retrieved from https://www.bain.com/insights/what-stops-women-from-reaching-the-top/. Accessed 15 June 2019.

Sanders, M., Zeng, J., Hellicar, M., & Fagg, K. (2015). The power of flexibility: A key enabler to boost gender parity and employee engagement. *Bain and Company*. Retrieved from https://www.bain.com/insights/the-power-of-flexibility/. Accessed 15 June 2019.

Sharma, S. (1990). Psychology of women in management: A distinct feminine leadership. *Equal Opportunities International, 9*(2), 13–18.

Uhl-Bien, M. (2011). Relational leadership and gender: From hierarchy to relationality. In P. H. Werhane & M. Painter-Moorland (Eds.), *Leadership, gender and organization* (pp. 65–74). Springer.

Waley, A. (Ed.). (1958). *The way and its power: A study of the Tao Te Ching and its place in Chinese thought*. Grove Press.

Walker, R. C., & Aritz, J. (2015). Women doing leadership: Leadership styles and organizational culture. *International Journal of Business Communication, 52*(4), 452–478.

Weyer, B. (2007). Twenty years later: Explaining the persistence of the glass ceiling for women leaders. *Women in Management Review, 22*(6), 482–496.

Wong, D. (2014). Comparative philosophy: Chinese and Western. *The Stanford Encyclopedia of Philosophy*. Retrieved from https://plato.stanford.edu/ archives/spr2017/entries/comparphil-chiwes/. Accessed 19 February 2018.

Xu, J. C. (2003). Poststructuralist feminism and the problem of femininity in the "Daodejing". *Journal of Feminist Studies in Religion, 19*(1), 47–64.

Yang, C. F. (2006). The Chinese conception of the self: Towards a person-making perspective. In U. Kim, K. S. Yang, & K. K. Hwang (Eds.), *Indigenous and cultural psychology: Understanding people in context* (pp. 327–356). Springer.

Chapter 8
Nurturing Empathy

Svetlana Holt

Abstract When enterprises are in tune with the needs of the world around them, they provide solutions which meet the desires of many, resulting in robust performance. The most ethically grounded decisions are made within a balance between logic and emotion. How organizations create challenges and learning opportunities to motivate the younger generations is of utmost importance as these cohorts place significant priority on developing initiatives that directly assist in alleviating social and economic problems. In the increasingly immediate, intimate world driven by rapid change, where everyone has to be proficient at identifying opportunities and solving problems, the case for empathy could not be stronger. This chapter discusses empathy as a critical leadership skill, which can grow only through personal relationships. Listening is the centerpiece of empathy and is vital for leaders of all styles. As any skill, it should be trained through consistent practice.

Keywords Organizational effectiveness · Leadership · Empathy · Diversity · Listening

> *If we have optimism, but we don't have empathy – then it doesn't matter how much we master the secrets of science, we're not really solving problems; we're just working on puzzles.*
>
> Bill Gates (2014)

The pandemic, racial injustice, economic uncertainty, political polarization, misinformation, and general daily ambiguity, – over the multitude of challenges 2020 has brought, empathy has been on everyone's mind more than ever. Yet opportunities to offer and take it still feel inadequate, with virtual get-togethers, air hugs, and masked heart-to-hearts not quite up to the task—and when we are so anxious with our own problems, we are not as attuned to other people's plights as we could or should be.

S. Holt (✉)
Woodbury University, Burbank, CA, USA
e-mail: Svetlana.Holt@woodbury.edu

J. Marques (ed.), *Innovative Leadership in Times of Compelling Changes*, Management, Change, Strategy and Positive Leadership, https://doi.org/10.1007/978-3-030-67258-4_8

Some leaders have discharged the gravity of the predicaments of their constituents, while ordinary Americans convey a lack of concern for others by refusing to socially distance and wear face coverings or disparage those who do. The fact that a recent Gallup poll (July 2020) (https://news.gallup.com/poll/1687/race-relations.aspx) showed that roughly a third of the USA does not believe there is a problem with race relations confirms that many individuals refuse to be concerned with others' perspectives. But it does not have to be this way. In this groundbreaking book, Jamil Zaki (2020) shares a cutting-edge research, including experiments from his own lab and stories of people who embody this new perspective and are fighting for kindness in the most difficult of circumstances, and argues that empathy is not a fixed trait—something we are born with—but rather a skill that can be strengthened through effort.

Empathy implies the ability to understand and take active interest in others by recognizing changes in their emotional states through reading body language and verbal clues and being insightful about the underlying reasons of these changes. By matching appropriate behaviors to social environments, leaders stimulate followers' motivation, which, in turn, results in greater organizational effectiveness. Accordingly, contemporary global organizations are challenged with the task of enhancing the emotional intelligence in their leaders, who must acquire and practice their empathy and social skills through self-learning as much as job-related training.

Leading with Empathy

Empathy is an essential aspect of twenty-first-century leadership and can no longer be ignored if we want to prevent continuation of ethical disasters in our world. On a regular basis, scholars have kept readers updated on the elements that determine good leadership in contemporary times, and empathy is a recurring theme. As an example, Schilling (2010) draws a significant inference from a study on some great twentieth-century leaders—John F. Kennedy, Martin Luther King, Jr., Mahatma Gandhi, Mikhail Gorbachev, Nelson Mandela, and Lech Walesa. While these leaders are often labeled as charismatic leaders, their levels of empathy, emotional intelligence, commitment, inspirational motivation, and trustworthiness were foundational in making them the remarkable individuals they became.

Empathy, viewed as the compassion for and attunement to others' emotions and circumstances, has been highlighted as an important aspect of effective leadership in the research literature for several decades. Originally described as "leader empathy," this type of connection encourages leaders to be better listeners, who understand their followers, thereby building belief that group members are being heard (Bass, 1960).

Leadership can be defined as a position, process, action, or state. Leaders take responsibility, inspire, influence, support, and take risks. Assuming leadership is a relationship grounded in trust, (Northouse, 2019), emotional management—which undeniably begins with empathy—is definitely a factor in leadership effectiveness. In recent years especially, leadership effectiveness has been examined extensively in connection with relational management as a critical factor for organizational success, with strong positive correlations found between managers' abilities to connect with others and their employees' motivation and productivity (Bartock, 2013; Drager, 2014; Park, 2013).

In the aftermath of corporate collapses resulting from leadership that was primarily focused on personal enrichment and magnificence, the adjectives used to describe the term "leader" have been shifting from result-driven and leader-focused to stakeholder- and relationship-centered. Responsible leadership (Voegtlin et al., 2012) considers the leader's effectiveness in terms of the ability to establish rewarding, consensual solutions rather than just financial performance. Spiritual leadership (Fry & Cohen, 2009) aims to achieve organizational transformation in such a way that employee well-being and corporate social responsibility are prioritized without neglecting the company's growth, profitability, and performance. What most of such theories have in common is their component of interdependency between leaders and stakeholders, which Hudson (2013) typifies as attachment theory.

Emotionally intelligent leadership focuses on achieving positive results through conscious decision-making—decisions incorporating logical and emotional data. Twenty years of studies on emotional intelligence (EI) in the workplace have solidified that high EI indicates better interpersonal skills and better professional performance. Leaders with high levels of EI are well-equipped for putting others at ease and solving problems, maintaining a high level of self-awareness as well as a responsible work-life balance while being honest, collected, and decisive (Greenockle, 2010). Empathy, specifically, is a critical component of EI in leadership because it establishes an unspoken mental and emotional connection that enables the carrier to understand the hidden meaning in and behind words.

Empathy Skepticisms

At the beginning of 2000s, a certain cynicism of empathy began to set in, particularly among younger individuals. Konrath et al. (2014) reviewed several decades' worth of studies and noticed that recently more younger people say it is not their problem to help persons in distress and not their responsibility to understand the world from someone else's standpoint. Their thinking seems to have transformed to the one that cutting someone off from empathy has a helpful value, a means to take a stance (Lanzoni, 2018).

Jamil Zaki (2020) seconds these observations that empathy is in short supply. He discusses how we find it hard work to appreciate people who are not like us, that it is easy to hate them, and how we are less considerate than we were even 30 years ago. Since 2006, when Barack Obama said that the USA was suffering from an "empathy deficit," the situation seems to have worsened (Zaki, 2020).

We often think of our capacity to experience the suffering of others as the ultimate source of goodness. Many of our wisest policy makers, activists, scientists, and philosophers agree that the only problem with empathy is that we do not have enough of it. Nothing could be farther from the truth, argues a Yale researcher Paul Bloom in his book *Against Empathy: The Case for Rational Compassion* (Bloom, 2016) maintaining that limiting our impulse toward empathy is often the most compassionate choice we can make. Bloom reveals empathy to be one of the leading motivators of inequality and immorality in society. Far from helping us to improve the lives of others, empathy is a capricious and irrational emotion that appeals to our narrow prejudices, the author argues. It muddles our judgment and, ironically, often leads to cruelty. Accordingly, we are at our best when we are smart enough not to rely on it, but to draw instead upon a more distanced compassion.

Basing his argument on groundbreaking scientific findings, Bloom (2016) makes the case that some of the worst decisions made by individuals and nations—whom to give money to, when to go to war, how to respond to climate change, and whom to imprison—are often motivated by honest, yet misplaced, emotions. He demonstrates how empathy distorts our judgment in every aspect of our lives, and that without empathy, our decisions would be purer, more reasonable, and ultimately more ethical (Bloom, 2016).

Psychologists and neurologists have started to look more deeply at how empathy works in real-life situations, when we are not consciously focusing on it. They have found that one of the strongest causes for human empathy is seeing a conflict between two other parties. In his new book, *The Dark sides of Empathy*, Fritz Breithaupt, a professor at Indiana University, explains that once we take a side, we are drawn into that perception, leading to very strong empathy and a strong divergence from the perspective of the other side (Breithaupt, 2019).

Researchers who study empathy also confirm that it is truly difficult to empathize with people who are different than ourselves and even harder with people we do not like. There is a natural way that empathy gets activated in the brain—our pain centers light up when we see another person in anguish, but According to Breithaupt (2019), out in the real world, it starts to develop more like tribalism, a method to strengthen our own point of view while hindering any others.

Empathy in Diverse Organizations

Although empathy is now perceived more and more as a professional ability, it is hard to quantify and difficult to measure, just like it is difficult to assign numeric values to companies' goodwill on their balanced scorecards, hence the scarcity of empirical studies on correlations between companies' efficiency and the role empathy plays in their organizational cultures. Nevertheless, such studies, which tie empathy to organizational success, are attempted more frequently, especially in studies of sales and product development, with terms like "empathy marketing" and "user empathy," becoming mainstream (Olson, 2013).

It is clear that businesses that do not espouse a bigger purpose than generating a profit will have a hard time maintaining relationships with their investors, customers, and surrounding communities. But when an enterprise is in tune with the need in the world, it can provide solutions which meet the needs of many, which results in robust profitability.

Using a combination of publicly available information and exclusive statistics drawn from its investigations and from social and financial broadcasts, focusing on global companies, the Global Empathy Index looked at CEOs' approval ratings among staff, the ratio of women to men on the board, frequency of complaints, the companies' performance on social networks, and the impact of controversy such as ethical lapses, scandals, and fines—among other metrics—to determine that five of the ten most empathic companies are based in Silicon Valley (Palomar, 2016). Intriguingly, they are also among the most profitable and the fastest growing compared to weighted average of 5.2% of all the companies in the index. The automotive industry is a particularly thought-provoking topic for discussion. Mercedes is 91st on the list, Toyota 94th, VW 95th, and Honda 108th. There are two outliers: Tesla in third place and Audi in 10th. It is important to note that Audi dramatically outperformed its parent company, VW, due to high scores for its CEO, while VW's score suffered with the ongoing emissions scandal and low approval ratings for its recently departed CEO, Martin Winterkorn. On the other hand, Satya Nadella, the CEO of Microsoft, says that the company's core business is connected with the customers' needs and that Microsoft would not be able to satisfy them if it did not have a deep sense of empathy (Nadella & Shaw, 2019). Microsoft has prioritized empathy, and this certainly factored into its high ranking in the Index. Facebook, Alphabet (Google), LinkedIn, Netflix, and Apple, also in the top 15, are taking concrete actions to grow empathy in their workplaces and with their clients (Palomar, 2016).

Indeed, in the increasingly immediate, intimate world driven by rapid change, where everyone has to be proficient at identifying opportunities and solving problems, the case for empathy in business could not be stronger. Companies make money by designing, producing, and selling what customers need (or want). Without understanding what the customers want, there is no business. Without empathy, the capacity to put oneself in others' situations, and meet these others where they are, there is no understanding of the customers' needs. And retaining existing ones is far less expensive than securing new ones. A similar logic can be applied to employees: happy employees are better than just employees, as profits are to a large extent a derivative of devoted staff (Hewertson, 2012; Keynes, 1964).

Empathy—cognitive and affective—combining understanding of both logical rationale and the emotional one (Hogan, 1969), is the driving power behind effective communication as well, so crisis stakeholders' communication strategies have gained increasing attention in recent research. A study by Bentley (2013), for example, discusses the power of effective apology, which, from the stakeholder perspective, includes such important components as expression of remorse, acknowledgment of responsibility, and promise of forbearance—a combination of words and behaviors which demonstrate empathy.

Hence the importance of understanding the multifaceted diversity in the communities served by businesses and adapting corporate practices and behaviors based on the constituents' values, work ethic, and business protocol. As poor understanding of the motives of others leads to unproductive conflict and sometimes even organizational failure, effective managers have to be open to learning new patterns of social interaction. As a result, their emotional skills, as well as the ability to leverage diverse points of view, are essential to successful communication (Colfax et al., 2010; Holt et al., 2009; Rahim & Marvel, 2011). Self-awareness juxtaposed against the emotional and logical profiles of others will help develop appreciation of these differences (Bentley, 2013; Boulouta, 2011).

Assuming the overall goal of multinational organizations is to embrace the common good, the leaders of these organizations must realize that fulfilling this objective can be achieved only by studying and understanding the environment in which they operate. Companies which aspire to enhance their leaders' effectiveness in the global arena accept the imperative to respect all countries and cultures in determining the selection of appropriate leadership styles. Multiple studies on global leadership suggest that perceptions of preferred leaders differ based on employees' cultural backgrounds, age, education, and, to some extent, gender (Dunn et al., 2012; Rahim & Marvel, 2011). While awareness of differences between cross-cultural leadership preferences is important, it is also important to seek similarities between them (Colfax et al., 2010; Sharma, 2012). Overall, the cultural implications of several studies suggest a certain cross-cultural commonality of expectations for leaders, and more than one component of emotional intelligence can be applied to match the needs of a particular culture (Holt et al., 2009; Bowles, 2011; Plante, 2013).

The basic theories within a free market economic system are tied to supply and demand, which are heavily influenced by emotions (Fama, 1970; McGregor et al., 2000). So perhaps it would be safe to suggest that today's global economic system would be better referred to as an "emotionomical system"—meaning supply and demand are not driven only by basic need but also by emotional tendencies. It would not be imprudent to further argue that emotionally intelligent global leaders, capable of recognizing and regulating these subconscious drivers in themselves and others, would be capable of generating tremendous power and wealth given the opportunity to properly channel those tendencies into tangible products (Acharaya & Yorulmazer, 2008; Fernandes & Ferreira, 2009). Thus, within the sphere of global enterprise, emotions can be useful as well as harmful (Hirshleifer, 2001; Hirshleifer & Shumway, 2003; Kida et al., 2001; Plante, 2013; Rahim & Marvel, 2011), and therefore, their role deserves a serious consideration.

Positive emotions have been found to encourage exploration and discovery, expand our thinking, help generate new ideas, and encourage us to consider various possibilities (Kibben, 2012). Negative emotions also have a place in our lives as they also enhance thinking, but in a different way: they encourage a clearer focus and attention to detail, motivating search for errors and imperfections (Bower, 1981; Fredrickson, 2001, 2003). How we feel, then, does impact our judgment (Mayer & Salovey, 1997), and the better the mood is matched to the message, the better we pay proper attention. Empathy, in turn, starts with self-awareness. Outside of lifting the mood and energizing a multicultural team through a humorous ice-breaking activity, getting in touch with one's moods and energy levels helps us not only understand our own mental states but also those of our colleagues.

One of the trademarks of a successful enterprise is its ability to harness creativity. Brenton and Levin (2012) explain the importance of nurturing the productivity of innovators and identify the drivers of innovation, one of which is the way innovators are treated at their workplaces. They suggest that great leaders will "fire people up and instill passion" (364). Among traits common to successful innovators, they name high levels of empathy, collaborative interpersonal style, and "mature intelligence" (365), which is understood as humility to abdicate the need to be "the smartest person in the room" (365).

A corporate culture of innovation accepts that there are appropriate uses for all emotions. Even anger could be put to good use: for example, when an instance of injustice needs to be rectified. Happiness, characterized by positive mood and high energy, is a suitable emotion when we need to have an open mind in order to accept and generate creative ideas through the use of original thinking (Salovey & Mayer, 1990). Indeed, when we are happy, we are less critical about our own actions and those of others. We are also better able to see the situation as a whole and pay less attention to small details (Caruso & Salovey, 2004). Experiencing pleasant mood and low energy is the best state to be in when meeting new people. As mentioned earlier, positive mood ensures open-mindedness, while low energy minimizes the risk of overbearing potential new friends by our own narration. Low energy and unhappy mood ensure attention to minute details because our mindset is critical. This mood, therefore, is suitable for checking and double-checking one's work for minor and major errors—especially when stakes are high (Caruso & Salovey, 2004).

Skillful relational management as applied to workplace situations implies recognizing the moods of our coworkers, knowing what moods would be appropriate for the task at hand, and, most importantly, having the skill to take colleagues from where they are to where they need to be by managing their emotions. Are they overly happy to be troubleshooting a financial issue? How can you bring them down? Are they sad, fearful, and indifferent? If you need them to be open for brainstorming creative solutions, how do you bring them up?

Especially in entrepreneurship, empathy is essential to sustainable achievement. From shareholders to investors, from customers to employees, entrepreneurs have to be able to tune into the needs and outlooks of all their stakeholders. Empathy allows them to create bonds of trust, and such connection, in turn, allows them to run their businesses most efficiently. It is essential, too, that stakeholders are confident that their interests are taken into account, and, consequently, entrepreneurs need to be able to empathize with their stakeholders' anxieties and perceptions. Therefore, modern enterprises are challenged with the task of enhancing the emotional management skills of their leaders, who must acquire and practice their empathy and social skills through self-learning as much as job-related training.

Cultivating "Selfish Empathy"

While empirical research has produced evidence that empathy, emotional intelligence, and other human skills are crucial to effective global organizational performance, few college curricula adequately address the emotional and interpersonal skills that prospective employers most want in their employees and organizations want in their leaders. The good news is that researchers believe that these capacities can, and should, be enhanced in the traditional classroom—both in faculty and in students (Chang, 2006; La Civita, 2003; Mertz, 2003; Ohm, 1998; Zadel, 2008).

Unquestionably, empathy is a valuable business commodity, and for those of us to whom it does not come naturally, there is good news—it can be cultivated. The reason for unethical behavior is not poor ethical reasoning but the lack of understanding and care about what others feel because we have never had similar experiences. Taking a personal interest in others, practicing being fully present, listening, and tuning into nonverbal communication clues are paths to training our "empathy muscles" (Martinuzzi, 2009).

Empathy starts with awareness of the thoughts and feelings of others. In a learning context, this means being present, seeing, and hearing what is going on. Effective listening, then, plays an important role in developing one's empathy. Nevertheless, few school curricula give development of student listening skills any significant emphasis. Indeed, college reading, writing, and speaking classes are part of all general education curricula, while we would be hard-pressed to find a course completely dedicated to listening at a school of any level. Consequently, as part of the quest for empathetic organizational leaders, it would be prudent, in addition to incorporating service learning into the curricula, to also integrate learning experiences which encourage students to hone their listening and interpretation abilities.

As Baby Boomers retire and Generation X moves into the upper echelons of their corporations, Millennials and Generation Z are left in the lower and middle tiers of the management ranks, where their parts change from gathering experience and testing organizational values to applying and establishing those values through corporate leadership. With the knowledge that in any given organization there are approximately two to three generations of workers spread throughout the hierarchy, can and should we apply the same style of leadership we used to motivate the previous generations to motivate younger workers—the generations of text messaging and instant gratification? Indeed, traditional leadership ideologies, such as maintaining positive attitudes, listening, supporting one's workers, leading by example, developing a corporate image, empowering employees, and being fair and consistent, have proven effective in most leadership situations. Though they are markedly more diverse and individual in their behaviors, the millennial generation matured with a strong sense of and desire for structure and supervision. Their parents as role models, they identify with leaders who have integrity, humility, and grit (Pollak, 2019).

Millennials and Generation Z are known for their different views on life compared to generations before them. This divergence transpired as a result of a blend of many factors, such as the accelerated speed of everything, the multiplicity of communication devices, increased traveling opportunities, and the greater amount of parental nurturing they received (Barrick, 2020). Many of these generations' parents are affluent middle-agers who are now confronted with progenies who are drawn to the "softer" side of life: art, poetry, music, and the surreal world of games. They are so strongly drawn to an unreal world in which they become a fictional character because it enables them to live out their wildest dreams and achieve a high level of skills appreciated by their peers. Younger generations are drawn toward challenge as a driving motive for performance, expressing the importance of not deviating from the purpose they set for themselves, indicating opening one's mind and overcoming fear of change as ways to connect with others (Mohammed, 2019). However, while many of them excelled in high school and college, they do not seem attracted to the current structured world of work. Many of them seem to explore their options, waiting for the right moment or opportunity to come along and not in a hurry to proactively chase it.

With the changed needs of today's corporations and communities, the increased awareness about environmental and stakeholder care, and the increased global competition, there is tremendous need for workers who dare to think creatively and critically and understand the need to resolve new problems in innovative ways (Ferrazzi & Weyrich, 2020). Given their affinity for electronic games, poetry, music, and the arts, the Millennials and those who follow them could be a timely and much needed asset to the urges of the corporate world.

Accordingly, consideration should be given to the diversity of the generational cohorts working within organizations today (Pollak, 2019). With younger employees, perhaps their biggest strength lies in their diversity. Unlike previous generations, they are well versed in seeking and gathering information from the media and, in turn, using that information to increase awareness and, when able, using that information to better society (Mohammed, 2019). Older generations tend to bypass, ignore, or are not even aware of the breath of media outlets available.

Although organizations' success depends on empathetic leaders who are able to adapt, build on the strengths around them, and relate to their environment, focus on empathy and employee and customer satisfaction frequently becomes a victim of obsession with short-terms corporate results. When enterprises fail, it is often because leaders have stopped focusing on understanding their environment intimately and instead stay insulated in their own operations. Successful leaders are receptive to disruption and innately aware of what is going on in their organizations both internally and externally (Ferrazzi & Weyrich, 2020).

In fact, in the same book Breithaupt (2019) discusses the dark side of empathy, and he also proposes a rather creative solution: give up on the idea that when we are "empathizing" we are being altruistic, or helping the less fortunate, or in any way doing good. What we can do when we do empathy, proposes the author, is help ourselves, purely so we can expand our own imaginations and make our own minds richer. It is "selfish empathy," not virtuous, but better than being alone. Our heart motivates us to do good, and our head determines how best to work to achieve that good.

Company values and the idea of corporate and social responsibility (CSR) are increasingly more important to this generation, and hiring the right talent is only part of the challenge organizations face today. How businesses create challenges and learning opportunities that motivate the younger generations to give of themselves to their potential is of the greatest importance, as the younger cohorts place significant importance on not only recognizing current issues affecting the world today but rather developing initiatives that directly assist in bettering those social problems (Ferrazzi & Weyrich, 2020).

Although diverse and idiosyncratic in behavior, these generations have grown up with structure and supervision. With parents as role models, this generation will most likely respond to leaders who have honesty and integrity. Millennials and Generation Z tend to examine leadership from a different lens than the generational cohorts that came before them. Their background of sheltered affluence and lifelong exposure to virtual reality have made them nonresponsive to static instructions. Practical experience is valued over title and rank, and their desire to take the wheel and learn by trial and error is what often leads the members of this generation down a road of discovery and learning (Barrick, 2020). Being well educated, highly skilled in technology, and self-confident, this generation expects stimulation, collaboration and compensation. Work needs to be interesting to them, and managing them successfully means allowing them to work in different ways (Buchanon, 2010; Gilbert, 2011). They will not automatically respect someone who is older or who holds a superior position—they will respect only those who show appreciation for them as well. Studies also show that Millennials are primed to do well by doing good: "Almost 70 percent say that giving back and being civically engaged are their highest priorities" (Buchanon, 2010, p. 169).

Successful leadership development programs must incorporate conceptual knowledge, gained through readings and observations, with simulations, case studies, experiential exercises, and, most importantly, practice—including role-playing (Mohammed, 2019). Four factors are involved in the process of mentoring diverse employees: the first is the influence factor, which means that learning occurs when leaders act as strong role models, with high standards of moral and ethical conduct, and the staff emulate those sets of values. The second factor is inspirational motivation, occurring as leaders communicate their high expectations of their workers. Managers need to continuously reinforce their respect for their employees by acknowledging their contributions to the learning process of their peers and by thanking them, when warranted, for doing quality work. Intellectual stimulation is the third factor in the process of mentoring, which implies encouragement to innovate and challenge one's own beliefs while engaging in creative problem-solving. Within the workplace, leaders do not only demonstrate challenging their own assumptions, but they should encourage all colleagues to provide constructive feedback to each other and reflect on this feedback during meetings. The fourth factor is individualized consideration, which is meant to capitalize on the manager's skill to provide a supportive climate and to coach each employee to be fully actualized.

While empathy is a foundational skill for every social competency important in any organizational setting, we live in a culture promoting instant gratification and the importance of being young, rich, and entertained. Empathy, therefore, should be a big topic in organizational learning—not only because it is the underpinning of respect but also because becoming curious about strangers opens our minds. There is a psychological basis for human beings to have empathy. In his 2016 *TIME* article, neurologist Michael Trimble described how the same areas of the brain become activated when we see someone who is emotionally aroused as when we are emotionally aroused ourselves. Put simply: when we truly listen to others, we are literally able to feel what they feel.

Therefore, empathy can grow only through personal relationships, and the importance of listening should not be underestimated. Listening, consequently, should be the centerpiece of leadership. Listening is a skill, and any skill can be taught through consistent practice. The listening skill is especially vital for leaders of any style, as they need to understand when to listen and to whom. Yet, while writing, speaking, and reading classes are standard requirements in any curriculum, we would be hard-pressed to find a class specifically dedicated to honing listening skills in college and university curricula. Arguably, students will jump only as high as the targets are set for them, so emphasis on attention to the smallest details shared by their peers in favor of lectures and textbooks is key, and the highest grades should be awarded to the best listeners—those who listen with the purpose to understand and remember—not to those who speak or write the most. It is no secret that most of the information gained through lectures and textbooks becomes outdated very quickly; how we connect with the world outside—and handle relationships—will remain with us and ultimately promote success.

In sum, companies do not do business with other companies. Instead, people within these companies do business with each other, and successful individuals, and companies alike, do not operate in a vacuum. Consequently, in order for organizations to be effective in a contemporary business environment, they must be empathetic to stakeholders' differences, appreciate the emotional makeup of other people, and know how to build and manage relationships and networks. Indeed, everywhere, individuals need to communicate, work in teams, and let go of the issues that interfere with their performance. Interpersonal skills, such as communication and relating to people from diverse backgrounds, are indispensable qualities for success in any workplace.

Chapter Takeaways

1. Leadership effectiveness has been examined extensively in connection with relational management as a critical factor in organizational success, with strong positive correlations found between managers' abilities to connect with others and their employees' motivation and productivity.
2. Businesses that do not espouse a bigger purpose than generating a profit will have a hard time maintaining relationships with their investors, customers, and surrounding communities. But when an enterprise is in tune with the needs of the

surrounding world, it can provide solutions which meet the needs of many, resulting in robust profitability.
3. Within both professional and personal spheres, emotions can be useful as well as harmful. Our feelings impact our judgment, and the closer the emotional state is matched to the purpose, the more productive the outcome.
4. Empathy can grow only through personal relationships, and the importance of listening should not be underestimated. Listening is the centerpiece of leadership and, as a skill, can and should be trained through consistent practice.
5. How businesses create challenges and learning opportunities that motivate the younger generations to give of themselves to their potential is very important. These cohorts place significant priority on not only recognizing current issues affecting the world today, but rather developing initiatives that directly assist in bettering these social problems.

Reflection Questions

1. During your next face-to-face interaction, challenge yourself to actively listen while the other person is talking for several minutes. Do not interrupt and do not attempt to think about how to respond. What happened? Please report on your experience/s.
2. Do you believe that empathy has no place in business? Why?
3. Do you agree that unless they are offered an interesting and memorable experience, the younger generations' attention will be hard to capture and retain? Please explain.
4. If as a manager of your department you were hiring, how would you feel about employing a worker who you know is not going to stay?
5. Do you choose high remuneration over social impact and work-life balance while looking for fulfillment outside of your workplace?

References

Acharaya, V., & Yorulmazer, T. (2008). Cash-in-the-market pricing and optimal resolution of bank failures. *The Review of Financial Studies, 21*(6), 2705–2742.

Barrick, V. (2020). *How not to become a millennial: Learning from America's largest sociological disaster*. Independently Published.

Bartock, A. L. (2013). Fight or flight, stay or leave: The relationship between emotional intelligence and voluntary turnover. (Order No. 3585950, University of Phoenix). ProQuest Dissertations and Theses, 312. Retrieved from http://search.proquest.com/docview/1512420679?accountid=13159. (1512420679).

Bass, B. M. (1960). *Leadership, psychology, and organizational behavior*. Harper.

Bentley, J. M. (2013). Talk Is Cheap: Organizational Apologies from the Stakeholder's Perspective" (Order No. 3587407). Available from ProQuest Dissertations & Theses Global; ProQuest

Dissertations and Theses A&I: The Humanities and Social Sciences Collection. (1426849370). Retrieved from http://search.proquest.com/docview/1426849370?accountid=13159
Bloom, P. (2016). *Against empathy: The case for rational compassion*. Ecco Publishing.
Boulouta, I. (2011). Corporate social responsibility: Its rationale and impact at multiple levels. (Order No. U585960). Available from ProQuest Dissertations & Theses Global. (1414910481). Retrieved from http://search.proquest.com/docview/1414910481?accountid=13159
Bower, G. H. (1981). Mood and memory. *American Psychologist, 36*, 129–148.
Bowles, S. & Gintis, H. (2011). *A Cooperative species: Human reciprocity and its evolution*. Princeton University Press.
Breithaupt, F. (2019). *The Dark sides of empathy*. (A. Hamilton, Trans.) Ithaca, NY: Cornell University Press.
Brenton, B., & Levin, D. (2012). The softer side of innovation: The people. *Journal of Product Innovation Management, 29*(3), 364–366. https://doi.org/10.1111/j.1540-5885.2012.00910.x
Buchanon, L. (2010). Meet the millennials. *Inc, 32*(6), 166–180.
Caruso, D., & Salovey, P. (2004). *The emotionally intelligent manager*. Jossey-Bass.
Chang, K. T. B. (2006). *Can we teach emotional intelligence?* Unpublished doctoral dissertation, University of Hawaii, Manoa.
Colfax, R. S., Rivera, J. J., & Perez, K. T. (2010). Applying emotional intelligence (EQ-I) In the workplace: Vital to global business success. *Journal of International Business Research, 9*, 989–998.
Drager, K. A. (2014). Examining the ability of emotional intelligence and work location to predict job satisfaction. (Order No. 3611231, Capella University). ProQuest Dissertations and Theses, 124. Retrieved from http://search.proquest.com/docview/1502015688?accountid=13159. (1502015688).
Dunn, T. E., Lafferty, C. L., & Alford, K. L. (2012). Global leadership: A new framework for a changing world. *SAM Advanced Management Journal (07497075), 77*(2), 4–14.
Fama, E. F. (1970). Efficient capital markets: A review of theory and empirical work. *Journal of Finance, 25*, 383–417.
Fernandes, N., & Ferreira, M. (2009). Insider trading law and stock price informativeness. *The Review of Financial Studies, 22*(5), 1845–1887.
Ferrazzi, K., & Weyrich, N. (2020). *Leading without authority: How the new power of co-elevation can break down silos, transform teams, and reinvent collaboration*. Currency Press, a Division of Penguin Random House.
Fredrickson, B. L. (2001). The role of positive emotions in positive psychology: The Broaden-and-build theory of positive emotions. *American Psychologist, 56*, 218–226.
Fredrickson, B. L. (2003). The value of positive emotions. *American Scientist, 91*, 330–335.
Fry, L. W., & Cohen, M. P. (2009). Spiritual leadership as a paradigm for organizational transformation and recovery from extended work hours cultures. *Journal of Business Ethics, 84*(2), 265–278.
Gates, B. (2014). Text of the 2014 Commencement address by Bill and Melinda Gates. Stanford report. https://news.stanford.edu/news/2014/june/gates-commencement-remarks-061514.html
Gilbert, J. (2011). The Millennials: A New generation of employees, and new set of engagement policies. *The Workplace* (September/October 2011).
Greenockle, K. M. (2010). The new face in leadership: Emotional intelligence. *Quest (00336297), 62*(3), 260–267.
Hewertson, R. B. (2012). Great financial leadership: Stand out among peers. *Financial Executive, 28*(10), 57–58.
Hirshleifer, D. (2001). Investor psychology and asset pricing. *Journal of Finance, 56*, 33–97.
Hirshleifer, D., & Shumway, T. (2003). Good day sunshine: Stock returns and the weather. *Journal of Finance, 58*, 1009–1032.
Hogan, R. (1969). Development of an empathy scale. *Journal of Consulting and Clinical Psychology, 33*, 207–216.

Holt, S., Bjorklund, R., & Green, V. (2009). Leadership and culture: Examining the relationship between cultural background and leadership perceptions. *Journal of Global Business Issues, 3*(2), 149–165.

Hudson, D. L. (2013). Attachment theory and leader-follower relationships. *The Psychologist-Manager Journal, 16*(3), 147–159.

Keynes, J. M. (1964). *The general theory of employment, interest, and money*. First Harbinger Edition, Harvest/Harcourt Brace Jovanovich.

Kibben, C. (2012). Humor and emotional intelligence: A correlational study of leadership. (Order No. 3534887, University of Phoenix). ProQuest Dissertations and Theses, 188. Retrieved from http://search.proquest.com/docview/1282638689?accountid=13159. (1282638689).

Kida, T. E., Moreno, K., & Smith, J. F. (2001). The influence of affect on managers' capital-budgeting decisions. *Contemporary Accounting Research, 18*, 477–494.

Konrath, S., O'Brien, E, & Hsing, C. (2014). Changes in dispositional empathy in American college students over time: A meta-analysis. *Stanford Report, 15*(2), 180–198.

La Civita, L. (2003). An examination of emotional intelligence factors: Their relationship to academic achievement and the implications of retention of the at-risk community college student. Proquest Dissertations and Theses. Capella University, Minnesota. (Publication Number: AAT 3102546).

Lanzoni, S. (2018). *Empathy: A history*. Yale University Press.

Martinuzzi, B. (2009). *The leader as a mensch: Become the kind of person others want to follow*. Six Seconds.

Mayer, J. D., & Salovey, P. (1997). What is emotional intelligence? In P. Salovey & D. Sluyter (Eds.), *Emotional development and emotional intelligence: Educational implications* (pp. 78–89). Basic Books.

McGregor, D. G., Slovic, P., Dreman, D., & Berry, M. (2000). Imagery, affect, and financial judgment. *Journal of Psychology and Financial Markets, 1*, 104–110.

Mertz, D. L. (2003). Online learning, attrition, and emotional intelligence: Perspectives of leaders in online teaching. D.M. dissertation, University of Phoenix, United States – Arizona. Retrieved from ProQuest Digital Dissertations database. (Publication No. AAT 3106497).

Mohammed, K. J. (2019). *How to Lead millennials: Lead in the new era of business*. Club Mo Publishing.

Nadella, S., & Shaw, G. (2019). *Hit refresh: The quest to rediscover Microsoft's soul and imagine a better future for everyone*. Harper Business.

Northouse, P. G. (2019). *Leadership: Theory and practice*. SAGE.

Ohm, P. J. (1998). *"Emotional intelligence": A different kind of smart. Teaching for success through an emotion-based model*. M.A. dissertation, Prescott College, United States – Arizona. Retrieved from ProQuest Digital Dissertations database. (Publication No. AAT 1391459).

Olson, G. (2013). Neuromarketing 101: Branding empathy. *Empathy Imperiled. SpringerBriefs in Political Science, 10*. New York, NY: Springer. https://doi.org/10.1007/978-1-4614-6117-3_7.

Palomar, B. (2016, December). The most empathetic companies, 2016. *Harvard Business Review*. Boston, MA: Harvard Business School Publishing.

Park, H. H. (2013). Determinants of mechanism of emotional marketing: Emotional intelligence, perception of emotional labor' action, efficacy and customer' coping strategy on customer satisfaction. (Order No. 3598952, Oklahoma State University). ProQuest Dissertations and Theses, 188. Retrieved from http://search.proquest.com/docview/1461742750?accountid=13159. (1461742750).

Plante, L. (2013). Are you ready? Practitioners from around the globe urged to build the skills executives need. *PM Network*, 1–12.

Pollak, L. (2019). *The Remix: How to lead and succeed in the multigenerational workplace*. Harper Business Publishing.

Rahim, M., & Marvel, M. R. (2011). The role of emotional intelligence in environmental scanning behavior: A cross-cultural study. *Academy of Strategic Management Journal, 10*(2), 83–103.

Salovey, P., & Mayer, J. D. (1990). Emotional intelligence. *Imagination, Cognition and Personality, 9*(3), 185–211.
Schilling, L. (2010). *A historical analysis of the relationship between charisma and the making of great leaders*. Ph.D. dissertation, Walden University, Minnesota, United States. Retrieved November 17, 2010, from Dissertations & Theses: Full Text (Publication No. AAT 3397897).
Sharma, R. (2012). Measuring social and emotional intelligence competencies in the Indian context. *Cross Cultural Management, 19*(1), 30–47. https://doi.org/10.1108/13527601211195619
Voegtlin, C., Patzer, M., & Scherer, A. G. (2012). Responsible leadership in global business: A new approach to leadership and its multi-level outcomes. *Journal of Business Ethics, 105*(1), 1–16.
Zadel, A. (2008). Do emotionally intelligent leaders have more satisfied employees? *International Journal of Management and Enterprise Development, 5*(5), 590–608.
Zaki, J. (2020). *The war for kindness: Building empathy in a fractured world*. Broadway Books.

Part II
Leading Innovatively to Address Strategic and Spiritual Challenges

Chapter 9
Inclusive Leadership in a Creatively Compelling World

Ginger Grant and Cheryl De Ciantis

Abstract The changes we now see, unprecedented in our lifetimes, call for extraordinary response and commitment to action. We see five areas of unprecedented opportunity for leaders to redefine greatness for the coming generations. These are not new ideas per se; rather, they represent a will to use the capacities and perennial wisdom we collectively possess and commit to proceed with honesty and inclusion of all stakeholders—and these stakeholders include everyone on the planet. These five opportunities are embracing change as imperative while committing to creating nodes of needed stability, putting people first by prioritizing the value of empathy and getting real about issues of power regarding who gets what and why, commitment to values by "walking the talk," making it real by ensuring all stakeholders have a place at the table, and re-mything ourselves: using every avenue available to us—from science to the arts—to re-create the narratives that valorize the truths we wish to live by as humans within an interconnected web of existence.

Keywords Empathy · Values · Mythopoesis · Phronesis · Episteme · Techne · Metis

Introduction

At the time of this writing, the entire world is roiling with the effects of a crisis of unprecedented magnitude: Covid-19. Populations worldwide, including organizations whether private or public, NGOs, volunteer associations, or government or municipal departments, who had already been facing the challenges of rapid and accelerating change, are facing the greatest collective crisis in history. Many are already collapsing under the existential pressure of pandemic. We are living in a

G. Grant (✉)
Humber College Institute of Technology and Advanced Learning, Mississauga, ON, Canada

C. De Ciantis
Kairios Independent Human Development Research and Practice Group, Tucson, AZ, USA
e-mail: cdeciantis@kairios.com

J. Marques (ed.), *Innovative Leadership in Times of Compelling Changes*, Management, Change, Strategy and Positive Leadership, https://doi.org/10.1007/978-3-030-67258-4_9

time of unprecedented crisis and unprecedented opportunity to re-create the terms of "greatness," articulated 20 years ago the groundbreaking work of Collins (2001), in a radical manner.

Traditionally, organizations had two sources of intelligence [IQ, EQ] and three types of capital at their disposal: financial, intellectual, and emotional. But being good is not good enough to endure and prosper. Organizations are being asked to re-vision their entire reason for being (Grant, 2005).

In service of this new compelling world, we propose a new source of intelligence and capital that can be described as "mythic." Of course, in fundamental ways this is not "new" at all; but we need the multivalent perspectives this form of intelligence makes available. This form of capital both causes and enables an organization to reconnect with its founding ethos, the archetypal pattern that expresses its unique purpose and its distinct voice (Grant, 2005). The mythic view, as proposed here, incorporates the concept of mythopoesis—the conscious re-creation of mythic stories to illuminate renewed values, giving us the ability to face present needs and create the capabilities to confront them.

Leaders of great organizations have understood the importance of invoking stakeholders to explore those activities that excite their passion and skills to deliver on their search for meaning. Employees in such companies are capable of developing myths, stories, and rituals to elicit creative responses from suppliers, customers, and investors. By firing on both intelligence cylinders (intellectual and emotional) and by utilizing all five forms of capital (material, rational, relational, spiritual, and mythic), greatness is more likely realized.

Five Compelling Opportunities for Leadership

1. *Embracing Change as Imperative*—Covid-19 has brought to the fore the most likely future scenario: change that is turbulent, deep, accelerating, pervasive, and now, potentially, perennially deadly as the factors fueling pandemic are exacerbated by climate change at the same time that divisive political movements inhibit necessary collective efforts. The ability to adapt to our current circumstances is key to our survival. We must also acknowledge the need for stability and to take on responsibility to actively engage in a change/stability dialectic. To do this, we need to get past default binary thinking—the manner of thinking that has seen us to this moment, where it is politically possible to deny the science of accelerating climate change and to deny our collective responsibility for ensuring the most fundamental life needs for all. In order to bring the planet and its inhabitants to a livable equilibrium, we need leadership to commit to the creation of nodes of stability within the reality of changing conditions: in policy and governance, in social safeguards, in ethical technologies, and in fair exchange.
2. *Putting People First*—Since the era of Jack Welch, we have lived in a fiction that places the shareholder first and insists on unending growth as the only true measure of value (Deming, 2017). Instead, putting people first means prioritizing

talent, commitment, experience, involvement, and a willingness to let go of measures of success that commoditize people and looking toward societal good over profit. This too requires we redefine how we think about power, in governance, in activism, and in design. In large economies, pandemic has refocused public attention on life-saving and caused a re-evaluation of the costs of ever-expanding economic growth against the value of individual human lives. Populations are increasingly seeking courage and decisiveness in their leaders and leading by example. People are also giving greater priority to those seeking empathy. They want to see leaders who show that they can imagine walking in another's shoes and firmly incorporate the value of human life into political calculus.

3. *Commitment to Values*—Being willing to see it through and "walking the talk." Younger people are seeking meaning in life, wanting to serve something of value that benefits more than just themselves. Being conscious of our values and consistently prioritizing the values we want to see reflected in real behavior points us in the direction of changing our reality. The demands of the planet now will not allow our habitual structures to sustain. Our value systems must also incorporate values that are grounded in structures that can support the flexibility required by change, values that need to be re-examined and redefined. What do equity and equality look like in a world in which we would like to believe that pandemic spares no one—even as we see stark evidence of impoverished and socially neglected communities being hit harder than others.
4. *Making it Real*—Willingness to work "on the ground" to verify data, models, measures, and assumptions against lived conditions and practice, to be willing to adjust to lived conditions, and to redefine values that have failed to serve the larger good. A global stage such as the Internet makes transparency the norm. There is nowhere to hide. At least, that is its real potential. Unfortunately, too prominent among its effects have been the cascading proliferation of disinformation, including on the part of actors working to discredit democratic structures, and in such massive quantities, it is difficult to pursue and refute these messages, especially when the will to do so is demonstrably lacking in the leadership of the corporations who profit from it. Making it Real means calling out and addressing the dynamics of power in operation at every node of interaction (Flyvbjerg, 2001). Political and corporate leaders alike need to become leaders in prioritizing transparency, actively promoting and taking part in discussions about the reality of power; owning up to the realities about the means by which a decision is actually taken; what are the actual—not covert or implicit—outcomes it means to achieve; and who will "win" and who will lose thereby and what are the consequences. Making it Real means empowering heretofore silenced stakeholders to take a seat at the table and influence real policies.
5. *Re-mything Ourselves*—As we look to the future we may forget to look to the past and the perennial wisdom of humanity. What is myth? Jean Houston, repeating the insight of the Roman poet Sallust, has said that *myth is something that never was, but is always happening*. Myth holds the seeds of wisdom in compressed forms; it is in effect an encoding of the deepest psychic forms and pat-

terns that govern the conditions of our embodied being. For the pre-Socratic Greeks (i.e., before the common era of our understanding of rationality as "truth") myth, which derives from *muthos*, "mouth," signified divinely inspired speech, *true* speech (De Ciantis, 2019, p. 61).

One of the functions of myth is to "to enforce a moral order within each successive coherent social group" (De Ciantis, 2017, p. 144). Our myths enshrine the bases of our normative cultural values. Yet, myths may drop away if their relevance to life is no longer felt. That myths survive is not because they are literally written in stone, but because they are elastic enough to continue to serve our deepest needs in changing circumstances. Further, we ourselves are the source of this elasticity: it is our job to reimagine and expand our myths, in a creative act Joseph Campbell (1968) called "mythopoesis," a term coined from Greek words meaning "myth-making." We co-create the myths that "live" us every day. Kenton Hyatt (2019) reminds us that the insights of philosophy have been reified by psychology and demonstrated by neurophysiology: we literally create the reality we live, through our perceptive filters in combination with the daily choices we make that establish neural pathways. We each have a responsibility to own this creativity and to recognize that we all have creative contributions to make, whatever our individual creative style. Different eras require makers: bards, artists, teachers, philosophers, composers, novelists, screenwriters, and visionary leaders to retell our myths, re-clothing them so that we can recognize ourselves as we are now. In the age of the Internet, we all have the potential to become storytellers and, by doing so, make a difference.

The Mythos of the Makers

An urgent example of the need for re-mything is the increasing speed of technology that has rapidly outpaced our ability to keep up with its potential consequences. In ancient Greek and West African mythology (the latter still vital in the orisha religions common to the African diaspora worldwide) mortals appeal to the maker gods Hephaistos and Ogun to make material life on earth successful for humans. The maker gods remain in connection with humanity and are concerned with human flourishing, specifically with regard to technology as a means of improving life.

In the *Iliad* Homer tells us that Hephaistos was "famed for his *techne*," which is the root of our English "technology," and classified by Aristotle among the three ways of knowing and finding our way in the cosmos. Homer tells us that Hephaistos created robots: AI is no new idea. Hephaistos also creates from clay a biotechnological woman, Pandora. Significantly, Homer also tells us that Hephaistos was famed for his *metis*, which is a quality well-known to the Greeks, but left out of the categories of knowing enumerated by Aristotle (that will be discussed below). Metis is difficult to contain in a definition; it includes resourcefulness, trickery, opportunism, also subtlety of mind and forethought, as well as experience and mastery of techne, which must be called on when opportunity suddenly presents itself (Detienne & Vernant, 1978, p. 2). "One does not approach the blacksmith's forge without preparation" (De Ciantis, 2017), and innovation requires not only techne but metis. Ogun tells us even more about the metistic flexibility required by the occupation of the smith. Ogun is revered in praise songs as the one who is "both hot and cool" (Barnes, 1997), referring to the dangerous heat of the forge, in which the blacksmith makes white-hot iron run like water; and the inflexible strength of iron once cooled after the smith has worked it into deft and fluent shapes.

It is in the mythic territory of the divine smith that we find ourselves at the crossroads of nonbinary thinking. The crossroad is also a locus for the exchange of information, through *phronesis*—another Greek term, one that we have inherited from Aristotle, meaning in essence acquiring practical knowledge through encounters with others. Aristotle's categorization of how we know has been embedded in Western culture. His categories are hierarchical by necessity, since they are based on the Greek belief that there is an ideal, a true reality, the material forms of which as we experience them every day are mere reflections (think of Plato's Cave, which is an illustration of exactly this concept). *Episteme* is the rational, philosophical, higher-order mode of knowing whereby we seek to grasp the nature of this Ideal. *Techne*—for which our mythic maker deities are famed—is how we learn the properties of physically manifested things by interacting with them and then encoding the knowledge gained thereby. It is inferior to *episteme* by definition, since in employing techne we are dealing with only distant reflections of the ideal according to Plato and Aristotle. Phronesis, "practical wisdom," is dialogue, the means by which we learn from each other through verbalizing and representing to ourselves and others the fruits of our experience and learning from that of others. Because of its subjectivity, Aristotle conceived of phronesis as the least reliable of the three categories of knowing (Fig. 9.1).

Fig. 9.1 Aristotle's ways of knowing. (Illustration by Cheryl De Ciantis)

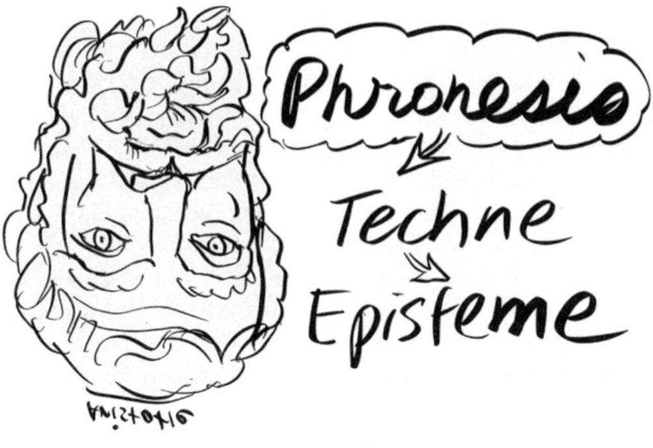

Fig. 9.2 Turning Aristotle on his head. (Illustration by Cheryl De Ciantis)

What if, instead, we turn this on its head? In our current world, phronesis acts as guide. What we know to be true by learning from each other through dialogue should be what informs our techne, especially with regard to developing a robust ethics of technology to focus our future visions through a lens of a phronetic prioritization on serving a common good—which we can only determine through continual dialogue. The relationship of phronesis and techne can then inform our episteme: what we know to be true of the world we have created based on shared values, a deep and continual conversation whereby we can co-create our own reality (Fig. 9.2).

Better yet, if we bypass hierarchical notions by taking a relational perspective, we are able to draw on all forms of wisdom, coming into relationship with all of the enormous challenges we face, in this time, on this planet.

The Challenge: Taking a Relational Perspective

At no other time in history has leadership been more important than it is now and into the future of a new reality.

If we invoke a relational perspective, assumptions that have been taken for granted and until recently remained implicit and unquestioned can be investigated and tested. However, if we default to either/or mindsets, we will be forever stuck in mechanistic, linear, and novelty-driven expectations which do not serve our evolutionary needs. Returning to the blacksmith deities mentioned above, they, as do their mortal counterparts, establish their forges at crossroads, where different commercial and practical interests may intersect and where diverse points of view find a locus of encounter. There, they impartially serve clients whose aims may be mutually inimical—for example, the farmer for whom the blacksmith forges his plow, the warrior her sword, and the ruler her or his scepter. The still-extant temple of

Hephaistos stands adjacent to the Athenian Agora, the marketplace where ideas and schemes intermingled amid cash exchange, and next to the Keramikos, the ancient quarter of the craft guilds whose techne drove the Athenian economy and who considered Hephaistos to be their patron god. In more than one ancient culture, oaths were taken on the blacksmith's anvil. Artist and writer Kenton Hyatt puts it this way: "blacksmiths forge relationships" (private conversation). The wisdom systems manifested in the ancient myths of technology shine a light on our human ability to hold more than one idea at a time in dynamic suspension, allowing more possibilities to enter our fields of consideration without pre-judgment. The psychologist James Hillman warned that when we lack the perspectives we may derive from such mythic archetypes, "we remain in a … model of consciousness which must be one-sided in its judgments and narrow in its vision, for it is unaware of the wealth and variety of psychological ideas" (Hillman, 1976, p.126).

Taking a relational perspective means first of all that we reconsider binary thinking habits and incorporate an internal "rheostat" to complement our heretofore over-reliance on an "on-off switch" style of thinking and decision-making that tends as well to over-rely on the quantitative at the cost of the qualitative. Expanded and increasingly qualitative models call for an expansion of our qualitative cognitive abilities. Our tendency is to visualize change and stability on the opposite ends of a continuum, and therefore cognitively irreconcilable. If, instead, we place these concepts on a more conceptually provisional x-y axis, we may then conceptualize a more dynamic and generative model (Fig. 9.3):

This model also reflects in a visual form the experience of moving toward wisdom. To know oneself requires circumambulation—the act of circling a referent—and defines boundaries of a space by relating to a center of value. Common in most religions, circumambulation is used to define a sacred space (De Ciantis & Grant,

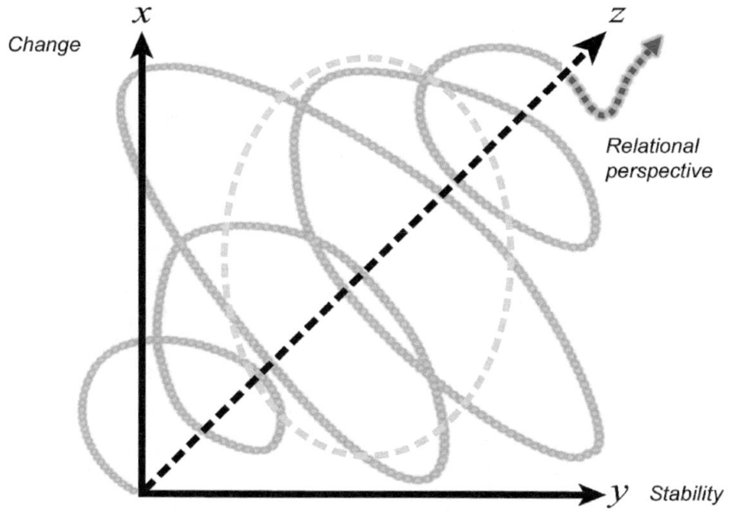

Fig. 9.3 Relational perspective

2019, p. 133). The process is inclusive, for the individual is constantly in dialogue with others along the path. Like peeling an onion, understanding progresses deeper, layer by layer until insight is reached. This model also gives us access to intersubjectivity, which allows us to mediate the Western assumption that "the individual is the center of her or his perceptual and cognitive universe" to the point of excessive egotism, even narcissism (Hyatt, 2019, p. 139).

A relational perspective also takes into account what Tomas Bjőrkman calls the collective imaginary, our uniquely human ability not only to imagine but to imagine collectively. We can communicate about the contents of imagination, but also activate it socially by hearing and internalizing rituals and narratives which become beliefs, held by large groups joined by social, political, economic, or religious bonds that exceed the limits of human intimacy and the ability to communicate person to person, allowing people who are "essential strangers" to "cooperate peacefully" in creating organizational structures that exceed individual grasp but extend our reach (Bjőrkman, 2019).

Mind the Gap

Embracing Change as Imperative

The reality we face in an era of climate change and global pandemic is change of an entirely different order than we have had to face within our present lifetimes. It also presents an unprecedented opportunity to recalibrate the way we think, value, and act. The essence of our era of post-modernism has been to embrace change as an end in itself and continually seek novelty for its own sake. We embrace the increasingly rapid advances in technology but lack a well-conceived, articulated, and shared ethics that will protect life and ensure equable access to the most foundational requirements for life. Embracing change—the x-factor in the model above—as imperative also means we embrace the y-factor: stability.

An example of engaging this dialectic is the support on the part of the Canadian government of new immigrants who are highly professionally trained, for example, physicians, but cannot be immediately certified in their fields upon arrival in a new regulatory environment. Canadian employers have consistently identified that internationally trained professionals (ITPs) are not hired for three key reasons: (1) lack of familiarity with Canadian workplace practices, (2) inability to effectively assess the relevance of work and education experience obtained abroad, and (3) lack of experience working in a typical Canadian team/matrix workplace environment. These barriers create significant underemployment for these highly skilled professionals who have immigrated to Canada. Due to increased immigration, Canada will require enhancing immigration policy development by developing broader knowledge-transfer systems; this will be important not just to manage immigration but ensure equitable knowledge transfer, positive governance of diversity, stability, integration, and inclusivity. In short, we need more skilled workers. The primary driver of this increased demand is the aging Canadian labor force, which is projected to have five million retirees by 2035 and almost no increase in the national birth rate. With the advent of the global economy that is characterized by a rapid pace and scale of change, the accompanying uncertainty and ambiguity that this has, and will create, is changing the skills needed to thrive. One of the key attributes most evident in new immigrants is their willingness to "pivot" and embrace change. From these new immigrants, we are learning much about the need for resilience in the face of the unknown.

Putting People First

Putting people first means prioritizing human values. When those values are made explicit, passion and purpose are evident. The capacity to learn, to be creative, and to seek meaning characterizes most people in an organization, not a small few. Currently, the standard conditions at work do not allow for the maximization of this human potential. It is probably the biggest wasted resource on this planet. One of the leading causes of a lack of cultural vitality and personal commitment in organizations is the poor example of leaders toward the opinions and feelings of employees. And the result is obvious. Assets now have feet (Grant, 2017).

Now, new leaders are emerging in North America and Europe with the rise of the Black Lives Matter movement, leaders who are bringing attention to core issues like ingrained, institutionalized racism. Public opinion is shifting in a way and to a degree that has not been experienced in our lifetimes. The very concept of leadership as individualized is being subsumed within a larger frame of citizens, employees, and previously excluded stakeholders taking on the power to demand change and the responsibility to reframe how we shape the future. The Black Lives Matter movement, which has spread far from its origins in protest against Black lives senselessly lost to police murder in the USA, may enable us to reach and extirpate the root of ingrained racism that can be exemplified by the recent statement by the US Senator of Arkansas, Tom Cotton, that slavery was a "necessary evil" in building the economy and nation of America, in his aim to discredit the current movement to teach the historical facts of slavery as an institution in the USA (Cole, 2020).

Commitment to Values

We find that a useful way of thinking of human values is to recognize three clusters: Foundation values, which ensure our ability to live and function; Focus values, meaning the energy we give to solving problems day to day, recognizing opportunities, and carrying out our personal and institutional missions; and Future values that pull us toward a more expansive view that encompasses the largest questions and greatest aspirations (and such values are never represented by a number, by earnings, or profits, but rather to what much greater, globally life-enhancing ends those resources will be dedicated).

While embracing change is necessary, sustainability requires a degree of stability. We term the set of values that support this as "Foundational" values. They must be in place for any structure to withstand the pressures of change even while value structures we call "Focus" and "Future" must be flexible enough to move with and through it. Many groups find the Foundation in the values expressed in their founding stories. They may also find these stories need to be re-evaluated in order to rebuild foundations that will stand into the future.

An example is a global consumer personal care product company founded in the nineteenth century when Great Britain and the Western European countries were at the height of their colonial power. Managers sent to open markets like Australia, in an era when communication took months or years, were selected for their ability to gather people and market intelligence and to make decisions that aligned with the company's overall mission to maximize sustained profit. By the twentieth century, the company was an established global player and the cachet of country managership was high in the organization. At the turn of the twenty-first century, corporate leadership invoked its founding-era story as a reminder of the strengths of individualistic and empowered country-based market managers, who were responsible for maintaining the strength of their brands and localizing the appeal to their markets by being in touch with and responsive to the unique cultural preferences of customers on the ground.

At the same time, corporate leadership was keenly aware that country brand leaders felt no responsibility to share success factors or market intelligence gathering methods with other managers and that the future of the company would be dependent on cross-pollination of best practices and innovative ideas so that long established brands as well as strategically introduced new products would be able to sustain the company's overall market share in an environment of rapidly changing demographics, magnified by the impacts of social networking. The efforts of the corporate leadership to integrate the definition of leadership as a shared value involving peer-to-peer communication, feedback at all levels, and responsibility to the corporate strategies and top line overall were initially resisted because they were felt to impinge dramatically on the freedom of the country managers to conduct their locally focused parts of the business.

Corporate leadership recognized the need to redefine and realign values that were based in the foundation story and conducted leadership development training that incorporated values alignment. Values alignment by necessity incorporates dialogue in order to mutually understand how values are defined locally. A company or team may say it values listening and trust, but what that means to each player in their own unique environments can vary greatly. The outcome of such a dialogue results in expanded understanding of a group's shared values and a much more depthful understanding of what a value means in practice. Values alignment permits the establishment of a spectrum of behaviors that are recognizable by superiors, peers, team members, subordinates, shareholders, regulators, and customers as effective expressions of a particular value.

The following visualization is adapted from a graphic created by the company's HR manager, who was a member of the executive team. This metaphor helped

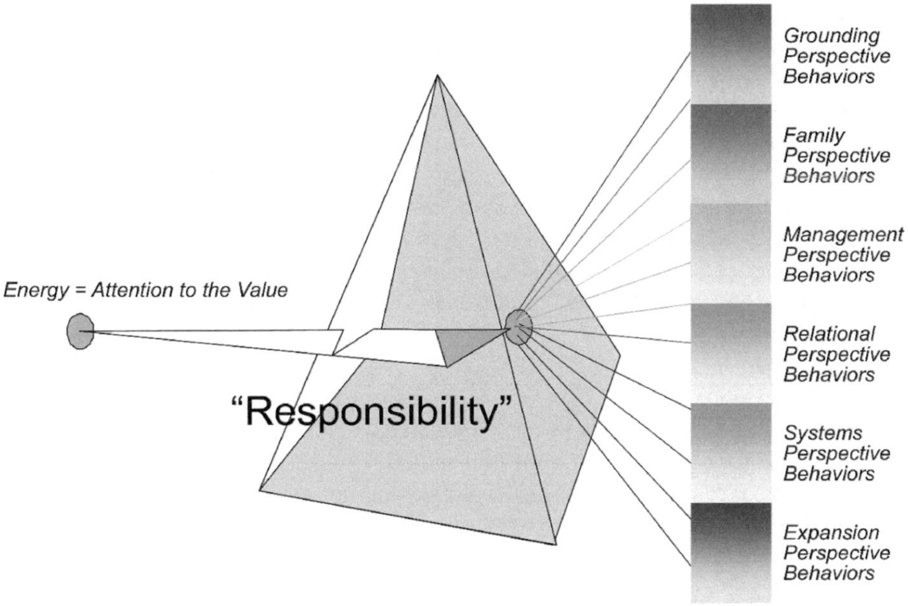

Fig. 9.4 Values can be recognized in a spectrum of behaviors (Hyatt & DeCiantis, 2014, p. 129)

people in the company to affirm the company's redefined values and see themselves in the values spectrum. Such a metaphor also accommodates the strength of diverse values definitions and corresponding behaviors. The key is dialogue whereby the values spectrum can be generated, understood, agreed upon, and mandated by ongoing appraisal and reward systems that are grounded in the company values. The company spent the next few years conducting small-group dialogue and action planning sessions to ensure the understanding of shared values company-wide (Fig. 9.4).

Making It Real

Whenever we have asked participants in leadership seminars, "What is your greatest leadership challenge?" the answer is most often "Creating a team culture." This is indeed difficult. But more so when corporate middle managers tell us that the "real deal" is that the true priority of higher management, no matter what values they publicly espouse, is invariably *results*. What then *is* real?

In 2018, the USC Viterbi School of Engineering launched a two-semester engineering course: Innovation In Engineering and Design For Global Crises. Its mission is twofold, to discern the real needs of real people and to create real-world solutions and to immerse students in meaningful and impactful experiential learning that makes a difference. In early 2020, just before USC suspended classes due to Covid-19, engineering students traveled to the Moria Reception and Identification Center in Lesvos, Greece, which houses 20,000 refugees awaiting asylum in a “space built for 3000” (Druhora, 2020). The students immersed themselves in the camp inhabitants’ daily lives in order to discern their most pressing needs. The team generated nine innovations that addressed unmet needs. These include an app for gathering, tracking, and storing refugee medical records; a life-skills educational app geared toward displaced teens that have piloted health and safety educational content; a “virtual mental healthcare platform for volunteers and aid workers in crisis zones that provides tele-counseling sessions with licensed mental healthcare professionals pro bono” which is being piloted in Greece and in Southern California to support pandemic health workers; and a low-cost system of soft, modular housing parts that aid temperature and humidity regulation in makeshift and emergency housing such as in the refugee camp and in homeless populations in urban environments (Druhora, 2020).

Burçin Becerik-Gerber, Dean’s Professor of Civil and Environmental Engineering, told participants in the virtual World Human Forum Conference that her intent and focus in launching the course had been on generating products. What happened instead, she realized, was that the program generated student empowerment and commitment that changed lives, not only the lives of the people affected by the solutions the team created but also the lives of the students themselves, who now see themselves as capable of making real and impacting change for the better. One student told the conferees, “Out of all my education, these 6 units changed my life,” and “I never realized my passion could overlap with my purpose” (World Human Forum, 2020).

Re-mything Ourselves

Among the five leadership “literacies” enumerated by futurist Bob Johansen (2017) is developing the ability to lead “shapeshifting” organizations that morph too quickly for command-and-control strategies to be effective. How do we re-myth ourselves?

Companies and leaders can be guilty of resting on their creative laurels: all the right people are in place; they innovate constantly and support their company’s position at the top of the market. At such times it is possible to forget the need to consciously re-examine the myths guiding the company’s soul. Case in point, a US-based company that led the field worldwide with a unique, beloved consumer product that relied on chemical processes. The technical team at the company was topnotch, and the team leader, who was also a subject matter expert, was excellent at directing talent toward innovative problem solutions. So innovative in fact that whenever a novel chemical variability problem arose that impacted the quality of the product, the lavishly budgeted team routinely “invented” a new molecule to solve it. Enter change, with the compound challenge of economic downturn and a rapidly manifesting displacement of the company’s signature product by attractively novel technical competitors marketing to a younger generation.

Given suddenly tight new constraints, the team leader was willing to experiment with very far out-of-the-box, nontraditional facilitated techniques to shake up the team's mindset. These included a dream-circle process. Team members received a dream "seeding," and the following day a dream circle was convened following the guidelines created by Montague Ullman (1990) for respecting the dreamer and contributors taking "ownership" of dream interpretations to minimize ad hominem projections and ensure psychological safety in the process. What emerged from this novel project were two significant insights: one a recognition of the company's hubristic culture, which made it unable to learn from competitors' approaches to the market, which they mostly ignored, and the realization that the chemical variability problem arose out of hand-off issues between functions and could have long before been solved by focusing on clear communication and building trust by asking questions and listening to the answers.

This second insight was offered by a member of the team who had been so effectively sidelined that he was on the point of resigning; and it was offered only after others had taken turns. He was the last to speak. He also happened to be in an HR liaison position and the sole African-American team member. He had pointed out the hand-off issue in the past but had simply been ignored, not through personal animus but simple neglect since he was not one of the scientists heroically producing new molecules; and people of color report often being treated as invisibles. The team did not address the racial diversity issue; instead they thanked the team member, asked what it would take for him to decide to stay, and waited for his response; and the last business of the meeting was analyzing and agreeing on the main points and accountabilities for a comprehensive plan to mitigate the hand-off issue. The female team leader acknowledged that she had focused too much on the science (and the scientists) and articulated her own detailed commitment to prioritizing inclusivity and listening to all of her team members and stakeholders as her key, continuing responsibility.

This example points out more than one kind of inclusivity. The inclusion of people who represent racial/ethnic, national, religious, age, or gender diversity is one aspect of inclusion. However, the team member who had been sidelined represented not only racial diversity but perhaps even more significantly, cognitive diversity (De Ciantis, 2017). Most of the technical team were ideators (a characteristic measured as Sufficiency of Originality by the Kirton Adaption-Innovation Inventory, meaning that their preference was to sidestep a problem definition such as chemical process variability to create novel chemistry each time it appeared). The sidelined team member was an Adaptor (in Kirton's terminology) with regard to creativity: closely observing a given situation to identify its local variables and offering small-scale, fine-tuned adjustments that in the case of the hand-off problem were agreed by the rest of the team to have the greatest short-term potential to solve a persistent problem in a way that made it much more likely to prove sustainable over time with less or no expense. He was also an introvert in a generally extrovert organizational culture which had an overall "friendly" aspect but also moved at a speed that made it difficult for introverts, who tend to spend more time coming to conclusions on evidence before speaking out, to contribute their insights.

Another kind of inclusivity the team's leader and its members exhibited was a readiness to adopt a different kind of novelty, in the form of dramatically nontraditional methods in order to break out of habits of thinking and problem definition. Many leaders are reluctant to try something that they fear team members will reject out of hand and shy away from interventions that will actively challenge status quo. We were hired by a global tech company as an innovative experiential learning design collaborative with an extensive track record in Silicon Valley to co-design innovative, meaningful communication and creativity experiences that would challenge the mindsets of young engineers only to have the company ultimately scrap our design recommendations, opting for learning technology that was 20 years out of date. It became clear they were more afraid of alienating the engineers and risking the loss of talent than they were of minimizing real dysfunction and getting the talent organized most effectively to support overall goals. Collaboration was not at issue, they claimed; the engineers are extremely collaborative—and we asked ourselves: then why were we hired to help solve a silo problem?

Traditional Challenge Coping Mechanisms

As outlined by Zohar and Marshall (2004), organizations have traditionally deployed three sources of capital and two types of intelligence to create wealth, sustain growth, and cope with the challenges and obstacles along its path. Zohar and Marshall proposed "spiritual capital" as a values-based business culture where a critical mass of individuals act from aspirational values that nourish the human spirit. We would like to go a further step to propose a Mythic Economy, based on a collective definition of who we are. Everyone has a stake in creating the conditions for a good life for all on the planet we share (Table 9.1).

Industrial Economy—based in the exploitation of material resources and the transformation through physical processes of raw material into consumable product: things that can be bought and sold in a marketplace. This corresponds to one of the three main intelligences, three categories of how we come to know about life

Table 9.1 Types of economic capital

Economy type	Attribute	Intelligence	Function	Capital
Industrial	Material	Physical (IQ)	What I see	Resources—raw inputs; financial, data
Knowledge	Mental	Rational (IQ)	What I know	Intellect as applied to systems and processes Information
Experience	Emotional	Emotional (EQ)	What I feel	Self-awareness and the ability to relate to others Knowledge
Spiritual	Intuitive	Reflective (EQ)	Who I am	Meaning-making in service of a global citizen. What we each contribute or not to our culture
Mythic	Perennial	Collective	Who We are	Archetype and perennial wisdom; self and other awareness; values alignment Mythopoesis

and the cosmos that we have inherited from Aristotle. It corresponds to techne, one of Aristotle's three categories of knowing. Techne is our way of learning about the world through manipulation of its physical properties, through experiment and evaluation. It results in quantitative properties that can ultimately be judged in terms of their effectiveness and the elegance of solutions with a minimum of means and expenditure of resource. It refers to products and solutions that can be replicated and transmitted by teaching and example; the scientific method is an example of this intelligence and the basis for the successes of the industrial economy.

Knowledge Economy—comes from our ability to use knowledge to create goods and services resulting in a change of the basic production structure from the manufacturing sectors to service sectors. This shift required that lifelong learning and skills renewal became a permanent necessity. This type of intelligence corresponds to Aristotle's *episteme*: understanding the "real" nature of things through emotionally detached, rational examination and getting as close as we can through data collection and abstract modeling to a fundamental reality that lies behind the apparent complexities of variable, subjective contextual manifestations.

Experience Economy—rooted in our emotional connections, to each other and to personal experiences, memories, and imaginative engagement with the kind of lives we desire to live day to day. The experience economy appeals to personal, focus-cluster values through language and image, for example marketplace branding that communicates identity and a sense of belonging. This kind of "intelligence" corresponds to Aristotle's *phronesis*: how we learn from each other about what the world is, for ourselves and others. This way of knowing comprises iterative, ongoing dialogue.

Spiritual Economy—expresses the desire to understand deeper psychic layers than the quotidian. We seek to know who we are in a fundamental way; we seek connection with something outside ourselves that is larger and all-encompassing. Through exercise of this intelligence, we may also awaken the emotion of compassion, both for ourselves and for others.

Now: Mythic Economy

"Economy" comes from the Greek *oikos* or household, and the concept recognizes our "house" as both a highly localized and equally a large, shared space. We are collectively responsible for what we prioritize in life at both the smallest and largest scale. At no time in human memory has this been more important to remember, as we face pandemic and climate change that will force the movement of human communities on a previously unimaginable scale.

A Mythic Economy is collective; it is founded in the perennial wisdom possessed by humanity. In this light, we may reconsider in a new light an idea that has been around for a while, the relationship between data-information-knowledge and wisdom. "Data does not equal knowledge," much less wisdom. We are overwhelmed with data; we are nevertheless developing skills in deriving useful information from it. But we lack competence in adequate means to make sense of information in holistic ways that might lead us to wisdom in forming policies and constructive social practices that benefit all. Leaders must focus on phronesis or practical wisdom in making the move beyond data, information, and knowledge. Practical wisdom is tacit knowledge acquired from experience that enables people to make prudent judgments and to take actions based on the actual situation, guided by values and morals. When leaders cultivate such knowledge throughout their organizations, they will be able not only to create fresh knowledge but also to make enlightened decisions (Nonaka, 2019, p. 21).

Knowledge needs a context in order to be created and then transmitted to others. Nonaka and Konno identified two types of knowledge, explicit and tacit (1998). Explicit knowledge can be readily transmitted by words and/or numbers and shared in the form of data, an operations manual, or the like. This is the primary form of knowledge transmission in the West. In the East, emphasis is placed on tacit knowledge, deeply rooted in personal values and experience over time. As such, it is harder to transmit. Nonaka and Konno believed that knowledge creation and transmission is a spiraling process between tacit and explicit knowledge and called their model SECI (short form for socialization, externalization, combination, and internalization). It is based on learning by doing with circumambulation at the core (Fig. 9.5).

Socialization—one to one: Here we see the initial interaction between teacher and student, expert and beginner. For example: take a task to be learned. The expert shows the novice the task to be mastered and shares his or her experiences of completing this task. The beginner can mimic the expert, imitating the aspects of the task at hand. The beginner can ask questions and a discussion can ensue. This initial knowledge is shared through the common experience, joint activities, and being in

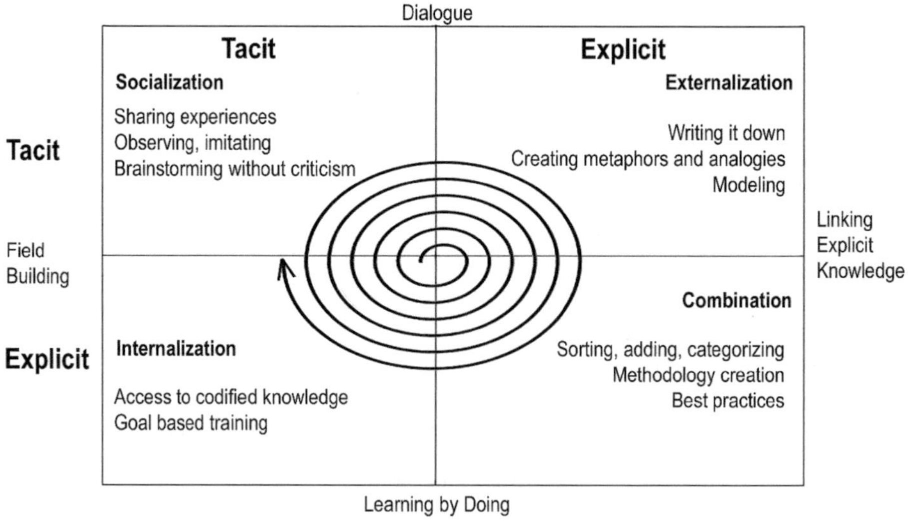

Fig. 9.5 Tacit and explicit knowledge (Nonaka, 2019)

the same environment as opposed to memorization from a textbook or manual. Socialization in this sense involves the sharing of the tacit knowledge between individuals.

Externalization—shared with a group or team: The translation of the tacit knowledge into comprehensible forms is undertaken so that others may share in the knowledge. Stories may be told, models or maps made, and manuals created. Ongoing dialogue takes place to support the physical creation of the knowledge. What was before tacit knowledge is now made explicit.

Combination—shared with an organization: Here new knowledge is shared within the organization by presentations or meetings whereby dialogue continues and the explicit knowledge is refined. The knowledge at this point may be edited or processed in order to make it commonly usable. This is explicit to explicit knowledge creation.

Internationalization—becomes praxis: The last stage is the conversion of the explicit knowledge into tacit knowledge. This internalization relies on two dimensions. First, the explicit has to be embodied into concrete action, such as through training programs. Second, the explicit knowledge is embodied through the doing—experiential learning is key. The knowledge then is internalized and no longer is consciously undertaken, but it is unconsciously adopted and becomes a matter of ongoing practice—the "ways things are done around here." The student now becomes the master and the cycle continues.

And when does knowledge become wisdom? We believe this is a mythic question. It occurs in the same imaginal space as myth. Tomas Bjorkmann speaks of the "collective imaginary." Kenton Hyatt describes the process whereby Western philosophy and ultimately psychology came to recognize the qualities of human knowing hidden within the unconscious. Science increasingly validates myth. Although we in the West may need to turn Aristotle on his head, we would do well to remember that he bequeathed us a notion of the "constructive phantasia," each of our capacity for mental representation that stands between "the outer world of experience and the inner world of knowledge" (De Ciantis, 2019, p. 75).

Chapter Takeaways

This is an unprecedented time in history that gives us all the opportunity and responsibility to re-create the myths we live by. This means re-evaluating and redefining principles that have become empty words and creating new narratives that guide both our daily decisions and our strategies for a survivable future. All aspects of our human capabilities—from science to the arts—must be put on the table for consideration through inclusive dialogues with the purpose of consciously co-creating the reality-based narratives that will guide our daily decisions, policies, and long-term strategies. The mythic view we propose incorporates the concept of mythopoesis—the conscious re-creation of mythic stories to illuminate renewed values, giving us the ability to face present needs and create the capabilities to confront them. In re-mything ourselves, we need to collectively embrace change as imperative, put people first, and commit to values and make it real.

What we have learned from our former experiences and our current contexts is that revalorizing the wisdom we already possess is both necessary and takes time. It cannot be obtained in a weekend retreat or a quick Band-Aid leadership program. Diversity requires honest dialogue and then time to reflect and absorb the ideas presented and then more dialogue "for the common good." If we commit to this process, perhaps Covid-19 is a blessing in disguise for it has forced all of us to slow down and start evaluating what really is essential for our survival.

Reflection Questions

1. What is your attitude toward change? Toward stability? What can you do to ensure needed stability without stifling needed change?
2. What does it mean in your life and work context to put people first? How do you define diversity? How are you contributing to a diverse environment? What commitments do you need to make in order to put people first?
3. What is most important to you? To your organization? How can you ensure that the values you and others hold are mutually discussed and fully understood? How can you "live" your most deeply held values?
4. How do you define what is "real"? How do you define power? How transparent are your policy-setting processes? How can you contribute to clear assessments of who benefits by decisions made and by what means?
5. How willing are you to face a future of uncertainty? What stories and exemplars give meaning to your life? How can you take personal responsibility for shaping the future?

References

Barnes, S. T. (1997). The many faces of Ogun: Introduction to the first edition. In S. T. Barnes (Ed.), *Africa's Ogun: Old world and new*. Indiana University Press.

Bjőrkman, T. (2019). *The world we create: From god to market*. Perspectiva Press.

Campbell, J. (1968). *The masks of god: Creative mythology*. Penguin.

Cole, D. (2020). Tom Cotton describes slavery as a 'necessary evil' in bid to keep schools from teaching 1619 Project. *CNN online*. Updated 11:11 PM ET, Mon July 27, 2020. https://www.cnn.com/2020/07/27/politics/tom-cotton-slavery-necessary-evil-1619-project/index.html

Collins, J. (2001). *Good to great*. Random House.

De Ciantis, C. (2017). The gait of Hephaistos: Crooked perceptions into consilience. Revista ICONO14. *Revista científica de Comunicación y Tecnologías emergentes, 15*, 128. https://doi.org/10.7195/ri14.v15i1.1048

De Ciantis, C. (2019). *The return of Hephaistos*. Kairios Press.

De Ciantis, C., & Grant, G. (2019). *Joan Marques, PhD., Editor. Awakening leadership: The outer reaches of inner space. The Routledge companion guide to management and workplace spirituality*. Routledge.

Deming, S. (2017). Making sense of shareholder value: 'The world's dumbest idea.' *Forbes*, Jul 17, 2017, 07: 29pm EDT. https://www.forbes.com/sites/stevedenning/2017/07/17/making-sense-of-shareholder-value-the-worlds-dumbest-idea/#1616e7282a7e

Detienne, M., & Vernant, J.-P. (1978). *Cunning intelligence in Greek culture and society. Trans. J. Lloyd. Atlantic highlands*. Humanities.

Druhora, D. (2020). Six innovative ideas to aid people in crisis zones. *Viterbi School of Engineering*. Posted May 28, 2020. https://viterbischool.usc.edu/news/2020/05/how-to-aid-refugees-during-covid-19-six-innovative-ideas/

Flyvbjerg, B. (2001). *Making social science matter: Why social inquiry fails and how it can succeed again*. Cambridge University Press.

Grant, G. (2005). *Re-visioning the way we work*. Trafford Publishing.

Grant, G. (2017). In J. Neal (Ed.), *The untapped power of imagination in the workplace. Handbook of personal and organizational transformation*. Springer.

Hillman, J. (1976). *Re-visioning psychology*. Harper.

Hyatt, K. (2019). *Radical creativity*. Kairios Press.

Hyatt, K., & DeCiantis, C. (2014). *What's important: Understanding and working with values perspectives*. Integral Publishers.

Johansen, B. (2017). *The new leadership literacies: Thriving in a future of extreme disruption and distributed everything*. Berrett-Koehler.

Nonaka, I., & Konna, N. (1998). The concept of "Ba": Building a foundation for knowledge creation. *California Management Review, 40*(3), 40–54.

Nonaka, I. (2019). *The wise company*. Oxford University Press.

Ullman, M. (1990). Guidelines for teaching Dreamwork. In S. Krippner (Ed.), *Dreamtime & Dreamwork: Decoding the language of the night*. Jeremy P. Tarcher.

World Human Forum. (2020). The echo of Delphi in Ludwigsburg 22 23 24 May 2020. *Virtual conference*. https://delphiecho.worldhumanforum.earth/wp/

Zohar, D., & Marshall, I. (2004). *Spiritual capital: Creating wealth we can live by*. Berrett-Koehler.

Chapter 10
Understanding and Reformulating Mental Models

Babar Dharani and Kurt April

Abstract Building simplified models using prior information from experiences and learnings from reality is a natural propensity of the mind. Inputs from any new stimuli encountered are processed through mental models for quick action towards the stimuli, serving a vital purpose for survival. However, since mental models are created using prior information, they are susceptible to errors if the information is incomplete, false, miscommunicated, misinterpreted, or if correct information is ignored. They are also at risk of an oversimplification of reality, stale knowledge, as well as misapplication of knowledge. The role of leadership is argued to facilitate changes to the mental model of the followers, either by 'exploitation' of them for gradual refinement and sculpting or by 'exploration' of new mental models by shattering existing ones. The balancing act of 'exploitation' of current mental models and 'exploration' of new mental models is the paradox for leadership for achieving an optimal pace of change for leading followers into new paradigms. From a self-leadership perspective, limiting stumbling blocks to reform mental models and facilitate their evolution through enablers can allow for an optimal degree of flexibility in mental models to be aspired towards to ensure their continued usefulness.

Keywords Design thinking · Exploitation · Exploration · Knowledge · Leadership

Introduction

In everyday language, a physical model is a depiction of an actual person, place, animal, or thing, which is typically a three-dimensional, smaller-scale, simplified representation of the original. The manageable scale of models assists in grasping aspects from reality where their scale can inhibit comprehension (e.g. models of the universe or the atom). Models also serve the vital purpose of allowing accessibility where the real objects are inaccessible (e.g. models of dinosaurs which allows for

B. Dharani (✉) · K. April
University of Cape Town, Cape Town, South Africa

J. Marques (ed.), *Innovative Leadership in Times of Compelling Changes*, Management, Change, Strategy and Positive Leadership, https://doi.org/10.1007/978-3-030-67258-4_10

learning about them despite never encountering one). Models can also provide a useful tool for obtaining experiential knowledge through a proxy (e.g. a walk-through model of a space station prior to an astronaut's visit to one). Similarly, models may also permit an enhanced understanding of future developments of things that currently do not exist (e.g. architectural models of buildings or miniature models of cars and aircrafts under development). Thus, models by representing historic, currently existing, as well as expected (projected) things from reality serve their users as a tool for representing information to enhance understanding.

Models can also be representative of concepts, where the models are analogous to the process or structure of a phenomenon, event, or situation. Such models are usually presented as a simplified diagram. Like three-dimensional physical models, conceptual models also serve similar purposes. In addition, they also allow for visualization of concepts that may be invisible, thus enhancing comprehension for the user (such as the water cycle, where evaporation is 'visualized' by the reader due to its diagrammatic depiction in the model). Not only do models represent simplified information to enhance understanding, they frequently serve the purpose of forecasting – to enhance predictability (such as weather forecasting, or behavioural models).

While a model is an external representation of an existing thing or phenomenon, Craik (1943, p. 61) theorized the human mind's tendency to construct such 'small-scale models of external reality' in the mind to process alternative reactions and to use the knowledge of past events to deal with the future, which he called 'mental models'. Craik's theory was that the mind acts like a machine, modelling or forming symbols for new external events and finding parallels from experience, and this process itself was the basis for thought and explanation (Craik, 1943). He thus effectively described what was to go on to become the central tenant of the field of cognitive science, the idea of the mental model as a computational structure (Jones et al., 2011). Rook (2013, p. 42), many decades later, similarly defined a mental model to be: 'A concentrated, personally constructed, internal conception, of external phenomena (historical, existing or projected), or experience, that affects how a person acts'.

The analogy with a model is significant, as similar to models, mental models also represent historic, currently existing, as well as expected (projected) things from reality and, as a result, mental models serve very similar purposes to a model. Mental models: '… enable individuals to make inferences and predictions, to understand phenomena, to decide what actions to take and to control its execution and, above all, to experience events by proxy; they allow language to be used to create representations comparable to those deriving from direct acquaintance with the world; and they relate words to the world by way of conception and perception' (Johnson-Laird, 1983, p. 397). Since mental models are socially constructed (Berger & Luckmann, 1966) using information obtained from prior experiences or learnings that is internally organised as a model, any similar representations that are encountered are associated to a mental model, and processed through it, which generates an appropriate or inappropriate action in response to the stimulus encountered.

The Fundamental Purpose of Mental Models

A foundational purpose of the mind is to detect threats to one's survival (Darwin, 1859; Howard, 2009). As such, a fundamental functioning of the workings of the psyche is to protect one from dangers that may harm an individual – either physically or mentally (Smit, 2014). To do so, whenever one encounters any external object or situation, the learnings from the experience are retained by the mind. Gradually, with increased experiences and learnings, the mind builds models based on these experiences and learnings and applies them to future experiences to predict outcomes. Personal constructivism theorises that people organize their experiences and learnings for sensemaking of everyday life, as well as psychologically anticipating outcomes (Pande & Bharathi, 2020). The mind, using the input from the stimuli through the senses, processes the information through an appropriate mental model regarding similar stimuli and aims to predict outcomes. For example, having had the experience of being bitten by a fox previously, the mental model may associate other animals with potential harm. Upon encountering another animal at a later point in time, such as a dog, the mental model processes the stimulus through the most similar and relevant mental model that it regards as appropriate for decision-making in the scenario faced. The response or reaction using the model is one deemed most appropriate for self-preservation, and a vital purpose of the mental model is to speed the reactions to stimuli, as faster assessments of threats can help to ensure survival. Thus, mental models act as a predictive tool to quickly assess the stimuli one encounters for increasing the likelihood of self-preservation.

Basic behaviourist theories explain behaviour based on respondent theory or classical conditioning (Pavlov, 1929), where: 'Behaviour is seen as directly (automatically) elicited by antecedent stimuli in the environment' (Thomas & Segal, 2006, p. 142) that are: 'processes that operate automatically and need not involve conscious reflective thought' (Thomas & Segal, 2006, p. 164). Alternatively, behaviour may be explained by operant theory: '… named for its emphasis on behaviour that is identified by its consequences in the environment (technically termed contingencies of reinforcement)' (Thomas & Segal, 2006, p. 142), where positive or negative reinforcement of behaviour leads to development consistent behaviour patterns (Lejeune et al., 2006; Skinner, 2009). Such consistent behaviour is indicative of formations of mental models by the psyche for processing of responses and dictating behaviour when encountering similar stimuli.

Featured Case in Point: Utilizing User's Mental Models for Technology Adoption

Due to their influence on behaviour explained earlier, mental models can help shape the approach to solving problems and performing tasks. As the world embarked on the fourth industrial revolution (Hewitt, 2017), more and more of our everyday requirements are moving onto digital platforms, which required human-computer interactions. However, mental models regarding operations of these tasks were founded outside the digital world. To facilitate technological adoption, metaphors were used to name various aspects of the digital interface, such as the top of a desk is used to name the interface a 'desktop', discarding of documents in 'trash', and saving documents in 'files' and 'folders', to name a few. These were named and designed to assist with the cognitive leap needed for techonological adoption by 'exploitation' of existing mental models (Riggins & Slaughter, 2006).

As such, when creating something unfamiliar, designers base it on the familiar to help the users make the connection by tapping into their mental models. Once people are more familiar with the new paradigm, only thereafter can designers start evolving the interface, as a means for a step-by-step developing or sculpting of the mental model held by the users. For example, note-taking moved from typically yellow, lined paper using a pen or a pencil onto the screen. To facilitate the adoption of technology, the application designed for note-taking was named 'notepad' and resembled the physical note-paper for faster association with note-taking. Similarly, digitalized contact lists had stark similarities to earmarked letters of the alphabet and leather-bound covers of contact books that were used for purposes before digitization. Once users grew accustomed to the new paradigm and its functioning, not having leather imagery on digital contact books, as well as doing away with alphabetical earmarks, and adopting a flat design rather than using buttons evolved.

Mental models are not only tapped into naming new techonological tools and their aesthetics but also as sets of experiences, of how to operate and the expectations of how to perform any task. The better aligned the new paradigm is to the mental models of the users, the easier it can be adopted, hence speeding up the adoption process and making it less likely for the paradigm to be rejected (not adopted by new users) (Renaud & van Biljon, 2008). Apple Technology Company, led by Steve Jobs, greatly tapped into basic mental models that were largely shared by the world population. This was one of the reasons for their products' success. Turning of pages by stroking the screen is similar to a physical paper or book, closing of application with the gesture of the finger as if it were being discarded, and other novel but basic manoeuvring made it optimally user-friendly. They were revolutionary compared to their competitors who tapped less into users' mental models, for example, pressing a button with an arrow to move to the next page or to scroll down the screen and clicking a button with a cross on it to close a screen. By tapping into shared mental models of the users, user-friendliness was greatly enhanced as operations of the system felt intuitive and led to reactions by the interface that was easily predictable by the user. This gave the company a significant advantage towards late adopters, such as the elderly and younger children, who did not need to embark on steep learning curves to adapt the technology (Renaud & van Biljon, 2008).

Problems with Mental Models

Since models are a useful tool, it is unsurprising that they form an integral part of several disciplines for which model-building rules and norms are devised so that it is accurately understood by its audience by following the norms of representation. For example, in theory building, academic models are built on prior knowledge, a philosophical structure of logical forms, obeying the formal rules for theories of reasoning and researching for their development to ensure an accurate reflection of what they represent (Shepherd & Suddaby, 2017). Also, many academic models aim to enhance predictivity, a process that uses data and statistics to forecast outcomes with data models (Davis et al., 2007). Despite formalized processes of developing academic models, review processes, and rigour, the world has seen proposals of certain models and their subsequent collapse due to the use of alternative reasoning and perspectives, exploring of nuances, and use of newer and more sophisticated research techniques.

What academia and other disciplines have formalized is a natural tendency for humans to create small-scale models of reality to anticipate outcomes. However, unlike models by disciplines, the foundational reasoning behind the development of mental models is not based on logical form (Johnson-Laird, 2013); as such, they are prone to unsubstantiated forms of reasoning, use of questionable information, and imperfect forecasting in a new scenario. Mental models are built on individual experiences, which are firstly random in the likelihood of occurrence and, secondly, subjective in the varied emphasis and understanding of different aspects of experiences. Additionally, the lack of testing, rigour, and validity that academic models embrace is led through subjective psychological evaluations and judgements in the case of personal mental models. Thus, mental models, void of foundational reasoning, testing, and critique, are prone to inaccuracies. As a result, mental models can be challenged by the notion that: 'We cannot be sure that we actually know [something] and haven't somehow been 'tricked' into believing it by our senses' (Buckingham et al., 2011, p. 13). Senge (1990, p. 8) took the theory into the organizational learning space and described mental models as deeply ingrained assumptions, generalizations, or even pictures of images that influence how we understand the world and how we take action. Those assumptions are developed from childhood, life experiences, socialization and culture, peers and family, as well as education and reading (April & April, 2007). Chapman and Ferfolja (2001) explore many such challenges of mental models which are briefly discussed below:

Mental Models Built with and without Cultural Knowledge

Indigenous knowledge in each culture has developed over centuries, and it is passed on between generations through watching adults, followership of customs, and learnings from stories or folklore. Folklore, due to the lack of written text but a verbal transfer of knowledge from one generation to the next, is highly susceptible to losing the knowledge that the tradition represented. For example, '*ulwaluko*' (Morrell, 1998) refers to the passage of boyhood to manhood in the isiXhosa language of South Africa. It includes male circumcision, and if administered with due care, the psychological transformation it perpetrates in boys is well understood, respected, and cherished by the community (Unterhalter, 2000). The mental model arising from it is that a man is considered a boy unless circumcised and having undergone '*ulwaluko*'. Such traditional knowledge remains relevant, and the mental model of associating '*ulwaluko*' with manhood or '*indoda*' (Mfecane, 2016) serves a purpose to that community. On the contrary female circumcision is a tradition followed by many cultures, but the knowledge of its purpose and use has been lost over the generations. The real origins remain obscure, even though the practice has been noted, by researchers, in Egyptian mummies in 163 BC, is speculated to have links to slavery, is believed to have been a religious requirement, is an outgrowth of human sacrificial practices, and sometimes is linked to ideas of early population control (Wilson, 2013). In the absence of knowledge, such a mental model of associating female circumcision with womanhood bears the risk of becoming a meaningless ritual, leading to serious repercussions on the well-being of women and for societies that follow them without questioning the knowledge and meaning behind the mental model. As a result, speculation and dangerous, alternative theories emerge to fill the void, e.g. as a way to control women's sexuality, to protect young girls from being raped, to ensure virginity before marriage and fidelity afterward, and to increase male sexual pleasure, and multiple claims about the supposed health benefits for females even though the WHO has expressly asserted that it carries no health benefits for females are extremely dangerous, and the practice only serves male hegemony through suppression of girls and women.

Stale Mental Models

It is argued that no two experiences are ever the same as, the Greek philosopher, Heraclitus expressed through the analogy of a river. While one can step into the same river numerous times, one cannot touch the exact same water when one steps into a river. As such, he argued against the concept of a river as a static constant (Buckingham et al., 2011). Similarly, mental models may be formed by prior experiences or learnt behaviour towards an external person, object, phenomena, or experience, but when the psyche acts on them based on prior knowledge in a new situation, based on Heraclitus' philosophical stance, the psyche is argued to always be projecting. Projection by the psyche is also embedded in the aim at survival, as a thorough investigation of all the qualities of a new stimulus requires time and projection allows for a quicker assessment of the qualities of new stimuli by drawing information from prior experiences and learnings and projecting them onto the new (Baumeister et al., 1998).

Since models use information from learnings or past experiences, while they can be highly relevant and useful, they are at risk of becoming acutely irrelevant and inaccurate under new circumstances and environmental changes (Chapman & Ferfolja, 2001). For example, stories of many mythical heroes who slew beasts to protect their romantic interests, loved ones, or their communities are common tales (Goethals & Allison, 2012). However, the context in many communities has changed, where attitudes have now shifted from 'protection *from* beasts' to 'protection *of* beasts'. Surges in the extinction of species and depletion of the natural environment they lived in have led to a greater emphasis on species and environmental protection, requiring a change in mental models that associate slaying of beasts with heroism to an association of conservation with heroism.

Mental Models Built on False Information

The world has always faced the risk of acquiring unsubstantiated and invalid information from unreliable sources (Chapman & Ferfolja, 2001). Amongst these are presumed facts, such as claims that one must drink two litres of pure water a day, historical claims of facts such as Napoleon Bonaparte was short compared to men of his era, and even observational discrepancies such as the Great Wall of China being visible from space, to name a few. Such information is fitted into the dominant mental models of the time, for example, associating drinking less than two litres of water with ill-health. Mental models associated with these are arguably more rigid and difficult to break away from due to these 'fake facts' regarded as basic knowledge. Despite being erroneous, they occupy the space of 'general knowledge' in everyday life. The risk of false information is greater in our day and age, as we live in an era of an abundance of information, which is available at the click of a button. However, a consequence of it has been that production of information has also been compromised, leading to a host of unreliable sources that may be trusted, and their reasoning, understanding, and information accepted as true, bearing with it the risk of developing mental models of false information.

Oversimplified Mental Models

The definition of a model entails that it aims to simplify the reality for ease of comprehension and allows the use of the mental model in new situations. Simplification is achieved by ignoring nuances and encouraging an understanding of the world through categorization into pigeonholes. While it allows people an enhanced perception of sensemaking of new stimuli encountered and avoids being overwhelmed in the exploration of the details (Riggins & Slaughter, 2006), it is at the risk of an oversimplification of reality. While nuances can allow for models to become more complex, it would entail that the complexification of the model is required to persist to a degree that the model is as complex as the reality in itself, thus failing at facilitate comprehension. An example of such simplification is a racial identity associated with overgeneralized behaviours (Rushton, 1995) without exploring intersectionality (Crenshaw, 1991) that recognizes the many identity constructs that form the identity of an individual. For example, oversimplified mental models have sketched an association between intelligence and race, ignoring the fact that race may be associated with an individual's socio-economic background that may not facilitate children of certain racial backgrounds to attend better schools or institutes of higher education, therefore, locking them out of powerful, informational networks, have less or no time from overworked/absent parents who could assist with homework and mentoring, may need to spend out-of-school time themselves working in the home or jobs. Such simplifications also do not account for family composition in patterning socio-economic inequalities – all of which can influence their academic opportunities and ultimate abilities. While simplication of reality is necessary to form models, the consequences of such over-generalised and simplified mental models are grave on those facing marginalisation due to them.

Mental Models Built on Miscommunicated and Misinterpreted Information

There may be a lack of congruity between the intended communication and its receipt, interpretation, and/or consequential interventions. This leads to misinterpreted experiences and information. When in receipt of the same source of information, there may be an assumed reassurance that others possess the same understanding. These assumptions of 'common knowledge' halt opportunities for learning from one another, as well as lead to interpersonal miscommunications. Based on varied reasoning and interpretations, people can develop a significantly different understanding of the same stimuli. For example, philosophical reasoning behind a mental model may be founded on rationalism (a scientific reasoning process to acquire knowledge of the world) or empiricism (that argues that one's knowledge of the world comes not from reason, but experience) (Buckingham et al., 2011) which can lead to different understandings of the information received. As such, a risk that information may be adjusted by the minds of people receiving them can lead to profound differences in mental models from the same source of information. Different mental models arising from the same sources of information are at an inherent risk of at least some of the models being incorrect.

Mental Models Built by Misapplying Valid Knowledge

Knowledge can be immensely useful for appropriate action for desired results. For example, the fundamentals of Darwin's theory of natural selection (Darwin, 1859) were successfully used to help eliminate a fatal genetic disease, Tay-Sachs, from the Orthodox Jewish community in Brooklyn. This was done by ensuring that all congregations underwent a blood test and marriages were endorsed by the faith, based on genetic compatibility for the avoidance of the disease in future children.

Ironically, a prominent example of the misapplied theory of Darwin also involves people of the Jewish faith, as it was drawn on by the Nazi government of Germany to create the concept of a master race, and an explaination for the genocide referred to as 'the final solution' (Mitchell, 1996). While it may be argued that the knowledge was intentionally twisted by the regime, its acceptance as a mental model by the Nazi-party followers is difficult to contest. As such, while the foundational knowledge may be reliable and accurate, models that fail in correct application of it can lead to catastrophic consequences.

Incomplete Mental Models

Acquiring complete information is a near-impossible task. Even when limiting the scope, for example, to an organization, it retains its difficulty. In reference to organizational knowledge, Chapman and Ferfolja (2001) state that access to information may be limited by organizational structures, such as departments or divisions that lead to compartmentalized knowledge, or only top management having a holistic view of the organization, referred to as power-knowledge. For example, the big four accounting firms (Deloitte, Ernst & Young, KPMG, and PriceWaterhouseCoopers) are some of the largest and most profitable partnerships in the world. They provide services such as audit and assurance, tax advisory, and compliance, as well as consultancy services, to name a few. Each division faces different levels of competition in different geographies, and, as such, cross-selling of services to the clients is a vital tool to ensure profitability. Yet, a major problem faced by the firms is the lack of knowledge of other service offerings to facilitate cross-selling to their customer base.

Mental Models Ignoring True Information

Acceptance of information as accurate is subject to a host of factors, including its reasoning. Illogical reasoning may not allow for information to be accepted. However, reasoning may be ill-presented, and fallacies that are convincingly 'sold' may be accepted. Similar to fake information that bears the risk of acceptance, reliable information may not be accepted should the reasoning disagree with any philosophical biases or if it is not argued convincingly. Such information may be rejected, generating incorrect mental models, or ignored, in which case a mental model is not impacted by it. This may be founded on personal or interpersonal reasons such as personality differences or a lack of trust. However, deeming a correct source unreliable could also be the result of fixed and predetermined ideas.

Mental Models and Leadership

Based on the above challenges, managing one's mental models emerges as a necessity because it is fundamentally embedded in survival and instincts. Many theoretical frameworks can assist regarding it, for example, by acknowledging the lack of universal validity of mental models, a cognitive awareness can develop regarding their shortcomings (Schraw, 1998); by understanding one's own behavioural response to stimuli, triggers can be identified that activate mental models for better personal control of the use of mental models instead of their use as an automated behavioural response (de Graaf, 2019); and self-reflection of the natural evolution of mental models within oneself can link it to the psyche's mental and physical protection notions associated with mental models (Hamilton, 1970). As such, self-leadership of mental models need to, firstly, thoroughly question the mental model's validity. Additionally, similar to physical or diagrammatic models, design thinking can assist in moulding mental models. 'In order to develop a capacity for design thinking ...[one] must first acknowledge and confront their built-in bias for exploitation and analytical thinking, their tendency to favor reliability over validity' (Leavy, 2010, p. 8). As such, even when validity is assessed in favour of the mental model, it is the degree of reliability that needs a cognitive assessment and interrogation through the rigorous divergent and convergent approaches of design thinking (whole brain thinking and the drawing in of multiple perspectives).

It can be argued that the role of a leader is to facilitate momentum for movement into new paradigms, thus advancing and developing/growing oneself in the case of self-leadership or followers in the case of leadership. To do so, mental models of the followers need to be challenged, critiqued, reformed, moulded, or shattered, based on the leader's assessment of the requirement at hand. The assessment of the requirement and desired pace of change to new paradigms can be argued to be the ongoing and necessary challenge for leadership. Since mental models are a natural working of the mind and form an integral part of information processing and organization by the mind that contribute to one's instincts, intuitions, as well as cognitive responses, they cannot be eliminated. Similar to the challenges of adoption of a novel design, where new designs leverage on mental models for enhanced acceptance (exploitation) or opt for a more dramatic shift in design to hurl adopters into a new paradigm (exploration), options for moulding mental models present an array between the polar opposite choices of exploitation and exploration. One of the attributes of design thinking is that it caters to attempts for achieving the most effective balance between these two. The balancing act of these opposing forces can be argued to be the nature of the paradox for leadership – the balancing of 'exploration' of new mental models and 'exploitation' of current mental models for achieving the optimal pace of change into new paradigms by leaders.

Mental models can also be reinforced through agreement by others with similar mental models. Though the psyche is more sensitive to reinforcement during childhood, positive or negative reinforcements of one's mental models can occur throughout life. Reassurances of mental models by those in leadership positions who may share one's mental models present an influential reinforcement. Leaders may either confirm one's mental models by voicing them out loud and lead society or organizations based on those or by designing things that operate in a way that provides positive reinforcement (Skinner, 2009). The reassurance of one's mental models boosts one's self-esteem by feelings of having been proved right, that is, through acknowledgement of accuracy of the information processing and organizational ability (Loughlin & Alexander, 2012), hinting towards one's wisdom. They also limit the need for exploration or challenging one's mental models, which can be anxiety-inducing. From a leadership point of view, tapping into people's mental models is founded on positive affect for the followers and can allow for enhanced willingness to transition to new paradigms (Guba & Lincoln, 2008), yet ensuring ease of transition by managing negative affect associated with change. By doing so, such leadership can help their followers, either for nations, civilizations, societies, communitites, or employees, by encouraging people to gradually absorb new information to slowly change their mental models to eventually lead to reformed ones and subsequent advancement to new paradigms.

However, there is an abundance of shortcomings of mental models, primary amongst these is epistemological challenges (Byrne, 2016) which question the sources, relevance, and scope of information used for building mental models, as well as the nature of the knowledge, its justification, and rationality. Shortcomings of mental models have led to immense suffering, including female circumcision, Nazi atrocities, as well as prejudice against groups of people, to name a few. Such pieces of evidence are stark warnings against tapping into people's superficial mental models or 'exploitation' of uncritical mental models, to propel oneself into leadership roles by reinforcement of flawed societal (Werhane et al., 2011) or shared in-group mental models (Tajfel & Turner, 1979). Such examples, together with fast pace change in paradigms the world faces today, justify the need for enlightened and conscientized leadership to shatter societal mental models and enforce the 'exploration' of new mental models for a radical leap to a paradigm shift (Riggins & Slaughter, 2006). While the pace of change of such a transition may leave some followers behind, the values-based cause (such as human rights violations, continued discrimination and gender inequality, or irrelevant/out-of-touch organizational approaches and stances) may well justify such an approach by leaders.

Enablers and Stumbling Blocks

According to neuroscientists, the treatment of lived experiences and perspectives as 'truths' reduces the load that mental models place on our working memories, but also raises the consequence of systematic errors in deduction – which we term as stumbling blocks. One of the tenants of stumbling blocks is the key limitation that individuals can only filter new information according to the closeness with what their mental models can perceive as the 'truth' and may simply reject evidence that does not comply with this (Hastie & Dawes, 2001). This is extended when we then actively seek out information that confirms our current understanding, a phenomenon described as confirmation bias (Klayman & Ha, 1987). Kahneman (2011) takes this further, describing our excessive confidence in what we believe we know and our apparent inability to acknowledge the full extent of our ignorance and the uncertainty of the world we live in (Kahneman, 2011). An example might be a white, privileged male who views others, particularly women and people of colour, in lesser terms (and stereotyped notions of credibility, competence, intelligence, and even humanhood) as a result of a deeply rooted system of self, reinforced through how history and the media have portrayed and continues to portray others, as well as through the lack of diversity in his personal networks and the US- and European-dominated literature he chooses to only engage with. Even emotions and moods, which become internal markers and prime individuals for future events through past decisions, are known to affect our mental models and memory, dictate and constrain which bits of information are used by individuals, and ultimately (often incorrectly) influence our choices and often cause us to repeat unhelpful behaviours (Friedman, 2004; Zey, 1992). Our research has unearthed several stumbling blocks, and we list a few salient ones here: individuals moving in social networks that reinforce their embedded beliefs and assumptions (treating it as 'common wisdom'), individuals hearing only what they expect to hear from others; individuals unable to accept the subjectivity of reality and 'truth,' when individuals have incomplete information they fill in the gaps with assumptions and their 'stories,' and, assuming that others, not in their close social network, look at the world the same way that they do.

Alternatively, an innate orientation towards learning and purposeful curiosity (April & April, 2007) serves to overcome stereotypical and irrelevant mental models – which we term as enablers. Such learning and curiosity could manifest latticed mental models emanating from such activities as, for example, exposure to the literary and performing arts (if technical in background) and to science (if artistic in background), exploring activities related to psychological archetypes which are different from one's own, having an interest outside of one's work expertise and technical domain, and a love for reading as broadly and deeply as possible from a multitude of disciples as suggested by the billionaire Chairman of Berkshire Hathaway, Warren Buffett. In our hypothetical white, male example above, we know from the intergroup contact theory research of Pettigrew and Tropp (2006) and others, for instance, that in-group and out-group identities can either be managed in ways that deepen prejudice and cause social conflict, or they can be facilitated in such a way that they create an understanding of the other and a willingness to compromise for the sake of shared values and the achievement of the common good. Our research has unearthed a number of other enablers, and we list a few salient ones here: individuals regularly share their ideas and are open to/ask for critical and constructive feedback from others and vice versa (reciprocal enquiry); individuals make their assumptions explicit for examination by others in dialogue; individuals purposefully seek out and regularly engage others who are different from themselves; individuals adopt an orientation of being willing to 'let go' (change acceptance) in order to be transformed by others' experiences and/or perspectives; and, individuals spend reflective time with themselves, conducting a robust interrogation of the 'truths' and assumptions which they hold. Munger (2005, p. 55) neatly summarizes the necessary orientation: '... just as multiple factors shape almost every system, multiple models from a variety of disciplines, applied with fluency, are needed to understand that system'.

Chapter Takeaways

While mental models are integral to how the mind operates and serve a vital role in survival, they are susceptible to errors arising from a host of aspects of their creation. In recognition of both the need for mental models and their susceptibility to failures, it can be argued that mental models need to be flexible. This entails that they need to be built, broken, and reformed as and when required, thus requiring self-leadership for managing one's own mental models or leadership for moulding followers' mental models. In a world that is changing at a faster pace than ever before, the risk of mental models going stale is higher, thus further supporting this need. By limiting stumbling blocks to their reform and facilitating their evolution through enablers, an optimal degree of flexibility in mental models can be aspired towards for ensuring their continued usefulness. From a leadership perspective, the paradox lies in balancing of 'exploration' of new mental models and 'exploitation' of current mental models for achieving the optimal pace of change to progressing towards new paradigms. Design thinking presents a helpful framework for attempting to achieve the most effective balance between these two.

Reflection Questions

1. Identify a situation/s where your mental model/s failed you to assess their degree of validity.
2. Evaluate instances of mental model failure/trauma that led to changes in your mental model.
3. Assess if there are scenarios where the new refined mental model is likely to fail again to test its reliability.
4. What enablers can assist you in the continual refining of your mental models to minimize failure and/or ensure that your ideas and perspectives remain relevant?
5. Which stumbling blocks may hinder your progressive refinement of your mental models or stop you from experiencing more/all of reality?

References

April, K., & April, A. (2007). Growing leaders in emergent markets: Leadership enhancement in the new South Africa. *Journal of Management Education, 31*(2), 214–244. https://doi.org/10.1177/1052562906297595

Baumeister, R., Dale, K., & Sommer, K. (1998). Freudian defense mechanisms and empirical findings in modern social psychology: Reaction formation, projection, displacement, undoing, isolation, sublimation, and denial. *Journal of Personality, 66*(6), 1081–1124. https://doi.org/10.1111/1467-6494.00043

Berger, P., & Luckmann, T. (1966). *The social construction of reality: A treatise in the sociology of knowledge*. Doubleday.

Buckingham, W., Burnham, D., Hill, C., King, P. J., Marenbon, J., & Weeks, M. (2011). *The philosophy book: The big ideas simply explained*. Dorling Kindersley.

Byrne, D. (2016). *Research project planner*. SAGE Publications.

Chapman, J. A., & Ferfolja, T. (2001). Fatal flaws situations. *Journal of Intellectual Capital, 2*(4), 398–409. https://doi.org/10.1108/EUM0000000006087

Craik, K. (1943). *The nature of explanation*. Cambridge University Press.

Crenshaw, K. (1991). Mapping the margins: Intersectionality, identity politics, and violence against women of color. *Stanford Law Review, 43*(6), 1241–1299. https://doi.org/10.2307/1229039

Darwin, C. (1859). *On the origin of species*. John Murray.

Davis, J. P., Eisenhardt, K. M., & Bingham, C. B. (2007). Developing theory through simulation methods. *Academy of Management Review, 32*(2), 480–499. https://doi.org/10.5465/amr.2007.24351453

de Graaf, F. J. (2019). Ethics and behavioural theory: How do professionals assess their mental models? *Journal of Business Ethics, 157*(4), 933–947. https://doi.org/10.1007/s10551-018-3955-6

Friedman, S. (2004). Learning to make effective decisions: Changing beliefs as a prelude to action. *The Learning Organization, 11*(2), 110–128. https://doi.org/10.1108/09696470410521583

Goethals, G. R., & Allison, S. T. (2012). Making heroes: The construction of courage, competence and virtue. In J. Olson & M. Zanna (Eds.), *Advances in experimental social psychology* (Vol. 46, 1st ed., pp. 183–235). Academic Press.

Guba, E. G., & Lincoln, Y. S. (2008). Paradigmatic controversies, contradictions, and emerging confluences. In N. K. Denzin & Y. S. Lincoln (Eds.), *The landscape of qualitative research* (2nd ed., pp. 255–286). Sage.

Hamilton, W. D. (1970). Selfish and spiteful behaviour in an evolutionary model. *Nature, 228*(5277), 1218–1220. https://doi.org/10.1038/2281218a0

Hastie, R., & Dawes, R. M. (2001). *Rational choice in an uncertain world*. Sage.

Hewitt, J. (2017). *This is the hidden risk of automation that no one is talking about*. Retrieved July 31, 2020, from World Economic Forum website: https://www.weforum.org/agenda/2017/11/automation-automated-job-risk-robot-bored-boredom-effort-fourth-industrial-revolution/

Howard, J. C. (2009). Why didn't Darwin discover Mendel's laws? *Journal of Biology, 8*(2), 15.1–15.8. https://doi.org/10.1186/jbiol123

Johnson-Laird, P. N. (1983). A computational analysis of consciousness. *Cognition & Brain Theory, 6*(4), 499–508.

Johnson-Laird, P. N. (2013). Mental models and cognitive change. *Journal of Cognitive Psychology, 25*(2), 131–138. https://doi.org/10.1080/20445911.2012.759935

Jones, N., Ross, H., Lynam, T., Perez, P., & Leitch, A. (2011). Mental models: An interdisciplinary synthesis of theory and methods. *Ecology and Society, 16*(1), 46–60.

Klayman, J., & Ha, Y.-W. (1987). Confirmation, disconfirmation, and information in hypothesis testing. *Psychological Review, 94*(2), 211–228. https://doi.org/10.1037/0033-295X.94.2.211

Leavy, B. (2010). Design thinking – A new mental model of value innovation. *Strategy & Leadership, 38*(3), 5–14. https://doi.org/10.1108/10878571011042050

Lejeune, H., Richelle, M., & Wearden, J. H. (2006). About Skinner and time: Behavior-analytic contributions to research on animal timing. *Journal of the Experimental Analysis of Behavior, 85*(1), 125–142. https://doi.org/10.1901/jeab.2006.85.04

Loughlin, S. M., & Alexander, P. A. (2012). Explicating and exemplifying empiricist and cognitivist paradigms in the study of human learning. In *Paradigms in theory construction* (pp. 273–296). Springer. https://doi.org/10.1007/978-1-4614-0914-4_15

Mfecane, S. (2016). "Ndiyindoda " [I am a man]: Theorising Xhosa masculinity. *Anthropology Southern Africa, 39*(3), 204–214. https://doi.org/10.1080/23323256.2016.1208535

Mitchell, M. (1996). Darwin's dangerous idea. *Complexity, 2*(1), 32–36.

Morrell, R. (1998). Of boys and men: Masculinity and gender in Southern African studies. *Journal of Southern African Studies, 24*(4), 605–630. https://doi.org/10.1080/03057079808708593

Munger, C. T. (2005). *Poor Charlie's almanack: The wit and widom of Charles T. Munger, Expanded*. Walsworth Publishing Company.

Pande, M., & Bharathi, S. V. (2020). Theoretical foundations of design thinking – A constructivism learning approach to design thinking. *Thinking Skills and Creativity, 36*(2019), 100637. https://doi.org/10.1016/j.tsc.2020.100637

Pavlov, I. P. (1929). In G. V. Anrep (Ed.), *Conditioned reflexes: An investigation of the physiological activity of the cerebral cortex*. Oxford University Press.

Pettigrew, T. F., & Tropp, L. R. (2006). A meta-analytic test of intergroup contact theory. *Journal of Personality and Social Psychology, 90*(5), 751–783.

Renaud, K., & van Biljon, J. (2008). Predicting technology acceptance and adoption by the elderly. *Proceedings of the 2008 Annual Research Conference of the South African Institute of Computer Scientists and Information Technologists on IT Research in Developing Countries Riding the Wave of Technology – SAICSIT '08, 338*, 210–219. https://doi.org/10.1145/1456659.1456684

Riggins, F. J., & Slaughter, K. T. (2006). The role of collective mental models in IOS adoption: Opening the black box of rationality in RFID deployment. *Proceedings of the 39th Annual Hawaii International Conference on System Sciences (HICSS'06), 8*, 184c–184c. https://doi.org/10.1109/HICSS.2006.479.

Rook, L. (2013). Mental models: A robust definition. *The Learning Organization, 20*(1), 38–47. https://doi.org/10.1108/09696471311288519

Rushton, J. P. (1995). *Race, evolution, and behavior: A life history perspective*. Transaction Publishers.

Schraw, G. (1998). Promoting general metacognitive awareness. *Instructional Science, 26*(1–2), 113–125. https://doi.org/10.1007/978-94-017-2243-8_1

Senge, P. (1990). *The fifth discipline: The art and practice of the learning organization*. Currency Doubleday.

Shepherd, D. A., & Suddaby, R. (2017). Theory building: A review and integration. *Journal of Management, 43*(1), 59–86. https://doi.org/10.1177/0149206316647102

Skinner, B. (2009). About behaviorism (1974). In *Foundations of psychological thought: A history of psychology* (pp. 261–278). Sage.

Smit, H. (2014). *The depth facilitatator's handbook: Transforming group dynamics*. Moonshine Media.

Tajfel, H., & Turner, J. C. (1979). An integrative theory of inter-group conflict. In W. G. Austin & S. Worchel (Eds.), *The social psychology of inter-group relations* (pp. 33–47). Brooks/Cole.

Thomas, J. C., & Segal, D. L. (2006). *Comprehensive handbook of personality and psychopathology: Personality and everyday functioning* (Vol. 2). John Wiley & Sons.

Unterhalter, E. (2000). The work of the nation: Heroic masculinity in South African autobiographical writing of the anti-apartheid struggle. *European Journal of Development Research, 12*(2), 139–156. https://doi.org/10.1080/09578810008426770

Werhane, P. H., Hartman, L. P., Moberg, D., Englehardt, E., Pritchard, M., & Parmar, B. (2011). Social constructivism, mental models, and problems of obedience. *Journal of Business Ethics, 100*(1), 103–118. https://doi.org/10.1007/s10551-011-0767-3

Wilson, A.-M. (2013). How the methods used to eliminate foot binding in China can be employed to eradicate female genital mutilation. *Journal of Gender Studies, 22*(1), 17–37. https://doi.org/10.1080/09589236.2012.681182

Zey, M. (1992). *Decision making: An alternative to rational choice models*. Sage.

Chapter 11
Nurturing Sustainability as a Future-Oriented Strategy

Roger Hilton and Diane McCann

Abstract Leaders must be aligned both spiritually and emotionally as well as delivering sustainable outcomes for the businesses that they lead. For a business, the commitment of all stakeholders including the board, employees, and suppliers means an obligation to deliver quality and service excellence to its customers to ensure satisfaction and long-term loyalty while ensuring meeting all necessary compliance and government regulations where applicable. All the stakeholders and particularly leaders must be conscious in delivering this commitment. Consciousness means being able to make choices, not from a reactive mind but an emotionally attuned place that supports the protecting of the planet and ensures all people enjoy peace and prosperity and economic survival. Company executives need to develop a strategy to create a culture of sustainable practice to balance profit, people, and the planet, and all leaders within the business from the senior management down to the shop floor and all customer-facing staff must be mindful and be a part of the deployment of this strategy. We are living in extraordinary times – a world of limited resources and challenges that need solving. Business has a huge role to play here as we transition from one way of "doing business" to another. These extraordinary times are not only due to the 2020 pandemic but general changes in society towards assessing climate change, diversity of leadership, and heartfelt communication. We can take the safe path and do what we are "expected" to do, make profit, etc. Or we can listen to a calling that comes from somewhere deep inside ourselves that asks for more. We are at a tipping point of a new future that will impact generations to come, and we can either destroy ourselves or create a whole new world, a world that works for everyone. Business can be used to improve lives; there is a movement happening, a movement of people helping people – being a pioneer in new areas, not even considered just a few short years ago.

R. Hilton (✉)
Lean Sigma Institute, Armadale, VIC, Australia
e-mail: rhilton@leansigmainstitute.com.au

D. McCann
Beyond the Ordinary, North Haven, South Australia, Australia
e-mail: diane@bto.net.au

J. Marques (ed.), *Innovative Leadership in Times of Compelling Changes*, Management, Change, Strategy and Positive Leadership, https://doi.org/10.1007/978-3-030-67258-4_11

Keywords Sustainability · Alignment · Heartfelt · Excellence · Consciousness

Introduction

The US Environmental Protection Agency defines sustainability as "meeting the needs of the present without compromising the ability of future generations to meet their own needs." In other words, sustainability attempts to balance the needs of people today with the future needs of our children and the natural systems that sustain all life. The *United Nations Sustainable Development Goals* are a universal call to action to end poverty, protect the planet, and ensure that all people enjoy peace and prosperity by 2030. The triple bottom line is a framework or theory that recommends that companies commit to focus on social and environmental concerns just as they do on profits. The triple bottom line posits that instead of one bottom line, there should be three: profit, people, and the planet. The triple bottom line seeks to gauge a corporation's level of commitment to corporate social responsibility and its impact on the environment over time.

In an evolving, more mindful consumer landscape, sustainability and business are now inextricably linked. There is a growing importance for businesses to focus on sustainability with shifting public opinion.

Leaders must be aligned to these Sustainable Development Goals, both spiritually and emotionally as well as delivering sustainable outcomes for the businesses that they lead. For a business, the commitment of all stakeholders including the board, employees, and suppliers means an obligation to deliver quality and service excellence to its customers to ensure satisfaction and long-term loyalty while ensuring meeting all necessary compliance and government regulations where applicable.

All the stakeholders and particularly leaders must be conscious in delivering this commitment. Consciousness means being able to make choices, not from a reactive mind but an emotionally attuned place that supports the protecting of the planet and ensures all people enjoy peace and prosperity and economic survival.

Company executives need to develop a strategy to create a culture of sustainable practice to balance profit, people, and the planet, and all leaders within the business from the senior management down to the shop floor and all customer-facing staff must be mindful and be a part of the deployment of this strategy.

We are living in extra ordinary times – a world of limited resources and challenges that need solving. Business has a huge role to play here as we transition from one way of "doing business" to another. These extraordinary times are not only due to the 2020 pandemic but general changes in society towards assessing climate change, diversity of leadership, and heartfelt communication.

We can take the safe path and do what we are "expected" to do, make profit, etc.

Or we can listen to a calling that comes from somewhere deep inside ourselves that asks for more. We are at a tipping point of a new future that will impact generations to come, and we can either destroy ourselves or create a whole new world, a world that works for everyone. Business can be used to improve lives; there is a movement happening, a movement of people helping people – being a pioneer in new areas, not even considered just a few short years ago.

In this chapter, we discuss the necessary conditions for businesses to adhere and nurture sustainability as a way of balancing profit, people, and the planet. This involves recognizing the need to continuously improve, innovate, and reimagine our businesses and how leaders play a significant role in this sustainability. Importantly, we also present the key characteristics of leaders and what constitutes spiritual and emotional leadership in driving a culture to nurture sustainability while recognizing that these changes and a new movement will be the new norm.

Nurturing a Culture of Balancing People, Profit, and Planet as a Future Strategy

In September 2015, the United Nations General Assembly adopted the "2030 Agenda for Sustainable Development," with 17 ambitious, universal goals to transform our world. UNESCO ensures that the role of culture is recognized through a majority of the Sustainable Development Goals (SDGs), including those focusing on quality education, sustainable cities, the environment, economic growth, sustainable consumption and production patterns, peaceful and inclusive societies, gender equality, and food security. UNESCO's work promoting cultural diversity and UNESCO's culture conventions are key to the implementation of the 2030 Agenda for Sustainable Development.

In an evolving, more mindful consumer landscape, sustainability and business are now inextricably linked. There is a growing importance for businesses to focus on sustainability with shifting public opinion to look after the planet and the people. Company executives need to be conscious and develop a strategy to create a culture of sustainable practice to balance profit, people, and the planet, and all leaders within the business from the senior management down to the shop floor and all staff must be mindful to ensure that the strategy is deployed and sustained.

Developing a culture of sustainability is important on the path towards sustainable development. The importance of cultural sustainability lies within its influential power over the people, as decisions made by leaders that are made within the context of society are heavily impacted by the beliefs of that society.

It is clear that cultural sustainability means different things to different companies. Certainly, no one can tell you what sustainability should mean for your company. There is an opportunity to create and nurture clever conversations about nurturing sustainability. These conversations need to be honest and authentic as they will help everyone feel ownership of the final outcome which will yield enormous dividends. The working environment needs to be safe to articulate these honest and authentic communication especially between leaders and their peers and their direct reports. A cross-functional mindset is critical to create a culture of sustainable performance.

Sustainable performance is enhanced through a number of key competencies as follows:

1. It is important that leadership exists at all levels of the organization, and these leaders need to be capable and confident in terms of both in hard and soft skills.
2. The culture of the organization needs to inclusive, positive, open, and trusting.
3. Change agents need to be competent both in hard and soft skills in order to obtain buy-in from all stakeholders to drive improvements in terms of minimizing waste and reducing errors in processes that are critical to all stakeholders.
4. Teams need to be formed by project leaders who are aware of team dynamics and tacit behaviors of team members and other stakeholders to ensure improvements are managed and embedded in the organization.
5. Good quality data needs to be available to monitor performance and present an overview of the status to the leadership and the level of sustainability in real time.

These change agents need to be generalists more than specialists to bring people together and drive a culture of cooperation on sustainability. This will have the benefit of creating a cohort of critical thinkers who can be rotated into varying jobs at all levels as a way to advance the sustainability agenda along the way, diffusing institutional knowledge throughout the company. To hire and promote generalists to drive a culture of cooperation on sustainability is not easy because it requires a new breed of executives in human resources. This is happening to some extent with a new breed of executives classified as leaders of people and culture.

Sustainability is a new way of thinking about old topics. And in a field with so much novelty, there is so much still to learn and nurture. In sustainability, the best is not that far ahead, and the worst is not that far behind as well. Companies must stay away from negativity when discussing sustainability, either internally or externally. Criticizing people for lack of compliance to or support of sustainability only serves to shut them down. In building a culture around sustainable performance, companies must stick to the positive. There is a choice – love or fear of everything we do. Thank people for their support, encourage engagement, and talk to the positive outcomes associated with behavior. Negativity and fear are a final line of defense if nothing else is working and should be used accordingly. People work better when they feel good and this creates energy and momentum. Companies should evaluate all of their conversations, gauge them for any hidden meanings and tone, and look for opportunities to shift the messaging when and where appropriate.

No matter where a company is on its sustainability journey, it can go further. The more its people are aligned, the faster the progress. In trying to set goals for your company, thinking about them in terms of people will help ensure success.

In the future, there will continue to be significant disruption for businesses and the people who lead them. The current 2020 pandemic is one such significant disruption. Within this disruption, businesses are losing sight of sustainable practices; they are moving to survival with a focus on economic and social issues; that is the bottom line and the safety of all the stakeholders. Businesses still need to continuously improve and innovate and nurture sustainability in the face of significant disruption to the supply chain, customer demand, and market need.

During significant disruption, sometimes business continuity plans will only be partly helpful. The current 2020 pandemic has blown many business continuity plans flying out of the window. Businesses have needed to reimage themselves from face to face to online, and some have needed help from governments, who have stepped to assist, but the legacy has been enormous for the generations to come.

In an era of population growth, increasing economic competition, and environmental challenges ranging from climate change to air pollution and decreasing water levels to rising energy costs, strategic planning is essential to our future and the well-being of our communities.

It is useful to understand the best sustainability practices currently in use and know how a community can move from an idea to a plan to successful actions thereby forming a future strategy to nurture sustainability. Clearly, climate action should be part of businesses future strategy. We need robust and accurate data and performance measurements to assess the contribution and impact on climate change for those businesses needing to do so. Software systems can help communities create inventories and analyze impacts of actions on traditional air pollutants and greenhouse gas emissions. Communities in which businesses operate need to assess their strengths and weaknesses regarding transportation, land use planning, open space protection, energy, air quality and climate, water supply, storm water and wastewater and solid waste, and recycling. Businesses need to build a coalition of stakeholders to support environmental and social aspects of the triple bottom line. Nurturing and educating the employees of sustainable practice is a must.

Even the most successful sustainability planning effort needs a systematic approach for managing and reducing environmental impacts. Environmental management systems (EMS) provide a vetted framework that allows communities to address both specific and broad environmental issues in order to realize desired outcomes. By addressing root causes and integrating environmental approaches into everyday operations, environmental stewardship can become a priority across your entire organization. Every EMS should follow Deming's continuous improvement Plan-Do-Check-Act cycle. The Plan phase is used to analyze current state of environmental impacts and legal requirements and then setting appropriate environmental objectives. The Do phase moves to implementing specific programs, projects, and processes to meet objectives. The Check phase includes internal auditing, monitoring progress, assessing successes and failures, identifying areas for improvement, and benchmarking. The Act phase is for reviewing progress, performing management reviews, and implementing improvements to the plan, which can start the planning process again.

Supply chains need to be sustainable through Green Product design, preparing for disaster logistics, sustaining procurement strategy, creating closed loops with reverse logistics, and sustainable packing strategies. Supply chains need to be resilient and adapt to the ever-changing environment both locally and globally. The food supply chain is booming and so is online retail. Some businesses are sustaining their economic, social, and environmental practices, but many businesses can only see the need to protect the cash flow and continued employment of their staff when there is significant disruption like the 2020 pandemic that has been a significant challenge by all nations and peoples.

Characteristics of Leaders to Lead the Nurturing of Sustainable Practice as a Future Strategy

Leaders must be aligned to these UN Sustainable Development Goals, both spiritually and emotionally as well as delivering sustainable outcomes for the businesses that they lead. For a business, the commitment of all stakeholders including the board, employees, and suppliers means an obligation to deliver quality and service excellence to its customers to ensure satisfaction and long-term loyalty while ensuring meeting all necessary compliance and government regulations where applicable. All the stakeholders must be conscious in delivering this commitment. Consciousness means being able to make choices, not from a reactive mind but an emotionally attuned place that supports the protecting of the planet and ensures all people enjoy peace and prosperity and economic survival.

The pandemic is also a challenge for leaders unlike any they have ever faced before, forcing an abrupt dislocation of how employees work, how customers behave, how supply chains function, and even what ultimately constitutes business performance. McKinsey in their latest article in July 2020 suggests that CEOs have shifted how they lead in expedient and ingenious ways. A good CEO is always scanning for signals and helping the organization deliver fine-tuned responses. A great CEO will see that this moment is a unique opportunity for self-calibration, with profound implications for the organization.

The interesting point is whether leaders continue with this new mindset. There are many facets to being a leader, and the difference between a great leader and a mediocre one is as vast as an ocean. Leaders definitely need heart and courage; however, it is also important to consider the human side of leaders and what goes on underneath the façade that everyone shows to the world, so let us take a journey from the outside into the heart of it all.

From an outside business perspective, one of the jobs of leaders and management is to encourage creative lateral thinking that will benefit the company and the people working in it. How to do that? Dr. R. Buckminister, author of many books (including Critical Path, first published 1981) spent 60 years rethinking and relentlessly challenging every assumption about structure, function, materials, technology, services, distribution, mobility, collaboration, information, and social norms. His major principle was doing "vastly more with invisibly less." His constant goal was a much more efficient equitable distribution of planetary resources to enable the survival and ongoing evolution of the human species. In his book *12 Degrees of Freedom*, he proclaimed there are 12 solutions to every challenge…so therefore one answer for leaders would be to surround yourself with people who are very different from you in all areas and explore all the offered solutions. Diversity of opinion is not a threat; in today's world, it is a necessity. We all have to have a purpose, and as Sinek (2011) says in his book *Start with Why*, people need a reason to get out of bed! Many times people who have much to offer the company they work for have bosses/leaders who do not want change because "it worked in the past!" that old adage "If it isn't broken, don't fix it" may have been true once, but in today's fast-changing world, we have to be willing to change in a split second, and not doing so does not allow the innovators to shine. Sometimes those same innovators get ridiculed, told it will never work, etc., and that in turn decreases their job satisfaction and happiness.

One of the authors knew a man who was headhunted from Europe. At first, he was excited to move his entire family from to Australia, but over a few years he became "dull, dry, and disheartened." He had no freedom to implement his ideas and thus became robotic in his job. He lost his joy, and this reflected in his family life; his kids were growing up fast, and he was too exhausted and empty to give them time when he came home so his relationship with them deteriorated as did the one with his wife, who felt she was doing all the parenting and loving of their two children. Then along came the lockdown of 2020, and suddenly he was home with his family; he started spending quality time with each of his kids. He would take his sons individually on walks every night and actually talk with them for the first time in a long time. His relationships all improved so much that when his state actually opened up, he realized he was not getting any pleasure from his job. He had reconnected with his kids who were thriving, his relationship was again passionate and intimate, and he felt alive again inside; the difference was so obvious that he knew he could not go back to the "grindstone" so he resigned. A wonderful man with many skills now lost to that company because their bottom line was more about profit and not honoring the needs of their employees, which in his case was to innovate without criticism, do what he was hired to do without having to fight for every inch of change, and have more family time.

All human beings are a product of their own environment from conception up. We have layer upon layer of suppressed emotions from the time we were first told to "Man up" or "Boys don't cry" as a little boy to "What are you crying about now?" to little girls. We learn to ignore our feelings and do as we are told, hiding our emotions for fear of being taunted at school or at home. It takes courage to do the work required to discover and then release those old pent-up emotions, but it absolutely needs to be done in order to be a fully authentic human being, who in turn makes a great leader because there is a safety around people who are emotionally available which allows others to grow and thrive, instigate, and innovate.

Likewise, there is little or no safety in people who cannot allow themselves to be vulnerable or who are unapproachable. These people are almost guaranteed to have difficult relationships with their children and of course their partners, not to mention co-workers. Men think that they are doing a wonderful job; they work hard, long hours, earn good money, and support a family, yet so many men come home 1 day to find their partner has left them, taken the kids, etc. or wants a divorce. How does that happen? They say: "I had no idea." The bottom line is that relationships, whether professional or personal, are not something people are taught how to do! When we are young, we think they just happen. Many people do not talk about what is important to them in a relationship, be it professional or personal. Men often assume that women want stability, a home, and financial security; however when asked, most conscious women say they would rather have intimacy and a "present" partner willing to talk about things from the heart not the head and to share the load of parenting. Even for couples who consider their relationship to be equal, it takes exceptional navigation on both parts to manage a tricky dual career. Leaders of both genders often find a lack in their emotional/sexual lives regardless of the success of their professional one, which leads to unhappiness or even affairs! In fact, there are increasing divorce rates in people in their fifties and sixties; 50% of these divorces are initiated by the women. Women leaders often quit their jobs as well as their marriages because of old patriarchal attitudes and a lack of recognition.

Let us Delve Deeper

The subconscious is where all the old stuff from childhood is stored. Did you know that only 2–10% of every day is spent being conscious? The rest is subconscious, and this is where we react from. Everyone has had experiences where something triggered you, maybe at home before you left for work, maybe on the road, or maybe a work situation when you arrived. Suddenly you find yourself reacting instead of responding. How many times have you spoken to someone (especially your kids) the way a parent spoke to you, and, if you are aware of it, you regret it instantly. Perception is everything, yet we are not our perceptions; we simply react through the filter of the lens we see through, and that lens was created through our past. Weissman and Montana (2013) creator of The LifeLine Technique says, "By raising our consciousness and processing the reactive emotions, limiting beliefs and traumatic memories that live within our subconscious mind, we are able to transform stress into growth. Our body runs off old memories and thus it is always being triggered by our past. Every 6–8 s our body jettisons into the past and we react from there. Memories create imprints and imprints are like fingerprints on our soul."

Science now knows that those memories may not even be ours; they could be our parent's memories or their parents or even their parents. What is inherited family trauma? Simply put by Wolynn (2016), many of us relive the tragedies from previous generations, and we rarely make the link often resulting in unexplained depression, anxiety, obsessive thoughts, and physical symptoms. Scientists are now calling it "secondary PTSD." We do not know why we feel this way, and yet we react from those feelings day in, day out. So, the job of a great leader is to continually process one's own emotions so that you can be consciously fully present in the moment, not in the past or in the future which is where most people live.

What we see above the water in Fig. 11.1 is not necessarily what is going on underneath, and healing what is underneath makes everyone a better human being, thus a better leader.

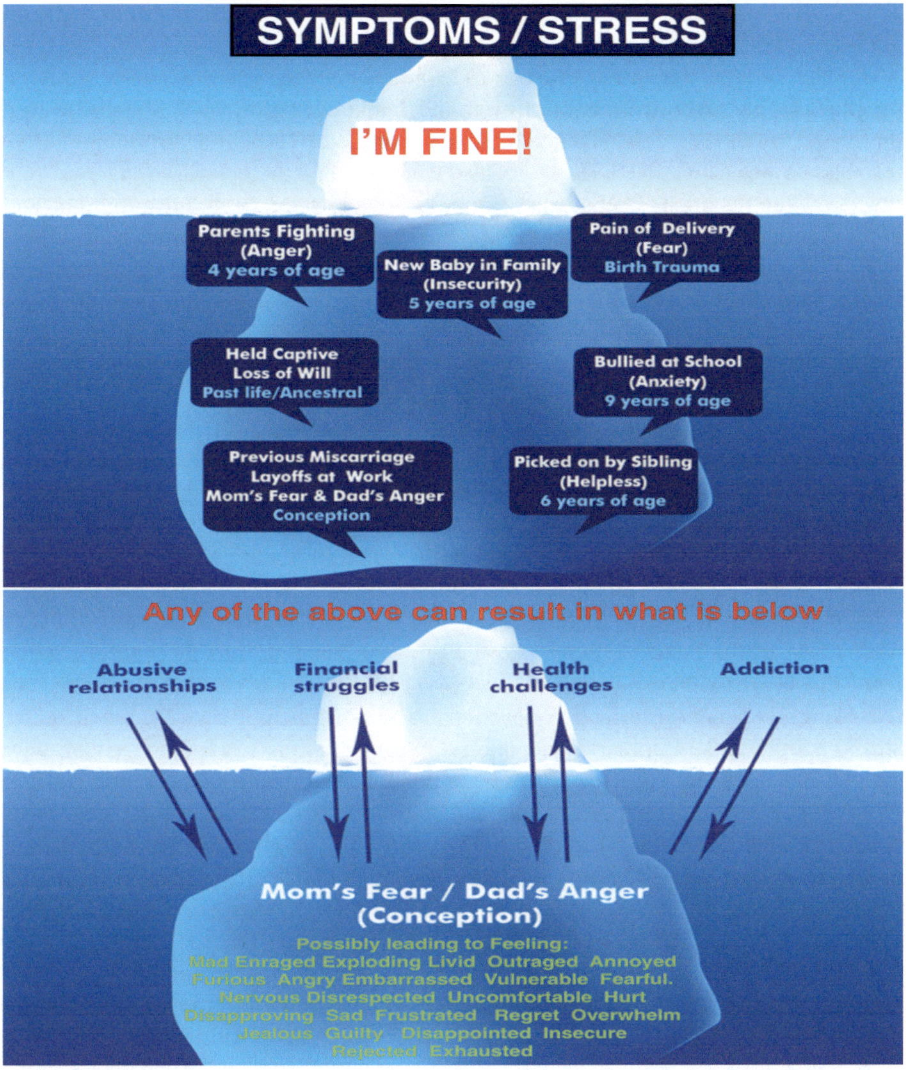

Fig. 11.1 Symptoms/stress reality

Bradshaw (1992), the father of family therapy, believes every family is dysfunctional in some way, shape, or form. For most of us, our environment did not serve us well as adults. Perhaps dad worked away all the time and was never around, and when he was home, he was emotionally unavailable. Perhaps mum was exhausted from child minding, cleaning, cooking, etc. and not emotionally available either. Maybe a parent died; maybe they divorced or fought. Maybe an addiction was involved. Each of which impinge on our ability to be who we really are. Three square meals and a roof over your head does not represent a healthy childhood, and yet that is what many of us got.

Rachel Yehuda, a neuroscientist from Mount Sinai Medical, did a great study on pregnant women who were at or close to the Trade Center on 9/11. She discovered that these mums as a consequence of 9/11 developed PTSD, and surprisingly, they also had babies who had PTSD. Holocaust survivors and their children share exactly the same gene changes in the exact same part of the same gene, meaning that you and I are more likely to have PTSD if one of our parents suffered from it, and thus, we are more likely to have melancholy personalities with bouts of depression. Perhaps not there all the time, but it shows up at major events in our lives, like getting married, becoming a parent, and breaking up in a relationship. What was your in utero experience like or your early childhood? Harmonize that and there is more of you available for your family and your job.

The HeartMath Institute (2020) created great computer programs designed to destress busy executives. You were probably taught that the heart responds to messages sent by the brain in the form of neural signals; however, the heart actually sends more signals to the brain than the other way around; these signals from the heart have a large substantial effect on brain function affecting many things from emotional processing to attention, perception, and problem solving. In essence the brain continually responds to the messages of the heart. During stress or negativity, the pattern of the heart rhythm is erratic and not ordered; thus the neural signals from the heart to the brain inhibit functions like thinking clearly, remembering, reasoning, and making effective decisions, a good indicator of why, when under stress, people make impulsive and often unwise decisions yet another reason why smart businesses and good leaders have in place modalities to support their staff.

Dr Bruce Lipton, scientist, ex-medical school professor, brought the science of epigenetics to the world. Lipton (2015) originally taught that the body was a machine, comprised of biochemicals which were controlled by genes; however, he discovered that our 50 trillion cells have their own intelligence, and it is that intelligence that creates the body. Our cells actually talk to us! We feel it through what we call symptoms or feelings or emotions. Business leaders often refer to it as a "gut feeling." We now know that the environment in utero does more to make us or break us than anything else.

So, what does all of this have to do with leaders? Well, depending on your experiences in the womb, your birth, and your first few years, it is now known that they literally impact how you "do" life. If you did not get nurtured enough, loved enough, cuddled enough; if you were talked down to, rejected, ignored, mistreated/abused; if you lived in an environment which was not conducive for healthy growth; etc., then shutting down the emotional self is the natural protective method all humans use to survive. This results in emotional unavailability, fears, depression, and not able to be "present," which in turn results in either a highly reactive personality (getting angry quickly, etc.) or a shutdown one; either way the outcome is dysfunctional relationships both at work and home. As adults how do we reopen those channels so that we may be all that we are and unlock our true potential?

To be a good leader, perhaps the first thing is to admit that all is not "fine" in one's world! Tell the truth to yourself about which areas need to be healed. Is it parental, sibling, emotional, sexual, financial, mental, or even spiritual? Then act on. Good leaders have mentors to assist them in business decisions, maybe a coach and absolutely a practitioner who can assist them to deal with the issues that inevitably come up for everyone on a daily basis.

There is a great documentary called "Reconnect" by Brian Rose from London Real, UK. He is in his 50s, runs marathons, has a screaming high D or A type personality, cannot relax, does not like holidays, and has to be the best at everything he does. He goes on a journey into his past, with the help of a South American shaman and discovers exactly why he does what he does, and the reason was a disconnection with a part of himself as a little 7 year old. If he had been told that beforehand, he would have denied it, but experiencing it actually released it and changed all his relationships into the future. So, a good leader is someone who is connected to himself and continually works on himself to release pent-up emotions.

Good Leaders from a Business Perspective

- Are great mentors and happy for those under them to rise above them.
- Have high EQ (emotional intelligence).
- Inspire and listen to everyone from the caretaker to the people on the floor.
- They are trustworthy, trust-giving, and loyal, and they walk their walk and talk their talk.
- They acknowledge staff often and from a place of authenticity making them feel valued.
- They are highly respected by everyone in the organization.
- They continue to learn both personally and professionally and innovate.

Good Leaders from an Emotive Perspective

- Have done and continue to do the work to peel off their layers, reparenting their inner child to the point where they feel safe as an adult, and thus are authentic in all their dealings, resulting in happier and more productive employees.
- Allow for the truth to be spoken, hearts to be open, fears to be shared, and tears to be shed, all without fear of vulnerability.
- Have empathy and compassion for their employees and create an environment that supports change on every level, e.g., provide resources like Massage, HeartMath technology, The LifeLine Technique, or various other modalities for the emotional well-being of staff. In the end that is much less expensive than lost hours of work through nonproduction and sick days.

- A good leader recognizes their own core which is one of loving who they are and living according to their real values and integrity thus making a difference in the lives of others.
- When a human being does what they do for a loving instead of a living, the business is successful.
- Passion for what you do is a gift, and people love seeing that passion because it is actually highly contagious.

Good Questions to Ask Leaders Are as Follows

1. Who are you?
2. In an ideal world, if you had an abundance of money and time, what would you be doing right now?
3. What are you here to give?

Some Simple Steps

To find your leadership ability, here are some simple steps.

- Find a practitioner to help us uncover what is under the layers of "I'm fine," the stress, and the lack of connection with ourselves; never mind other people.
- Join a men's group or a woman's circle, somewhere you can be fully validated just by being there. Many people have a knee jerk reaction to that idea; however, to be in a safe place where you can speak from "I" or not is an incredibly freeing experience which requires huge courage, but these spaces offer a sense of connection and release which is why they are growing exponentially. No one asks what you do for a living or what car you drive or footie club you support. All that matters is what is in your heart.

Businesses generally offer lots of How-To workshops and corporate events, but perhaps they should offer personal development seminars to begin the process of unravelling so that people are happier and more productive. I once had a participant at my workshop for women who was from Ireland and worked for a huge multinational company. Her job was Energy Manager, and I jokingly asked her if she went around switching on lights!! She said her job description involved speaking with employees daily to determine where they were at and were they happy, sad, stressed, or thriving, and whatever she determined, she directed them to either a masseuse (on premises), a HeartMath session, or other modalities. That company knew that if the employees were happy, the business would flourish and prosper.

One of the two authors of this chapter worked with a large organization in WA. The general manager was an ex-army major who was insistent that his way was the only way. People feared his reactions which were derogatory, unnecessary, and downright rude. We suggested the GM gather every employee from the top down in a circle, set forth some rules which were as follows: only one person could speak at a time, absolutely no interruptions, and everyone had to speak. However, they could only speak the truth about how they felt about their work environment in all of its aspects, including the GM. He opened up the floor. No one spoke. For 10 min there was deathly silence. He offered the rules up again. One employee said: "Okay, you want the truth, well here it is." He proceeded to point out his intense dislike of the GM with his intolerance to ideas of others, his arrogance, and his lack of kindness or acknowledgment and finished by saying how much he hated working there. Every person followed suit with similar grievances. Ninety minutes later when every employee had their say, "Terry" the GM was stunned, shocked into silence. He had absolutely no idea he was perceived as being so ruthless, obnoxious, and hard-nosed. He thanked them and said he would do the work on changing to be a better boss. They lost a lot of production in that 90 min, but amazingly by the end of the week, they had not only caught up but surpassed their normal requirements in terms of output. Terry did "the work," found a modality that worked for him, healed a lot of his past, and became a completely different, more open, more vulnerable human being adding value to both his employees and the profitability of the business.

Chapter Takeaways

- Be kind to yourself, your peers, your direct reports, and your managers.
- Notice every day how you can become a leader of sustainable practices both at home and at work.
- For the world to change, you must be willing to change.
- Take responsibility; move out of lay blame/justify and denial.

Reflective Questions

1. Which UN Sustainable Development Goals are you going to strive towards?
2. How will you lead your organization towards a vision of sustainable continuous improvement?
3. Are you an agent for change?
4. Do you acknowledge those close to you every day?
5. Do you teach your children to be emotionally intelligent?

References

Bradshaw, J. (1992). *The homecoming: Reclaiming and championing your inner child.* Bantam Books.

Lipton, B. (2015). *The biology of belief.* Hay House Publishers.

Sinek, S. (2011). *Start with why*. Penguin Books.

The HeartMath Institute (2020). *Introducing our Personal Well-Being Survey*™. Retrieved from https://www.heartmath.org/

Weissman, D., & Montana, C. (2013). *Heart of the matter*. Hay House Publishers.

Wolynn, M. (2016). *It didn't start with you.* Penguin, Putnam. https://www.heartmath.com/. Accessed 2020

Chapter 12
Letting Go as a Liberation

Pamela Kay Caldwell and Oluseye David Akintunde

Abstract Studying leadership, one begins to see the various theories, approaches, and styles. However, with the vast research on the topic of leadership, institutions and systems are characterized by poor and ineffective leadership and leaders. This has and will continue to boggle the business professionals. Because of this, business professionals and scholars continue to as to ask the questions, "why, how, and what?" Why is it that regardless of the current reseearch and knowledge that we have on leadership, we continue to have discussions on the topic of ineffective and innovative leadership? How as business scholars and professionals do we move into a more effective style of leadership? What do we embrace, to have effective and responsible leaders and leadership? This chapter discusses the why, how, and what that we need to let go to be liberated.

Keywords Innovative leadership · Value-based leadership · Millennials · Changing of mindsets · Disenchantment in business

Introduction

Even with the numerous leadership theories, styles, and approaches, the world still experiences situations and outcomes from ineffective leadership. Regardless of how many times we experience these situations, it seems like not much time passes before it happens again. Seeing this cycle, we must wonder how to get past and stay past these situations. Changing the way we view leadership will first start with a change in how we think. This idea of it starts in the mind was written by James Allen, in his first edition *As A Man Thinketh* (Allen, 2019). Moving through the history of leadership, this idea seems to have been forgotten and moved away from what a person is to what they say. Because of recent conflicts, the question of "Can

P. K. Caldwell (✉)
Jilin University Lambton College, Changchun, Jilin, P. R. China

O. D. Akintunde
Jiangsu University, Zhenjiang, Jiangsu, P. R. China

J. Marques (ed.), *Innovative Leadership in Times of Compelling Changes*, Management, Change, Strategy and Positive Leadership, https://doi.org/10.1007/978-3-030-67258-4_12

leadership be done a different way?" has been asked along with "What is the better or different way?" This chapter looks at the idea that letting go could be the first step of changing the idea of leadership. This idea of "letting go" is more than a cliché from some liberation theorists trying to gain relevance in the field of business. A theology of "letting go" is a progressive idea useful for broadening how we study and understand the world. It is asking stakeholders to be socially conscious in the study of rules and the forces that are shaping the world particularly that of business. Letting go has the impact of allowing freedom of all people and societies, moving the world into a more inclusive leadership that can ensure sustainability of today's societies.

Why We Need to Let Go

For us to have a chance at liberation, first we must let go. For us to let go, we must know why we need to let go. If we do not understand or know the way, then the changing of our mindset is only a temporary change and not a change that will be sustainable. Understanding why comes with understanding what caused us as a business society to even begin thinking we need to let go and change. What caused us to as a society to ask these questions are recent scandals, pandemics, and global chaos. What caused us to ask these questions is the disenchantment of how business is conducted.

Disenchantment to Making Business Better

The race to open "the pandora box" is relatively new for business and has been described as primitive but growing (Day et al., 2014). For decades, the understanding of leadership, executives, and effective performance in the workplace and business are said to be influenced by politics, sociology, and social psychology (Conger & Kanungo, 1987). These topics focus on how perception, emotions, cognition, and observed behaviors such as charisma, transformative, and aggressiveness affect leadership performance. This effects can be seen in the performance of self, teams, groups, organization, and societies (Conger & Kanungo, 1987). However, "the disenchantment of the world" spoken by Max Weber combines ethics, religion, and capitalism. These are said to be related to a number of discontents and issues seen within business, the workplace, and society (Grosby, 2013). These discontents are rooted in the impacts of VUCA, which means volatility, uncertainty, complexity, and ambiguity (Schoemaker et al., 2018). These discontentments are not just based on corporation; they include individuals as well. It brings the issue of why business exist, the role of ethics, and support for social justices into questions. Wondering how businesses can remain profitable along with being ethical and supporting social injustices (Bartlett & Preston, 2000; Primeaux & Stieber, 1994).

Separating the economic value of the business for both shareholder and owners from social goals is still heavily criticized. This is because big business executives hold responsibility for polluting environments and other such practices which impact people and the societies (Schwartz & Saiia, 2012). The idea and logic that business demands profits and innovative thinking continue to grow. The idea that large corporation and capitalism is the blame of society social problems is therefore considered unjust (Fritsch, 2017). However, with movements as "conscious capitalism," Edward Freeman's "a new story of business" and stakeholder theory, and Michael Porter's shared values, the corporate world is still divided on the purpose of business. The implication is business and executives reflect on a higher and inner purpose for going into business, while others consider interests of stakeholders in balancing profits and social goals (Sternad et al., 2017). However, this is not to mean that all corporations have turned to greater purpose, inner lights, or stakeholder's responsibility infused into their businesses. Such changes may be constructed at times within the map of conscience or corporate sovereignty of business executives. One of the concerns today is how corporations can engage in pursuit of business self-interest and still be socially responsible.

Case in Point

US Volkswagen has a corporate responsibility culture of "it pays to give" and had even won Green Power Leadership Award in 2013. The scandal involving the Volkswagen "Diesel Cheat" in 2015 shocked many global customers and US citizens about what big corporations do in the name of social responsibility (3BLMedia, 2014). However, corporations face the drive to balance cost of new entries into the market, technology, innovations, and competition for resources, local regulation, and at the same time social concerns as making employees happy and productive. The first concern is how to balance or survive this relationship and still stay competitive. The second is adjusting to leadership demands of super-diverse and junior employees categorized as "millennial" with different perspectives on issues about workplace relationship and how VUGA challenges that characterize business climate should be handled.

Analysis of Business Environment and Leadership Challenge

When referring to VUCA business environments, some words that have been used are "dynamic changes," "haziness of reality," "mixed meaning of conditions," "fluidity," "greater confusion," and "dilemmas" and "perplexity of matters and solutions" (Kornelsen, 2019). The environments are characterized by events and issues being linked and unfolding at such a fast pace beyond people, societies, and leadership capacities to absorb, understand, or make sense of and provide solutions.

Researchers also speak about crises influencing corporations and societies and what kind of leadership is needed (Sarkar, 2016). Here, businesses create super wealthy shareholders and chief executives that must coexist with equalities, ethics, and social goods as far as employee's welfare, inequalities, labor right, privacy, and planet concerns are concerned (Linnenluecke & Griffiths, 2010). How and the extent businesses incorporate social responsibility and stakeholder interest have been debated many years and still ongoing (Jose & Lee, 2007). Customers' criticism, today's media about controversial issues has forced organizations to be transparent on how their mission, vision, values, and goals ensure conformity regarding social repsonsiblity (Shabana et al., 2017).

Business environment is characterized by accidental events such as terrorist attack, natural disasters, pandemic, flooding, earthquakes, and financial meltdown of 2008. In essence, what is required of business leaders is a lot of strategic thinking, planning, and preparing all business departments to adequately prevent these accidents or respond effectively when these accidents occur. What comes to mind are pictures of "Captain America," "Superman," and "superheroes" becoming common today but with qualities like those of Greek mythology gods except in physical appearance (Hafci & Asliturk, 2017). These are images in the fabric of Western societies through comics and cinemas culture to prevent these crises. The arts and films industries have borrowed from how arts and films impact leadership construct and behavior. It is evidenced that leaders either in the political or business fronts want to appear tough and resilient rather than weak or compromising in the face of business threats. The narrative becoming common among business managers and supervisors today and which is good is that effective leadership must focus on risk, crisis, and security in business (Engemann, 2018).

The external environment has one of the greatest influences on performance and productivity than the internal (Benson et al., 1978). Business executives and supervisors have the option to adapt and be responsive or discretionary. Since the external environment can turn unstable rapidly, individuals become concerned with what conditions will allow organizations and executives to respond effectively to this pressures and crises. The unstable environments can become more complex, making it exceedingly difficult under the "complex adaptive system" for management or leaders and the strategies available to operate (Benson et al., 1978). This will necessitate that businesses decentralize their decision-making structure from the top-down approach (Mason, 2007). Decisions will be shared by perception of managements including the chief executive officer, directors and supervisors, information processing system, department preference, and resources available. The business models matter. Other business skills which are needed include anticipating, challenging, learning, interpreting, designing, and aligning with changes occurring in the environment businesses operate.

Case in Point

This section gives cases that explain these issues and how they impact corporations and leadership using two climates, the United States and China. Business operates in different climates with their peculiarities that are subject to change. Public trust has become a topic in business and leadership. China's opening and integration into the World Trade Organization has been declared beneficial to the global trading system (Gwyther, 2015; Lardy, 2004). The opening provided markets for businesses from many countries. In 2013, GSK's China crisis grabbed the headlines of national dailies such as The Telegraph and Chinese media. Senior executives and a fraud investigator of GSK's China had been implicated in a cover-up in what has been tagged the biggest corruption scandal to hit a foreign firm in years. The British-headquartered pharmaceutical company was eventually fined $490 m (297 m pounds). The Chinese government since joining the global trade system World Trade Organization 2001 has launched several offensives against corruption and graft particularly among the political class (Wedeman, 2005). When the Chinese public security cracked down on the GSK bribery and corruption case, it shows a trend towards scrutiny of activities of foreign corporations in China and the corporation's lack of foresightedness about legal reforms in the country.

The second has to do with social media such as Twitter and Facebook enabled by technological innovation. There is increased social networking and cheap and modern advertising for small businesses. Individuals and governments however are worried about access, user protection and unregulated media, breach of privacy, and fraud in electoral campaigns (Cambridge Analytica and Online Manipulation, n.d.). There is nothing morally wrong about these tools; however, the concern is how to resolve issues of regulation and functionality. Zuckerberg though promised to fix Facebook; the organization since 2018 has been found guilty of privacy issues in Mexico, Germany, and Belgium law courts. In 2019, the US Federal Trade Commission fined a $5b penalty on Facebook which in many ways affected the company (FTC Imposes $5 Billion Penalty and Sweeping New Privacy Restrictions on Facebook, 2019).

How to Move Towards Liberation

Letting go and moving towards liberation start with how one thinks. This was portrayed in James Allen's book *As a Man Thinketh* (1903) and is still prevalent today as seen in the value-based leadership styles. When letting go, how do we do this in a way that is sustainable not only for ourselves but sustainability in a way that we can teach others and can be adjusted for future use? The areas that we will discuss are mindset, learning and perception, and change for improvement.

Mindset

When one contemplates change, one will begin to think about how to change. To think about change activates our mind into processing knowledge, events, and history of our actions. This process usually leads us into accepting the change and moving forward or not accepting the change and accepting the consequences from not making the change. These are the two alternatives to our decision. Looking at these alternatives, we can conclude that since we thought about it, we activated our mind, and our mindset either remained or changed (Dweck, 2006; Gupta & Govindarajan, 2002; Thum, 2012).

Doing a Google Scholar search on "mindset" on Tuesday July 28, 2020, yielded a response with 667,000 sources. From the yielded responses, there were some that had been cited mutliple times. however, there were a few sources that were cited or appeared multiple times. These included Carol Dweck, Myrko Thum, and Gupta and Govindarajan (2002). Looking further at each one, a definition of mindset becomes clearer. For a basic definition, Webster's Dictionary defines mindset as "a mental attitude or inclination"(Dweck, 2006; Gupta & Govindarajan, 2002; Thum, 2012). Webster's Dictionary defines attitude as a settled way of thinking or feeling about someone or something and inclination as a person's natural tendency or urge to act or feel in a particular way, a disposition. Attitude has also been defined in academic textbooks, as a learned tendency to consistently respond positively or negatively to people and event (Merriam-Webster, 2008). The second definition of attitudes gives us an understanding that an attitude is not only negative but a way that we learn and a way that we respond to people and events (Merriam-Webster, 2008). If an attitude is something that is learned followed by an action, then we know that we can unlearn an attitude and reactions. Also noted is that it can be positive or negative, meaning that just because we respond to something positive may not make it right. Understanding attitude, which is a part of mindset, we can define mindset. Started earlier was three individuals Dweck, Thum, and Gupta and Govindarajan that was seen cited multiple times and will be used to define mindset.

Carol Dweck states that we have two types of mindset, fixed and growth (Dweck, 2006). She furthers defines both of them as (1) individuals that have fixed mindset, see individuals as superior or inferior, and lack the need to change and (2) individuals with a growth mindset that see individuals as capable of improving along with self. Individuals with a growth mindset are constantly improving and letting go of old ideas (Dweck, 2006).

Myrko Thum defines mindset as "Your mindset is the sum of your knowledge, including beliefs and thoughts about the world and yourself in it. It is your filter for information you get in and put out. So it determines how you receive and react information" (Thum, 2012).

Gupta and Govindarajan, when defining mindset, concluded that (Gupta & Govindarajan, 2002):

1. Our mindsets are a product of our histories.
2. Our current mindset guides the collection and interpretation of new information.

3. After the collection of new information, if consistent with current mindset, then our mindset is reinforced.
4. After collection of new information, if different than current mindset, then our mindset either remains the same or is changed. If our mindset is to change, it will be determined on our self-awareness of our current mindset.

When we have an enhance understanding of mindset, how it is developed, and how it can be change; when we are letting go to liberate we know that it is not just changing our mindset. It is changing our mindset as well as having a high level of self awareness of our mindset, the influences on our mindset, and why we have fears of letting go of the current and moving to the new. Looking back at the initial definition of mindset seen in Webster's Dictionary that included attitude, and attitudes are either positive or negative reactions, we must look deeper into the idea of letting go and what we are letting go of.

Perception and Learning

With the process of change, first, it is the mindset that starts the path of either changing or not. When we think of letting go, to be liberated, understanding the definition of perception and learning allos us to see how this is part of the process of letting go. Perception is "the process by which we receive and interpret information from our environment," and learning is "an ongoing process through which individuals adjust their behavior based on experience" (McKee et al., 2012; Neck et al., 2018). We may know that we need to let go of some old ideas and ways of doing and reacting. Although we may know, we may not know what to let go. This may cause individuals to become fearful and resistant to change. Studying change process, fear is a reason for people to be resistant (McKee et al., 2012; Neck et al., 2018).

Looking back at the previous section, it starts with a change in mindset. After the change what happens? Do individuals just think, what we have been doing is not good now, so what do we do, stopping here. Or does the process continue, and the decision of how becomes part of the solution? Letting go must include ongoing actions.

Change for Improvement

One central issue today is the style of leadership that would be required to deal with these opportunities and how to embrace them. When discussing leadership style, one soon learns that there are many styles. One also learns that no leader uses only one style. This can be seen when discussing situational leadership, meaning the situation will determine the style of leadership. With the latest pandemic and other social issues that have happened during the year 2020, we can see that different leadership styles would be an advantage for dealing with the year 2020. As organizations and leadership, looking back over the current situation of the world, how do organizations as well as these leaders learn to adapt to a changing environment?

First, corporations and executives need to sense changes and when there is need for them to change as well. Second, corporations and business executives must determine threats and seize opportunities to transform the internal culture and adapt to external environment where their businesses operate. When it comes to leadership, the authoritarian style of leadership even in the non-Western society has been argued to be less successful (Chiang et al., 2020). Suppression of subordinate feelings and a climate of emotional suppression can create emotional exhaustion and can negatively affect team performance and business success. Responsible leadership is inclusiveness and combines ingredients of transformation, servant, and authentic leadership and as a substitute for the superior-subordinate exchange leadership traditions. In this case, empowerment of workers or subordinates can help businesses create an environment where creativity and innovation can thrive (Chiang et al., 2020).

Furthermore, talent or skill attraction, deployment, and retention are crucial. Businesses need to treat employees particularly subordinates as important as top management. Executives must thoroughly and carefully examine themselves to determine what is their motivation for leadership. Doing this may allow them to move away from a style that does not embrace their mood, emotions, and values (Shu, 2015). Traditionally, employee's welfare and particularly paychecks were incentives for attracting the best talent and boosting organizational productivity. Business managers are interested in how they can use them to motivate employees to improve workers' performance and profits. However, millennial employees are not falling for this reward strategies, but looking for a more work-life balance. This has not been seen much in earlier generations, where the concern was more on stability than the work-life balance (Chiang et al., 2020; Griffin & Griffin, 2019; Myers & Sadaghiani, 2010).

Millennials Letting Go and Embracing Ideas of Leadership

Millennials entered the workforce and, like from the past generation, changed the workforce behavior. Millennials, also known as Generation Me, are individuals born between 1982 and 1999 and are the youngest generation in today's business and workplace (Twenge et al., 2008, 2010). The growing populations are considered prospects for business leadership and are rising to offer solutions to today's social disenchantment. The millennials view the world differently given their passion for technology, how workplace should be organized, and what purpose business should serve in both Western and Eastern societies (Griffin & Griffin, 2019). They are stereotypically labelled as being self-centered, unmotivated and disloyal at work, and too ambitious because of their interest to change in ways things are done. These are evidenced in their distinctive values and behavioral tendencies on teams, their communication style with supervisors, and their savvy communication technologies

(Myers & Sadaghiani, 2010). The fundamental questions when it comes to the millennials are their ability to have a functional relationship with older employees at work, the leadership style or management that best motivate them to work, and type of leaders they would become.

Since 2008, business professionals have become curious on how to fit the millennials into the workplace. Articles become normative in nature focusing on how to prepare or "fix" young skills and talents entering the workforce traditional dominated by Generation X and baby boomers. For example, there are studies as how academics provide career development opportunities for business graduates (Beard et al., 2008). Universities were also curious about whether business schools are responsible for producing millennial narcissistic employees and how they can provide millennial students career development (Westerman et al., 2012). The mindset is that the millennials are not motivated at work and switch jobs easily. Business professionals hoped universities could do their job well by preparing the millennials for the corporate world which had traditionally structured as hierarchical, time bound, and profit-driven (Westerman et al., 2012). However, research have shown that the millennials do not consider job or work advancement conditions as less significant but seek to balance work and life meanings together or make impacts in their societies (Buzza, 2017). Johnson Center's 2020 Report on Philanthropy shows that millennials desire more intrinsic motivation than external. These internal motivations are flexibility at work, work and life balance, relationships with managers, and strategies that measure quality and not quantity (Johnson Center, 2020). The millennials not only want more for themselves but want more as leaders and from leadership. It has been seen that millennials prefer value-based leadership styles, which are styles that were mentioned before as being considered as leading from the inside to the outside. On leadership culture and the millennials, there's emerging study on what sort of leadership millennials prefer and offer at corporate business. Current research shows that millennials who occupy leadership positions are utilizing distinct value-centered systems. The millennials believe in social needs, tight peer bonds, and stronger team orientation, and this is why they prefer an inclusive and value-based leadership style (Chou, 2012). They are also more likely to prefer a two-way communication approach in which people are at the center of the information sharing system. Based on the characteristic traits of the millennial generation, their leadership styles of choice are the ones that emphaisis value-centered leadership. Value-centered leadership are ones that are more inclusive, collaborative, and committed to people rather than the task based and organization mission leadership ofolder generation (Maier et al., 2015).

What to Embrace

The research on leadership has given us many styles, theories and discussion of how to be an effective leader. Leadership has gone through many styles, and discussion of what is the best. As we continue to grow and understand leadership, we are learning that the best style or the best way is one that encompasses a variety of leadership styles. We are beginning to liberate ourselves in knowing that leadership start with self. We are learning that putting self into leadership shows authenticity from the leader, a place where the leaders' thoughts, feelings, and beliefs are displayed (Gardner et al., 2011; McKee et al., 2012). We are moving away from the idea that leadership is a list of character traits that one need to possess or to develop and moving towards the idea of leading from the inside out, leadership being ethical and socially responsible (Cashman, 2008; George, 2003) What we are moving towards are leadership styles that are value-based such as authentic, spiritual, servant and ethical leadership as well as leading with emotional intelligence (Avolio & Gardner, 2005; Fry et al., 2005; Gardner et al., 2011; George, 2003).

Authentic Leadership

Authentic leadership and authenticity are nothing new, and a review of history will show that it can be traced back to Greek philosophy ("To thine own self be true"), Maslow's hierarchy of needs with self-actualization, and emotional intelligence (Avolio & Gardner, 2005; Gardner et al., 2011; Ilies et al., 2005; Luthans & Avolio, 2003; Walumbwa et al., 2008). Authenticity is owning one's personal experiences and acting according to self-feelings and beliefs (Luthans & Avolio, 2003). Along with leading from knowing self and acting the same way, authentic leaders' main desire is serving, empowering others, and leading with purpose, meaning, and values (George, 2003). Authentic leadership is turning leadership inside out and urging leaders to first know self and then act on those values and beliefs. This is going beyond what we have been taught and what organizations have demonstrated in the past where leadership was a list of traits that individuals need to possess to be determined successful or effective (George, 2003). It is calling for leaders to serve alongside of the followers, building relationship with the followers, and being part of the leadership process. Authentic leaders are said to have these 5 qualities: (1) understanding their purpose, (2) practicing solid values, (3) leading with heart, (5) establishing connected relationship, and (6) demonstrating self-discipline (George, 2003).

Spiritual Leadership

Spiritual leadership, a value-based leadership style, is a style that involves motivating and empowered followers (Fry & Slocum, 2008). This type of leadership style begins with the leader's understanding of their own spirituality, values, and beliefs, also considering the wellbeing of the followers (Fry & Slocum, 2008). Like authentic leadership, spiritual leadership starts from the inside where the leader is grounded in self-identity, self-concept, and self-awareness (Fry et al., 2005, 2007). These types of leaders tend to have a high level of emotional intelligence and be able to understand their own emotions, their follower's emotions, and how each is part of the environment. Spiritual leadership goes beyond one religion, although some of the concepts can be seen in the Christian religion (Fry et al., 2005, 2007). Spiritual leadership as proposed by Fry et al. (2005) is said to include following 5 descriptors: (1) vision, (2) hope/faith, (3) altruistic love, (4) meaning/calling, and (5) membership. Vision is what the leader or organization wants to achieve in the future and why they want to achieve these goals. Hope/faith can be viewed as the belief and thinking that the goal will be achieved. Altruistic love is seen as harmony, self-love, and love for others. Meaning or calling is the belief that all lives are meaningful and equal, and membership is the feeling of belonging and inclusion (Fry et al., 2005). Spiritual leadership is another style that is changing how the relationship between the leader and follower is viewed. It shows that to move towards effective leadership, leaders and followers must work together, motivate each other, and be concerned with each other's wellbeing. This style is calling for us to let go of the ideas that leaders do not care for their followers; leadership is a list of traits one emulates, and self is not a part of leadership. Spiritual leadership is liberating us to believe that love has a place in leadership, that leadership comes from within, and that self is part of leadership.

Servant Leadership

Servant and ethical leadership are both classified as value-based styles of leadership. Servant leadership is a style that is not new and formulated by Robert Greenleaf in his work *Servant Leadership: A Journey Into the Nature of Legitimate Power and Greatness* (1977) (Farling et al., 1999; Gregory Stone et al., 2004; Sendjaya & Sarros, 2002; van Dierendonck, 2011).This style of leadership emphasizes the needs of the followers and changing the influence from the leader to the follower (van Dierendonck, 2011). Like the other value-based leadership styles, it changed how leadership is done; instead of the leader being the focus, the focus shifts to the followers. The purpose of the leadership again changes to starting from within the leader. The leaders display their values and beliefs in leadership.

Emotional Intelligence

Learning about value-based leadership styles, the notice of similarities is seen. The focus of leadership begins to take a different perspective, becoming more of being aware of one's emotions, other emotions, and the importance of relationships. This new perspective on leadership is embracing emotional intelligence (EI), embracing the idea that emotions are a part of business and leadership. EI is a construct that links emotions and cognition with improving relationships (Jordan & Lawrence, 2009; Mayer & Salovey, 1993). The four areas of EI are self-awareness, self-regulation, motivation, empathy, and social skills (Jordan & Lawrence, 2009; Mayer & Salovey, 1993; McKee et al., 2012). EI is not just the emotional intelligence of the leaders, but others as well.

Case in Point on Value-Based Leadership Styles

Although we are talking about value-based leadership styles, let us understand that these styles are nothing new. However, we are advocating that we need to embrace the using of these styles regularly. Some cases that have shown effective leadership while using value-based leadership styles have been demonstrated by Carlos Rodriguez, Ursula Burns, Jamie Irick, and Jordan Peterson.

Servant and Ethical Leadership. A case in point on the style of servant and ethical leadership is Carlos Rodriguez-Pastor. His mission for his leadership was to "to build a brighter future, day by day, for all Peruvian families" (Tuck-Alumni Stories, n.d.). He used this same idea when he decided to start a school Innova Schools. This school system he decided would be "affordable, high-quality K-12." His focus was on the emerging of the middle class, not only helping them in business but their children as well. The emphasis of the school was on three mandates: affordability of middle class, high-quality instruction, and an effective curriculum. The model includes a blended style of learning, where students spend 70% in group learning and the rest of the time self-learning using various learning programs (Tuck-Alumni Stories, n.d.).

Authentic Leadership. A case in point on the style of authentic leadership is Ursula Burns. During her tenure as CEO of Xerox, she was known for using emotional intelligence in her leadership. Attending engineering school, she soon learned that this was a male-dominated field, and she was usually the only female and minority in the room. Instead of using this as a crutch, she used it as a way to be her true self; she used this as an opportunity to distinguish herself from the crowd. Doing this was the reason behind her success, which included being the first Black woman to run a business featured in the Fortune 500.

Spiritual Leadership. An example of spiritual leadership being used in business is Jordan B. Peterson. Peterson a clinical psychologist and social commentator provides answers to life suffering, purpose, and dark times to young adults (Peterson, 2018). He uses his own spiritual learning to teach his program ***12 Rules for Life***. He does not classify himself with a religion, but focuses on the interconnection of man, higher power, and being.

Do Interests Merge in Crises and How Does "Letting Go" Enable a Better World?

The business environment particularly the external environment still has resemblance of order where stakeholders must determine how to negotiate what values are important and what responsibility in the shared world. Already discussed is what appears as a dividing of ideas of doing business. Edward Freeman gave credit to the idea or concept of "stakeholder theory" which holds that corporations including the leadership spectrum should take cognizance of groups that can affect them. We also agree on what "stakeholders" should be. Are terrorists, sometimes seen as freedom fighters also stakeholders? As well as governments, shareholders, employees, community, and societies? However, one of the basic choices is to understand what values are important to the survival or sustainability of the society and make them parts of business. Economic value as profit is not sustainable in a social world where employees and customers who are members of societies had been driven to poverty because of business practices which cause environment havoc.

Furthermore, corporations are also waking up to the idea of "shared value." The idea of shared values is that corproations with the help of society, and using their business models; can indeed solve the most important social problems and engage society. It all starts with purpose of our existence more than making money or profits. Leading the letting go are millennials who are wanting to address social problems and using business to change the world.

Chapter Takeaways

- Letting go does not mean what we were doing before was wrong.
- The generation millennials are on the frontlines when it comes to sustainable leadership change.
- Leadership is no longer emotional-less.
- Leadership is more of a relationship-building interaction.
- Societies want businesses to be accountable and responsible.

Reflection Questions

1. How can individuals and businesses be educated on the need for more value-based leadership styles?
2. How can individuals and businesses be educated on the idea of leading from the inside out?
3. How can we use authenticity to reduce or eliminate global uncertainty?
4. What is the true reason for conducting business?
5. With letting go of the old ways of leadership, how can this liberation be sustainability for all societies?

References

Allen, J. (2019). *As a man thinketh*. Penguin.

Avolio, B. J., & Gardner, W. L. (2005). Authentic leadership development: Getting to the root of positive forms of leadership. *Leadership Quarterly, 16*(3), 315–338. https://doi.org/10.1016/j.leaqua.2005.03.001

Beard, D., Schwieger, D., & Surendran, K. (2008, April). Preparing the millennial generation for the work place: How can academia help? In *Proceedings of the 2008 ACM SIGMIS CPR conference on Computer personnel doctoral consortium and research* (pp. 102–105).

Bartlett, A., & Preston, D. (2000). Can ethical behaviour really exist in business? *Journal of Business Ethics, 23*(2), 199–209. https://doi.org/10.1023/A:1006037107565

Benson, J. K., Pfeffer, J., & Salancik, G. R. (1978). The external control of organizations. *Administrative Science Quarterly*. https://doi.org/10.2307/2392573

Buzza, J. S. (2017). Are you living to work or working to live? What millennials want in the workplace. *Journal of Human Resources Management and Labor Studies, 5*(2), 15–20. https://doi.org/10.15640/jhrmls.v5n2a3

Cambridge Analytica and Online Manipulation—Scientific American Blog Network. (n.d.). Retrieved July 31, 2020, from https://blogs.scientificamerican.com/observations/cambridge-analytica-and-online-manipulation/

Cashman, K. (2008). Leader for life. *Leadership excellence*.

Chiang, J. T. J., Chen, X. P., Liu, H., Akutsu, S., & Wang, Z. (2020). We have emotions but can't show them! Authoritarian leadership, emotion suppression climate, and team performance. *Human Relations*. https://doi.org/10.1177/0018726720908649

Chou, S. Y. (2012). Millennials in the workplace: A conceptual analysis of millennials' leadership and followership styles. *International Journal of Human Resource Studies, 2*(2), 71. https://doi.org/10.5296/ijhrs.v2i2.1568

Conger, J. A., & Kanungo, R. N. (1987). Toward a behavioral theory of charismatic leadership in organizational settings. *Academy of Management Review, 12*(4), 637–647. https://doi.org/10.5465/amr.1987.4306715

Day, D. V., Fleenor, J. W., Atwater, L. E., Sturm, R. E., & McKee, R. A. (2014). Advances in leader and leadership development: A review of 25 years of research and theory. *Leadership Quarterly, 25*(1), 63–82. https://doi.org/10.1016/j.leaqua.2013.11.004

Dweck, C. (2006). *Mindset: Changing the way you think to fulfil your potential*. Hachette UK.

Engemann, & J, K. (2018). The Routledge Companion to Risk, Crisis and Security in Business (First edition.). Taylor and Francis. Retrieved from https://gen.lib.rus.ec/book/index.php?md5=3d42b011f729ad5aec8c83d103209177

Farling, M. L., Stone, A. G., & Winston, B. E. (1999). Servant leadership: Setting the stage for empirical research. *Journal of Leadership and Organizational Studies, 6*(1–2), 49–72. https://doi.org/10.1177/107179199900600104

Fritsch, M. (2017). The theory of economic development – An inquiry into profits, capital, credit, interest, and the business cycle. *Regional Studies, 51*(4), 654–655. https://doi.org/10.1080/00343404.2017.1278975

Fry, L. W., Matherly, L. L., Whittington, J. L., & Winston, B. E. (2007). Spiritual leadership as an integrating paradigm for servant leadership. In *In integrating spirituality and organizational leadership* (pp. 70–82). ISOL Foundation.

Fry, L. W., & Slocum, J. W. (2008). Maximizing the triple bottom line through spiritual leadership. *Organizational Dynamics, 37*(1), 86. https://doi.org/10.1016/j.orgdyn.2007.11.004

Fry, L. W., Vitucci, S., & Cedillo, M. (2005). Spiritual leadership and army transformation: Theory, measurement, and establishing a baseline. *Leadership Quarterly, 16*(5), 835–862. https://doi.org/10.1016/j.leaqua.2005.07.012

Gardner, W. L., Cogliser, C. C., Davis, K. M., & Dickens, M. P. (2011). Authentic leadership: A review of the literature and research agenda. *Leadership Quarterly, 22*(6), 1120–1145. https://doi.org/10.1016/j.leaqua.2011.09.007

George, B. (2003). *Authentic leadership: Rediscovering the secrets to creating lasting value*. Josey-Bass.

Gregory Stone, A., Russell, R. F., & Patterson, K. (2004). Transformational versus servant leadership: A difference in leader focus. *Leadership & Organization Development Journal, 25*(4), 349–361. https://doi.org/10.1108/01437730410538671

Griffin, N. S., & Griffin, N. (2019). A millennial methodology? Autoethnographic research in do-it-yourself (DIY) punk and activist communities. In *Forum Qualitative Sozialforschung* (Vol. 20, p. 3). Institute for Qualitative Research. https://doi.org/10.17169/fqs-20.3.3206

Grosby, S. (2013). Max weber, religion, and the disenchantment of the world. *Society, 50*(3), 301–310. https://doi.org/10.1007/s12115-013-9664-y

Gupta, A. K., & Govindarajan, V. (2002). Cultivating of global mindset. *Academy of Management Executive, 16*(1), 116–126. https://doi.org/10.5465/AME.2002.6640211

Gwyther, M. (2015). Leadership in crisis. *London Business School Review, 26*(4), 40–43. https://doi.org/10.1111/2057-1615.12076

Hafci, B., & Erbay Asliturk, G. (2017). SUPERHEROES: MYTHS OF MODERN AGE? Idil Journal of Art and Language, 6(30), 497–510. https://doi.org/10.7816/idil-06-30-02

Ilies, R., Morgeson, F. P., & Nahrgang, J. D. (2005). Authentic leadership and eudaemonic well-being: Understanding leader-follower outcomes. *Leadership Quarterly, 16*(3), 373–394. https://doi.org/10.1016/j.leaqua.2005.03.002

Johnson Center at Grand Valley State University (2020). 11 Trends in Philanthropy for 2020. Retrieved from https://archive.johnsoncenter.org/wpcontent/uploads/2020/01/11-Trends-for-2020-Report.pdf

Jordan, P. J., & Lawrence, S. A. (2009). Emotional intelligence in teams: Development and initial validation of the short version of the Workgroup Emotional Intelligence Profile (WEIP-S). *Journal of Management and Organization, 15*(4), 452. https://doi.org/10.5172/jmo.15.4.452

Jose, A., & Lee, S. M. (2007). Environmental reporting of global corporations: A content analysis based on Website disclosures. *Journal of Business Ethics, 72*(4), 307–321. https://doi.org/10.1007/s10551-006-9172-8

Kornelsen, J. (2019). The quest to lead (with) millennials in a VUCA-World: Bridging the gap between generations. In *Contributions to management science*. Physica. https://doi.org/10.1007/978-3-319-98884-9_2

Lardy, N. R. (2004). Integrating china into the global economy. In *Integrating china into the global economy*. Brookings Institution Press. https://doi.org/10.2307/20033216

Linnenluecke, M. K., & Griffiths, A. (2010). Corporate sustainability and organizational culture. *Journal of World Business, 45*(4), 357–366. https://doi.org/10.1016/j.jwb.2009.08.006

Luthans, F., & Avolio, B. (2003). Authentic leadership development. In *cerf.radiologie.fr*. Retrieved September 29, 2020, from https://cerf.radiologie.fr/sites/cerf.radiologie.fr/files/Enseignement/DES/Modules-Base/Luthans %26Avolio%2C2003.pdf

Maier, T., Tavanti, M., Bombard, P., Gentile, M., & Bradford, B. (2015). Millennial generation perceptions of value-centered leadership principles. *Journal of Human Resources in Hospitality and Tourism, 14*(4), 382–397. https://doi.org/10.1080/15332845.2015.1008386

Mason, R. B. (2007). The external environment's effect on management and strategy. *Management Decision, 45*(1), 10–28. https://doi.org/10.1108/00251740710718935

Mayer, J. D., & Salovey, P. (1993). The intelligence of emotional intelligence. *Intelligence, 17*(4), 433. https://doi.org/10.1016/0160-2896(93)90010-3

McKee, A., Kemp, T., & Spence, G. (2012). *Management: A focus on leaders*. https://books.google.com/books?hl=en&lr=&id=NRLiBAAAQBAJ&oi=fnd&pg=PP1&dq=management+a+focus+on+leaders+&ots=efi3r0WHvD&sig=KeKaW4uSjgRGEMANvjf3ojloaxU

Merriam-Webster, I. (2008). *Merriam-Webster online dictionary*. Author.

Myers, K. K., & Sadaghiani, K. (2010). Millennials in the workplace: A communication perspective on millennials' organizational relationships and performance. *Journal of Business and Psychology, 25*(2), 225–238. https://doi.org/10.1007/s10869-010-9172-7

Neck, C., Houghton, J., & Murray, E. (2018). *Organizational behavior: A skill-building approach*. https://books.google.com/books?hl=en&lr=&id=knl_DwAAQBAJ&oi=fnd&pg=PP1&dq=Organizational+Behavior:+A+Skill-Building+Approach&ots=NSF_R0uBrF&sig=ahmT-AkSzBa_a5ELgbjLGdP9OyY

Peterson, J. B. (2018). 12 rules for life: An antidote to chaos. Penguin UK.

Primeaux, P., & Stieber, J. (1994). Profit maximization: The ethical mandate of business. *Journal of Business Ethics, 13*(4), 287–294. https://doi.org/10.1007/BF00871675

Sarkar, A. (2016). We live in a VUCA World: The importance of responsible leadership. *Development and Learning in Organizations, 30*(3), 9–12. https://doi.org/10.1108/DLO-07-2015-0062

Schoemaker, P. J. H., Heaton, S., & Teece, D. (2018). Innovation, dynamic capabilities, and leadership. *California Management Review, 61*(1), 15–42. https://doi.org/10.1177/0008125618790246

Schwartz, M. S., & Saiia, D. (2012). Should firms go "beyond profits"? Milton Friedman versus broad CSR. *Business and Society Review, 117*(1), 1–31. https://doi.org/10.1111/j.1467-8594.2011.00397.x

Sendjaya, S., & Sarros, J. C. (2002). Servant leadership: Its origin, development, and application in organizations. *Journal of Leadership & Organizational Studies, 9*(2), 57–64. https://doi.org/10.1177/107179190200900205

Shabana, K. M., Buchholtz, A. K., & Carroll, A. B. (2017). The institutionalization of corporate social responsibility reporting. *Business and Society, 56*(8), 1107–1135. https://doi.org/10.1177/0007650316628177

Shu, C.-Y. (2015). The impact of intrinsic motivation on the effectiveness of leadership style towards on work engagement. *Contemporary Management Research, 11*(4), 327–350. https://doi.org/10.7903/cmr.14043

Sternad, D., Kennelly, J. J., & Bradley, F. (2017). Digging deeper: How purpose-driven enterprises create real value. In *Digging deeper: How purpose-driven enterprises create real value*. Routledge. https://doi.org/10.4324/9781351283809

Thum, M. (2012). The right mindset: Change your mindset in 6 steps.

Tuck Dartmouth University (n.d.). Tuck-Alumni Stories. Retrieved from https://www.tuck.dartmouth.edu/mba/alumni-stories

Twenge, J. M., Campbell, S. M., Hoffman, B. J., & Lance, C. E. (2010). Generational differences in work values: Leisure and extrinsic values increasing, social and intrinsic values decreasing. *Journal of Management, 36*(5), 1117–1142. https://doi.org/10.1177/0149206309352246

Twenge, J. M., Konrath, S., Foster, J. D., Campbell, W. K., & Bushman, B. J. (2008). Egos inflating over time: A cross-temporal meta-analysis of the narcissistic personality inventory. *Journal of Personality, 76*(4), 875–902. https://doi.org/10.1111/j.1467-6494.2008.00507.x

van Dierendonck, D. (2011). Servant leadership: A review and synthesis. *Journal of Management, 37*(4), 1228–1261. https://doi.org/10.1177/0149206310380462

Walumbwa, F. O., Avolio, B. J., Gardner, W. L., Wernsing, T. S., & Peterson, S. J. (2008). Authentic leadership: Development and validation of a theory-based measure. *Journal of Management, 34*(1), 89–126. https://doi.org/10.1177/0149206307308913

Wedeman, A. (2005). Anticorruption campaigns and the intensification of corruption in China. *Journal of Contemporary China, 14*(42), 93–116. https://doi.org/10.1080/1067056042000300808

Westerman, J. W., Bergman, J. Z., Bergman, S. M., & Daly, J. P. (2012). Are universities creating millennial narcissistic employees? An empirical examination of narcissism in business students and its implications. *Journal of Management Education, 36*(1), 5–32. https://doi.org/10.1177/1052562911408097

Chapter 13
Leading with a Moral Compass

Virtuous Leadership and Health Management in Turbulent Times: Meeting the Challenges of New Pandemics

Aikaterini Grimani and George Gotsis

Abstract Within the last two decades, there have been several large outbreaks of infectious diseases. However, the COVID-19 pandemic has caused huge disruption to the medical, social, and economic systems and highlighted the need to reinvent the healthcare systems to meet the new reality. Nevertheless, this is also a period of intense innovation, collaboration, and problem solving, in relation to search for vaccines, expansion of capacity to ventilate, or moving much of the routine work of public services online. Leadership is key to mobilizing people who are facing new demands and must receive motivation and direction on how to deal with adversity while continuing to deliver critical services. Virtues are gaining traction within leadership scholarship. They reflect moral character, which is made up of numerous dispositions, not just compassion and fidelity versus practical wisdom but also honesty, justice, steadfastness, humility, courage, integrity, etc. This chapter discusses the virtuous leadership and healthcare management in turbulent times while identifying the challenges of new pandemics.

Keywords Virtuous leadership · Virtues · Healthcare leadership · Pandemic · COVID-19

A. Grimani (✉)
University of Warwick, Coventry, UK
e-mail: grimaniaik@phs.uoa.gr

G. Gotsis
National and Kapodistrian University of Athens, Athens, Greece

J. Marques (ed.), *Innovative Leadership in Times of Compelling Changes*, Management, Change, Strategy and Positive Leadership, https://doi.org/10.1007/978-3-030-67258-4_13

Introduction

Within the 20 years of the twenty-first century, there have been numbers of large outbreaks, such as SARS, Ebola, and now COVID-19. However, the COVID-19 pandemic has challenged healthcare systems across the world and had an impact on service delivery and viability. This pandemic has highlighted the gaps in safety that still exist in hospitals, reshaping the narrative about healthcare safety and shifting the responsibilities of future healthcare leaders. The loss of life has been tragic, communication errors have increased significantly, and some of the logistical challenges relating to testing and provision of protective equipment have seemed insurmountable. As COVID-19 has exposed the weaknesses of the last two centuries' healthcare models, it has accelerated the need for effective transforming and information sharing. This will require a combination of short- and long-term solutions built on system-level resilience and leader effectiveness. Prioritizing engaged leadership, and emphasizing a more team-oriented approach to care delivery and collaboration across institutions, will improve systems in the short term and, ultimately, set conditions for long-term change.

Now more than ever, in the midst of the COVID-19 pandemic, we need the virtues and the insights that virtue ethics afford us. Leaders are commonly identified as role models, whose actions and reputations, both moral and immoral, have a profound impact on the ethical climates of their organizations. The actions and behaviors of those in positions of power and influence inform the actions and behaviors of their counterparts and organizations. Virtue and discrete virtues are gaining traction within leadership scholarship, but there remains a lack of clarity regarding exactly what virtue is and precisely how virtues inform leadership (Newstead et al., 2019).

Existing leadership literature supports the notion that virtues inform the goodness of good leadership (Wang & Hackett, 2016). This notion is supported implicitly by theories of leadership that reference the importance of specific virtues. Implicit evidence of the centrality of virtue to good leadership is found in those theories of leadership that reference discrete virtues such as care, compassion, justice, and integrity as desirable leader characteristics. Furthermore, over 60 virtues were identified in a review of moral, ethical, spiritual, servant, charismatic, transformational, and visionary leadership theories (Hackett & Wang, 2012). In order to help leaders draw on their virtuous motivation, there is a need to refine their behavioral practices of virtue and increase the frequency with which they are observed as demonstrating virtues and leading in ways that are effective and ethical. The current evidence has laid the foundations for further work on virtue-based leadership development by focusing greater attention on the role of virtue in informing the emergence, enactment, and attribution of good leadership and by building a clear conceptualization of good leadership as informed by virtue in multiple domains (Newstead et al., 2019).

Virtuous Leadership: Definition of the Construct

Virtuousness has its roots in Aristotelian ethics. Aristotle considered virtues as enablers of action which empower the individual who holds them to achieve happiness, increase societal welfare, or stimulate human flourishing (Crossan et al., 2013). Virtuousness is a construct associated with a constellation of virtues in the aggregate. As such, virtuousness serves the moral goals of an organization and not simply bottom-line goals such as profit, power, and persistence. Organizational virtuousness implies that intended positive human effects which transcend the instrumental desires of the actor are produced (Nikandrou & Tsachouridi, 2015). Virtues refer to situationally appropriate behaviors that are widely considered emblematic of good leadership. Some of these virtues are personality traits, such as conscientiousness and openness which predispose individuals to behave in certain ways (Crossan et al., 2017). The virtue ethical framework begins with an examination of the intrinsic qualities that make someone admirable, excellent, or virtuous.

Overall, the practice of courage, temperance, justice, prudence, and humanity, as a part of a virtuous life, is anticipated to produce the greatest happiness. Specifically, courage is a virtue between cowardliness and recklessness. Temperance enables the control of desires for instant gratification even when there are no externally imposed restraints. Justice enables leaders to be respectful and fair in the treatment of others while allocating valued resources, even when conflicting interests are involved. Prudence enables leaders to make a right assessment and/or decision even in the face of the needs of a plurality of stakeholders as in complex business environments, so that resources are used in an efficient, effective manner. Finally, humanity is a virtue between the deficiency of shyness and the excess of shamelessness (Crossan et al., 2013; Nassif et al., 2020).

Accordingly, virtuous leadership has been defined as distinguishing right from wrong in one's leadership role, taking steps to ensure justice and honesty, influencing and enabling others to pursue righteous and moral goals for themselves and their organizations, and helping others to connect to a higher purpose (Pearce et al., 2008). Accepting virtuousness as a key attribute of responsible leadership provides at least two functional benefits. One benefit is the role virtuousness plays in creating a fixed point in decision-making, while another benefit is the increases in performance that virtuousness produces in organizations. In particular, responsible leadership, as represented by virtuousness, is leadership that can effectively manage the turbulence and instability characterizing the current external environment (Cameron, 2011).

Antecedents and Outcomes of Virtuous Leadership

Several researchers have developed theoretical models of virtuous leadership which include potential antecedents and outcomes. Pearce et al. (2008) identified two potential antecedents of virtuous leadership: the personal characteristic of responsibility disposition and environmental cues. The leader's responsibility disposition plays a key role in how virtuous one behaves as a leader. Leaders can be classified according to two types of need for power: socialized and personalized. The key distinction between these types of need for power lies in the leader's underlying responsibility disposition. Socialized leaders tend to have a high responsibility disposition, whereas personalized leaders have a low responsibility disposition. Individuals with a strong sense of responsibility have beliefs and values reflecting high moral standards, a feeling of obligation to do the right thing, concern about others, and a high degree of self-judgment or critical evaluation of one's own character. In contrast, leaders high in a need for personalized power, often described as narcissistic, desire positions of power for their personal benefit, rather than the benefit of the larger group or organization. These types of narcissistic leaders often have great difficulty in building a team because of their counterproductive need for personal power over others (Pearce et al., 2008).

Environmental cues, which seem to be predictive of virtuous leadership, feature the concept of situational strength. Strong situations are characterized as providing very clear cues as to appropriate behavior, while weak situations are characterized as being ambiguous with regard to what constitutes appropriate behavior. Researchers have specifically articulated the importance of managing one's environment in support of effective leadership. At the organizational level, cues can take on many forms, from ethics codes, to leadership selection and development systems, to the manner in which rewards are distributed (Pearce et al., 2008).

Drawing on empathy literature and moral affect theory of gratitude, Li (2013) explored whether leaders' moral emotions (leader empathy and leader gratitude) predict ethical leadership behaviors. Since moral emotions capture morality, they are natural moral reactions to certain situations, and they are likely to provide for a more ethical leader for their high relevance to leaders' tendency to perform ethical leadership in the workplace. Briefly, empathy refers to a generalized tendency of individuals to take others' points of view and to feel warmth, compassion, and concern for others. In addition, gratitude is defined as "a generalized tendency to recognize and respond with grateful emotion to the roles of other people's benevolence in the positive experiences and outcomes that one obtains" (Li, 2013).

A variety of antecedents of ethical leadership have been proposed by Brown and Treviño (2006) such as situational influences and individual influences. They identify three situational factors that are likely to influence employees' perceptions of a leader as an ethical leader: ethical role modeling (childhood role models, career mentors, and top managers), the organization's ethical context, and the moral intensity of the issues that the leaders face in their work. In particular, leaders who work in strong ethical contexts that support ethical conduct will be better prepared to handle morally intense situations and demonstrate their ethical leadership. Childhood models were the most commonly reported type of ethical role model, followed by career role models and, finally, by top management models according to Brown and Treviño (2014).

Individual characteristics (e.g., personality characteristics (agreeableness, conscientiousness, and neuroticism); Machiavellianism; moral reasoning; locus of control) of leaders are also likely to be associated with ethical leadership. Agreeableness reflects the tendency to be trusting, altruistic, and cooperative, while highly conscientious individuals exercise self-control, carefully plan, and are well organized and reliable. On the contrary, neuroticism reflects the leader's tendency to experience negative emotions such as anger, fear, and anxiety (Brown & Treviño, 2006). The following two traits, leader agreeableness and conscientiousness, have also been found to be related to follower ratings of ethical leadership (Kalshoven et al., 2011). Other research on antecedents by Jordan et al. (2013) found that ethical leadership is positively related to the leader's cognitive moral development and is maximized when the leader's cognitive moral development diverges from and is greater than the follower's cognitive moral development.

In addition, Mayer et al. (2012) examined antecedents of ethical leadership by testing whether one source of motivation for leaders to exhibit ethical behaviors arises from moral identity. Moral identity is defined as a self-schema organized around a set of moral trait associations (e.g., honest, caring, compassionate). Existing research proposed that moral identity influences moral behavior by acting as a self-regulatory mechanism rooted in people's internalized notions of right and wrong. People whose moral identity is self-important should be motivated to act in ways that are consistent with their understanding of what it means to be a moral person (e.g., demonstrating some responsiveness to the needs and interests of others). Moral identity has two dimensions: symbolization (public aspect) and internalization (private expression). Moral identity symbolization is positively related to ethical leadership because these leaders are more likely to demonstrate morally positive behaviors. Moral identity internalization represents moral traits that are imbedded in an individual's self-concept. Leaders who are high in moral identity internalization are more likely to pay attention to correct and punish unethical behaviors (Mayer et al., 2012).

Mayer et al. (2012) also explore consequences of ethical leadership at the work-unit level. Many potential outcomes of virtuous leadership are likely. In particular, the authors examined unethical behavior (e.g., behavior that is morally unacceptable to the larger community) and relationship conflict (e.g., interpersonal strife associated with differences in personalities or matters unrelated to a job). Leaders set the ethical tone of an organization and are instrumental in encouraging ethical behavior and reducing interpersonal conflict from their subordinates. However, authors indicated that not only do leaders have to be moral individuals but also have to go one step further and actively model ethical behaviors and use reward and punishment systems to influence followers' behaviors.

Based on ethical leadership literature and theories of creativity, Li (2013) examined employee creativity as an outcome of ethical leadership. Creativity refers to the generation of novel and useful ideas or problem solutions (Detert et al., 2008). Ethical leadership, which creates high levels of psychological safety and certainty, was found to have a direct positive effect on employee creativity. Moreover, ethical leaders influence ethics-related conduct such as employee decision-making and prosocial and counterproductive behaviors through modeling and vicarious learning processes. The followers of ethical leaders are more likely to focus on the ethical implications of their decisions and make more ethical decisions as a result. In addition, they are more likely to perceive themselves as being in social exchange relationships with their leaders because of the fair and caring treatment they receive and because of the trust they feel. Given the social exchange relationship employees are likely to have with ethical leaders, followers should wish to reciprocate the caring and fair treatment they receive and the trust in the relationship, making counterproductive behavior less likely. Ethical leadership is to be related to positive follower attitudes, such as satisfaction, motivation, and organizational commitment, because of ethical leaders' honesty, trustworthiness, care and concern for employees and other people, and their fair and principled decision-making (Brown & Treviño, 2006).

Pearce et al. (2008) focused on two specific outcomes: the relationship between virtuous vertical leadership on the development of virtuous shared leadership and the link between vertical and shared virtuous leadership and organizational learning. The authors indicated that virtuous vertical leadership is positively related to the development and display of virtuous shared leadership as well as to organizational learning. In addition, virtuous shared leadership is positively related to organizational learning. Nassif et al. (2020) investigated the association between virtuous leadership and the following business-related outcomes: leader effectiveness, follower in-role and extra-role performance, follower ethicality, as well as happiness and life satisfaction among leaders and followers. The more affective-laden outcomes were leader happiness and follower life satisfaction. Similarly, Wang and Hackett (2016) found that virtuous leadership is positively predictive of a range of desirable leader and follower outcomes, including ethical conduct, general happiness, life satisfaction, and job performance. Honesty, transcendent meaning, caring and giving behavior, gratitude, hope, empathy, love, and forgiveness, among other virtues, have been found to predict desired outcomes, such as individuals' commitment, satisfaction, motivation, positive emotions, effort, physical health, and psychological health. A series of studies in which indicators of virtuousness and of performance outcomes were assessed in organizations across 16 industries (e.g., retail, automotive, consulting, healthcare, manufacturing, financial services, not-for-profit) (Cameron, 2011).

The Virtues Project (TVP), as a leadership development program, identified two key leader outcomes following the training, both of which arose from mechanisms enabled by leaders' developmental readiness: the content mechanism and the process mechanism. Leaders adopted and adapted TVP strategies that enabled them to engage in more positive communication strategies both in terms of sending messages and listening to others (Newstead et al., 2020). In addition, Hendriks et al. (2020) indicated that an immediate supervisor's virtuous leadership as evaluated by the subordinate positively influences all three considered dimensions of work-related well-being (job satisfaction, work-related affect, and work engagement) for a wide variety of employees.

Leading with Virtue in Healthcare Organizations

Health Management and Leadership: A Review of Current Developments

Leadership can substantially influence the quality of healthcare systems in many significant respects (Xing et al., 2020). In view of organizations' attempt to adequately influence the health outcomes of a population, they must align with the wider community's interests to shape a prosocial strategy that encompasses the psychosocial and environmental factors that contribute to one's health (Caldararo & Nash, 2017). These new societal commitments can be substantiated in management and leadership styles that would gradually diverge from competency-based models focused on individual training, so as to better encompass longer-term initiatives reflected on the primary systemic goals of accountability, innovation, and learning (Kwamie, 2015). Enriching traditional approaches to healthcare management consists in broadening the perspective of conventional wisdom about decision-making, cost-effectiveness, service quality, and equity through concepts of mission and vision that are in a position to promote collaboration, engagement, and common sense (Adinolfi & Borgonovi, 2017).

Contemporary challenges to the global health management tend to focus on efficiency-saving, change, and human resource management. In this new context, the role of health managers is constantly expanding to properly meet new emerging priorities. Concomitantly, ensuring contemporary health leaders have the capabilities to respond to a new demanding landscape is of the utmost importance (Figueroa et al., 2019). In this respect, healthcare leadership has to promote a shared vision, develop organizational governance models that reduce barriers to coordinated action, and foster capabilities to address substantial organizational challenges (Balser & Stead, 2015). In so doing, we are in need of a potential transition from individually focused to collectively focused leadership that envisions public health as a common good in itself (Fraser et al., 2017). Kumar et al. (2015) summarize the leadership competencies required to attain societal goals as follows:

- *External environmental skills* involve new initiatives that anticipate and adapt to change in alignment with networking that considers societal good.
- *Team and organizational skills* involve shared vision through coaching, motivating others, mentoring, and empowering them.
- *Self-management skills* consist in integrity, self-awareness, a sense of deep commitment, constant openness to new ideas and learning prospects, social and emotional competencies, and achievement of work-life balance.

A variety of leadership styles has been employed as appropriate for or akin to behaviors that affirm the principle of human dignity in healthcare conditions, taken for granted that leadership and management quality are the cornerstones in effective health systems (Pfeffermann, 2012). Ruth, Gaare and Alan (2008) found that principled leadership, one that integrates ethics into managing ethical tensions and meeting conflicting obligations within healthcare systems, fosters a practical ethics approach to public health practice that focuses on shared values and vision. Undoubtedly, ethics is a fundamental component in healthcare organizations, and leaders have to encourage ethical behavior by adopting ethical leadership styles that can promote an organizational service climate and motivate employees accordingly (Zappalà & Toscano, 2020).

Low et al. (2019) advocate a relational leadership style through a team-based approach as more akin to HIM professionals in healthcare services. Communicative leadership styles could help managers to positively influence employee's well-being in view of shaping a more humane working environment (Bäckström et al., 2016). Holder and Ramagem (2012) posit that strengthening management capacity of health systems through transformational leadership styles is deemed an important factor for achieving greater efficiency and responsiveness, ultimately improving health outcomes. In a similar vein of reasoning, Guerrero et al. (2020) seek to advance leadership theory in the healthcare sector, highlighting the role of middle managers' implementation leadership in mediating the effects of top managers' transformational leadership on staff attitudes.

Wong and Walsh (2020) advocate an authentic leadership model because of the relevance of its basic tenets to the particularities of healthcare work environments. In this respect, they contend that authentic leadership offers the sound basis of leadership development within healthcare organizations founded on the desire for authenticity and the maintenance of high ethical standards in leadership practice.

The role of servant leadership has been viewed as critical to shaping a positive work climate that enhances eudaimonic and psychological well-being in healthcare organizations (der Kinderen et al., 2020). A servant leadership model for instance is in a position to nurture personal and professional growth, empowering healthcare professionals to assume a leadership role and thereby increasing collaboration, satisfaction, and mutual respect within working environments (Sturm, 2009). Collaborative leadership practices thrive in synergistic work environments in which different health agents pursue an ideal conducive towards the enhancement of healthcare management practices and processes (VanVactor, 2012). In sum, developing synergistic relationships through collaborative leadership facilitates co-production of social science knowledge and its translation into practice, a fact that proves beneficial to better health quality (Marston et al., 2020).

Stapleton and Opipari (2020) hold the view that inspirational leadership fosters resilient behaviors, self-care practices, and role modeling as integral to organizational strategies that support effective and cohesive healthcare teams. Other contributions center on complexity leadership, for instance, as more pertinent to the complex initiatives and environments that characterize the unfolding healthcare networks and systems (Porter-O'Grady, 2020). The adoption of distributed leadership in healthcare organizations has been also supported, given its efficiency in significantly reducing communication and knowledge barriers, as well as enhancing continuity of care in primary healthcare delivery (Okpala, 2020). The principal constituents of distributed leadership in this context encompass leadership coalitions among members of primary healthcare teams, a collective approach to decision-making processes, and shared accountability.

The Potential of Virtuous Leadership in Informing Healthcare Management Policies

As demonstrated earlier, virtuous leadership is frequently founded on virtue ethics traditions. Meawad (2016) advances the view that the application of virtue ethics to healthcare ethics is particularly promising. This is contingent on the ability of virtue ethics to properly address systemic disadvantage that has negatively affected certain ethical considerations in the health sciences broadly and bioethics specifically. Worthy to note is the capability of virtue ethics to shape observable, pragmatic, and informed solutions for its adherers and a common denominator through which healthcare ethics could be informed by certain religious discourses on the dignity and the intrinsic worthiness of the human person.

Hendriks et al. (2020) showed that subordinates who perceive their supervisors as more virtuous trust their leaders more and, in turn, display higher work engagement, job satisfaction, and work-related affect. The findings of this study suggest that organizations seeking to promote the psychological well-being of their employees may strongly benefit from stimulating virtuous leadership and employee perceptions thereof. This perspective may also apply to the respective personnel in healthcare organizations.

Meyer and Hühn (2020) demonstrated that neo-Aristotelian leadership and positive leadership can explain why companies who draw on value-laden language reminiscent of a higher organizational purpose tend to outperform companies whose reports employ the conventional rhetoric of profit maximization. Neo-Aristotelian leadership is based on Aristotle's virtue ethics, while positive leadership is a more pragmatic approach primarily based on research in the fields of positive psychology and positive organizational scholarship. These two approaches to leadership development highlight the role of values as drivers of human behavior and the importance of leader character and ethos. Furthermore, they are based on the premise that organizations do well by doing good, because they are viewed as communities of value-driven individuals. In this respect, virtuous behavior is deemed an effective means to simultaneously do well financially and to fight the ongoing process of dehumanization of the business world.

For Meyer, Sison, and Ferrero (2019: 399), the ethical qualities of a leader are considered a major determinant for success in positive and neo-Aristotelian leadership. An organization that seeks to foster ethical behavior should primarily focus on ethical human development through which employees are afforded the opportunity to thrive as persons in their wholeness. Within such work environments, the leader is perceived as a role model of ethical conduct by motivating and empowering his subordinates accordingly. Virtuous leadership is a strong predictor of leader happiness (Nassif et al., 2020) and is invested with a potential for positive follower outcomes, in particular life satisfaction and eudaimonic well-being.

Newstead et al. (2019) provide a robust conceptualization of the ways through which virtue informs good leadership practices. They thus proceed to elucidate the core synergistic components of virtue-based leadership development, namely, how a virtue approach accounts for ethical leadership effectiveness; the fact that virtue and leadership can be enabled through learning; the relationship between virtues, character, and leadership; the unity and universality of virtue; and the channels through which virtue bridges the gap between the individual and the common good.

The above analysis can offer permeating insights on how healthcare leadership could be improved through an emphasis on leader virtue and character. At the individual micro-level, virtuous leaders can motivate and empower their subordinates, facilitating their personal fulfillment and personality growth, as well as by promoting the psychological health and well-being of healthcare personnel. At the meso-organizational level, virtuous leaders are in a position to shape more humane and ethical work environments from which all participants, personnel staff, and patients can significantly benefit. Last but not least, at the macro-social level, virtuous leadership is in a position to embed healthcare organizations in their societal context in a way that is respectful of the expectations of all stakeholders, organizations, patients, and local communities.

Healthcare Management in a World of Pandemics

The unprecedented challenges brought on by the COVID-19 pandemic have inflicted tremendous strain on healthcare human resources, thus culminating in a series of ethical decision-making dilemmas to be effectively met by the respective personnel (Menon & Padhy, 2020). In this novel situation, the implementation of processes and practices to support healthcare personnel is more than necessary (Adams & Walls, 2020). This may even necessitate a major paradigm change in established views on conventional health management practices (Garraud, 2020).

In these new contexts, HRM research has to properly adapt to encompass societal expectations of multilevel actors by managing under uncertainty, facilitating international and even global work, and redefining organizational performance criteria (Caligiuri et al., 2020). Latest research showed that albeit the pandemic is negatively experienced for most career trajectories, it might under certain conditions allow for more positive vocational outcomes (Akkermans et al., 2020; Cho, 2020). At the macro-level, the pandemic necessitates an endeavor towards realization of more equitable and sustainable societies in order to prevent a major humanitarian crisis (van Barneveld et al., 2020).

In the light of the recent COVID-19 pandemic, organizations seek to navigate an unprecedented situation by thereby finding new solutions to challenges arising across many areas of their operations and in human resource management (HRM) in particular, through facilitating their workforce endure and adjusting to this entirely altered work environment (Carnevale & Hatak, 2020).

Yang and Ren (2020) showed that both moral obligation and public leadership were conducive to collective action for COVID-19 prevention and control insofar as these two critical factors could substantially strengthen each other's positive role in initiatives aiming at mitigating COVID-19's perilous consequences. Stoller (2020) evokes five core commitments as constituents of effective leadership in a pandemic crisis, namely, challenging the process, inspiring a shared vision, enabling others to act, modeling the way, and encouraging the heart.

More importantly, in these turbulent times, a tension between two primary responsibilities of healthcare participants arises: their primary responsibility to safeguard the health rights and interests of individual patients seems to enter into conflict with the responsibility to protect the public's health rights and interests in public health emergencies (Zhu, 2020). Such a view of leadership comprises the government's willingness to draw on expertise knowledge and ongoing effort to mobilize the population as well as to enable coping behaviors: these factors make the difference in times of pandemics insofar as they build the trust in leadership required by transformative, collective action (Wilson, 2020).

Discussion

The Political Economy of COVID-19 Pandemics

The COVID-19 crisis has severely affected the functioning of market economies in multiple respects. The era of new pandemics has afflicted not only entrepreneurial pursuits, business activities, and supply chain management (Brown & Rocha, 2020; Donthu & Gustafsson, 2020; Kraus et al., 2020; Pantano et al., 2020; Sharma et al., 2020) but has also a tangible impact on organizational processes and outcomes (Kramer & Kramer, 2020), flexible work arrangements (Spurk & Straub, 2020), and consumer behaviors and attitudes (Sheth, 2020).

Liu et al. (2020) designate the importance of resilience, strategic agility, and entrepreneurship in the context of the fight against COVID-19. They also underline the need to develop predictive models that take into consideration uncertainties and risk factors in the proactive dynamic planning of supply. They in turn argue in favor of greater collaboration between governments, industries, and societies to ensure minimum disruption in global supply chains and the proper functioning of markets.

He and Harris (2020) offered an outline of how the ongoing COVID-19 pandemic influences corporate social responsibility, consumer ethics, and marketing philosophy. They thus argued that the COVID-19 pandemic may offer a unique opportunity for businesses to undertake a decisive shift towards more genuine and authentic CSR attitudes and contribute to address current social and environmental issues by encouraging more responsible and prosocial economic behavior. Under a different perspective, Crick and Crick (2020) draw on resource-based theory and on relational views to delineate coopetition as an effective marketing strategy during a pandemic. Coopetition activities comprise cooperative and competitive practices in which decision-makers have to properly choose which competitors they would collaborate with, due to potential detrimental outcomes on their performance. They then suggest that such a perspective incorporates a strong potential to benefit the firms involved in such types of partnerships. Interestingly, issues of whether these coopetition strategies will persist in a post-COVID-19 world still remain inconclusive. Again, virtuous leadership founded on the primary virtue of wisdom may offer invaluable insights on how to tackle with such cases. Managerial wisdom and discretion are in a position to facilitate firms and organizations to successfully cope with these new challenges.

Prospects for Health Management in a Post-COVID-19 World

Health management is subject to substantial transformation due to the experience accumulated gradually during this latest pandemic. We have thus far argued that virtuous leadership as a highly contextual approach is in a position to substantially benefit healthcare personnel facing a situation of extreme necessity.

Admittedly however, health management in times of pandemic may assume new, unprecedented dimensions. One of them involves the fact that health management is then elevated to crisis management that has to successfully and effectively balance conflicting societal demands and, in particular, the need for public health based on security premises and the respective need for individual liberties and, among them, economic freedom. In this case, a social utility dilemma arises: Should we have to protect a common good, public health, perhaps at the expense of equally important individual rights founded on democratic legitimacy? How can we handle such competing aspects of social life?

Effective paradox management presupposes the respective skills and competences required to solve such social dilemmas. Christensen and Lægreid (2020) outline the ways through which the Norwegian government managed to control the pandemic by employing suppression and control strategies based on a collaborative and pragmatic decision-making style, ensuring successful communication practices with the public, mobilizing necessary resources, and securing a high level of citizen trust in the government. In this view, the success of the Norwegian authorities was based on the relationship between displaying a high crisis management capacity and maintaining democratic legitimacy. To mitigate tensions between these competing demands, the authorities had to draw on cultural factors (bonds of trust, accumulated social capital), structural factors (coordination and regulatory capacity), and evidence-based knowledge about the new pandemic. Huang (2020) highlights the systemic variables that helped Taiwanese endeavor launch related initiatives, mobilize the public, and engage private resources to implement policies enhanced by multiple collaborative behaviors.

In a similar vein of reasoning, Moon (2020) explores the strategies adopted by the South Korean government to effectively mitigate the threat posed by COVID-19. South Korea employed adaptive, transparent actions that precluded a harsh forced lockdown: this strategy was grounded on a policy of transparency in communicating risk and citizens' voluntary cooperation with the authorities. The author suggests that Western societies should strive for alternative ways of managing uncertainties and complexities. Evidence-based heuristics as well as strong governmental and societal capacities are deemed as critical factors contributing to maintaining a high level of quality of life in open, free, and more humane societies.

Virtuous leadership is an invaluable resource in situations of extreme necessity. As already implied, virtue incorporates the doctrine of the mean, the primary principle to avoid both excess and shortage of an inner disposition. At the social level, if we align with the doctrine of the mean, we are in a position to effectively solve social dilemma situations and handle paradox management, by avoiding the two extremes, the two opposing poles that seem to contradict each other. Public health and individual liberty are two ultimate ends in themselves, in a wide spectrum of terminal values such as social welfare, social justice, and democratic liberty.

In our case, virtuous leadership may indicate the mechanisms through which the common good of public health is entirely compatible with the need for individual liberty in all areas of social life. Harsh measures imposed upon the society through public health management may yield negative long-run effects (such as citizen's addiction to measures that preclude social deliberation and curtail basic liberties), as well as a considerable reduction of citizens' prosperity and psychological subjective well-being. A society that focuses only on one pole of a dilemma and underestimates the other runs the risk of either endangering the health of its citizens or turning into an authoritarian regime that ultimately violates shared values and long-held ideals of enlightenment cultural heritage to our contemporary world.

Practical Implications and Conclusions

Despite its ongoing significance nowadays, there still remains a relative paucity of research regarding the development programs designed for healthcare middle managers (Whaley & Gillis, 2018). The importance of incorporating education for community and health actors into health sector leadership development programming has been recently recognized (Aini, 2018; Ayeleke et al., 2019; Sikipa et al., 2019), especially in post-COVID-19 framework of management education (Beech & Anseel, 2020; Budhwar & Cumming, 2020).

Furthermore, leadership has to provide new psychological services in view of managing the innate tensions, existential threats, and needs experienced by the frontline medical staff (Zaka et al., 2020). Virtuous leadership is in a position to significantly mitigate these tensions and support the psychological needs of those engaging in healthcare services, thus reducing uncertainty and enhancing personal fulfillment through the pursuit of the common good.

In sum, virtuous leadership opens a new pathway to more humane healthcare organizations that respect the dignity of the human person and consider the needs of local communities through enactment of more sustainable practices. This chapter encourages new empirical research on virtuous leadership in healthcare organizations, especially in a post-COVID-19 world, to demonstrate the potential, promises, and prospects, but also the possible limitations of this relatively new approach to leadership development in the healthcare sector.

Chapter Takeaways

- Many potential antecedents of virtuous leadership have been investigated, such as the personal characteristic of responsibility disposition and environmental cues; leader empathy and leader gratitude; moral identity; leader's cognitive moral development; leader's agreeableness, conscientiousness, and neuroticism; and situational influences and individual influences.
- Many potential outcomes of virtuous leadership are likely: employee creativity; satisfaction, motivation, and organizational commitment; organizational learning; leader happiness and follower life satisfaction; positive emotions, effort, physical health, and psychological health; and employee decision-making, prosocial, and counterproductive behaviors.
- Virtuous leadership is in a position to substantially benefit healthcare personnel facing a situation of extreme necessity by reducing uncertainty and enhancing personal fulfillment through the pursuit of the common good.
- Virtuous leadership may indicate the mechanisms through which the common good of public health is entirely compatible with the need for individual liberty in all areas of social life.
- Virtuous leadership is in a position to significantly mitigate the tensions and support the psychological needs of those engaging in healthcare services.

Reflection Questions

- How can we face the challenges in healthcare management in a world of pandemics?
- How important is moral compass for healthcare leaders?
- What are the antecedents and outcomes of virtuous leadership?
- How effective is virtuous leadership in healthcare organizations?
- How can virtuous leadership contribute to healthcare management policies?

References

Adams, J. G., & Walls, R. M. (2020). Supporting the health care workforce during the COVID-19 global epidemic. *JAMA – Journal of the American Medical Association, 323*(15), 1439–1440.

Adinolfi, P., & Borgonovi, E. (2017). *The myths of healthcare: Towards new models of leadership and management in the healthcare sector*. Springer.

Aini, Q. (2018). Management skill and leadership: A case study from hospital managers of charity business in health. *Journal of Social Sciences Research, 4*(12), 478–482.

Akkermans, J., Richardson, J., & Kraimer, M. L. (2020). The COVID-19 crisis as a career shock: Implications for careers and vocational behavior. *Journal of Vocational Behavior, 119*, 103434.

Ayeleke, R. O., North, N. H., Dunham, A., & Wallis, K. A. (2019). Impact of training and professional development on health management and leadership competence: A mixed methods systematic review. *Journal of Health Organization and Management, 33*(4), 354–379.

Bäckström, I., Ingelsson, P., & Johansson, C. (2016). How communicative leadership influences co-workers' health. A quality management perspective. *International Journal of Quality and Service Sciences, 8*(2), 143–158.

Balser, J.R., & Stead, W.W. (2015). How academic health centers are transforming in leadership, administration, and management: A case study. In: *The transformation of academic health centers: Meeting the challenges of healthcare's changing landscape* (pp. 23–28). Academic Press.

Beech, N., & Anseel, F. (2020). COVID-19 and its impact on management research and education: Threats, opportunities and a manifesto. *British Journal of Management, 31*(3), 447–449.

Brown, M. E., & Treviño, L. K. (2006). Ethical leadership: A review and future directions. *The Leadership Quarterly, 17*(6), 595–616.

Brown, M. E., & Treviño, L. K. (2014). Do role models matter? An investigation of role modeling as an antecedent of perceived ethical leadership. *Journal of Business Ethics, 122*(4), 587–598.

Brown, R., & Rocha, A. (2020). Entrepreneurial uncertainty during the COVID-19 crisis: Mapping the temporal dynamics of entrepreneurial finance. *Journal of Business Venturing Insights, 14*, e00174.

Budhwar, P., & Cumming, D. (2020). New directions in management research and communication: Lessons from the COVID-19 pandemic. *British Journal of Management, 31*(3), 441–443.

Caldararo, K. L., & Nash, D. B. (2017). Population health research: Early description of the organizational shift toward population health management and defining a vision for leadership. *Population Health Management, 20*(5), 368–373.

Caligiuri, P., De Cieri, H., Minbaeva, D., Verbeke, A., & Zimmermann, A. (2020). International HRM insights for navigating the COVID-19 pandemic: Implications for future research and practice. *Journal of International Business Studies, 51*, 697–713.

Cameron, K. (2011). Responsible leadership as virtuous leadership. *Journal of Business Ethics, 98*(1), 25–35.

Carnevale, J. B., & Hatak, I. (2020). Employee adjustment and well-being in the era of COVID-19: Implications for human resource management. *Journal of Business Research, 116*, 183–187.

Cho, E. (2020). Examining boundaries to understand the impact of COVID-19 on vocational behaviors. *Journal of Vocational Behavior, 119*, 103437.

Christensen, T., & Lægreid, P. (2020). Balancing governance capacity and legitimacy – How the Norwegian government handled the COVID-19 crisis as a high performer. *Public Administration Review, 80*(5), 774–779.

Crick, J. M., & Crick, D. (2020). Coopetition and COVID-19: Collaborative business-to-business marketing strategies in a pandemic crisis. *Industrial Marketing Management, 88*, 206–213.

Crossan, M., Mazutis, D., & Seijts, G. (2013). In search of virtue: The role of virtues, values and character strengths in ethical decision making. *Journal of Business Ethics, 113*(4), 567–581.

Crossan, M. M., Byrne, A., Seijts, G. H., Reno, M., Monzani, L., & Gandz, J. (2017). Toward a framework of leader character in organizations. *Journal of Management Studies, 54*(7), 986–1018.

der Kinderen, S., Valk, A., Khapova, S. N., & Tims, M. (2020). Facilitating eudaimonic well-being in mental health care organizations: The role of servant leadership and workplace civility climate. *International Journal of Environmental Research and Public Health, 17*(4), 1173.

Detert, J. R., Treviño, L. K., & Sweitzer, V. L. (2008). Moral disengagement in ethical decision making: A study of antecedents and outcomes. *Journal of Applied Psychology, 93*(2), 374.

Donthu, N., & Gustafsson, A. (2020). Effects of COVID-19 on business and research. *Journal of Business Research, 117*, 284–289.

Figueroa, C. A., Harrison, R., Chauhan, A., & Meyer, L. (2019). Priorities and challenges for health leadership and workforce management globally: A rapid review. *BMC Health Services Research, 19*(1), 239.

Fraser, M., Castrucci, B., & Harper, E. (2017). Public health leadership and management in the era of public health 3.0. *Journal of Public Health Management and Practice, 23*(1), 90–92.

Garraud, O. (2020). COVID-19: Is a paradigm change to be expected in health care and transfusion medicine? *Transfusion Clinique et Biologique, 27*(2), 59–60.

Guerrero, E. G., Frimpong, J., Kong, Y., Fenwick, K., & Aarons, G. A. (2020). Advancing theory on the multilevel role of leadership in the implementation of evidence-based health care practices. *Health Care Management Review, 45*(2), 151–161.

Hackett, R. D., & Wang, G. (2012). Virtues and leadership. *Management Decision, 50*(5), 868–899.

He, H., & Harris, L. (2020). The impact of COVID-19 pandemic on corporate social responsibility and marketing philosophy. *Journal of Business Research, 116*, 176–182.

Hendriks, M., Burger, M., Rijsenbilt, A., Pleeging, E., & Commandeur, H. (2020). Virtuous leadership: A source of employee well-being and trust. *Management Research Review, 43*(8), 951–970.

Holder, R., & Ramagem, C. (2012). Health leadership and management competencies: A systemic approach. *World Hospitals and Health Services: The Official Journal of the International Hospital Federation, 48*(3), 9–12.

Huang, I. Y. (2020). Fighting COVID-19 through government initiatives and collaborative governance: The Taiwan experience. *Public Administration Review, 80*(4), 665–670.

Jordan, J., Brown, M. E., Treviño, L. K., & Finkelstein, S. (2013). Someone to look up to: Executive–follower ethical reasoning and perceptions of ethical leadership. *Journal of Management, 39*(3), 660–683.

Kalshoven, K., Den Hartog, D. N., & De Hoogh, A. H. (2011). Ethical leader behavior and big five factors of personality. *Journal of Business Ethics, 100*(2), 349–366.

Kramer, A., & Kramer, K. Z. (2020). The potential impact of the COVID-19 pandemic on occupational status, work from home, and occupational mobility. *Journal of Vocational Behavior, 119*, 103442.

Kraus, S., Clauss, T., Breier, M., Gast, J., Zardini, A., & Tiberius, V. (2020). The economics of COVID-19: Initial empirical evidence on how family firms in five European countries cope with the corona crisis. *International Journal of Entrepreneurial Behaviour and Research, 26*(5), 1067–1092.

Kumar, S., Kumar, N., Adhish, V. S., & Reddy, R. S. (2015). Strategic management and leadership for health professionals: Skills to leverage resources to achieve health goals. *Indian Journal of Community Medicine, 40*(3), 158–162.

Kwamie, A. (2015). Balancing management and leadership in complex health systems: Comment on "management matters: A leverage point for health systems strengthening in global health". *International Journal of Health Policy and Management, 4*(12), 849–851.

Li, C. (2013). *Ethical leadership in firms: Antecedents and consequences*. University of Alabama Libraries.

Liu, Y., Lee, J. M., & Lee, C. (2020). The challenges and opportunities of a global health crisis: The management and business implications of COVID-19 from an Asian perspective. *Asian Business and Management, 19*(3), 277–297.

Low, S., Butler-Henderson, K., Nash, R., & Abrams, K. (2019). Leadership development in health information management (HIM): Literature review. *Leadership in Health Services, 32*(4), 569–583.

Marston, C. A., Matthews, R., Renedo, A., & Reed, J. E. (2020). Working together to co-produce better health: The experience of the collaboration for leadership in applied health research and care for Northwest London. *Journal of Health Services Research and Policy, 26*(1), 28–36.

Mayer, D. M., Aquino, K., Greenbaum, R. L., & Kuenzi, M. (2012). Who displays ethical leadership, and why does it matter? An examination of antecedents and consequences of ethical leadership. *Academy of Management Journal, 55*(1), 151–171.

Meawad, S. (2016). Virtue as mediator: Informing health care issues through virtue ethics and scripture. *Ethics and Medicine, 32*(2), 95–107.

Menon, V., & Padhy, S.K. (2020). Ethical dilemmas faced by health care workers during COVID-19 pandemic: Issues, implications and suggestions. *Asian Journal of Psychiatry, 51*, 102116.

Meyer, M., & Hühn, M.P. (2020). Positive language and virtuous leadership: Walking the talk. *Management Research. Journal of the Iberoamerican Academy of Management, 18*(3), 263–284.

Meyer, M., Sison, A. J. G., & Ferrero, I. (2019). How positive and neo-aristotelian leadership can contribute to ethical leadership. *Canadian Journal of Administrative Sciences, 36*(3), 390–403.

Moon, M.J. (2020). Fighting against COVID-19 with agility, transparency, and participation: Wicked policy problems and new governance challenges. *Public Administration Review, 80*(4), 651–656.

Nassif, A. G., Hackett, R. D., & Wang, G. (2020). Ethical, virtuous, and charismatic leadership: An examination of differential relationships with follower and leader outcomes. *Journal of Business Ethics*.

Newstead, T., Dawkins, S., Macklin, R., & Martin, A. (2019). We don't need more leaders: We need more good leaders. Advancing a virtues-based approach to leader(ship) development. *Leadership Quarterly*.

Newstead, T., Dawkins, S., Macklin, R., & Martin, A. (2020). Evaluating the virtues project as a leadership development programme. *Leadership, 1742715019899845, 16*(6), 633–660.

Nikandrou, I., & Tsachouridi, I. (2015). Towards a better understanding of the "buffering effects" of organizational virtuousness' perceptions on employee outcomes. *Management Decision, 53*(8), 1823–1842.

Okpala, P. (2020). Increasing access to primary health care through distributed leadership. *International Journal of Healthcare Management*.

Pantano, E., Pizzi, G., Scarpi, D., & Dennis, C. (2020). Competing during a pandemic? Retailers' ups and downs during the COVID-19 outbreak. *Journal of Business Research, 116*, 209–213.

Pearce, C. L., Waldman, D. A., & Csikszentmihalyi, M. (2008). Virtuous leadership: A theoretical model and research agenda. In *The virtuous organization: Insights from some of the world's leading management thinkers* (pp. 211–230). World Scientific.

Pfeffermann, G. (2012). Leadership and management quality: Key factors in effective health systems. *World Hospitals and Health Services: The Official Journal of the International Hospital Federation, 48*(3), 18–20.

Porter-O'Grady, T. (2020). Complexity leadership: Constructing 21st-century health care. *Nursing Administration Quarterly, 44*(2), 92–100.

Ruth Gaare, B., & Alan, M. (2008). Principled leadership in public health: Integrating ethics into practice and management. *Journal of Public Health Management and Practice, 14*(4), 358–366.

Sharma, P., Leung, T. Y., Kingshott, R. P. J., Davcik, N. S., & Cardinali, S. (2020). Managing uncertainty during a global pandemic: An international business perspective. *Journal of Business Research, 116*, 188–192.

Sheth, J. (2020). Impact of COVID-19 on consumer behavior: Will the old habits return or die? *Journal of Business Research, 117*, 280–283.

Sikipa, G., Osifo-Dawodu, E., Kokwaro, G., & Rice, J.A. (2019, April). Better board education for better leadership and management in the health sectors of low and middle income countries. *Frontiers in Public Health, 7*, 67.

Spurk, D., & Straub, C. (2020). Flexible employment relationships and careers in times of the COVID-19 pandemic. *Journal of Vocational Behavior, 119*.

Stapleton, F. B., & Opipari, V. P. (2020). The current health care crisis-inspirational leadership (or lack thereof) is contagious. *JAMA Network Open, 3*(6) e208024.

Stoller, J. K. (2020). Reflections on leadership in the time of COVID-19. *BMJ Leader, 4*, 77–79.

Sturm, B. A. (2009). Principles of servant-leadership in community health nursing: Management issues and behaviors discovered in ethnographic research. *Home Health Care Management and Practice, 21*(2), 82–89.

van Barneveld, K., Quinlan, M., Kriesler, P., Junor, A., Baum, F., Chowdhury, A., & Rainnie, A. (2020). The COVID-19 pandemic: Lessons on building more equal and sustainable societies. *Economic and Labour Relations Review, 31*(2), 133–157.

VanVactor, J. D. (2012). Collaborative leadership model in the management of health care. *Journal of Business Research, 65*(4), 555–561.

Wang, G., & Hackett, R. D. (2016). Conceptualization and measurement of virtuous leadership: Doing well by doing good. *Journal of Business Ethics, 137*(2), 321–345.

Whaley, A., & Gillis, W. E. (2018). Leadership development programs for health care middle managers: An exploration of the top management team member perspective. *Health Care Management Review, 43*(1), 79–89.

Wilson, S. (2020). Pandemic leadership: Lessons from New Zealand's approach to COVID-19. *Leadership, 16*(3), 279–293.

Wong, C. A., & Walsh, E. J. (2020). Reflections on a decade of authentic leadership research in health care. *Journal of Nursing Management, 28*(1), 1–3.

Xing, L., Song, J., & Yan, F. (2020). How can leadership influence the quality of care in a healthcare organization? *Frontiers of Nursing, 7*(1), 19–22.

Yang, L., & Ren, Y. (2020). Moral obligation, public leadership, and collective action for epidemic prevention and control: Evidence from the corona virus disease 2019 (COVID-19) emergency. *International Journal of Environmental Research and Public Health, 17*(8), 2731.

Zaka, A., Shamloo, S. E., Fiorente, P., & Tafuri, A. (2020). COVID-19 pandemic as a watershed moment: A call for systematic psychological health care for frontline medical staff. *Journal of Health Psychology, 25*(7), 883–887.

Zappalà, S., & Toscano, F. (2020). The ethical leadership scale (ELS): Italian adaptation and exploration of the nomological network in a health care setting. *Journal of Nursing Management, 28*, 634–642.

Zhu, J. (2020). Is it ethical to be a 'whistleblower' during COVID-19 pandemic? Ethical challenges confronted by health care workers in China. *Journal of Advanced Nursing, 76*, 1873–1875.

Chapter 14
Leadership as Merit Making: The Case of Myanmar and Applications for Western Organizations

J. Andrew Morris, Aung Chan Aye, David Lingelbach, and Wah Wah Than Oo

Abstract Western leadership theory has overemphasized the role of the leader. As a result, leaders have become overly self-focused and self-interested. In this chapter, we suggest that leadership grounded in Buddhist thought can help overcome these problems. Drawing upon our experience as educators in Myanmar (Burma), we build upon the Buddhist concepts of merit and merit making to present a version of leadership that inspires collaboration and common purpose. Centering this approach within the complimentary areas of evolutionary economics and evolutionary psychology, we then highlight how three areas of leadership as merit making has application in modern organizations. Lastly, we develop two exercises that we have used to illustrate a more others-directed leadership style.

Keywords Leadership · Buddhism · Merit making · Others-directed · Evolutionary economics

Introduction

> *For the good of many, for the happiness of many, out of compassion for the world*
> ~ Siddhartha Gotama

J. A. Morris (✉)
CSU Channel Islands, Camarillo, CA, USA
e-mail: john-andrew.morris@csuci.edu

A. C. Aye · W. W. T. Oo
Monywa University of Economics, Monywa, Myanmar

D. Lingelbach
University of Baltimore, Baltimore, MD, USA

J. Marques (ed.), *Innovative Leadership in Times of Compelling Changes*, Management, Change, Strategy and Positive Leadership, https://doi.org/10.1007/978-3-030-67258-4_14

These are difficult times. A global pandemic, social unrest, and climate change have left people feeling afraid and uncertain. In times of crisis, leadership matters more because small errors can cause exponential consequences. Recent evidence suggests that many leaders are not rising to the challenge. We suggest that part of this failure to lead occurs because too many leaders have forgotten who they serve and why they are serving. Leaders have become overly self-focused and self-interested.

Over the last several decades, leaders have been viewed as idols, heroes, and magicians, but this fascination with leaders and leadership is giving way to anger, frustration, and feelings of betrayal as financial scandals, rising inequality, and physical well-being become increasingly endangered (Walsh, 2020). The question becomes "How are leaders to grow to meet the increasingly difficult challenges they face?" Leadership is needed that governs without charismatics or heroes. The teachings of the Buddha show us one possible alternative. We suggest that part of the answer lies with a rediscovery of the teachings of the Buddha and its focus on leadership as service to others. In essence, a leadership style that is not based on personal achievement or glory but rather one that is centered on collaboration and common purpose.

Buddhist thoughts on leadership are extensive, and many scholars have written on this topic (Marques, 2017; Spiro, 1970; van den Berg, 2019). In this chapter, we will briefly explore Buddhism and Buddhist thoughts around leadership and merit making. We will draw upon our experiences as educators in Myanmar (previously known as Burma) to show how a more others-directed leadership has demonstrated in Myanmar. In addition, we draw upon Buddhism and the concept of merit to show how "leadership as merit making" might help reimagine Western concepts in the leadership process (a reconceptualization that is highly consistent with and influenced by research findings in evolutionary economics). In addition, we introduce two exercises that we have used to illustrate the human capacity for merit and being others-directed. We close with several reflective questions around these concepts and exercises.

Buddhist Leadership and Merit Making

Buddhism is one of the most time-tested philosophies available to humanity. Drawing upon Buddhist principles could help address many of the problems facing leadership in modern organizations especially the overemphasis on selfish outcomes and underemphasis on leadership as compassion and service to others (being others-directed). Buddhism is the major religion of many Southeast Asian countries, although the Buddha himself never considered it a religion. The Buddha believed his teachings to be a philosophy of self-actualization based on principles of love, kindness, and compassion (Nhat Hanh, 1999). Buddhism teaches that human suffering is largely the result of false belief and false perception. Practice of the noble eight-fold path can help overcome these delusions. Simply put, people suffer because they narrow down their "selves" too much and detach this from the well-being of others. The teachings of the Buddha often run counter to current management theories with their focus on strictly utilitarian principles. Buddhism emphasizes self-development, nonviolence, kindness, love, and compassion. It rejects the self-serving focus common to modern management and suggests the greatest well-being is obtained through compassion and service to others.

Buddhism does not reject economic progress. In fact, progress that alleviates suffering is greatly valued (unless it stimulates attachment and greed). However, the Buddha advised leaders not to live in the lap of luxury but to live a simple wholesome life to serve people rather than pursuing idle pleasure. Further, leaders cannot earn the trust and respect of people if they do not set a right example. Buddha believed that leading by virtue differs from leading by law and order. Leading by virtue does not require punishment but rather mutual love, respect, and virtuousness (van den Berg, 2019). Leadership that focuses on virtue and respect for others is consistent with the modern management practices of decentralization, flat organizational structures, and democratic governing.

Buddhist principles can contribute to the development of leaders who make a beneficial contribution to society. Buddhist thought helps leaders develop wisdom. Wisdom is gained through mindful focus on self-development and ethical conduct. A leader who engages with the noble eight-fold path will mindfully focus on decision-making that improves the quality of life of all stakeholders not just themselves. A key part of the mindful leadership path and its focus on respect and compassion is the concept of merit and merit making.

Merit and Merit Making Merit is fundamental to Buddhist ethics. A beneficial and protective "energy/force," merit accumulates as the result of good (right) deeds, acts, or thoughts. The act of doing good deeds is merit making. Merit differs from karma although the two are related. At its simplest, karma arises as the consequences of one's actions. Good actions and thoughts lead to good karma, while bad actions and thoughts lead to bad karma. It is important to understand that karma is not punishment but rather consequence, and if karma is consequence, then merit is just effect. In other words, whatever you do creates karma, but the merit you acquire from these actions is the effect of the positive causes you have made (Spiro, 1970).

Merit making is key to Buddhist practice since it determines the quality of one's life and contributes to a person's growth towards enlightenment. Indeed, Buddha Gotama explicitly states, "There are, O monks, three ways of making merit. What three? There are ways of making merit by giving, by virtue, and by the development of meditation." Later sources suggested seven additional ways of making merit. These are polite and modest conduct; offer service to do the common good; involving others in doing good deeds; rejoicing in the good deeds of others; listening to the teachings of the Dharma; explaining the teachings of the Dharma; and learning to see things as they really are so that one attains right view.

Generosity is the most common way of making merit and is a key way to avoid unwholesome thoughts based on greed. Buddhism teaches that attachment to things is an unwholesome behavior and generates unfortunate results. In other words, generosity helps reduce the emotional attachment to material things and thus becomes a way of reducing greed. However, there is often confusion around the merit making value of generosity when one's motivations are selfish or self-interested. Certainly giving for the wrong reasons is possible. For example, George Orwell described in his book *Burmese Days* the manipulation of earning merits as a sort of compensation for one's own wrong deeds done to others in society. Yet the Pali Canon is clear here. It suggests that only by performing ethical actions with a mind based on loving kindness can the benefits of giving generate merit (Spiro, 1970). Interestingly, these issues connect to current discussions in Western social science regarding differences between altruism and hedonistic behaviors. In general, Western social scientists do not require the intent of "loving kindness" for an act to be considered altruistic – only that the action have greater benefit for others (Ridley, 1997).

The second way that the Buddha taught merit was through virtue. According to the Pali Canon, virtue arises by following different percepts. Individuals follow five basic percepts, nuns follow eight precepts, novices follow 109 precepts, and monks follows 227 precepts. The five basic precepts include refraining from killing living beings, refraining from taking what is not given, refraining from non-celibate conduct, refraining from false speech, and refraining from drugs and drinks that would cloud one's mind. Following these precepts is not only making merit by virtue but also helps avoid unwholesome actions that arise from the three defilements of greed, hatred, and delusion (Spiro, 1970).

The third way of making merit is through meditation or mental development. Buddhism identifies two kinds of meditation: tranquility or concentration and insight or wisdom. This type of making merit emphasizes self-consciousness and mindfulness. Self-consciousness and mindfulness help one gain wisdom (a better understanding of impermanence, non-self, and suffering). The Buddha discovered through self-experimentation that any attempt to freeze the world or grab on to it is inherently impossible. One of the aims of meditation is to see the nature of change, without overstating and over-conceptualizing it, but experiencing it as phenomena arising and passing away. From an awareness of constant change, the concept of non-self is found. Buddha taught that the personal self or "I" is fundamentally empty of an intrinsic reality of its own, but a product of the conceptualization of one's mind and thus the cause of many false beliefs. Key to these false beliefs is the concept of suffering. Indeed suffering and the cessation of suffering is the heart of the Buddha's teaching (Nhat Hanh, 1999). Buddhism does not say "life is suffering"; however, it does say "life, as we normally live it, involves suffering." The realization of impermanence and non-self as gained through meditation becomes the foundation upon which to reduce our suffering and the suffering of others.

In summary, Buddhism is a time-tested philosophy that is based on principles of love and compassion for oneself and others. A key part of Buddhist ethics is merit and merit making – the effects of doing "good" actions. Merit making involves giving, virtue, and self-awareness. We suggest in this chapter that drawing upon the concept of merit making can be a way to help redirect leadership study from one of influence and self-interest to service and compassion. Leaders who see their roles as merit making should be less likely to engage in misconduct since they are more aware of how their behaviors harm others. In the sections to follow, we provide both an example of leadership that takes merit making seriously and ways to apply a more others-directed merit-centered approach to leadership. Interestingly, our approach grounded in Buddhism finds support from recent research in evolutionary economics (Fehr & Gintis, 2007).

The Case of Myanmar

Myanmar was given the prestigious title of the number one giving nation in the world for 4 years running (2014–2017; it dropped to number nine in 2018) by Charities Aid Foundation. As Dove (2017) notes, there are many reasons for this generosity, but the widespread practice of Theravada Buddhism (87.9% of the population) and its focus on merit making are critical to the nation's generosity. Indeed, many Buddhists in Myanmar consider themselves very fortunate to be able to practice giving in ways highlighted in the Pali Canon (Dove, 2017; Spiro, 1970). Myanmar's achievement as one of the top giving countries is even more surprising in that Myanmar is one of Asia's poorest countries (Thant, 2019). The fact that Myanmar, while ranking as one of the least developed countries in the world, can demonstrate such strong generosity is an economic paradox.

The daily practice of charitable deeds is a critical component of everyday life in Myanmar. Food, water, and flowers are offered at local monasteries and to Buddhist images. Depending on their means, Buddhists will also make other donations, such as inviting the monks to their homes and offering food, training their young sons as novice monks, special giving on birthdays and anniversaries to monasteries or private interests such as children's homes or animal shelters, and donating materials to the monastery. While the amounts given may be small, they still have significant religious meaning, and many people give daily, regardless of income. Further, by supporting the monasteries that provide education to children, the community members are able to ensure the continued teachings of the Buddha, a key aspect of merit making.

Interestingly, the individual practice of charity in Myanmar finds expression in Burmese institutions and business organizations (Thant, 2019). For example, companies give gifts of schoolbooks, meals to orphanages or homes for the elderly, and medical equipment or glasses for those who cannot afford them. As educators in Myanmar (two of us were Fulbright Scholars there, and two were Burmese faculty at Monywa University of Economics), we saw on multiple occasions our university (both as individual members and as a collective) engage in acts of giving. Indeed, one of the most important days in the life of our university was the ceremony in which monks from a local monastery were invited to the campus to receive offerings from each academic program. After the offering and comments from the Abbott, hundreds of students, faculty, and staff joined a loud, wildly joyful procession around the campus. For two of us, this was truly a unique experience. In asking questions of why this process and why this importance, we were told two things: (a) students and faculty valued it because it reflected their individual spiritual practice, and (b) senior administrators believed that it reflected the larger purpose of the university. In speaking with the rector, it was clear that he believed that the purpose of the university, its faculty, and ultimately the students was one of service to the larger community not just their own self-interests. Theirs was a mission to enhance the well-being of the community and the nation state. Specifically the rector writes on the university webpage, "Monywa University of Economics is the auspicious ground of producing economists who are reliable by the State... It is gladly and proudly seen that economists are serving the State in their positions dutifully..... I encourage you to be a righteous, good-spirted, well-qualified and reliable economist of the country by nurturing yourself." What truly stands out here is just how explicit the rector is in describing a community-based purpose.

Applications and Exercises

Our focus on merit and merit making finds support within the emerging literatures of both evolutionary economics and evolutionary psychology. Consistent with the Buddhist concept of the "middle way" and the understanding that people are neither good nor evil but both, these research areas indicate that human behavior is a complex mix of hedonism and altruism and, under certain conditions, may exhibit a high propensity for others-directed behavior (Ghosal, 2005) as evidenced in Myanmar. In this section, we explore ways a fuller, more complete understanding of the human capacity for others-directed behaviors (as grounded in merit making) can affect leadership and organizations. Drawing from this understanding, we then introduce two exercises that educators can use to illustrate these points.

Motivation Buddhism and the concept of merit can be used to reevaluate and reconsider self-interest models of motivation. Business education presents the utilitarian model as the primary model for understanding work behaviors. This model makes several key assumptions to include individuals are rational, more is better, and people always seek to maximize their subjective utility function. At its core, the model assumes a world of very intelligent individuals, termed *homo economicus*, who behave in amazingly simple ways. Evidence, however, suggests a substantially different agent operating in a significantly different environment: a cognitively limited person coping with an incredibly complex world, where decision-makers must consider more than self-interest in order to maximize expected utility since utility is largely dependent upon the behaviors of others as well as their own.

Evolutionary economists are showing that economic agents will make choices that are not self-serving. Fehr and Gintis (2007) observed that thousands of subjects, from several cultures who engage in activities which result in monetary gains or losses, simply do not behave as traditional economic theory predicts. For example, the Ultimatum Game provides one of two participants (the "proposer") with ten one-dollar bills. The "proposer" is then informed that he or she must offer some fraction of the money to the "receiver," whose identity may or may not be hidden from the proposer. The proposer may offer any amount, from nothing to the entire ten dollars. The receiver may then accept or reject the offer. If the offer is accepted, the cash is shared according to the offer made. If the receiver rejects the offer, however, no one receives any money. Assumptions of rationality and self-interest indicate that the proposer should make an offer significantly less than five dollars, and the receiver should accept almost any offer, as something is better than nothing! The "rational" proposer, convinced that all human behavior is influenced by the rational pursuit of self-interest, would then make a relatively simple resource allocation decision: offer $1, as the game is played only once under "take it or leave it" conditions. Results consistently demonstrate, however, that most proposers offer about 40% of the money, either believing this is fair or worrying that a smaller offer will be rejected. Approximately half of all receivers reject offers at the 20% level, even when the stakes are financially significant. Here, Fehr and his associates argue that receivers reject low sums because the sums are perceived as unfair.

The central role of fairness and justice in exchange relationships suggests a greater need to explore the exact conditions that influence and direct judgments made when individuals attempt to determine if they are being treated fairly or acting fairly with others. Buddhism suggests and evolutionary economics research confirms that many individuals do not adhere to maximization perspectives. Indeed, in a world of nonzero sum outcomes, helping others often leads to better overall outcomes. This is not to deny that people can be selfish; they often are, but rather we suggest that drawing upon the concept of merit and its demonstrations of merit making in Myanmar indicates that placing an exclusive emphasis on self-interest is detrimental to understanding and modeling leadership.

Leader Humility In contrast to the heroic or visionary style often associated with business leaders, humble or servant leadership is conceptualized as a natural feeling that one wants to serve first, rather than be a leader first (Greenleaf, 1977). Research on leader humility (Owens et al., 2013) provides evidence for the utility of humility in leadership. Leader humility influences both organizational outcomes such as employee retention and individual performance. Morris and his associates (Morris et al., 2005) defined leader humility as a two-dimensional construct involving (a) the ability to honestly and truthfully appraise one's talents, strengths, and weaknesses and (b) an awareness of and respect for the influence of situational factors in determining outcomes. According to Van den Berg (2019), leader humility is a fundamental aspect of Buddhist practice through its contribution to the development of "leading with wisdom": leadership that is others-directed, moral, authentic, and strategic. The possibility that humility is critical to Buddhist and effective leadership offers a new lens through which to view and understand the leadership process. For example, research (Morris et al., 2005; Owens et al., 2013) suggests that humble leaders will create more fair reward systems, develop more supportive relationships with others, and use power in a manner that differs from that of leaders who are low in humility. Greater compassion and thus a focus on merit making is also likely to be one consequence of leader humility since humble leaders are more likely to understand that much of their success is due to the contributions of others. As such, these leaders should be more likely to give to others since they are more likely to be mindful of all that has been given to them. By transcending categories such as "leader" and "servant," Buddhism offers the possibility of showing how humble/servant leadership can be implemented, particularly in entrepreneurship. In the next section, we focus on that topic.

Entrepreneurship Entrepreneurship is defined as the identification and development of new opportunities (Shane, 2004). These opportunities can be discovered from existing problems or market gaps or created through new products, services, or processes that address yet unknown problems or provide new delights or satisfactions. From a Buddhist point of view, the role of the entrepreneur is to achieve moral objectives through economic means balancing the tensions between economic, religious, and social objectives (Valliere, 2008). Within the startup community, there has been increasing practitioner interest in the application of Buddhist principles and practice to entrepreneurship (Ives, 2018). While most of that interest has centered on meditation, we argue that merit making also influences entrepreneurial activity.

Entrepreneurship can be either an antecedent or consequence of merit. First, as an antecedent, entrepreneurship can lead to wealth creation that allows a startup founder to act charitably to a greater extent monetarily than he/she could otherwise do. For example, in Myanmar we can observe wealthy entrepreneurs building new temples as tangible evidence of their charity and therefore as an obvious means to generate merit. Second, entrepreneurship can lead to merit when a startup is operated consistent with Buddhist moral principles. As mentioned previously, these principles are abstention from killing living beings, stealing, sexual misconduct, lying, and intoxication. If followed strictly, these five principles would prohibit business activities in industries such as arms manufacturing or meat processing. More generally, these principles suggest virtues such as kindness, compassion, generosity, renunciation of lust and desires, contentment, honesty, dependability, mindfulness, and responsibility. An entrepreneur acting in accordance with these virtues would adopt them for him or herself, as well as for the startup that he or she owns. Thus, the new venture would generate merit for the founder. Third, entrepreneurship can generate merit through meditation. Meditation creates mindfulness, which can cause stress reduction in employees. Thus, founders that enable mindfulness practice among their workers can generate merit for themselves and these associates. Given the high stress nature of many startup environments, such practices are likely to be useful for both stress reduction and consequent productivity improvement.

Until recently, entrepreneurship has been a minor feature of the Myanmar economy. Many of the Myanmar entrepreneurs who have applied merit concepts in their startups have emphasized morality and philanthropy, although most do not explicitly state that they are seeking merit. Two examples illustrate these applications. Inle Heritage (http://inleheritage.org) is a social enterprise located on the shores of Inle Lake in Myanmar's Shan State. Inle Heritage's mission is to preserve the lake and the cultures of the ethnic groups living around it (Carruthers, 2019). Its philanthropic activities are 100% funded by its business activities, which include accommodations, a restaurant, a gift shop, and cooking classes. Inle Heritage exemplifies the application of merit concepts in a social enterprise. A second example, Sharky's restaurants https://www.sharkys.com.mm), is headquartered in Yangon, Myanmar's largest city. Founded in 1996 by U Ye Htut Win (nicknamed Sharky), the business's restaurants, delicatessens, and manufacturing operations produce and serve food that is organic, artisanal, locally sourced, and made from whole foods. These interlinked commitments to sustainable agriculture and healthy foods indicate a moral foundation, as well as a viable business model. Its morality provides an example of merit making.

Two Exercises The concept of merit making as described above, along with recent findings in evolutionary psychology and evolutionary economics, provides a new lens for educators to understand, model, and teach about human behavior and leadership. We believe that we can offer two exercises that some readers of this chapter may wish to incorporate into teaching or training practices. Educators can use exercises such as the Ultimatum Game and Wason Tests, which are described below, to great effect at both the undergraduate and graduate levels in courses such as principles of management, organizational behavior, and leadership. These exercises offer a terrific way to illustrate problems with self-interest models as well as the possibility of others-directed behavior in organizations. It should be emphasized that grounding these exercises explicitly within both an evolutionary framework and Buddhist concepts helps students gain a better general understanding of fairness as well as their personal reactions to unfair allocations. In particular, the exercises help illustrate the automaticity of behavioral reactions to unfair behavior and the value of compassion.

Wason Test We have used Wason Tests in both graduate and undergraduate classes in organizational behavior and principles of management courses to illustrate the human sensitivity to cheating behaviors and concerns for justice. Instructors typically introduce the exercise during discussions of decision-making; the versions that are used most frequently include the following instructions:

> *Consider the following problem – cards with a letter on one side have a number on the other. A logic rule of "if D then 3" is put into place. Students are then shown the following cards: D F 3 7 and are asked: "At a minimum which of the cards must be turned over to establish the truth of the logic rule?"*

D	F	3	7

Most students choose either the D card or the D card and the 3 card. The correct answer, however, is D and 7. The problem asks nothing of F, and the 3 card is irrelevant since the logic rule states that D's have 3's, not that 3's have D's. The 7 card is crucial, however, since if a D were displayed on the obverse side, the rule would be false.

If the format of the problem remains exactly the same, but the content of the information is altered so that the numbers and letters are replaced with real-world events that are both contextually relevant to participants and also framed as detecting cheaters in social exchange, participants become significantly better at generating the correct answer. For example, students are instructed:

> *"Let's assume the city of Los Angeles has enacted a law that states 'If a person goes into Los Angeles, then that person must take public transportation.'" Students are then shown cards that have information about four Los Angeles residents. Each card represents one person. One side of the card provides a person's destination; the other side of the card displays the method of transportation used to travel to that destination. Students are then asked to indicate only those card(s) that must be turned over to determine if any of these people have violated the law.*

Los Angeles	Malibu	Bus	Car

In the second version, approximately 80–85% of students correctly respond Los Angeles and car. The law asks nothing of Malibu, and the bus is irrelevant since the law states "If Los Angeles, then public transportation." It does not state that all public transportation must go to Los Angeles. Results consistently show that most students struggle to solve the first abstract logic problem, but most perform exceedingly well when the problem is re-framed as one of fairness.

Ultimatum games have been used in a number of disciplines to demonstrate concepts such as bargaining strategies and concerns for fairness. Drawing upon Buddhist principles and an evolutionary framework, however, helps instructors better explain allocation decisions to students, as well as to help students understand their own reactions to unfair allocations. In effect, the concept of merit making allows educators to better explain that what appears to be an irrational choice in the game, an individual turning down "free" money (often with a sense of righteous anger), can actually be a very rational decision within the cooperation-defection dynamic. Instructions for one version of the Ultimatum Game which draw from the Fehr and Gintis (2007) research program follow:

> *You and your classmate have been chosen to participate in an experiment in which you could earn real money (games with significant stakes, 20 dollars or more, seem to work particularly well). In this experiment, you will be given 20 one-dollar bills, but you must offer some amount of that money to your classmate. If your classmate accepts your offer, the experiment is over. If your classmate rejects the offer, neither of you will receive any money. Again, if you classmate rejects your proposal, all the money is returned to me. Are the rules clear? OK, take a moment to think about it, and then make your offer.*

Personal experiences with the game (which include a version known as the Dictator Game in which no offer can be rejected) indicate that no player has ever offered only one dollar. Typically, students offer between 30 and 40% of the available money, and no student has ever accepted less than 20%.

Leadership as Merit Making Lessons

> The critics of selfish schools have a point, for everything becomes normative. If people are not rational maximizers of self-interest, then to teach them that such behavior would be logical is to corrupt them. (Ridley, 1997; 145)

Buddhist traditions and emerging research in evolutionary economics and psychology offer business educators an alternative perspective by which to understand and explain leadership within organizations. Both suggest that selfishness is not the human norm but rather that people have the capacity to be both caring and cooperative when rightfully mindful. The extent to which that capacity is utilized, however, is largely influenced by cultural institutions and spiritual and ethical traditions. Current business models fail to capture this more complex and robust understanding of human behavior, and as a result we appear to have produced far too many leaders who focus on their own narrow self-interest. We have argued that drawing upon the Buddhist principles of merit and merit making offers a way to overcome this failure.

We draw upon our experiences in Myanmar to illustrate examples of leadership that take merit seriously. Further, we highlight three different ways the concept of merit making might influence how we learn about or teach leadership. We concluded with two very practical exercises that educators might use to demonstrate merit making and human concerns for fairness and compassion. We argue the exercises can be used to address as well as to begin to overcome the problematic normalization of self-interest and in so doing help create leaders that lead "for the good of many, for the happiness of many, out of compassion for the world."

Chapter Takeaways

- Western leadership theory overemphasizes the role of leader, and as such too many leaders are too self-focused.
- Buddhism offers an alternative approach to leadership.
- Leadership as merit making revises the role of leader from one of self-interest to one of service but service that has individual benefits.
- Myanmar offers examples of leadership grounded in merit making.
- Leadership as merit making changes how we approach and think about motivation, humility, and entrepreneurship.
- Approaching leadership as merit making is strongly consistent with research findings in evolutionary economics and evolutionary psychology. Both suggest that being others-directed can often lead to the better outcome.

Reflection Questions

Here are a few questions to supplement your reflection on how the Buddhist concept of merit making could influence leadership in Western organizations:

1. How might confusion over Buddhism as ethical philosophy rather than religion impede application of Buddhist concepts such as merit and merit making?
2. What is likely to happen to giving practices in Myanmar as its economy develops? Rising expectations of a stronger wealthier government for basic services may reduce giving. On the other hand, perhaps people give even more as their wealth and income increase. Traditional economic theory predicts one outcome. What does the reader believe? Why?
3. Was the discovery that Buddhism and evolutionary economics arrive at a shared understanding of a human nature surprising? How might a more complex view of human economic behavior (one that is more focused on fairness, justice, and compassion) influence how leadership is taught in business programs?
4. What does the future hold for merit making in entrepreneurship? It promises a kinder, gentler alternative to the toxic organizational climates in contemporary startups, yet it is not clear that merit making will contribute to a startup's sustainable competitive advantage. How might merit making enhance competitive advantage?
5. What should students learn from the Wason Test? Why was the first problem so much harder than the second problem? How might a focus on kindness and concern for others influence one's willingness to perceive things as fair or unfair? How might a focus on kindness and concerns for others influence motivation to address perceived unfairness?
6. What does the Ultimatum Game teach students about human behavior? At work? In life? How do the outcomes shown in your version of the game agree/conflict with economic theory? How would previous interaction and possible future interaction influence resource allocation? Why do students make the offers they do? How would concerns with fairness and compassion influence allocation decisions? How might the game help students be more mindful of concerns for fairness and justice?

References

Carruthers, M. (2019). Making sustainability work for nature and people. TTGAsia, August, 5th.

Dove, C. (2017). Giving trends in Myanmar: More than merit making. *Austrian Journal of South-East Asian Studies, 10*(2), 205–222.

Fehr, E., & Gintis, H. (2007). Human motivation and social cooperation: Experimental and analytical foundations. *Annual Review of Sociology, 33*, 43–64.

Ghosal, S. (2005). Bad management theories are destroying good management. *Academy of Management Learning & Education, 4*, 75–91.

Greenleaf, R. K. (1977). *Servant leadership: A journey into the nature of legitimate power and greatness*. Paulist.

Ives, M. (2018). Jack Dorsey, posting on Twitter, is accused of being tone deaf. *New York Times,* December 10th.

Marques, J. (2017). A mindful moral compass for twenty-first century leadership: The noble eightfold path. *The Journal of Values-Based Leadership, 10*(1), Article 7. https://doi.org/10.22543/0733.101.1177

Morris, J., Brotheridge, C., & Urbanski, J. (2005). Bringing humility to leadership: Antecedents and consequences of leader humility. *Human Relations, 58*(10), 1323–1350.

Nhat Hanh, T. (1999). *The heart of the Buddha's teaching: Transforming suffering into peace, joy & Liberation: The four Noble truths, the Noble eightfold path, and other basic Buddhist teachings*. Broadway Books.

Owens, B., Johnson, D., & Mitchell, T. (2013). Expressed humility in organizations: Implications for performance, teams, and leadership. *Organization Science, 24*(5), 1517–1538. https://doi.org/10.1287/orsc.1120.0795

Ridley, M. (1997). *The origins of virtue: Human instincts and the evolution of cooperation*. Viking.

Shane, S. A. (2004). *A general theory of entrepreneurship: The individual-opportunity nexus*. Edward Elgar.

Spiro, M. (1970). *Buddhism and society: A great tradition and its Burmese vicissitudes*. Harper & Row.

Thant, M. (2019). *The hidden history of Burma: Race, capitalism, and the crisis of democracy in the 21st century*. Norton.

Valliere, D. (2008). Exploring Buddhist influence on the entrepreneurial decision. *International Journal of Entrepreneurial Behavior & Research, 14*(3), 172–191.

van den Berg, P. (2019). Leading with wisdom and Buddhist practice. In T. Tu & T. Thein (Eds.), *Buddhist approach to global leadership and shared responsibilities for sustainable societies*. Vietnam Buddhist University Series.

Walsh, J. (2020). Contextualizing the attention to managers and leaders since 1890 and our infatuation with leaders since 2007: A commentary on Kniffin, Detert & Lerory. *Academy of Management Discoveries*. Published Online: 4 May 2020 https://doi.org/10.5465/amd.2020.0074

Chapter 15
Living the Power Shift in Business and Beyond

Jo Aschenbrenner

Abstract The goal of this chapter is to expand awareness about the power shift needed in the world of work to let self-organization for-purpose flourish and ultimately to safeguard mankind's wellbeing and the sustainment of planet Earth. This shift requires new rules – rules in service of freedom – inside of our organizations, as well as intra-personally, inside the people doing the work. This chapter covers the new organizational form of the For-Purpose-Enterprise and discusses how individuals can calm down their anxious ego and grant purpose more power in business and in their lives.

Keywords Power · Purpose · Self-organization · Holacracy practice · Leadership and management hierarchy and concepts

The World Needs a New Understanding of Power

To safeguard mankind's wellbeing and the sustainment of our planet Earth, the world needs a new way of doing business. Truly pursuing company purpose in a self-organized manner puts an end to maximizing profits, to overusing natural resources, and to the supremacy of our selfish, anxious egos in business. To succeed in self-organizing the company for purpose, the company and its members need a new understanding of power. This power shift is the prerequisite for truly changing the way business is done and for reaching a new level of consciousness.

Living the power shift also is a key condition for an evolutionary society. When humanity learns to calm down the personal need for control, for external recognition, and for conventional forms of success it paves the way for true purpose and for

J. Aschenbrenner (✉)
Self-employed Coach and Mentor for Lawyers, Law Worx, Germany

encode.org, LLC, NV, USA
e-mail: hello@law-worx.com; https://www.linkedin.com/in/joaschenbrenner

J. Marques (ed.), *Innovative Leadership in Times of Compelling Changes*, Management, Change, Strategy and Positive Leadership, https://doi.org/10.1007/978-3-030-67258-4_15

"re-enchanting the materialistic world view of modernity through non-religious spirituality" (Laloux, 2014).

This chapter illustrates what the power shift means in the context of business entities and how it can be pursued. The practice examples of *Hypoport Group* and *NRG Circles* used in this chapter are meant to illustrate both the organizational and the personal journey of developing into the power shift.

Job Opening

If *living the power shift* issued a job advertisement and invited people around the world to join the movement, it would have only very few lines (Fig. 15.1):

Job Opening

Posting Title:	DISTRIBUTED POWER AND PERSONAL POWER
Job Code Title:	Pitch for roles to pursue company purpose
Department/Office:	Look for open positions among the companies of the PowerShift Economy
Duty Station:	VIRTUAL / LOCAL TBD
Posting Period:	2021 - forever
Job Opening Number:	21-power shift-PURPOSE-forever

Living the Power Shift Core Values: Purpose, Power, Autonomy, Transparency.

Responsibilities:
Pursue company purpose in alignment with individual purpose.

Competencies:
Step into your own power: integrate your shadows and wounds. Move from fear to love. Know your purpose. Act from within.
Exert systemic power: transfer your personal power over others and your personal decision-making authority to the power of a system, the decentralized, purpose-driven self-organizing system of the company.
Leadership: lead yourself and your work. Stop leading others, the rules take care of that.

Education:
Self-awareness, mindfulness, courage.
Any educational background, autodidact.

Work Experience:
Experience working in a powershifted self-organized company is highly desirable.
Experience in differentiating and integrating role and person is a distinct advantage.

Fig. 15.1 Job opening

The Conventional Understanding of Power

Max Weber, a German sociologist, defines power as "every chance to assert one's own will within a social relationship, even against reluctance, no matter what this chance is based upon" (Herb, 2008). Every human being is out to dominate others in order not to be dominated himself (Macchiavelli, 2009). To prevent being dominated, he or she is prepared to enforce any means, even illegal ones, is what Macchiavelli postulates.

According to Crozier and Friedberg's organization theory, power develops in the relationship between actors in a specific situation, and therefore power varies from person to person and from situation to situation. Power is always reciprocal, because every single person only has as much power as the other person grants them in a certain situation. Often, but not always, the possibilities of influencing others in a relationship are asymmetrical. As such, power is both relational and situational.

Power in the Conventional Sense Is Influence Over Others

A lot has been written about how to acquire conventional power in organizations and the corresponding social relationships (c.f. Pfeffer, 2010). Crozier and Friedberg find the source of power in the ability to control what they call "zones of uncertainty." These include the availability of information, access to financial or other resources, as well as formal conditions such as hierarchy or stable relations with the industry, the clients, and the whole environment of the company (Crozier & Friedberg, 1980). According to Pfeffer, there are distinct approaches to become powerful. This includes, for example, the development of specific personal qualities such as ambition, energy, and focus. But it also includes finding access to resources (as is also described in the "zones of uncertainty" presented by Crozier and Friedberg), and becoming a good networker is key in your personal power game.

Fighting for influence, power games, and micro-politics are "business as usual" in most companies. If you want to reach the top in organizations, you have to master the rules of power (Pfeffer, 2010; Pfeffer, 2015; Neuberger, 2003). "Welcome to the real world," is what Jeffrey Pfeffer states in his book *Power: Why Some People Have It – and Others Don't*. If you oppose power plays, this will be your largest obstacle to obtain powerful positions. However, when power is your motive, you not only get to the top, you even receive better performance ratings (regardless of your actual performance) and are presumed to be an effective leader. Studies repeatedly demonstrate that female stereotypes are less favorable than male stereotypes on the way to conventional power. Other studies suggest that there is a higher number of sociopaths and narcissists in top positions. They are simply well-equipped for the power games and have an advantage as they do not shy away from using dirty tricks to get ahead (see the research of Robert D. Hare).

On your way to the top, you should act in a strategic manner and be able to endure defeats. The price is high, but it is worth it, says Pfeffer (2010). Do not question whether your power-oriented behavior is detrimental to the company, Pfeffer recommends, since "the company doesn't care about people either" (Pfeffer, 2010).

Power Relations Are Reflected in the Management Hierarchy, Social Interactions, and the Legal Foundations of the Company

In conventionally run companies, these above described power relations are reflected in a company's organization chart. At the very top, you find the owners and investors, having both formal and informal power over the organization and its people. They are followed by the top and middle management, and at the bottom, we find the employees who have little to no power. The organizational pyramid structure delegates decision-making authority from top to bottom.

Even if the involved managers truly want to empower their subordinates, the formal pyramid structure is much more powerful. It hinders true self-efficacy and often shuts down intrinsic motivation. Moreover, the employees look up to the CEO when it comes to decision-making and no longer feel responsible or accountable themselves. In addition, the formal internal structure (the pyramid or the organizational chart) seldom depicts the real structure, because all companies have an informal power structure that is formed by "personal relationships and political moves" (Robertson, 2015). Sometimes, the informal power structure can be even more influential than the formal structure.

A company's legal foundations (such as the Operating Agreement or by laws) also reflect this old power structure. Shareholders make the relevant decisions, the management is the trustee of the shareholders and maximizes the profits for the owners, while the employees have little say. For them it can be psychologically unsafe to address their problems in such a structure, be they work-related or personal in nature, as they may be reprimanded for speaking up. The shareholders and CEOs have much power and information; others have to request involvement.

Like it or not: this is what power looks like in many conventional organizations.

Management and Leadership in the Old Economy

This understanding of power results in a distinct understanding of leadership and management. A leader or a manager has more power than the regular employee and has power over others. Leaders and managers can make important decisions, define the strategy and business model, transform the internal structure, change the course of action, and decide whether to invest money. They lead, motivate, and inspire others and provide direction for the "non-leaders." But they also have the power to dismiss people.

Furthermore, the legal owners of the company decide upon the so-called core transactions of the company in the members' meeting (the legal governing body). This power of the owners is grounded in the number of shares, as they are the power base.

In sum, in the conventional understanding, power over others is attributed to people high up in the management hierarchy (managers and leaders) and to those who own the company (namely, the shareholders). This power hierarchy and its reflection in leadership and management has proven to be too slow in reacting to (disruptive) change and too demotivating and disempowering for the people energizing the work of the company. It hinders the self-organization of work and the unfolding of company and individual purpose (cf. Petriglieri, 2020).

The Journey of Self-Organization

The global emergence of new forms of organizing and running a business has been on the agenda for decades. The early pioneering companies such as Gore (1957) and Morningstar (1970) demonstrated that it was possible to structure work in radically new ways with new rules and new underlying assumptions decades ago. Frederic Laloux's seminal study about the patterns of how organizational systems evolve over time and the breakthroughs and shadows they brought to humanity provided momentum to the movement of self-organized, purpose-driven, and holistic businesses. In addition, the agile movement that started in software and small service companies has now reached the corporations of this world.

We currently experience a growing number of managers, leaders, and organizations experimenting with new forms of organizing and running a business. Sociocracy, Holacracy practice, self-organization, Teal, Scrum, Lean, Responsive Org, Conscious Capitalism, and Agile are all examples of solutions and movements that present alternatives to the conventional management approach of maximizing shareholders profits, aiming for unlimited growth, and following the commands of our selfish, anxious egos. What "can unfold when we embrace this journey is beautiful to behold" (Seuhs-Schoeller, 2020).

Success or failure of self-organization in pursuit of purpose depends on making the shift from *conventional power to a new understanding of power* as reflected in the company's work hierarchy, the legal rules, and the social interactions, as well as intra-personally – inside the individuals doing the work.

Shifting Power

The premise of this chapter is the shared willingness to safeguard our wellbeing and the sustainment of planet Earth by using new forms of organizing and running a business. Companies of all industries, size, and offerings are regarded as the change- and peace-makers and will, step-by-step, change our world "for purpose." Whatever approach, system, or methodology is chosen, there will be no success without *truly shifting power*(Fig. 15.2).

The Dimensions of Shifting Power

The power shift leading to successful self-organization in pursuit of company purpose occurs in two main dimensions:

1. The organization: Every member of the organization exerts systemic power instead of power over others to fulfill the tasks of the organization in pursuit of purpose.
   (a) Work context: Introduction of new work hierarchies, use of decentralized decision-making authority, and introduction of decentralized (systemic) power.
   (b) Legal context: Changing the ownership structure to reflect decentralized power instead of owners outside of the organization determining the course of the company to reflect their own needs.
   (c) People context: Going beyond an unhealthy parent-child dynamic present in many leadership constellations and moving towards healthy relationships.
2. The individual: Stepping into your own personal power instead of shying away from your responsibilities, strength and personal power (Fig. 15.3).

Shifting Power in Organizations

Starting and running a business requires three things: capital, work to be done, and people. These three areas are governed by specific rulesets:

1. The Operating Agreement or bylaws of the enterprise define the financial rules and ownership rights.
2. The rules for the organization and execution of work determine work governance, decision-making authority, decision-making procedures, and internal coordination.
3. The social rules and norms when interacting inside the company concern, for example, feedback, conflict resolution, and personal growth.

Two Current Examples of Self-Organizing Companies

Hypoport Group (www.hypoport.com) is a network of technology companies for the credit, real estate, and insurance industries with a workforce of approx. 2,000 employees based in Germany. It is grouped into four segments: Credit Platform, Private Clients, Real Estate Platform, and Insurance Platform. Within the Hypoport Group, Hypoport SE performs the role of a strategic and management holding company with corresponding central functions. Hypoport SE's objectives are the advancement and expansion of its family of subsidiaries. The shares of Hypoport SE are listed in the Prime Standard segment of the Frankfurt Stock Exchange (Deutsche Börse) and have been included in the SDAX since 2015.

NRG Circles is a self-managed and purpose-driven organization in the Oil & Gas Industry, based in the South of the Netherlands with a workforce of 18 people. Its current purpose is: "transforming the oil and gas industry in inspiring to liberate potential to create and transform". NRG Circles started out with a more internal purpose that focused on the individual and this has evolved into a purpose that serves an entire industry and with that, has a global scale.

Fig. 15.2 Two current examples of self-organizing companies (I)

In a conventional enterprise, these three rulesets establish conventional power – namely, power over others. Owners have power over managers and over employees as defined in the legal charter, and managers have power over their subordinates. They define the vision, mission, strategy, and company goals and set up the business plan and the corporate incentive systems; they determine the internal structure of the company. As leaders, they motivate and lead others, they dismiss some and promote others. Powerful people influence less powerful people to assert their own will. Certainly, this is often done with the best intentions, and many leaders state that they wish to empower others (known as the "servant leadership"). In sum, though, empowering others is also a form of *power over* (see Robertson, 2013.)

In a powershifted enterprise, the abovementioned three sets of rules anchor the power shift and establish systemic power. They invite individuals to embark on this personal journey of trusting the system of self-organization as the source of systemic power and realizing their own personal power.

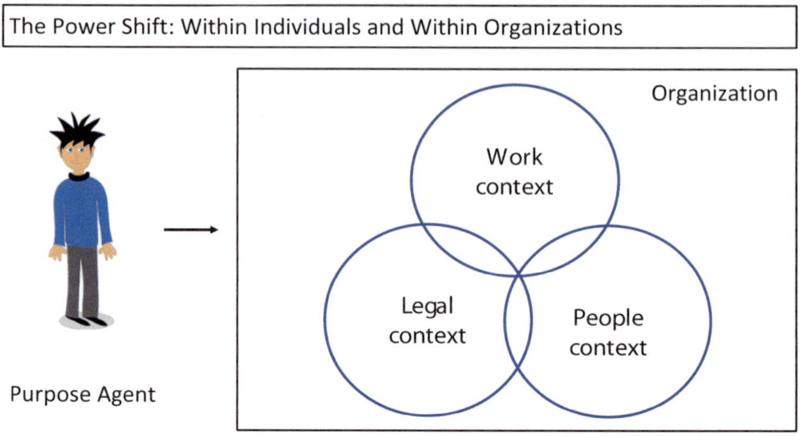

Fig. 15.3 The two dimensions of shifting power. (© Lori Rock, Jo Aschenbrenner)

The company encode.org defined the criteria of the systematic power shift in organizations – known as the PowerShift© – as follows:

1. Clearly written rules.
2. The rules bind everyone in the company in the same way. There are no privileged classes, no one is outside the rules, and nobody is above the law.
3. The rules construct power systemically, instead of assigning power to individuals or positions (like the leader, the head of, the COO, or the founder). The company has therefore completely detached itself from a linear leadership model of power over any other person or over the rules themselves.

The *For-Purpose-Enterprise* (FPE) as developed and tested by the company encode.org is a powershifted solution to self-organize work in pursuit of company purpose. It is "a compound structure with new rules for legal, liability, and capital matters; linked to an organizational operating system to express the work itself; and at long last, a clear set of agreements for the people doing that work" (Aschenbrenner, 2019).

The powershifted operating system of the For-Purpose-Enterprise incorporates the powershifted rules in all three contexts (work, people, and legal) of the company.

Work Context

Self-organization distributes authority in the company systemically across all shoulders, despite roles. In a For-Purpose-Enterprise, you apply the Holacracy practice to execute work in pursuit of company purpose. The conventional management hierarchy is left behind and work is managed, not people. The system itself therefore becomes the ultimate source of power. It is very important to understand that this step does not mean that an organization is without management or without leadership. Instead, the system of self-organization *manages and leads the work* in pursuit of purpose, and people *lead themselves and their work*. There is no more personal power over others present. These new definitions of power and leadership pave the way for the new way of organizing (cf. Seuhs-Schoeller, 2020).

Those who have been in powerful positions in a conventional organization need to learn to trust the system of self-organization to take over "control" or "power" from them. They need to adapt to their new role as *one powerful individual among other powerful individuals* in steering the company towards company purpose relying on the chosen system of self-organization. With this transfer of power inside the organization, there are no longer positions such as CEO, COO, or Director available which confer and attribute power personally to an individual (and not onto others). Neither are there informal positions of power ("oh, there comes the founder, stop criticizing"). It is a huge transformative personal step to let go of conventional power as it is so closely tied to our self-esteem and self-worth.

Those who have been at the bottom of the hierarchical management pyramid also need to learn to trust the system of self-organization. They need to experience that the system protects their systemic and personal power, authority, and autonomy and that the decisions they make based on their authority conferred by the new rules of self-organization are respected by their previous bosses.

People Context

Within the For-Purpose-Enterprise, members sign an *Agreement of Association*, which provides specific social norms for the interactions between the people doing the work in a powershifted system. These social norms of a For-Purpose-Enterprise create a *safe place* for all its members to grow into exerting systemic and personal power (you can see an example of both of the required competencies in the job opening above). Both dimensions are interrelated and positively influence each other.

Legal Context

The Operating Agreement of a For-Purpose-Enterprise sets up new legal rules for ownership, investment, and legal competencies. Currently, no legal form in the world (as far as I know) satisfies the three criteria of the PowerShift completely. Encode.org embarked on the journey to redesign existing legal forms in such a way that they encode the systemic PowerShift into the legal foundations of the company (Fig. 15.4).

Hypoport:

In 2016, the Hypoport leadership team realized that self-management and decentralization would be key strategies for its continual growth in the future. In search of a framework that would be robust and scalable enough to serve its needs, the Holacracy practice was identified as the main candidate to try. Within the Hypoport Group *Dr. Klein Privatkunden* was among the first to implement the Holacracy practice starting in 2017, others followed soon thereafter, with the remainder picking up the practice two years later. Currently, seven of the fifteen subsidiaries are practicing Holacracy: *Dr. Klein Privatkunden, Europace, Qualitypool, Smart InsurTech, Vergleich.de, Dr. Klein Ratenkredit,* and the holding company *Hypoport SE* itself. Roughly 1.000 people within the Hypoport Group practice Holacracy (as of June 2020). Since the subsidiary companies are relatively autonomous in their business decisions, the decision for or against the Holacracy practice as an operating system is not mandated from the holding but remains in the hands of each individual CEO.

Once a company decides to take the leap, they receive support from the "*hola::be*" circle which is embedded in the central services unit of the holding. People get onboarded with Holacracy "taster" workshops and are thoroughly trained in internal practitioner trainings to build the skills necessary to facilitate the meeting processes that the Holacracy constitution requires. A team of *hola::be* coaches supports the adoption and answers any questions.

Three years into the journey, the Holacracy practice is gaining traction within the company network with more and more companies expressing interest in adopting and shifting the power relations among colleagues and at work. Although at Hypoport the powershift has not transformed the layer of legal agreements (yet), it is an encouraging example that demonstrates that self-management is scalable. And while there is no definite proof that Holacracy is at the root of the company's stellar success (stunning growth rates and awards as a top employer in Germany) one can at least conclude that it did not cause harm or slow down innovation - quite the contrary.

Fig. 15.4 Two current examples of self-organizing companies (II)

NRG Circles:

In 2016, with the purpose of bringing wholeness into the organization and to embrace the individual as a whole, the Holacracy practice was implemented within NRG Circles as a self-management tool. This created the **first systematic powershift**.

Because the Holacracy practice organizes around work and not around people, there is by design no space for interpersonal or personal tensions. In order to create a safe space and common ground for people to come together, initial steps were taken in defining and implementing the organization's core values. During this period, which lasted nine months after the implementation of Holacracy, 30% of organization's work force left due to non-alignment with the system and the new culture.

In a workshop in March 2018 the company members realized the urge to create a people context - a safe space - that embraces the individuals in all their complexity. Individual coaching and feedback processes were established and a focus on personal development was implemented. This supported NRG Circles in creating that desired safe space around people, helping them process personal and interpersonal tensions. This approach ran separately and yet interdependently from the enterprises' context, where the work lived and created the **second systematic powershift**.

To anchor the power shift into a legal structure, NRG Circles has implemented the For-Purpose Enterprise structure. This makes purpose the only boss in the organization, by introducing a new decentralized model of ownership and financial rules. The For-Purpose-Enterprise structure makes the interdependence of the three contexts of work, people, and legal explicit, and creates with that the **third systematic powershift** by including all necessary levels to make NRG Circles a solely purpose-driven enterprise.

Fig. 15.4 (continued)

Shifting Power Within Individuals

There are a number of rules designed to shift power within organizations. The Holacracy practice as developed by Brian Robertson and Thomas Thomison has been applied in organizations for more than 10 years. The For-Purpose-Enterprise and its two additional rulesets (legal/financial and social norms) are in business since 2015. As a living laboratory, encode.org tested and implemented the rules from a minimum viable product to a ripe version that is safe to try. The powershift ecosystem is constantly growing. The powershifted operating system is applied (in various degrees) by NRG Circles (Netherlands); the Hypoport Group (Germany); PowerShift Capital, LLC (USA); PowerShift People, LLC (USA); Energized.org (Netherlands); Xpreneurs (Switzerland); and dwarfs and Giants (Austria).

What is holding people back from applying these rulesets at a larger scale? My hypothesis is the complexity of the power shift inside the individual. In a power-shifted, purposeful company, everyone is invited to step into their own personal power. Personal power to me means being yourself, acting from within, expressing your true self, and being aware of the interconnectedness of everything. Christiane Seuhs-Schoeller (2020) writes that it is ultimately about "accepting our new reality: we represent the power that is, inside us and around us – interconnected and interdependent."

To step into your own personal power and to discover who you truly are is a lifelong journey. This journey crosses the borders of many "countries": your conscious self and your sub- and unconscious self (cf. Kelley, 2009); your core self, your developed self, and your contextual self (Berens, 2010); the biologically and socially acquired parts of your personality (cf. Roth & Ryba, 2016); and your ego and your higher wisdom or soul knowing your personal purpose. It involves self-awareness (cf. Holmes & Holmes, 2013), the willingness to face our shadows, and understanding our ego blocks, as well as connecting with our inner wisdom or soul to unleash the power of our personal purpose. Exploring the facets of your personality and discovering your purpose is needed to step into your own personal power and to act from within.

Tim Kelley, founder of the True Purpose Institute, has developed an approach for how to find the purpose that is unique to you. He also says that some part of you already knows what it is (Kelley, 2009). He calls this part "inner wisdom", "trusted source" or "soul" without applying any religious borrowings. If you succeed in making contact with this very personal part of yourself, you will discover what your purpose is. The Austrian psychiatrist Viktor Frankl regards man as a being in search of meaning. Man wants to know what he is in the world for. This distinguishes him from the animal. This understanding of purpose goes beyond who we are as a person. The American author Daniel Pink (author of the book *Drive*, 2009) says that deeply motivated people combine the fulfillment of their own needs with motives that go beyond themselves (Pink, 2011) (Fig. 15.5).

Tim Kelley differentiates between four aspects of your higher purpose:

NRG Circles:

After establishing the focus on personal development and a safe space for the people of the organization (see above), the emotional maturity level of the NRG Circles tribe increased. This made a rational decision in favor of a personal higher purpose easier.

NRG Circles went on through a purpose discovery process with the True Purpose Institute, based in California, USA. In this process, the organization's members discovered their own individual purposes. This raised the question as to whether the purpose the NRG Circles had was still up to date. In fact, what had happened during the individual development and evolvement, the organization's purpose evolved as well.

With the rise of self-awareness, self-love and consciousness levels, a mind-set shift occurred, which is considered the **individual powershift**. The increased levels of consciousness allowed for the question of personal purpose to arise, and with that the question of the alignment to organizational purpose.

Fig. 15.5 NRG Circles and the individual powershift

- *Essence*: The first aspect is the pure dimension of being. What purpose do you radiate by simply being? Kelley calls this "essence." For example, a coach might recognize: "I am the impulse for change."
- *Blessing*: Secondly, living your purpose has a transforming effect on others – whether you are aware of it or not. Kelley calls this "blessing." The coach could say: "Where there is uncertainty, I bring clarity about the next step."
- *Mission*: Thirdly, what is your task in life? What should you do, even if it is not easy? Kelley calls it "mission." Perhaps the coach will answer: "I am there for people who are on the margins of society and offer them perspectives for a self-determined life."
- *Message*: Finally, you can understand your purpose as a message to the world. The message includes the knowledge that you have been given by life and that you share with others (Kelley calls this "message"). It can rarely be put into one sentence and, according to Kelley, is often the last aspect of purpose that people find out for themselves (Kelley, n.d.).

So far so good. But it is not that simple, because some other parts of our personality are not so open to these questions of calling. It is not unusual for our ego to object to our desire to explore and pursue our purpose. Frederic Laloux writes in *Reinventing Organizations* that when we overcome the fears of our ego, we are free

Every cell in the body, when functioning properly, collaborates with other cells in serving a purpose that is greater than both: namely, the healthy functioning of the organ of which they are part.

When a cell forgets that -- when it loses connection to its natural intelligence and instead of collaborating with other cells goes off to pursue its own thing without regard to the higher good of the larger organ – then it is malignant.

And that's what has happened to the human race: modern consciousness rests on the false belief that we're here alone, to do our own thing regardless of how it fits into the larger intelligence of unfolding life. Thus, modern consciousness is malignant, and can only be healed by the realization that we are here together to collaborate together to serve together. This idea is treacherous to the ego, which IS the false belief in separation. But of course the ego defends against such realization, because within it lies the death of the ego. The truth is facing us now as never before: the selfish ego will die, or we will.

Outtake from Oprah's SuperSoul Conversations: The Spiritual Purpose of Relationships on 13.07.2019 with Marianne Williamson

Fig. 15.6 Marianne Williamson at Oprah's SuperSoul Conversations in 2019

inside to ask questions about our vocation and to experience what is really important to us (Fig. 15.6).

Overcoming the fears of our ego is an interesting journey of self-discovery that is rewarding and refreshing. Tim Kelley suggests to regard our ego as a friend and to negotiate with it to set up conditions under which it agrees to pursuing our purpose. While this may sound strange, I can tell you from my own experience it works – even for me as a rational, technical business lawyer!

Conclusion

As you have now learned, living the power shift needs new rules to exert systemic power within an organization and requires individuals who are prepared to listen to their calling and their souls. The rules inside the organization have to satisfy the three criteria of the PowerShift(C) in order to be effective game-changers. Embarking on this journey of individual powershift promises an intense experience of self-development, a sense of freedom, and an experience of great self-efficacy. As Christiane Seuhs-Schoeller (2020) said: what "can unfold when we embrace this journey is beautiful to behold."

All over the world, we can see a pattern of how organizational systems evolve with time – a developmental trajectory of hope, if you will. I take comfort knowing there is an inevitable evolutionary march towards a bigger embrace of purpose, self-organization, and human wholeness. The organizational model of the For-Purpose-Enterprise is one visionary example of how this way of doing business can thrive in our world.

Chapter Takeaways

- The rules change the functioning of our companies to truly pursue purpose and to live the power shift.
- Such companies can change the world to the better.
- They need individuals ready to assume their personal power, to follow their purpose, and to exert systemic power.

Reflective Questions

1. What are your beliefs about leadership and which beliefs do you have about power?
2. Do you reflect upon an inner life of people and yourself?
3. Can you confront uncomfortable truths about yourself?
4. Do you feel a pull or a push to find your deeper meaning and purpose?
5. What does the organization of your dreams look like, and what does the world of your dreams look like?

References

Aschenbrenner, J. (2019). *For Purpose. Ein neues Betriebssystem für Unternehmen.* Vahlen Franz GmbH, Munich, Germany (Aschenbrenner, J. (2020), The For-Purpose Enterprise. A Powershifted Operating System to Run Your Business).

Berens, L. V. (2010). *Understanding yourself and others: An introduction to the 4 temperaments.* InterStrength Press.

Crozier, M., & Friedberg, E. (1980). *Actors and systems: The politics of collective action.* University of Chicago Press.

Herb, K. (2008). Machtfragen ("Questions of Power"). *Die Politische Meinung,* p. 68ss.

Holmes, T., & Holmes, L. (2013). *Reisen in die Innenwelt ("parts work: An illustrated guide to your inner life")*. Kösel.
Kelley, T. (2009). *True purpose: 12 strategies for discovering the difference you are meant to make*. Transcendent Solutions Press.
Kelley, T. (n.d.). *The true purpose model.* https://www.truepurposeinstitute.com/about-true-purpose-institute/true-purpose-model/
Laloux, F. (2014). *Reinventing organizations: A guide to creating organizations inspired by the next stage of human consciousness*. Diateino.
Macchiavelli, N., (first published in 1532 / 2009). *Il Principe*. Hamburg, Germany: Nikol.
Neuberger, Oswald, Mikropolitik, Schäfer-Poeschel 2003.
Petriglieri, G. (2020, June 18). Are our management theories outdated? *Harvard Business Review*. https://hbr.org/2020/06/are-our-management-theories-outdated
Pfeffer, J. (2010). *Power: Why some people have it- and others don't*. Harper Collins.
Pfeffer, J. (2015). *Leadership BS: Fixing workplaces and careers one truth at a time*. Harper Collins.
Pink, D. (2011). *Drive: The surprising truth about what motivates us*. Riverhead Books.
Robertson, B. (2013, May 1). *The Irony of Empowerment.* Holacracy. https://blog.holacracy.org/the-irony-of-empowerment-4f0d312559d6
Robertson, B. (2015). *Holacracy: The new management system for a rapidly changing world.* Henry Holt and Company.
Roth, Gerhard; Ryba, Alicia, Coaching, Beratung und Gehirn, Klett-Cotta 2016.
Seuhs-Schoeller, C. (2020, March 9). *Leadership and Powership*. Medium. https://medium.com/swlh/leadership-and-power-shift-b2d7ef9db29c
O.. (Executive Producer). *Oprah's SuperSoul Conversations: Marianne Williamson* [Audio Podcast]. OWN. https://podtail.com/en/podcast/oprah-s-supersoul-conversations/marianne-williamson-the-spiritual-purpose-of-relat/.

Part III
Leading with a Future Oriented Mind

Chapter 16
Crisis Preparedness as a Sustainability Strategy

Robert S. Fleming

Abstract This chapter considers how organizational crisis preparedness strategies developed and implemented in the interest of ensuring organizational resilience in times of crisis can also contribute to achieving an organization's commitment to sustainability. While the importance of crisis preparation and organizational resilience has been clearly and convincingly demonstrated as individuals, organizations, and nations around the world have conscientiously sought to navigate the uncharted waters of the COVID-19 pandemic, it is important to recognize the more frequent, but less severe and consequential, future crisis situations and events that organizations should anticipate and prepare for in their strategic planning activities. This chapter discusses the role of crisis preparedness within the overall crisis management process and how organizations can prepare to "weather the storm" of future crisis situations and events through informed decision-making and planning. A strategic approach to developing and implementing crisis preparedness strategies in support of an organization's mission, including its commitment to sustainability, is advocated. Responsible leadership that is both innovative and inclusive is discussed as an essential enabling factor in achieving organizational resilience and sustainability in times of crisis.

Keywords Crisis preparedness · Inclusive leadership · Organizational resilience · Responsible leadership · Sustainability

Introduction

This chapter was written during the unprecedented COVID-19 pandemic that occurred in early 2020 and quickly spread to nations around the globe. The realities of this devastating health crisis in terms of its severity and spread require little explanation, nor does the fact that as of this date the world's medical community

R. S. Fleming (✉)
Rowan University, Glassboro, NJ, USA

J. Marques (ed.), *Innovative Leadership in Times of Compelling Changes*, Management, Change, Strategy and Positive Leadership, https://doi.org/10.1007/978-3-030-67258-4_16

and pharmaceutical companies are aggressively striving to discover the essential vaccines to prevent individuals from contracting the virus, as well as viable treatments for those individuals who unfortunately do.

The current pandemic has significantly changed our lives, work, and travel. It has likewise expanded our vocabularies as we receive updated information about the pandemic and discuss it with others. While many would have already been familiar with terms such as asymptomatic and vaccine, most of us have expanded our Coronavirus lexicon to include community spread, confirmed positive case, contact tracing, personal protective equipment (PPE), presumptive positive case, screening, self-quarantine, social distancing, and, lest we forget, the overall challenge that we all face of "flattening the curve."

While we all hope and pray that through miraculous medical and pharmaceutical discoveries, we will soon be able as a nation and world not only to flatten the curve but also eradicate the virus and end this horrific worldwide health crisis that has resulted in an astronomical number of positive cases and deaths around the world, we fully recognize the importance of being prepared for both the anticipated and unexpected crisis situations and events that are likely to occur in the future. While most of these future challenges will likely be more localized, less severe, and of shorter and more predictable duration than the current pandemic, we all now recognize the critical importance of crisis preparation as individuals, organizations, nations, and the world. The COVID-19 pandemic, unlike many past crisis situations that tend to fall off our radar fairly quickly after their conclusion, will be indelibly embedded in our minds and very beings for the foreseeable future.

The current pandemic has obviously resulted in unprecedented public recognition of the importance of crisis preparedness and interest in the specific measures that various organizations, including businesses and governmental entities, are taking to address the current crisis that we are experiencing as well as to prepare for and ideally prevent or minimize the impact of future crisis events. This chapter focuses on crisis preparedness as an integral and essential component of an organization's strategic planning activities. After considering the nature and reality of crises in the contemporary world in which we live, work, and travel, the topics of organizational vulnerability and resilience will be discussed.

A crisis management process will be introduced, as will the importance of considering potential crisis situations and incorporating necessary crisis preparedness strategies in the development and implementation of an organization's strategic plans. While this chapter includes examples of crisis situations within the business world, it is important to realize that crisis preparedness strategies can and should be incorporated into the planning initiatives of any organization, including governmental agencies or entities.

This chapter discusses the importance of sustainability in our contemporary world. In addition to considering the traditional "pillars" of sustainability, we will make the point that the actions that an organization takes to survive during crisis events within an organization or its external environment likewise should be considered an important "sustainability" responsibility that organizational leaders have to the various stakeholders of an organization, including its customers, employees, and owners.

This chapter concludes with several sections that tie together the concepts of crisis preparedness, organizational resilience, and sustainability. The importance of organizational leaders, particularly those in senior management positions, engaging in responsible leadership where they both "talk the talk" and "walk the walk" will be discussed, as will the value of understanding stakeholder expectations and involving stakeholders in an organization's planning processes in advance of crisis situations and its information dissemination activities during a crisis.

While this is just one chapter in this collected work, we trust that you will recognize that what you will learn in this chapter along with the others that accompany it will provide you with strategies and tools that will prove useful as an organizational leader or someone preparing to assume a leadership role in the future. You will also learn that ensuring crisis preparedness requires an "all hands" approach, wherein through responsible and inclusive leadership, all of an organization's stakeholders are afforded the opportunity to contribute to its crisis preparedness strategies and plans and to understand how such initiatives afford a "mission-driven" organization the ability to continue its pilgrimage towards realizing its mission, goals, and sustainability commitment. Successfully navigating any crisis situation requires the dedication, commitment, and innovation of both organizational members and leaders. It requires "innovative leadership" as suggested in our book's title.

Crisis Events in the Contemporary World

Crisis events or situations are obviously not new in the twenty-first century. Among the many historical crisis events have been a number of major conflicts, some of which have escalated to wars, as well as a series of epidemics and pandemics which many of us are for the first time hearing about in the extensive media coverage of the current pandemic. It is important to understand the difference between these two types of health crises. The Merriam-Webster Dictionary defines an epidemic as "an outbreak of disease that spreads quickly and affects many individuals at the same time," such as a seasonal influenza outbreak, and a pandemic as "a type of epidemic (one with greater range and coverage), an outbreak of a disease that occurs over a wide geographic area and affects an exceptionally high proportion of the population." The COVID-19 health crisis is therefore properly categorized as a "pandemic."

As we move forward in our consideration of crisis preparedness, it is important to have a working definition as context for the discussions that will follow. We will use the definition provided in the Oxford Advanced American Dictionary which defines a crisis as "a time of great danger, difficulty, or confusion when problems must be solved or important decisions must be made." (Hornsby, 2010). Once again, there is likely no argument that the current pandemic should be considered a crisis.

Crisis situations can be categorized by type and include health crises, natural disasters, weather-related events, emergency incidents, terrorist attacks, economic and financial crises, technological crises, and organizational crises. Crisis situations and events can be further categorized based on their frequency, severity, scope, duration, and impact or consequences. More will be said about this later in this chapter. Crisis situations can begin as one type of crisis but go on to cause multiple types. There is much that can be learned from studying past crisis situations, and becoming a student of crisis management will greatly enhance an organizational leader's knowledge, skills, and confidence to enact their responsibilities in each of the steps in the crisis management process, as well as in each of the phases of crisis management.

Three major crisis situations serve to illustrate the lessons that can be learned through review and analysis of past crisis situations. The attacks that took place on September 11, 2001, illustrate the major impact that crisis events can have. Prior to that day, the conventional wisdom in crisis preparation was to prepare for the worst, recognizing that it was unlikely that the worst would ever occur. That tragic day changed the world in which we live, work, and travel when the worst did occur in New York City, Arlington (VA), and Western Pennsylvania. The many lessons learned from the September 11 attacks include the fact that the first 30 minutes in managing a major incident is crucial; that roles and responsibilities must be defined in advance; that a common incident management system was needed; that integration and coordination of local, state, and federal resources can prove challenging; and that effective information dissemination was essential. Governmental and public safety officials have proactively and successfully addressed these and numerous other issues.

The lessons of Hurricane Sandy (2012) included that a major weather event can have an extensive impact in a multistate area as a result of damaged and otherwise compromised critical infrastructure systems and facilities. The impacted region, including New Jersey and New York City, faced many challenges related to flooding, utility outages, and transportation issues. The business impact of this major storm included the loss of customers and contracts, reduced sales and revenues, reduced market share, reduced profits, and in some cases business failures. The ability of businesses to continue to operate as well as survive was in many cases determined by the extent and length of their business interruption. Perhaps one of the most important lessons learned from Hurricane Sandy was that teleworking, as well as benefiting employees as traditionally thought, could also allow many businesses to get back in business by having their employees work from remote locations. This understanding was important as during the pandemic 8 years later employers utilized remote working to get the trains running again in many businesses where a physical presence was not necessary.

The COVID-19 pandemic clearly has changed the world in which we live, work, and travel. It has presented a multitude of challenges including its worldwide impact, rapid spread, highly contagious nature, ability to impact vulnerable populations, and severity. The most daunting unknown of this catastrophic health crisis is the uncertainty of when it will end, its challenges for our healthcare system and medical professionals, and when mission-critical vaccines and treatments will be available. The lessons learned so far from the current pandemic include that it is a worldwide health crisis requiring worldwide cooperation, that we are all in this together and must work together to reduce the spread of the virus and flatten the curve, that our healthcare systems can become overwhelmed, and that new treatments and vaccines will be instrumental in containing, minimizing, and eradicating the pandemic.

Organizational Vulnerability and Resilience

Successful crisis preparedness strategies, while intended to reduce organizational vulnerability to crisis situations and events, must be developed and implemented based on a comprehensive understanding of the potential crises that could confront the organization. This analysis must include consideration of crisis situations emanating from within the organization, such as a major recall of a defective product or discovered improprieties in businesses practices, financial dealings, and/or reporting, as well as those originating in the external environment in which the organization conducts business, such as an economic downturn or financial crisis, natural disaster, or health crisis.

Developing a full understanding of potential crisis situations or events is an essential starting point in the development of an appropriate crisis preparedness strategy and plan. The potential frequency, severity, scope, duration, and impact of each potential crisis should be thoroughly understood and should serve as a basis for formulating appropriate strategies for crisis preparedness and the related crisis management activities that will be discussed shortly. Environmental scanning should be used to identify both organizational strengths and weaknesses with respect to various crisis situations, as well as the degree and impact of each crisis situation on the survival and continued success of the organization. Organizational strengths would include the existence of decentralized operations, effective controls, risk management, and contingency planning, whereas the absence of any of these would be considered a weakness of an organization in terms of its preparedness to endure crisis situations and events. The degree of exposure presented by various potential crisis situations or events would be determined by how centralized or decentralized an organization's operations are, where mission-critical activities are performed within the organization, and the task interdependencies that exist within the organization. The impact of exposure to a crisis situation will relate to its ability to operate and possibly survive. The extent and length of a business interruption, along with operating costs during a crisis, are important factors to consider.

"Organizational resilience," a relatively new term in business parlance, captures the intent of crisis preparedness. Organizational leaders have a responsibility to various stakeholder groups to ensure the continued success and survival of an organization. While the primary stakeholder groups that have related expectations for these managers who have been entrusted with the present and future wellbeing of an organization will include customers, employees, and owners, the stakeholders of crisis management strategies that contribute to organizational resilience, survival, and continued success also include suppliers, creditors, and communities.

Crisis Management

Crisis management is defined in the Oxford Advanced Dictionary as "the process by which a business or other organization deals with a sudden emergency situation." (Stevenson, 2010). An understanding of crisis management will enable you to enact your organizational leadership roles and responsibilities successfully before, during, and after a crisis, regardless of your management level.

Successful crisis management involves anticipating and preparing for potential crisis situations, preventing crisis situations or minimizing the impact of a crisis, leading decisively through a crisis, and recovering successfully from a crisis. As with any successful management initiative, the goal is to resolve the situation effectively, efficiently, and safely.

While the chapter title refers to crisis preparedness, crisis preparation, while an absolutely critical step in the crisis management process, is only one of five steps. These sequential steps include (1) crisis prevention, (2) crisis preparation, (3) crisis recognition, (4) crisis resolution, and (5) crisis recovery.

The first step in the crisis management process is crisis prevention. During this step potential crisis situations are identified in the interest of gaining the necessary understanding to develop crisis preparedness strategies and plans later in the crisis management process. Once identified, each potential crisis situation is evaluated and prioritized based on likely frequency and severity. The potential impact and consequences of each crisis situation are contemplated, including its potential impact on the normal business activities of the organization, its continued ability to operate, and associated business costs and related issues. The comprehensive understanding developed in this critical first step in the crisis management process will determine the success of an organization's crisis preparedness strategies and plan. Skills in information management, decision-making, problem-solving, and planning are of crucial importance in enacting crisis prevention activities.

The second step in the crisis management process is crisis preparation. It builds on and utilizes the information gathered and analyzed in the prior step and involves developing a viable plan for dealing with any crisis situations or events that an organization is not able to prevent or avoid. A crisis management plan is developed during this step in the crisis management process. This plan defines the roles and responsibilities that will need to be enacted during a crisis and assigns those roles and responsibilities to respective individuals within the organization. Those who will be expected to perform roles and responsibilities identified in the plan are provided the necessary training to prepare them to enact those roles and responsibilities successfully. Those with associated responsibilities are also prepared to engage in effective and efficient decision-making and problem-solving during a crisis event and to make necessary adjustments in planned tasks should changing developments, circumstances, or outcomes dictate the need to do so.

The third step in the crisis management process is easy to overlook, but of utmost significance. It involves crisis recognition. While an organization may have been successful in identifying and evaluating potential crisis situations, along with appropriate strategies to address them should they occur, unless an organization's leaders recognize, acknowledge, and "own" a crisis situation, nothing will be done to embrace and address that crisis. This requires that an organization ensure that monitoring potential crisis situations identified in its crisis management plan is an ongoing priority of all with associated roles and responsibilities in an organization. In reality, while senior managers often should and will be the first to learn about the occurrence of a crisis situation, there will also be times that those in other management levels will be in a position to detect an existing or impending crisis situation first. The importance of timely identification and tracking of crisis situations cannot be overstated. This also means that, regardless of one's management level in an organization, all employees should operate within an organizational culture wherein they are expected to bring any signs of an impending crisis to the attention of appropriate organizational leaders.

The fourth step in the crisis management process is what some might think would be the only step. This is the point in the sequential process where the organization engages the crisis in the interest of resolving it. Failure to recognize the importance of the previous three steps will most certainly compromise an organization's ability to prevent many crisis situations and to prepare properly to address those that do present themselves. During this step the individuals who have been previously assigned roles and responsibilities delineated in the organization's crisis management plan will be expected to enact those roles utilizing the training and resources that the organization has provided. An essential activity during crisis resolution is to ensure that stakeholders are kept properly informed. While ideally the strategies mapped out in the crisis management plan will prove successful in resolving the crisis situation, this will not always be the case, particularly when a crisis situation is rapidly developing as in the case of the current pandemic. Monitoring the situation closely and discerning and implementing any necessary adjustments in planned strategies is essential throughout any crisis.

The final stage in the five-step crisis management process is referred to as crisis recovery. During this step a variety of actions will be taken to return things to their pre-crisis state. There will obviously be crisis situations in which that will be possible and fairly easy to accomplish, as in the case of a retailer reopening after a major snowstorm that caused the location to close down for several days. The challenges of reopening certain businesses after certain crisis situations such as the current pandemic will often prove both challenging and at times problematic. The challenges of reopening a business where all business activities are conducted remotely or online are obviously very different than those of reopening a retail store or restaurant where an in-person presence is necessary. Similar to resuming activities after the September 11 attacks, businesses and other organizations around the world will likely be returning to a "new normal."

In addition to understanding the various steps in the crisis management process, it is also important to recognize that there are three phases during which crisis management activities are performed. These phases are time-specific and related to activities before, during, and after the occurrence of a crisis. The crisis prevention and crisis preparation activities that comprise the first two steps in the crisis management process should take place before a crisis. Failure to recognize the importance of dedicating the time and resources to do so will undermine an organization's ability to address a crisis situation successfully.

Likewise, the crisis recognition and crisis resolution activities that comprise the next two steps in the crisis management process enable an organization to proactively and aggressively recognize, confront, and resolve a crisis situation on behalf of the various organizational stakeholders that are counting on organizational leaders to do so effectively and efficiently. These steps obviously commence once a crisis has been detected. Crisis recovery, the final step in the crisis management process, takes place after the crisis situation has been resolved. This is an important juncture at which to review and evaluate how the organization faced the crisis and to discern lessons that will enhance the ability of the organization and its leaders to better prevent, minimize, and address future crises.

Sustainability in Times of Crisis

Societal interest in sustainability has grown in recent years as has that of individuals who choose to support organizations committed to sustainability through either investing in them as an owner, working for them as an employee, or patronizing them as a customer. Sustainability involves ensuring that the present decisions that an organization's leaders make in the interest of such traditional business goals as short-term financial performance are not compromising the ability to meet the needs of future generations. Although this ideal is not popular with some investors who expect organizations in which they invest to put their interests first in terms of producing a desired return on their investment, a growing number of enlightened investors have recognized the responsibilities that successful businesses should have with respect to future generations.

In operationalizing the concept of sustainability, preserving resources in a number of areas serves as a focus and metrics for an organization's commitment to setting and achieving sustainability goals. The concept of sustainability was initially framed to consist of three components or pillars identified as economic, environmental, and social. With time the pillars became referred to as profits, planet, and people. This led to the concept of the "triple bottom line," which advocated that organizations should devote as much attention to environmental and social issues as they do to profit. Some have suggested that there are actually four pillars of sustainability rather than three. The four pillars include economic sustainability, environmental sustainability, human sustainability, and social sustainability.

The commitment to sustainability of many contemporary organizations is now demonstrated through inclusion in organizational mission statements that articulate the value they attached to corporate social responsibility and sustainability. Their commitment to sustainability is further illustrated in their corporate goals. But the business practices they engage in accompanied by the decisions that their leaders make are the true demonstration of their commitment to sustainability as the right thing for successful businesses to do.

As with most things, it is often easy to do the right things when times are good. Even the most committed organizations will at time face challenges, such as those imposed by the current pandemic that may require that they take a momentary pause in many things that they desire to do as they struggle with the inherent challenges of a crisis. The important thing is that, while an organization might have to take its foot off the gas temporarily, the truly committed and engaged organization will never hit the brake or fail to return to forward motion as soon as possible and practical. While one could argue that organizational stakeholders will not continue to support sustainability initiatives in times of crisis, that would not seem to be true in the case where individuals have been drawn to and have supported organizations in large part because of their known commitment to sustainability.

Crisis Preparedness as a Sustainability Strategy

Successful contemporary organizations recognize the role that strategic planning plays in enabling them to gain and sustain a competitive advantage. They chart an appropriate strategic direction through delineating a mission statement and supporting goals. Both the mission statement and corresponding goals are developed in light of the understanding of the strengths and weaknesses of their organization in light of the environmental opportunities and threats that it faces, revealed through comprehensive environmental scanning activities. In formulating strategies most organizations seek to build on their strengths and address their weaknesses while taking advantage of opportunities and avoiding threats.

Increasingly, the goals of a growing number of organizations include goals related to more than one of the pillars of sustainability. In addition to environmental scanning and strategy formulation, involving the drafting of a mission statement and goals and strategies that support it, organizations must successfully implement strategies and through strategic control metrics and measures ensure that strategies are being implemented as planned and progress is being made towards accomplishing the stated goals.

Potential crisis situations or events represent threats that astute organizational planners must take into account in their strategy formulation. Once potential crises have been identified and evaluated, appropriate crisis preparedness strategies should be developed and implemented as part of the organization's crisis management plan. The potential that crises have to challenge and compromise an organization's success and at times its survival attests to the importance of crisis management activities. While the importance of crisis preparedness is obvious in terms of achieving many of the financial or economic goals of an organization, these same preparedness strategies can also contribute to the continued accomplishment of sustainability goals that correspond with the other recognized pillars.

Crisis preparedness is thus a must for contemporary organizations. Properly crafted and executed, these strategies are capable of addressing many of the business challenges and consequences of crisis situations and events discussed earlier. By their very nature, crisis preparedness strategies contribute to the continued well-being of an organization as well as that of its three primary stakeholder groups: customers, employees, and owners. Interestingly, all three groups have a common interest in seeing an organization get "back in business" following the business interruption that often results from a crisis. Customers are obviously interested in the restoration of a business's ability to provide the products and/or services that they desire. Employees are interested in returning to work for various reasons, including maintaining their income stream. Owners likewise want to see things up and running to enable the organization to once again fulfill their expectations with respect to the investment that they have made in the business.

By resuming its operations, an organization can once again work towards achieving its goals, including those that relate to the sustainability pillars. Crisis preparedness is therefore an essential competency of any contemporary business that desires to weather the storms of potential crises. All stakeholders of the contemporary organization have an interest in the responsible actions that the organization takes to fulfill its intended purpose of today while recognizing its responsibility to future generations. Crisis preparedness strategies in many ways also serve as sustainability strategies in that both contribute to achieving the overall goals of an organization, including those that address each of the pillars of sustainability.

Responsible and Inclusive Leadership

Successful organizational leadership in the challenging world of contemporary business demands that organizational leaders be prepared to engage in the responsible leadership necessary to position their organizations with a sustainable competitive advantage and to prepare for and address the many crises and other environmental threats inherent in a dynamic environment. These leaders fully recognize, embrace, and enact their roles and responsibilities with respect to ensuring that their organizations are prepared to engage in the comprehensive set of crisis management activities necessary to ensure continued organizational success and survival. They are committed to doing everything within their power to ensure that their organization does not create or contribute to crisis situations in the present or the future and are thus committed to instill in all organizational members the importance of their organization's commitment to the various pillars of sustainability and passing on to future generations the fruits of their sustainability labors.

These leaders are passionate about their organizations and ensure that they steer their organizational ships in a proper direction. They recognize the importance of inclusive leadership and ensure that there is always opportunity for the various stakeholder groups to understand what the organization is doing and to provide their input to organizational leaders. They discover that stakeholder engagement can represent both a strategy designed to contribute to goal and mission attainment and a goal in itself that corresponds in a sense with the sustainability pillars.

While recognizing the ongoing importance of communicating with relevant stakeholders, they particularly acknowledge the importance of ensuring that stakeholders, including employees, customers, owners, and suppliers, are kept in the loop during crises. These enlightened leaders recognize that stakeholders expect transparency and greatly prefer to receive official information from an organization that is accurate, complete, credible, professional, and timely. Otherwise they are forced to rely on other sources that may disseminate inaccurate, confusing, or misleading information. In summary, successful organizational leaders in times of crisis, and for that matter at other times as well, recognize the need to be innovative, inclusive, and responsible. They are the key to their organizations realizing success in all of the areas of sustainability.

Case in Point

A Commitment to Sustainability

Sharon, the president of a Midwest family-owned business with 36 retail locations, has for many years described herself as "a lifelong student of business." While she credits what she learned in college as contributing to her professional success as well as the impressive growth of her company which had only 20 retail outlets when she took over the reins when her father retired 5 years ago, she also recognizes and credits the valuable real-world business lessons that she continues to learn each and every day.

She has leveraged her preparation in marketing to ascertain continually through formal and informal means the expectations of her customers and whether her organization is meeting those expectations. She is joined by management and employee teams that share her commitment to fully meeting and ideally exceeding all reasonable customer expectations. She likewise periodically assesses through employee surveys, focus groups, and informal conversations whether her company is likewise succeeding in fully meeting and ideally exceeding the expectations of its employees. She considers her team to be the company's most important resource, and the instrumental role that they continually play is evidenced in the company's ongoing customer satisfaction surveys and periodic focus groups. Sharon is a "hands-on" leader and can frequently be found interacting with employees and customers in the various store locations.

About 10 years ago, with the encouragement of her father, Sharon facilitated the company's first strategic planning retreat and developed their first strategic plan. A mission statement, goals for a 5-year planning period, and the necessary strategies to achieve each goal were agreed upon and documented in this written plan. Both Sharon and her father recognized the limited value this work and resulting plan would have if it was not shared with the organization's team and utilized as a roadmap that mapped out the necessary route of travel to achieving the organization's mission. Highlights of the company's strategic planning process and current plan are likewise available for interested stakeholders, including current and potential customers and suppliers to review.

Since the initial strategic planning retreat, the plan has been reviewed and updated, as necessary, at the end of each year. The company sponsors a holiday party each year during which Sharon briefly recaps the business year, always thanking her team for all they do to make the company a success. This event is well attended, and all of the store locations are only open in the morning that day to allow employees to attend the afternoon party during which they collectively celebrate another successful year.

While over the years the organization's goals have changed, the company has remained steadfast to its mission which clearly articulates its commitment to the communities served by its growing chain of retail stores. Several years ago, Sharon introduced the concept of sustainability to the organization's management team after attending a related seminar. Before doing so, she had shared the idea with her father who indicated that he thought that their customers and employees would expect the company to be socially responsible in this regard. As she anticipated, the management team enthusiastically embraced the concept and suggested that it would make sense to afford their employees, and later their customers, the opportunity to weigh in on whether or not the company should revise its mission statement and goals to reflect a genuine commitment to the pillars of sustainability that she had initially learned about in the seminar and further researched before sharing the idea with her father and bringing it to her team.

It came as no surprise when both the employees and customers overwhelmingly endorsed the idea. This led to the company having an off-cycle strategic planning retreat during which a minor revision was made to their mission statement to articulate clearly the company's commitment to sustainability. The goals that were then developed in support of the revised mission statement included goals related to sustainability as well as crisis preparedness. The development of a much needed crisis management plan, while a goal in and of itself, also served as a strategy in support of the company's two sustainability goals.

To make a long story short, the company committed to these goals in support of their newly revised mission statement 3 years ago, and any concern about the business impact of their actions has vanished in light of the phenomenal growth and business success that the company has experienced since then. The fact that a commitment to sustainability was not only the right but also prudent, business decision has been clearly and convincingly demonstrated, as has the value of having a crisis preparedness plan. While challenging winters are nothing unusual in the Midwest, a major storm that challenged regional businesses for more than a week proved the value of having a comprehensive crisis preparedness plan to guide both managers and their employees during that particular crisis.

As well as becoming a believer in the role that sustainability should play in running a successful business, Sharon has assisted other regional business leaders as they too have taken a leap of faith and revised their mission statements to make sustainability a major role of their organizations and as they operationalized this commitment by developing and implementing related goals in crisis preparedness and sustainability. She has likewise been invited to speak at business association luncheons and deliver guest lectures at the college that played an important role in her preparation to lead this growing business enterprise. Several of her presentations have been titled, "Crisis Preparation as a Sustainability Strategy."

Chapter Takeaways

- Contemporary organizations exist in a dynamic, ever-changing environment that, while offering many opportunities for organizations to succeed, can similarly present challenges that can compromise an organization's success and, at times, its survival.
- The leaders of successful organizations recognize the critical importance of understanding their organization's strengths and weaknesses in light of the environmental opportunities and threats that it faces, as they formulate goals and strategies designed to achieve the mission of their organization.
- It is essential that organizational leaders recognize the potential crisis situations and events that may impact their organization in both the present and future and develop and implement crisis preparedness strategies to address these potential threats to organizational success and survival.
- It is important to understand and fully utilize the crisis management process and take the time to properly enact each step in that process.
- Proactive planning is a must in successful crisis management.
- Successful organizations recognize that they have a responsibility to future generations that can only be fulfilled through embracing and committing to achieve all of the pillars of sustainability.
- Stakeholders are increasingly interested in patronizing, working for, and investing in socially responsible organizations that espouse and deliver on their commitment to sustainability.
- Crisis preparedness strategies contribute to both a sustainable competitive advantage and to achieving an organization's mission and goals, including its commitment to sustainability.
- Successful crisis preparedness and sustainability strategies can only be fully realized through the commitment and efforts of engaged stakeholders empowered by organizational leaders who "walk the walk" as innovative, inclusive, and responsible leaders.

Reflection Questions

1. Discuss the role that crisis preparedness plays in organizational success and survival.
2. Discuss the role that crisis preparedness plays as a sustainability strategy.
3. Discuss how crisis preparedness contributes to organizational resilience.
4. Discuss the role that responsible and inclusive leadership play in developing and achieving an organization's sustainability goals.
5. Discuss how an organization's crisis preparedness strategies can position it for present and future success while achieving its sustainability goals.

References

Hornby, A. S. (Ed.). Crisis. (2010). In *Oxford Advanced Learner's Dictionary*. https://www.oxfordlearnersdictionaries.com/us/definition/english/crisis_1

Stevenson, A. (Ed.). (2010). Crisis management. In *Oxford Dictionary of English* (3rd ed). Oxford University Press.

Chapter 17
Imagination and Communication Toward Future Realization

Manuel Y. Fernandez and Vram Ismailyan

Abstract This chapter focuses on how imagination can lead to great innovation, if leaders demonstrate this trait themselves or help foster an environment that will unearth the inner creativity that lives inside everyone. The authors focus on and highlight a few methods that allow people to demonstrate their inner creativity through empathy, design thinking, and diversity. This chapter is enriched with personal stories from the authors that underscore how these creativity evoking methods can be used in practice and the learnings that can result from them. A dissection of speeches or talks given by influential leaders is also discussed in this chapter as a means to demonstrate how the use of subtle language can actually take an audience on an imaginative journey. Overall, the need for leaders to be imaginative when it comes to future trends, to keep themselves informed, and to communicate, not only toward learning and understanding facts and trends but also in making ideas understandable to team members, is the critical message in this chapter.

Keywords Innovation · Imagination · Communication · Empathy · Diversity

Introduction

How can leaders unearth creativity from deep within their psyche to help validate data and effectively communicate? Is asking the right questions more important than having the right answers? Paradigmatic eclecticism empowers leaders to leverage empathy and imagination in making ideas, both current and future, understandable to its stakeholders.

M. Y. Fernandez (✉)
Capital Group, Los Angeles, CA, USA

V. Ismailyan
Identifee, Los Angeles, CA, USA

J. Marques (ed.), *Innovative Leadership in Times of Compelling Changes*, Management, Change, Strategy and Positive Leadership, https://doi.org/10.1007/978-3-030-67258-4_17

This chapter focuses on the integration of empathy and diversity as critical elements that are catalysts for leaders to be radically imaginative and drive innovation with a shared vision. The backdrop on the importance of imagination that everyone has at some point in their lives will be examined. This chapter challenges common approaches to how some leaders have directed or continue to direct a *vision* for a program, product, or even organizational structure that, at times, may result in solving the wrong problem, thus resulting in increased costs and unsatisfied stakeholders. This chapter borrows and expands on elements of design thinking and discusses how elements of the design thinking process, coupled with tools from business analysis, equip any leader to dig into their own imaginative innovation or, better yet, help unlock radical innovation from any team member they are collaborating with. The first section will discuss how and why empathy is such a crucial element before anyone can even start to promote ideas, yet alone stand up an effort and implement. The second section will dive deeper into the power of imagination, which unlocks an endless possibility of ideas that can inform and align leadership and any team member toward a shared purpose and goal. The final section will weave in the element of diversity that extends beyond race or sex to compliment the level of empathy and ideation where true imagination can be unlocked.

Shifting the Paradigm and Setting the Tone

Imagine bright green mountains against a riveting sunrise as the rays of the sun glisten on the lake. Imagine sitting on a porch savoring the perfect cup of coffee as you absorb the aroma of those Arabica beans while taking in the majestic beauty around you. Often, it is so easy to describe a perfect getaway, vacation, or meditation spot, and yet people, including leaders at any level, neglect to imagine and communicate what their product, team, or organization should be. They lack the opportunity in describing every facet, such as what the product or culture should look like, feel like, or even taste like. How should the product, team, or culture make you feel? What are the top descriptors? Instead, there is a sense of command that is handed down the hierarchy where the assignee or team just takes the task at hand, project, or problem statement that is given at face value without bothering to question it and dig deeper to ensure they are solving for the right problem or achieving the right outcome. Many take the objective, given that is handed from up high, develop a list of milestones, confirm it with the governing bodies, develop timelines, execute, confirm the milestones were achieved, close out the effort, and call it a success. This might sound all too familiar and, in some cases and industries, works quite well. However, when trying to solve for complex problems or achieve a new level of innovation, leaders must give up the urge to command the outcome, sometimes based on limited or insufficient knowledge of the root cause, target market, segment, or persona.

What if leaders communicated a hypotheses of the problem statement, collaborated with teams to dissect the problem statement, and checked in with users of the actual product or service or team members of the organization to validate whether we are trying to solve for the right problem? What if we questioned the hypothesized problem statement and walked a mile in the shoes of the actual users or team members in order to confirm and maybe adjust? Research needs to go beyond sales figures and surveys. Research needs to include a deep level of empathy, followed by a shared vision, so that we provide products, services, or cultures that people love.

Toward a Deeper Level with Empathy

Empathy

Meriam-Webster defines empathy as the action of understanding, being aware of, being sensitive to, and vicariously experiencing the feelings, thoughts, and experience of another of either the past or present without having the feelings, thoughts, and experience fully communicated in an objectively explicit manner. Simply it is putting oneself in another person's shoes.

Building a deeper level of empathy can be more difficult than one would think, at least for many. As the authors, Doorley, S., Holcomb, S., Klebahn, P., Segovia, K., & Utley, J. from the Hasso Plattner School of Design points out in their design thinking bootleg, "your viewpoint carries assumptions and personal beliefs"; therefore, it is critical to remove these personal beliefs and biases and pretend that you do not know anything, thus starting from the beginning (2018).

This is a crucial part of any process where leaders and team members are trying to solve for a problem by coming up with new processes, policies, or products. It is important to acknowledge that developing this sense of empathy does in fact take time and may in fact be one area where we must spend the most time. If one were to compare this to traditional project management, this would be similar to the planning phase, which should always take the most time before launching into an effort. As the Project Management Institute and Harvard Business Review Staff point out, the planning phase of a project should involve the need to "Determine the right problem," which again, if done with care and an open mind, empathy will lead to a better problem definition and better results (2016).

From personal experience, one of the authors shares an instance of a project he was involved with where the project was already kicked off, and it was his job to gather requirements so that organization could configure an off-the-shelf product to be used by an operations team for crucial workflows where billions of dollars were involved in the day-to-day work. The author started as with any project, by talking with key users, gathering requirements, and then working with the vendor to see how the solution could be configured to meet the needs of the users. As the team started to configure and show the users initial configurations, the author could see the look of fear and disappointment in their faces around the room. Being that our culture is quite polite, the users expressed concerns, but he could tell that they were holding back. The author shared these concerns with his manager and asked if he could observe and shadow the users for a few weeks. He received much needed support from the manager and other leaders albeit there was risk to a timeline. During those weeks, the author recalls sitting with users and started off by just watching what they were doing and observing body language, facial expressions, sighs, deep breaths, and even moments of smiling and laughing. As the days of the weeks continued, as with any effort, he mapped processes and asked for more specifics to fill in some notes so that he could understand how they were using systems, what made them frustrated when he observed certain bodily reactions, and what made them happy when he saw smiles and laughter. To take it a bit further, he asked the IT department for special access to a sandbox environment that imitates the current system, but in a non-production way. This allowed him to witness and feel how the current system works and how it accounts for existing workflows and try to resemble what the users currently go through when experiencing the highs, lows, excitement, and stress. This literally helped the team to walk in their shoes and deeply understand their needs before implementing a new off-the-shelf solution.

Our project, or product team as it eventually became, borrowed from the design thinking approach to map out user journeys and created personas where they could summarize different types of users that would be interacting with this new off-the-shelf system and new processes. At the end of this internal anthropologic journey, the results and recommendations sent the program leadership into a bit of shock when they were informed that the off-the-shelf solution could not accomplish everything that this team performs for the firm. The recommendation was to augment the system with a custom in-house digital product to make up for some of the gaps. This was not an easy sell, but the research that was performed by building a deep sense of empathy with the users allowed the team to paint a current state picture that was so vivid that any audience members could feel the stress, adrenaline, and excitement that the team feels during various parts of a process. Once the story was painted, the project team demonstrated how the vendor solution would need to be used and where the gaps were and then showed a paper prototype of how the proposed custom product would improve and fill in the gaps, resulting in a process that not only maintains internal teams happy but positions the firm for more scalability because of how data could be structured more efficiently.

The takeaway from this sharing is that if it were not for that deep sense of empathy, the firm could have implemented a solution that met requirements on paper, basically the *what* that the team needed, but the *how,* for using the system would have slowed people down, caused undue stress and potentially led to miscommunication of data costing the firm opportunities in the market. The *how* gets to a deeper sense of what makes people happy, stressed, etc. and where user experience becomes critical.

When observing or building empathy, it is crucial to consider diversity of the sample. Diversity can include race, ethnicity, gender, direct users, and indirect users. Diversity of input allows leaders to truly build empathy and again reduces preconceived notions and biases. Failing to take time to observe, listen, and even do the work for which you are trying to solve a problem can lead to higher costs, user or employee dissatisfaction, and more work. However, doing the deeper research of empathy allows leaders to better understand the problem and then engage with users to be imaginative on how to fix the problems and unlock creative power to ideate.

Leveraging Empathy and Charisma

Is empathy a core component of leadership? How can leaders use empathy to influence their stakeholders' need for achievement? Choi (2006) states that there are three key elements to charismatic leadership: envisioning, empathy, and empowerment.

> The term 'charisma,' whose initial meaning is 'a gift' in Greek, has been frequently used in politics and religion to adduce legitimacy to power. Weber (1968) defined it as an individual's personality quality (or at least, specifically exceptional powers or qualities) by virtue of which he/she is set apart from ordinary people and which thus legitimizes his/her exercise of influence. House (1977) developed a theory of charismatic leadership which is among the first attempts to build a comprehensive theoretical basis for studying the topic.

A charismatic leader who is empathetic invokes trust and creates an emotional bond with stakeholders. This type of leadership comes in many forms dictated by contextual factors such as organizational factors, task factors, and stakeholder factors. Think about the last time you were with your family or friends and someone stepped into a leadership role to drive results. Think about the last time you watched a competitive team sporting event who emerged as a leader. These are two entirely contrasting settings that require different approaches. In the family setting, the leader who emerge demonstrates more empathy toward their family and friends which stimulates affiliation. In a competitive team sporting event, the leader who emerges will demonstrate envisioning behavior to influence the team's needs for achievement. This can be as simple as the player embodying what he/she is asking of his/her teammates such as working harder on the defensive end of a basketball game. In both situations, the leader who emerges must empower stakeholders with his/her own empowerment practices. By empowering stakeholders, they have a clearer understanding of their role, improved effort, increased satisfaction, and increased self-leadership within the organization.

Can leaders use specific words to build a deep sense of empathy? Yuan et al. (2000) examined the relationship between positive and negative words and leadership talent, using a formal interview. A sample of 804 high-level executives from a variety of public and private organizations were part of the study. Leaders used 6 positive words for every 100 words spoken during the interview while using only 1.5 negative words for every 100 spoken words. More important than the number of positive and negative words used is a positive mental mindset. The study found that a positive mental mindset has a big impact of how effective a leader is in building a deeper sense of empathy with their stakeholders. Think about the last time you were in a situation, whether personal or professional, whether negative or neutral. When you had conversations with specific individuals, did you feel a deeper sense of alliance with the person who was deeply empathetic toward you and used a positive approach or with the person who piled on the negativity surrounding your circumstances? One of the authors of this chapter recalls his childhood who, as a kid, loved to play and coach basketball. He learned firsthand that it usually wasn't the work ethic or desire to win that his players lacked, it was more about a mental block that prevented them from achieving confidence in their abilities, which ultimately resulted in limiting their basketball playing abilities. He took the approach of focusing on what each player did extremely well. He would keep a note card with each player's name and a scorecard (1 to 5, low to high) of key elements required to assemble a winning team; these included shooting, passing, defense, rebounding, leadership, hustle, speed, size, and other intangible qualities. Once he had enough time to evaluate each player's strengths and weaknesses through practices and games, he began to have one-on-one conversations with each person. The ensuing conversations were not about basketball. Instead, he spent time to get to know the individual from where they grew up, major milestones in life, things they enjoyed doing, family, friends, and everything that made them the individual they were; he already knows them as a basketball player. The goal in having those one-on-one conversations was to show his players a deep sense of empathy toward their personal stories outside of basketball. The author's foundation as a friend and coach with each player was based on trust. By using a positive mindset and building alliances, he was able to not only put his players in positions to succeed on the court, but they had the trust in him as a coach, and the confidence in themselves, to do what they were already good at. That simple approach was contagious as players began to spend time together off the court and formed bonds beyond basketball.

During his tenure as head coach, there were instances where he needed to listen to the players and pivot from one strategy to another in order to increase their chances of winning each game. This posed a small challenge as he had envisioned a specific path for success but had to let go of the preconceived vision in efforts to be successful; this was not easy. Was it personal fear of failing as a coach? Was it a fear of losing the game? Was it a fear of losing respect among the players? Webb and Mann (2018) discusses the personal rise and fall of Brandon Webb, a former Navy Seal. He experienced rock bottoms when he lost his business and filed bankruptcy, and ultimately, his wife filed for divorce. While he managed to pull himself up and out of rock bottom, just a few months after landing a six-figure salary job, Brandon was itching to start another business. His friends told him that he had a stable job earning nearly two hundred thousand dollars with benefits and can provide for his kids. They told him not to do it again, but Brandon felt like his job was his coconut. Brandon's friend from the Philippines shared a story with him about how they trap monkeys in his country. They dig a hole and place a coconut in it; the monkey reaches in and grabs the coconut, and his fist is now too big to pull back out. He iss trapped. All he has to do is let go of the coconut. But he won't do it. Why not? What keeps that monkey's fist clenched? Fear. He is afraid of losing what he has. So he keeps the coconut and loses his freedom. Brandon did not want to keep the coconut and lose his freedom. What prevents people from taking the risks they need to take in order to achieve the things they dream of achieving or, in the author's case, giving up control to his players in critical situations so they could win? The author could not let go of the coconut. They could have more success as a team if the author reciprocated the trust his players showed in him by empowering them to make the right decision in specific game-winning situations. Brandon writes that "mastering fear starts with a decision, then proceeds through rehearsal, so that you'll be as prepared as possible to make that jump into the unknown and take action in the face of your fear. But nine times out of ten, when the time comes to make the jump, something keeps people from actually doing it. Something they're holding on to." The author decided to let go of the coconut and empower his players resulting in more games won.

Diversity as a Galvanizing Force

Empathy is a catalyst for leaders to drive innovation toward a shared vision within an organization. There are circumstances that will impact how effective a leader's empathy is with each stakeholder. The foundation for effective leadership to drive an imaginative and innovative shared vision is understanding diversity. While some aspects of diversity is visible to the naked eye, other much more important forms of diversity that impact the daily lives of our stakeholders are not. As one of the authors who has held various roles in a large organization ranging from an individual contributor, to a mentor, and a leader, nothing has been more critical to their success than recognizing diversity among the people they work with. One of the simple things the author shares in doing from the beginning was get to know each person they interacted with on a personal level; this was important because he wanted to understand what they were getting out of bed for each morning and what made them want to perform at their highest level. Some individuals were driven by competition, others by money or recognition, some just to provide for their family, and others by a corporate career path to the top. Whatever the driving force was behind the why, it helped the author to understand the approach he needed to take with each individual in every single interaction. Whether it was a professional interaction or personal, empathy allowed the author to interact dynamically to ensure he had a genuine interaction with each other and walk away feeling positive. In his role as the Head of Product and Strategy at Identifee, the author spent time to master his art of communication with two key executives, the Founder and CEO, Vigen Ismailyan, and Head of Client Success, Kevin Miyamoto. While the communication style needed to be different with his two colleagues due to their differing roles, there was similarity in that both are fathers who love to spend time with their families. In his TED Talks, Ricardo Semler, a successful Brazilian businessman, talks about asking "why" three times so you can get to the real reason about why you are doing something. He notes that usually when you ask why once, it is easy to come up with an answer; the second time, it gets harder; and usually, by the third time, if you can answer the question, then you can move on to the more important question, which is "what for?" Mr. Semler is known for his radical management style of allowing people to work from home when it was not commonplace back in the 1990s. He also gave employees complete access to know what everyone in the company earned along with comparing what the market salary value is for the same position; he believed in transparency and giving up control. Furthermore, Mr. Semler asked his employees to vote on their manager every 6 months, and if the manager did not have effective leadership or 70%+ approval, they would demote the individual and place the person the group wanted. Mr. Semler goes on to talk about how children and adults learn differently, and we cannot place them in our preferred method of teaching. He founded Lumiar School as a result of his beliefs for kids ages 0 to 14. Li (2013) highlights the attributes of Lumiar School; this unique way of offering the school experience is organized in six pillars: mosaic curriculum, multi-age groups, active learning, tutors and masters, participatory management, and integrated assessment. The school offers no core curriculum but a mosaic curriculum, no classrooms but learning spaces, and meetings are not run by only faculty members but with students. There are two types of educators – tutors and masters. The tutor works with the kids in their learning skills and their discovery. Then masters are brought in, once the students express interest in a topic and need an expert in that field. Mr. Semler's approach to education is the definition of how understanding diversity can have a large impact to effectively teaching children from an early age. Rather than a one-size-fits-all model, Lumiar embraces diversity as a galvanizing force for educating children from a young age. In business, a simple understanding of one's culture, hobbies, or favorite foods can often be the fine line between effective and ineffective leadership. Mr. Semler's unconventional management style and education approach are foundations for unlocking and fostering innovation.

Imagination as a Crucial Building Block for Ideation

The ability to problem-solve goes beyond theory, mathematical equations, or lessons in history. Critical thinking and imagination play a major role for trying to solve problems rooted within human psyche. In business, many times we are trying to solve or fix problems related to processes or procedures, which were originally developed by humans. This is usually accomplished by studying how we work and documenting the steps and process. The creativity and imagination surface when trying to iterate through the processes and reimagine how we can make them better and more efficient. One could argue that tools like lean six sigma can help improve processes, which it can. However, when tools like this are coupled with imagination and creativity, it results in bigger innovation because when we combine the research that we gained with building deep empathy for the people for who we are trying to help or improve their lives for, we get to real problem statements and dream up bigger and grander ideas.

Imagination is defined by Merriam-Webster as the act or power of forming a mental image of something not present to the senses or never before wholly perceived in reality (2020). However, if you keep reading through other definitions from Merriam-Webster, it mentions that imagination is the ability to confront and deal with a problem; yet many people shy away from using the word *imagination* when in a meeting. An article in The Telegraph discusses the importance of imagination for children and their development. The Telegraph explains that "when children use their imagination in play they are developing crucial psychological and emotional capacities that help them understand the world in which they live and their relation to it; they are learning to solve problems, create new possibilities, even change the world," which should extend far beyond child play (2018).

It seems that as time passes and children grow to teenagers and adults, the art and importance of imagination erodes as humans take on critical classes where the emphasis is on theory, equations, and science. Imagination still exists inside of us, but we must relearn how to unlock it so that it does not remain suppressed. Borrowing again from the playbook and philosophy of design thinking, there are different activities that any leader or workshop or sprint facilitator can use to unlock the suppressed ability to imagine and ideate for the benefits of solving the right problem.

As defined or explained by Hasso Plattner School of Design in their design thinking bootleg, ideation is the mode in which you generate radical design alternatives. Ideation "is a process of 'going wide' in terms of concepts and outcomes—a mode of 'flaring' instead of 'focus'" (2018). This ability to go wide or "flare" requires creativity and, most importantly, imagination. This is an amazing opportunity where leaders or associates of an organization, product team, or program can pretend to be 5 years old again and harness the imagination and creativity from that time period and go big. The team can always constrain things later, but being completely imaginative in the beginning helps us imagine true possibilities and begins to unlock innovation.

This is not necessarily a new concept but perhaps something that gets overlooked because great leaders often share their grand ideas and visions that they imagine, just not necessarily use that term. Great leaders that come to mind are ones like Steve Jobs and Martin Luther King Jr.

When Steve Jobs first unveiled the iPhone in 2007, his choice of language is quite interesting because it plays on the sense of empathy and human psyche, and he tries to invoke deep feelings. When describing how a user or customer would use the iPhone, he stated "We're gonna touch this with our fingers. And we have invented a new technology called multi-touch, which is phenomenal. It works like magic" (Jobs, S. 2007; Wright, M. 2015). His language inherently requires us to imagine using our fingers and believing it is magic. One could argue that this clever technique had many people imagining the same thing all at once, resulting in the plethora of apps and allowing innovation to flourish in the field of technology.

If we pivot and think back to the famous speech by Martin Luther King Jr., there comes a moment where he vividly says "I still have a dream. It is a dream deeply rooted in the American dream. I have a dream that one day this nation will rise up and live out the true meaning of its creed:…" The speech captivates the audience or reader, and Dr. King did a remarkable job of delivering with such passion that it is truly inspiring to this day.

It takes time and practice to deliver a speech or address like Steve Jobs or Martin Luther King Jr., but being able to clearly and vividly share imagination and dreams about a project, product, or cause is crucial to inspire innovation and creativity. In efforts to truly unleash creativity and innovation from people, it is important for them to be heard. This is not always easy in a large setting, especially if someone is on the quitter side. There are methods to avoid one person from taking control of a brainstorm or ideation session. One of the authors shares learnings from Sprintwell, a company that focuses on design thinking and design sprints. He learned about the power of "working alone together" in these settings. The idea and concept as with any design thinking playbook is that you don't shout out ideas during these types of ideation sessions. Instead, we work together, silently, and we draw our ideas. It doesn't matter if they are stick figures or works of art. By drawing out your ideas, it unleashes a larger sense of creativity and imagination that lets others actually "see" what you mean. So often, we communicate ideas, and the vision that is in our minds may not be the narrative or scene that others are picturing, but by drawing your ideas, it helps put everyone on the same page. Most importantly here, we draw silently so that there isn't an alpha or dominant person in the room taking over the conversation. People are not just agreeing with the person speaking the most; people are aligning and agreeing to ideas, instead. Some ground rules here are ones that we can borrow from improv. The power of "yes and." As others start sharing the ideas they have drawn, think of how to improve upon the idea by saying "yes and." Many times we are quick to say, "yes but" or "no but," which immediately diminishes or minimizes another person's idea and could limit innovation.

Chapter Takeaways

- The integration of empathy and diversity can be a catalyst for leaders to be radically imaginative and drive innovation with a shared vision.
- Leaders should consider communicating a hypotheses of a problem statement, collaborate with their teams to dissect the problem statement, and check in with users of the actual product or service or team members of the organization to validate whether we are trying to solve for the right problem.
- Building a deep level of empathy is important but can be more difficult than one would think. This is due to the fact that our viewpoints carry assumptions and personal beliefs.
- A deep sense of empathy can propel a firm from implementing a solution that meets requirements on paper to accomplishing goals while keeping people happy and less stressed.
- A charismatic leader who is empathetic invokes trust and creates an emotional bond with stakeholders. This type of leadership comes in many forms dictated by contextual factors such as organizational factors, task factors, and stakeholder factors.

- Empathy is a catalyst for leaders to drive innovation toward a shared vision within an organization.
- The foundation for effective leadership to drive an imaginative and innovative shared vision is understanding diversity.
- Critical thinking and imagination play a major role for trying to solve problems rooted within human psyche. Imagination comprises the ability to confront and deal with a problem.

Reflection Questions

1. What are some ways in which you try to draw out your creativity?
2. The chapter emphasizes the importance of empathy. Consider this phenomenon: what, in your opinion, are three major advantages and three major concerns of applying empathy in workplaces?
3. Do you consider empathy and charisma each other's supplements or opposites? Please explain your stance.
4. This chapter explains that Ricardo Semler suggests asking "why" three times to get to the real reason for doing anything. Consider a problem or decision you are currently facing, and implement this practice. Share your findings below.
5. Do you consider a diverse workforce an advantage or a disadvantage to creative problem-solving? Please explain your rationale in detail.

References

Choi, J. (2006). A motivational theory of charismatic leadership: Envisioning, empathy, and empowerment. *Journal of Leadership & Organizational Studies, 13*(1), 24–45.

Doorley, S., Holcomb, S., Klebahn, P., Segovia, K., & Utley, J. (2018). *Design thinking Bootleg*, 3–4, 7–8. Retrieved from https://static1.squarespace.com/static/57c6b79629687fde090a0fdd/t/5b19b2f2aa4a99e99b26b6bb/1528410876119/dschool_bootleg_deck_2018_final_sm+%282%29.pdf

Empathy. (n.d.). *Merriam-Webster*. Retrieved from https://www.merriam-webster.com/dictionary/empathy.

Harvard Business Review Staff. (2016, Nov 3). The four phases of project management. *Harvard Business Review*. Retrieved from: https://hbr.org/2016/11/the-four-phases-of-project-management

Jobs, S., & Wright, M. (2015). The original iPhone announcement annotated: Steve Jobs' genius meets Genius. *NextWeb.com*. Retrieved from https://thenextweb.com/apple/2015/09/09/genius-annotated-with-genius/

King, M. (1963). I have a dream. *Americanrhetoric.com*. Retrieved from https://www.american-rhetoric.com/speeches/mlkihaveadream.htm,

Li, T. (2013, Sept 22). Ricardo Semler's Lumiar Schools - The Mosaic Curriculum. *Open Ideo*. Retrieved from https://challenges.openideo.com/challenge/creative-confidence/inspiration/ricardo-semler-s-lumiar-schools-the-mosaic-curriculum

Semler, R. (2014, Oct). How to run a company with almost no rules. *TED.com*. Retrieved from https://www.ted.com/talks/ricardo_semler_how_to_run_a_company_with_almost_no_rules?language=en

Webb, B., & Mann, J. D. (2018, Aug 26). I am a former Navy SEAL Sniper, and there is something I fear much more than being waterboarded or shot. *BusinessInsider.com*. Retrieved from https://www.businessinsider.com/what-navy-seal-sniper-fears-more-than-waterboarding-2018-8

Why imaginative play is important for a child's development. (2018, 29 June). *The Telegraph*. Retrieved from https://www.telegraph.co.uk/lifestyle/family-time/imaginative-play-benefits/

Yuan, H., Clifton, D. O., Stone, P., & Blumberg, H. H. (2000). Positive and negative words: Their association with leadership talent and effectiveness. *The Psychologist-Manager Journal, 4*(2), 199–214.

Chapter 18
Heading for the Future with the Proper Mindset

Victor Senaji Anyanje and Thomas Anyanje Senaji

Abstract The need for leaders to be imaginative when it comes to future trends, to keep themselves informed, and to communicate, not only toward learning and understanding facts and trends but also in making ideas understandable to team members, continues to increasingly elude society. Leaders have imperiled both themselves, their followers, and the society through failure to positively imagine, communicate, and clarify the path to the desired future state or the organizations they lead. In this chapter, we explore imagination, communication, and future realization. The guiding questions are as follows: Why is imagination important? How can communication be improved? How can the execution be unlocked to realize the future? In the process, we discern gaps and suggest improvements.

Keywords Imagination · Communication · Envisioning · Leadership · Future realization

Introduction

The role of a leader is to envision the future, inspire, and motivate followers to pursue and achieve both individual and shared goals. This is important because organizations of all types are formed for particular purposes and are guided by goals. In order to effectively deliver on their mandate, leaders need to communicate and remove barriers in the way of the followers. These barriers can be physical, social, and even psychological. The leaders should communicate authentically and be perceived and seen to lead by example. They need to anticipate future trends and share their insights with followers. They also need to appreciate that there always will be

V. S. Anyanje
High Court of Kenya, Nairobi, Kenya

T. A. Senaji (✉)
The East African University, Nairobi, Kenya

J. Marques (ed.), *Innovative Leadership in Times of Compelling Changes*, Management, Change, Strategy and Positive Leadership, https://doi.org/10.1007/978-3-030-67258-4_18

tension between the vision that they may be passionate about but which may be unclear to the followers. In this regard, frustration may set in both on the side of the leader to whom the vision is clear and the followers who may be wondering what the vision is all about. This is where communication comes in: the need for communicating the vision about the future with clarity and how that future will be realized becomes crucial. Alongside the vision and the path to the desired future is the need to empower the followers and those who will be affected by the vision that is being pursued. We contend that the *future* is the unseen that continues to shape our decisions today, and that imagining is the process of conceiving a progressive future for the society. This conception of the future is *vision*. Further, *future realization* is how the imagined ideal future is actualized. We next discuss imagining, communication, and future orientation and conclude with some suggestions for improvement.

Imagining

Arguably, every human being has aspirations for a better future, if not, just a future. They therefore engage their minds to envision this future. They imagine a future desirable state and would like to see and live that future. If we suppose that the aspirations are for a just and peaceful society with opportunity for everybody, then this is a positive aspiration. The vast majority of people have this aspiration for the future. Imagination is the faculty or action of forming new ideas or images or concepts of external objects not present to the senses or drawing from the senses to create new ideas, images, or concepts distinct from those available including through reference to past experience. It is the ability of the mind to be creative or resourceful.

To be creative is to come up with new ideas which then act as a resource to shape the future state of things or events. Creativity could also take the form of modifying existing ideas into an amalgam consisting existing and envisioned input. In this context, creativity becomes a resource which should be harnessed to propel and launch society into realms of prosperity such high social, economic, and political development. It means that human beings should apply their creative minds that is "imagine" the desired future together with what it would take to realize that future. It may be argued that the highest level of imagination is that which leads to the realization of a better society at peace with itself despite the diversity that exists or may exist as society evolves. This said, a question that begs answers is whether society is increasingly becoming at peace with itself or descending into conflict and what the role of imagination is or should be.

It is also possible that within the society, there may be those that can be described as self-centered and whose future outlook is that of depriving and excluding others in as much as they can. This situation can be seen as debauch imagining of the future. Given these two almost polar opposites, "positive or negative" imagination, there may be those that are in between along this continuum. This notwithstanding, it can be said that majority of society is perpetually yearning for a "good future" and any individual, in their small way, is continually (consciously or otherwise) progressing toward a future – a future that needs to be shaped through appropriate imagination. However, the question remains to be what it is it that people are imagining and how it can be realized.

To put the notion of imagination and realization into perspective, it is plausible to situate them in the context of leadership and followership in society. Specifically, the following questions are pertinent:

- How can people imagine positively?
- How are leaders aiding followers in imagining constructively?
- How can the imagination be realized?
- Suppose the imagination is pervert, should it be realized?

From a theoretical and practical perspective, leadership is conceived of in the context of the leader, the follower, and the context in which it is practiced. This implies that while the primary role of the leader is to inspire and motivate, that of the followers is predominantly to support the leader by being effective followers.

To be an effective follower is to actually participate in the leadership ecosystem by executing the leaders' legitimate vision and providing constructive feedback to the leader in the prevailing context which can take various forms. It may be an organization of any type such as a local community, state government, regional community, civil society, and learning Institutions, among others. Conversely, an example of an ineffective follower is a passive follower who may neither question the leader's actions respectfully nor provide any constructive feedback including genuine criticism.

As seen earlier, to aspire to lead implies willingness to constructively imagine (envision) and effectively communicate the vision of the desired future to the followers. It is the charting of a path or roadmap to the realization of the desired future. It also implies the willingness to empower others by sharing the power the leader has with the followers. It involves creating other leaders. It demands generosity and more often than not magnanimity in dealing with followers, peers, and superiors. In other words, it calls for magnanimous (selfless) imagination of the future and the ability to communicate and "sell" this imagination with other people around them. It also implies the willingness to bear and accept failure when and if it occurs as a learning opportunity.

Communication

Communication is the act of conveying meanings from one entity or group to another through the use of mutually understood signs, symbols, and semiotic rules. The main steps inherent to all communication are the formation of communicative motivation or reason, message composition, message encoding, message transmission, and finally, decoding of message at the receiver end. It is emphasized that communication is not complete until there is feedback. In the present case, we would be dealing with the formation of a vison for the future by constructively imagining it, articulating the vision in written form, converting it into clearly understandable form, choosing the best medium to convey the message, and finally conveying it to the target audience. The audience may be the people that are expected to act on the message by ways of taking various actions that are implied in the message in order to realize the desired future that is inherent in the vision being communicated.

It may be argued that beside appropriate imagination, the greatest task of leader is communication. Without effective communication even a leader's noble vision will fall flat! So, how should a leader communicate in order to have their vision effectively shared, embraced, and enacted by the followers to realize the desired "imagined" future?

This question appears to be as old of the cradle of mankind and continues to beg answers even as the environment changes: the basic issues around leading with vision remains perpetual. A related question is how positive imagination or envisioning can be nurtured in societies particularly among the leaders.

This notwithstanding, imagination is just one side of the coin: communicating with authenticity and enacting this vision in pursuit of realization of a desired future is even a more daunting task. In essence, since communication defines the success or failure of any noble idea as can be with a leader's or collective imagining of the future, the notion of mindful communication appears to be a rich area of interest to aid in understanding why and how imagination can lead to future realization. Similarly, it may be plausible to suggest that communicating should form that greater part of the preoccupation of not only leaders but also followers.

Mindful Communication

Mindful communication can be said to be sensitive and empathetic at the very least. By sensitivity, we mean one that respects diversities of people across gender, race, religion, age, ability, and aspirations of the target of the communication, among other attributes of the target. It also involves the framing and conveyance of the message. At this point it is important to observe that politicians have mastered the art of framing which they exploit to their advantage but to the detriment of the society they purport to be representing. An example is that of marinating chronic corruption in some parts of the world, where upon being pursued for accountability, the "leader" suspects often retreat to their communities "crying more than the bereaved" that their communities are being targeted.

Far from this example, it is important to observe that a very noble vision of the future that is not mindfully communicated may fail at the implementation stage. This being the case, it is desirable to interrogate some of the barriers to mindful communication. Such barriers include stereotypes, individual biases, and other cognitive dispositions that are not amenable to effective communication of a noble imagination. We can observe here that the conquest of self is one of the greatest of all conquests: a situation where we identify our limitations including cognitive ones, confront them, and effectively deal with them in a manner that avoids the blurring our vision of a desired future. When we do this, we are able to seek necessary help to overcome them – after all, no one lacks "skeletons in their closets."

Future Realization

Future is an expectation of advancement or progressive development (Meriam-Webster Dictionary, nd). From an organization perspective, we encounter a vision, mission, core values, and objectives that guide operations. To back up these statements of direction and purpose, structures are created, responsibilities described, and suitable people assigned to carry out certain functions to realize the vision. Some quotes on the "future" are as follows:

Quotes

> The future is always unknowable. The future is never realized because change, paradoxically, is constant. The future is happening now. It's contingent on the past and, just like history, it never ends. It's too busy beginning.[1] (Sir Bob Geldof, 2018) (EY New Zealand, nd.)
>
> The future belongs to those who prepare for it today. (Malcolm X, influential African American human rights activist (1925-1965))[2]

The vision is usually stated in very lofty and ethereal terms and is usually an ideal to be realized. The resounding words of Africa's celebrated son and icon President Nelson Mandela's 3-hour speech "I Am Prepared to Die" during his trial alludes to what conviction to ideals is:

> I have cherished the ideal of democratic and free society in which all persons live together in harmony and with equal opportunities. It is an ideal which I hope to live for and adhere. But if need be, it is an ideal for which I am prepared to die. (*Nelson Mandela, President of the Republic of South Africa)*

This speech "I Am Prepared to Die" suggests two themes "democracy and freedom," where democracy underpins choice and freedom implies absence of domination of any kind – political, economic, social, cultural, religious, ideological, etc. Democracy is essential for effective imagination, and "free society" is the bedrock of innovation and enterprise. It is a prerequisite for self-determination. Though one question to ask is how many are virtuous, another lingering question remains whether we have men and women of sufficient conviction and virtue or how we can increase the reservoir of effective leaders to guide society for future realization.

Besides all the advantages of democracy and free society disposition, lip service to these ideals is everywhere abound. For example, it is not lost to an average observer what is happening in the USA with regard to what appears to be racial

---

[1] https://www.ey.com/en_au/future-realised

[2] https://ec.europa.eu/education/knowledge-centre-interpretation/sites/kci/files/communities/yia_speech.pdf

undertones regarding the dispensation of justice in relation to people of color. There are several incidences manifesting the extent of active service to these ideals including the whacking of George Floyd on May 25, 2020, in Minneapolis, Minnesota, and the suggestion that looting should beget shooting which did not help matters given the fact Breonna Taylor a black woman and aspiring nurse was whacked by police in Louisville, Florida, in March 2020 (Washington Post, May 24 2020).

These disturbing examples suggest that the realization of a free society still remains a mirage in the world. In China for example, black people were persecuted in the wake of the novel coronavirus disease (COVID-19) outbreak and pandemic. African people were forced by the Chinese to sleep in the streets after eviction from their dwellings and prevented from accessing shops and restaurants (The Guardian, April 27 2020). But more disturbing was the lackluster response by the African Union to such discriminatory and racially motivated subversion of basic freedoms of the Africans. There are also persecutions on the basis of religion where freedom of worship is not guaranteed such as is the case in Egypt, Russia, India, Indonesia, and Turkey where restrictions on religion has heightened.

> Religious violence is undergoing revival ranging from "Islamic extremists waging global Jihad and power struggle, between Sunni and Shia Muslims in the Middle East to persecution of Rohingya in Myanmar and outbreaks of violence between Christians and Muslims across Africa." (Muggah & Velshi, 2019 Feb 25)

It is noted that "religious" violence is not religious at all but rather perversion of the teachings (Cavanaugh, 2009). Given these events which impact society's freedom, it is not clear where humanity can find sanctuary to fully realize the desired future potential and all dimensions of well-being; after all the essence of life on earth is to live happily and exit without suffering. However, this is not always the case due to strife, conflict, oppression, violence, environmental degradation, disease, and hunger among other life vagaries which can be significantly mitigated or avoided through appropriate imagination, communication, and directed action toward the desired common future.

Conflict, violence, and even strife can result from poor communication. For example, once issues are not accurately framed and communicated with clarity, the intended effect is lost, and the opposite may likely be the outcome. In turn, this curtails the possibility of realizing future aspirations. Further, if the desired future is not comprehensively and accurately "imagined" or envisioned, the result is a "blurred vision" which becomes difficult to articulate let alone to communicate. The result of this is certain: nothing clear to aim at and no future realization.

Leadership and Future Orientation

Leadership can be described as an enduring conviction and commitment by an individual or a group of people to the realization of a better society. It implies a clear focus by a leader or leaders on a future desired state. In this regard, a high premium is placed on the ability of leaders to plan for the future and execute the plan in a bid to move from the current situation to the next in an organizational context. Leaders are thus said to be effective if they can achieve this feat despite the obstacles that they may encounter. Consequently, leadership effectiveness continues to preoccupy researchers, practitioners, and scholars. The popular press and academia constantly lament the absence of effective leaders, which is particularly reflected in the mistrust of those in positions of authority (Senaji et al., in press). The essence of leadership is to guide organizations of all types to achieve the goal for which they are established. When effective, leadership offers the opportunity to bend personal motivations, group norms, and environmental opportunities toward organizational objectives (Senaji et al., 2016). Such leadership can facilitate implementation of plans aimed at realizing desired future for both organizations and individuals in these organizations. Meanwhile, though the search for effective leadership remains elusive, it may also find respite in the spiritual realm. This fact is articulated by Cardinal Vincent Nichols in Hollensbe et al. (2014) that:

> The deepest resources for the transformation of business, as for society as a whole, lie within the human heart. It is there we have to seek what it is we truly value and yearn for, and where we can harness the strongest motivation to change— ourselves, our organizations, and our world—for the better. (p. 1227)

Spirituality is a broad concept with room for many perspectives. In general, it includes a sense of connection to something bigger than ourselves, and it typically involves a search for meaning in life. As such, it is a universal human experience – something that touches us all. Spirituality is the state of having a connection to God or the spirit world; an example of spirituality is praying every day (http://www.yourdictionary.com/spirituality). It also has different definitions; one of these is "a quality that goes beyond religious affiliation that strives for inspirations, reverence, awe, meaning and purpose, even in those who do not believe in any God" (Murray & Zenter, 1989, p. 259). While some people find it in monotheistic religion as is the case with most religious traditions such as Judaism, Christianity, and Islam, others find it in meditation as is the case with most oriental cultures.

The importance of spirituality in leadership is aptly asserted by Fry (2003, p. 693) that "The purpose of spiritual leadership is to create vision and value congruence across the strategic, empowered team, and individual levels and, ultimately, to foster higher levels of organizational commitment and productivity." Further, leadership effectiveness is considered to be what followers ascribe to their leaders based on whether these leaders exhibit the qualities that the followers perceive to be attributes of effective leadership. Some of these leader dispositions may be in the realm of spirituality and may include having a vision, being compassionate, and enduring in the face of adversity or difficulty (e.g., Fry, 2003; Lituchy et al., 2013). Further, "spiritual leadership theory is inclusive of the religious- and ethics and values-based approaches to leadership" (Fry, 2003, p.693). In a study on leadership in Africa and in the African diaspora, Lituchy et al. (2013) found that Ugandans suggested that a good leader was "honest and trustworthy"; while Canadians and respondents from the USA said "being inspirational/charismatic," and Barbadians cited "being a visionary" (p. 201). From extant literature it is apparent that inspiration, honesty, trustworthiness, and vision underpin leadership effectiveness and that vison, which is a mental image of the desired future, has important implications for spirituality. "The four r spirituality dimensions that largely capture spiritual dispositions that an individual may have are belief in God, search for meaning, mindfulness, and feeling of security" (Hardt et al., 2012 cited in Senaji & Anyanje, 2021, p.196). It is suggested that this disposition may be instrumental in leadership effectiveness toward future realization. It is also recognized that the polar opposite of effective leadership is toxic leadership (Lipman-Blumen, 2005, p.1) which is "a process in which leaders, by dint of their destructive behavior and/or dysfunctional personal characteristics inflict serious and enduring harm on their followers, their organizations, and non-followers, alike." "Toxic" leaders engage in one or more of the following behaviors and in similar others:

> Leaving their followers (and sometimes non-followers) worse off than they found them by deliberately undermining, demeaning, seducing, marginalizing, intimidating, demoralizing, disenfranchising, incapacitating, imprisoning, torturing, terrorizing, or killing them; violating the basic human rights of their own supporters and others; and engaging in corrupt, criminal, and/or other unethical activities (Lipman-Blumen, 2005, p. 2)

Perils of Nations

That nations have been imperiled required no elaboration. This is evident in levels of poverty, political upheavals, civil strife, and degradation of the planet that abound globally. One may be forgiven for suggesting that life has become a "treacherous travail through hell." The fact that leadership can address these challenges leads to a question to which there appears to be no ready answers: *how many people are adequately self-aware as to richly or appropriately imagine the future for self and for the greater good of society?* Why, for instance, have some countries still remained worse off than they were before attaining political autonomy? Is it that some societies long lost the ability to discern who an effective leader should be?

For such countries, and they are many, does the concept of "leader" apply to the people at the helm? Or should it be replaced by more suitable concepts that are descriptive of how they imperil their society with their exploitative or limited imagination? One would be excused to make these observations because of lack of evidence of a visionary person who ever treaded such parts of the world. Another disturbing question: whence cometh the salvation of these countries?

From the forgoing, it may be appropriate to suggest that since imagination is either pervert/exploitative (such as amassing wealth and impoverishing others) or even totally absent, there is nothing to communicate. Consequently, the erroneously referred to as "leaders" become discreet and at the very least mysterious – some playing alpha and omega – or even "God's gift to Mankind" as they scheme "immortality" by "dying on the throne." In such situations, there is neither rich imagination nor communication of vision and hence no future to be realized for society except the "future in the mind of a despot" masquerading as a leader. This is a tragedy. As if the words of President John F. Kennedy were prophetic: "those who make peaceful revolution impossible will make violent revolution inevitable." The Arab spring which swept Tunisia and even Egypt expectedly falls on deaf ears as despots and dictators enjoy field days in many parts and places of the world. But this has a flip-side: is it a follower problem – where society allows its future to be squandered by miscreants – people without vision masquerading as leaders. This brings to the fore the role of society in imagining its future, communicating it through effective activism (leadership), and enacting the imagination in pursuit of a desired future.

It remains an open question how society can be empowered to shape their desired destiny. This calls for the ability of society to discern virtuous men and women, entrust them with leadership roles, imagine together for shared future – destiny, and work together to attain it in the framework of a holistic human well-being from economic, social, political, and spiritual perspectives.

Imagination, Communication, and Future Realization: Business Perspective

The unseen continues to shape our decisions today. That hope or belief that a tomorrow is imminent and that many other tomorrows within the term of one's life will come to pass or will come by encapsulate *future*. The future consists of that yet to come in time. In religion, it comprises the faith that beside the present, there is a new opportunity to experience immortal existence in a time to come other than the current. Businesswise, it is projected in terms of aspirations usually encompassed in an organization's vision. Both are characterized by an anticipation of more time in time other than the current. Based on different persuasions, the future may be interminable. Thus, what happens is that once a person (living or corporate) exhausts their life term, for example, through death or dissolution, it is their mortal existence (in the case of natural persons) that ceases or their business aspirations (in the case of corporates) that are extinguished. Their legacy or objectives may then be pursued by those surviving them or be abandoned altogether. Because life after death is a phenomena unexperienced, this chapter limit its discussion of the future to the mortal existence henceforward.

A vision undisclosed is no good than a personal secret, one that would disappear with the possessor. It is wiser to share such vision if continuity or realization is to be achieved. To live in the moment may be fashionable, but to plan for the unseen is wise. A leader ought to be forward-looking and, whenever possible, recounting the past in order to garner holistic insight toward the future: for only then can one be prepared for the unforeseen or the unseen even where no contingency is initially visualized. This highlights the notion of preparation, positioning the mind for the unexpected such as to somewhat mitigate or lessen the effect of adversity if they occur, even though this may not always be possible as in the case of pandemics such as COVID-19 that caught most a populace off guard.

Imagination appeals to intrinsic perceptions of the leader or a person and especially their ability to conceive, perceive, envision, or implement courses of action or strategies that would contribute to the attainment of their overall vision. If it were a journey, for example, at the very basic, such person or leader would want to at least bear or have a mental conception including the destination, duration of stay, activities to partake, resources required, and contingencies required to make the trip achievable. The contingency will likely cushion from the unforeseen should they occasion. In the business realm, an analysis of the pros and cons attaching to a desired objective is usually conducted in the formulation of strategy where potential threats are mapped and mitigation measures proposed, the strengths, weaknesses, opportunities, and threats (SWOT) analysis constituting one such model of evaluation.

During the imagination process, both hindsight and foresight must be evoked. The former will recount the missteps and progress resultant of prior conduct and decisions, while the latter will be mirrored and reflected in part through the lessons of the past. Hence, to envision tomorrow is our pension scheme bequeathed to posterity as what we perceive today for tomorrow may well constitute our contribution to history when tomorrow will be the mandate of others; and the lessons they draw therefrom may well shape the future of the descendants to come.

Unlocking/Decoding the Execution

But imagination alone cannot complete the cycle, for whatever is envisioned must be unleashed to certain quarters for it to be pursued toward realization; the key, communication. Communication is notoriously critical for the successful execution of a vision or strategy. It is the linchpin that glues the present to the future, and how well the vision is communicated will somewhat determine the extent to which it is ultimately realized; the measure of success (or realization) then taking the form of the vision (at the initialization stage, being after communication) vis-à-vis (as compared to) the level of achievement (based on indicators initially envisioned by the originators such as revenue earned) and the degree to which the vision or strategy has been implemented (to the letter or otherwise) with variations thereof considered as adjustments necessary or amendments to the initial vision or strategy (as the case may be) that address the shortfalls or omissions in the initial vision or strategy or account for dynamism such as technological changes that are exponential.

Thus, communication plays the significant role of *promissory* continuity, since circumstances may require ringing the changes on the initial vision or execution strategy and those entrusted with execution may also opt out over time, but a well-crafted and communicated vision should survive such alterations and should be considered as good if the deviations account for no more than a third of the initial vision (with likely measures including extension of time, increase in number of personnel required for execution, cost overruns). On opting out, continuity of the vision may depend on the commitment of those entrusted and mandated to steer execution; thus, their role in the realization of the vison is prominent requiring equally elaborate safeguards such as nondisclosure agreements and non-competition clauses upon exit among others. Conversely, where the vision is embraced, a subscriber to the vision can dedicate tremendous effort toward realization of the vision in a journey that may ultimately yield business success usually acknowledged by employers through rewards.

Today, servant leadership has had the tendency of enthusing team members especially where supervisors embrace acts of selflessness, sacrifice, or at the extreme resort to public relations in the quest for coalescing working teams (those capable of executing a vision to realization). The latter approach may however be short-lived as relapses to the natural self may be seamless, and this could impact teams negatively. In the modern workplace therefore, team members should be sufficiently empowered and entrusted to execute tasks, and self-supervision techniques, for example, through goal-setting with minimum superior interruptions should be encouraged. Businesses aspiring to realize their goals should thus leverage on human emotionalism (but not exploit) either through natural conduct or tactful improvisation that enthuse the workforce especially in the form of call to action.

The current trend within the workforce is that the team has augmented a stronger sense of inclusivity compared to the leader. The leader's primary role therefore is to pursue an assemblage of people who are diverse including in opinion, skill, tact, experience, and character to steer a common agenda, one that will, to varying degrees, contribute toward realization of the overall vision. Within and through such teams, a vision can also be borne, owned, and implemented such that in fullness of time it is realized.

Yet still, there are times when a totalitarian or despotic approach saves the day. This has, in political literature and history, manifested in various political eras that may well not be palatable to recount especially in the wake and prominence of an increasingly human rights-based society that, among others, protect the victims of such political occurrences. In times of calamity as has been the case presented by COVID-19, it may well be prudent to impose measures strict enough to uphold the greatest public good.

Jeremy Bentham described utility as "that property in any object" which "tends to produce benefit, advantage, good or happiness" and the utility principle as "that principle which approves or disapproves of every action whatsoever, according to the tendency which it appears to have to augment or diminish the happiness of the party whose interest is in question."[3]

Thus, a leader can be defined or described by how well their vision outlives them. The combination of their imagination (vision), the communication (continuum), and how this is achieved (strategy) ultimately delineates the prowess of a leader in

[3] https://plato.stanford.edu/entries/bentham/

terms of visionary status. The length of time taken to achieve the vision may also depict how effective the communication was if all factors are held constant.

Future realization will thus be significantly dependent on how the initial idea is embraced by those expected to execute the vision. An employee who feels *included* within the workplace is motivated and committed to the overall business goals of the organization and is likely to expend commensurate energy toward the realization of the business objectives of the organization. The opposite holds for an employee ravaged by consistent bureaucratic or rigidly hierarchical working conditions that stifle their involvement in decision-making and progressive independent thinking who would not be as enthused to contribute to the business objectives intended. The neutrals could swing either side or remain the balance. It is therefore crucial for a vision to be sufficiently cascaded to all levels of influence and execution as would be necessary to invoke significant realization of the vision.

We also posit that communication must be sufficiently linked to include some sense of ownership in the vision which albeit not actual *strictu* sensu amply invokes positive energy toward action or conduct that would lead to the realization of the vision.

Even though realization may not be constant or universal, the roles of imagination and communication in the realization of vision are to make one think ahead of time and to invoke our unique faculties of intellect, perception, and knowledge so as to illuminate what the future may likely demand and how best we can adapt to ensure survival or significance. As nature abhors the rigid, continuous effort toward preparedness for the unknown is necessary. It is through such that business parlance would attribute tenets of competitive advantage.

But imagination is not free. It comes at a cost of significant intellectual, perceptual, and conceptual value, for if it were served on a silver platter, then it would not demand so much investment as quiet time, sifting through knowledge, analyzing previous experience, and attempting to live tomorrow today while still having to live today. In the history of man, the most laborious of tasks may arguably be tackling the unknown, and it is little wonder that our source of being is a mystery still dominating religious and nonreligious discussion. Hence, within the process of demystifying the unknown, a body of new knowledge almost certainly emerges, and this should always be preserved. The effort that feeds into new discovery is what is sometimes protected under the law of intellectual property, primarily to spur further innovation that would offer solutions to life challenges or at least ease burden, elevating the status of technology in the imagination process for future realization.

Of what good then is the mind? If not utilized to better the world and societies? When primarily, human existence is extensively underpinned by satisfaction? Should the comfort of the existing be so prevalent as to encumber us from pursuing that beyond the currently available? We think not. For surely, there can be few decisions lower in rank than that of voluntary retirement of the mind.

Discussion

There appears to be a deep desire to get out of the morass that continues to curtail future realization. Consequently, the importance to avert the tragic exposure of society to the poignancy of toxic leadership cannot be belabored. Society continues to poignantly traverse hell on earth under the weight of such "leaders." In pursuit of an opportunity to lead, these individuals first purport to have the interests of followers and even those of non-followers at heart but turn out to be the proverbial "wolves in sheep's skin."

At national government levels, examples of leadership failure abound with its negative impact on society across the world where dictators have had a field day leaving society in ruins in their wake. Further, at organizational level, such as in business, reports are replete with corporate scandals and their devastating effect on employees and society at large. Instances of pollution of rivers and other water sources, corruption, financial impropriety, and trading in counterfeit products are just a few examples of perverse imagination and stewardship on the part of people at the helm of the affected organizations.

The belief in life after the present and in the possibility of punishment for wrong doing (sin) while here and the prospect of reincarnation as a creature on the receiving end depending on how one lives in the present and treats others in the present life may be a motivation for leaders to do good in order to guarantee a "blissful" future abode. This notwithstanding there is a dearth of evidence on the relationship between spirituality and effective leadership that is instrumental to desired societal change which ushers society into the desired shared future that provides opportunity for all and sundry.

In most of African cultures, such as among the people of western Kenya, metaphors are used to explain most social phenomena, and leadership has never been an exception. Among *vadiriji* (the Tiriki in English), a Luhya sub-tribe of Bantu grouping from Western Kenya such as those from *Ijemaga* and *Ishigomoli* villages in Gisambai location, Hamisi division, Vihiga County, *"ingoi ivoona malakha"* which literally translated as "a leopard inherits its parents' spots" or "a leopard begets a leopard." This is instructive in the sense that the well-being or otherwise of a community or society is a reflection of the leadership that it has. Similarly, according to the Luo, a lake Nilotic community of Western Kenya, "Fish rots from the head"; this metaphor suggests that if leadership is not right, everything else crumbles under the weight of bad leaders.

It should therefore not be lost that African countries were at the same level of development in the 1960s and 1970s as the present-day "Asian tigers" which include Singapore and South Korea. However, an examination of the current difference in socioeconomic development is akin to comparing death and sleep! This monumental difference can be attributed to leadership failure. This being the case one of the questions to be addressed appears to be how to detect and stop toxic individuals in their tracks before they rise to any leadership position in organizations of all types:

government, business, community-based organizations, and nongovernmental organizations, among others.

Though the situation both at country and organizational levels may be grim as to suggest complete preclusion of any possibility of realizing aspirations for a better tomorrow, there is a glimmer of hope. In particular, there are several rays of hope as evidenced by successfully led organizations such as the mobile service providers in Africa including Safaricom, under the leadership of Michael Joseph and Bob Collymore in Kenya that continue to bring about positive social innovations. Further, Aliko Dangote, Nigerian businessman who is worth USD 8.3 billion, founded Dangote Group which is positively empowering society in Africa and far afield across the world.

In addition, mainstream religious organizations and philanthropists also continue to positively impact society, and there appears to be a thread that binds them – spirituality. This realization continues to beg the question: *Is spirituality an antidote for future realization? If so, how and why?* Stated differently, *does the solution lie in the soul?* (e.g., Hollensbe, et al. 2014, p. 1227).

Suggestion for Imagination and Communication for the Future

It is suggested that leaders draw from their spiritual reservoirs for positive imagination and from their empathetic realms for communication. They then need to draw from their imaginative and artistic abilities to rally the creative efforts of society and orchestrate them in consonance with societal good in order to realize a shared bright future for the present and future generations. Further, since leadership is conceived in the context of the leaders, the follower, and the context, it is suggested that effective followership is crucial to the realization of a desired future since such followership checks excesses of the would-be "toxic" leaders.

Chapter Takeaways

- Realization of the best interest of society depends on collective positive imagination.
- Realization of a noble vision for the future is curtailed by poor leadership and ineffective communication.
- Human beings experience difficulties, while navigating through change and mindful communication of desired changes is imperative for this process to succeed.

- Future realization depends on effective implementation of required actions along the way; it requires both effective followership and leadership.
- A sustained search for solutions and mechanisms is needed to deter toxic leaders from imperiling society.

Reflective Questions

1. What is it that impairs positive imagination among leaders and followers?
2. Why do "toxic" leaders perpetuate themselves with abandon, yet they conspicuously imperil society at all levels: corporations, countries, etc.?
3. What makes followers helpless in the face of ineffective leaders?
4. How can effective followership be nurtured so as to influence the collective realization of a desired future?
5. What is the role of spirituality in future realization?

References

Cavanaugh, W. T. (2009). *The myth of religious violence: Secular ideology and the roots of modern conflict*. Oxford University Press. Merriam-Webster Dictionary (nd). Future. Retrieved 30 May 2020 from https://www.merriam-webster.com/dictionary/future

Fry, L. W. (2003). Toward a theory of spiritual leadership. *The Leadership Quarterly, 14*(6), 693–694. Retrieved 1 Sept 2020 from https://www.sciencedirect.com/science/article/pii/S1048984303000547

Hollensbe, E., Wookey, C., Hickey, L., George, G., & Nichols, C. V. (2014). Organisations with a purpose. *Academy of Management Journal, 57*(5), 1227–1234. https://doi.org/10.5465/amj.2014.4005

Lipman-Blumen, J. (2005). Toxic leadership: A conceptual framework. *Encyclopedia of Executive Governance, 2005*, 1–13. Retrieved 1 Sept 2020 from https://www.researchgate.net/publication/252792577_Toxic_Leadership_A_Conceptual_Framework_1

Lituchy, T., Ford, D., & Punnett, B. J. (2013). Leadership in Uganda, Barbados, Canada and the USA: Exploratory perspectives. *African Journal of Economic and Management Studies, 4*(2), 201–222.

Muggah, R., & Velshi, A. (2019, Feb 25). Religious violence is on the rise. What can faith-based communities do about it?. *World Economic Forum*. Retrieved 30 May 2010 from https://www.weforum.org/agenda/2019/02/how-should-faith-communities-halt-the-rise-in-religious-violence/

Murray, R. B., & Zenter, J. B. (1989). *Nursing concepts for health promotion*. Prentice-Hall.

Senaji, T. A., Knight, N. S., Melyoki, L. L., Galperin, B. L., Lituchy, T. R., & Punnett, B. J. (in press). Am I included? Lessons from leadership research in Africa and the African Diaspora.

Senaji, T. A., Lituchy, T. R., Metwally, E., Acquaah, M., Corbin, A., Michaud, J., Galperin, B. L., Melyoki, L., Ngunjiri, F., Muthuri, J., Adedoyin-Rassaq, H., Mukanzi, C., & Bagire, V. (2016). *Leadership in Africa: Insider and outsider perspectives*. Symposium IAABD Proceedings. Strathmore University, Nairobi, Kenya.

Senaji, T. A., & Anyanje, V. S. (2021). Elusive happiness: Does spirituality matter? In J. Marques (Ed.), *The Routledge companion to happiness at work*. Routledge.

Websites

https://www.theguardian.com/world/2020/apr/27/china-fails-to-stop-racism-against-africans-over-covid-19

https://www.washingtonpost.com/nation/2020/05/29/trump-minneapolis-twitter-protest/

https://www.ey.com/en_au/future-realised

https://plato.stanford.edu/entries/bentham/EY New Zealand (nd.). Future Realized. Retrieved July 9, 2021 from https://www.ey.com/en_nz/future-realised

Chapter 19
Nurturing Creativity in a Culture of Care

Ginger Grant

Abstract We are in the throes of finding our "new normal." Organizations depend upon capable leadership, to a noticeably increasing extent, to guide them through these unprecedented changes, especially in these times of economic turmoil. And yet, even some of the best companies are failing to adapt to change and implement their strategic plans successfully, especially in these times of economic turmoil. Current research indicates that most senior leaders believed that the next generation of managers is not ready to take over as leaders. Several studies highlight the gap in leadership capabilities among frontline managers and emerging leaders and in particular attribute this gap to lack of training programs or programs of poor quality. These statistics have significant implications for leadership develop programs. Certainly, responding to the complexity and inclusive diversity of the new knowledge paradigm of the twenty-first century is imperative to the sustainable economic viability in any country.

Keywords Meaning · Creativity · Collaboration · Culture of care · Leadership

Introduction

Organizations depend upon capable leadership, to a noticeably increasing extent, to guide them through unprecedented changes, especially in times of economic turmoil. And yet, even some of the best companies are failing to adapt to change and implement their strategic plans successfully, especially in times of economic turmoil. Current research indicates that most senior leaders believed that the next generation of managers is not ready to take over as leaders. Several studies highlight the gap in leadership capabilities among frontline managers and emerging leaders and in particular attribute this gap to lack of training programs or programs of poor quality. These statistics have significant implications for leadership develop programs. Certainly, responding to the complexity and inclusive diversity of the new

G. Grant (✉)
Humber Institute of Technology and Advanced Learning, Toronto, ON, Canada

J. Marques (ed.), *Innovative Leadership in Times of Compelling Changes*, Management, Change, Strategy and Positive Leadership, https://doi.org/10.1007/978-3-030-67258-4_19

knowledge paradigm of the twenty-first century is imperative to the sustainable economic viability in any country. There has been a great deal of research about what skills will be needed (Alterio & McDrury, 2004; Ayas & Zeniuk, 2001; Barell, 2010; Beaumont & Frank, 2003; Brockbank & McGill, 2012; Dweck, 2006; Grant, 2017; Hyatt & De Ciantis, 2015; Kay, 2010; Mishra & Mehta, 2017; Neuberger-Fernandez & Barton, 2017; Robinson, 2015; Rotherham & Willingham, 2010; Wagner, 2010, 2012). Essential themes that arise from all of this research shows that employees will need to demonstrate mastery of a variety of twenty-first century skills including creative thinking and problem-solving, collaboration and teamwork, agility and adaptability, curiosity and imagination, the ability to take the initiative, effective communication, and digital and data management (diagrammed below). I would add another: a passion for lifelong learning which Carol Dweck calls a "growth mindset" (2006) (Fig. 19.1).

With the advent of a global digital economy that is characterized by a rapid pace and scale of change, the accompanying uncertainty and ambiguity that this has and will create is changing the skills needed to thrive. To meet and supersede the demands of the changing paradigm, a number of beliefs will need to underpin the development of this mindset (adapted from Grant, 2017):

1. In our current context of this global pandemic (2020), as twenty-first century learner/leaders, we need to inspire as opposed to motivate. This ability to inspire is determined by our integrity of character (who we are, what we stand for, and how we act), our alignment of purpose, and our ability to create the presence of trust.
2. Authenticity and integrity occur when we develop self-awareness through ongoing self-reflection together with an ability to pay attention to others (empathy) and the current context in which we find ourselves. This attentiveness enables us

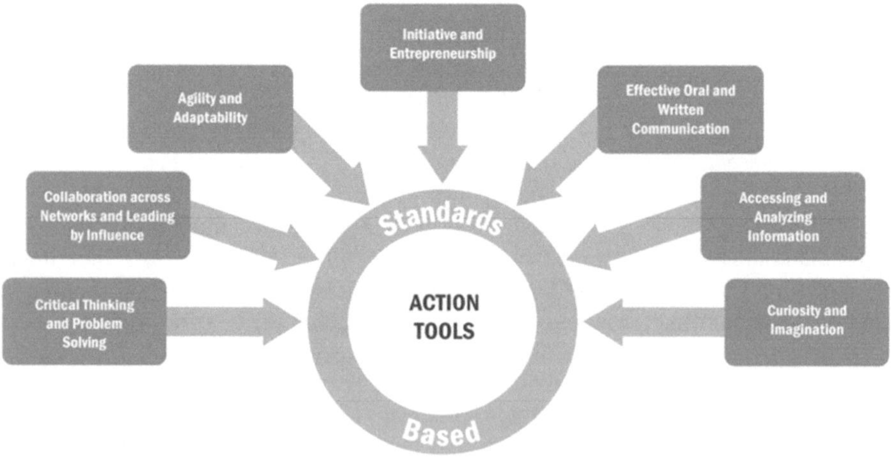

Fig. 19.1 Action tools

to examine a situation from all angles and communicate a clear vision of what needs to be done. We "walk our talk."

3. As twenty-first century learner/leaders, we need tools to help us become more reflective and attentive. We need to journey into our own hearts, minds, and psyches to discover our core beliefs and perceptual filters to better understand and use the shared myths and stories that align and inspire an organization to perform beyond the norm.
4. Organizational transformation is achieved one person at a time. We as leaders and our organizations must focus on nourishing our human assets as human beings or, better still, as human becomings. Ever evolving. Ever adapting. We need to develop our people's inner capacity for self-awareness and conscious choice making, otherwise old behavioral patterns, which cause resistance to change, will persist. Never forget – your assets now have feet.
5. Our organizations will not achieve the results we desire unless our practices, policies, and procedures reflect our espoused values and purpose. Those values need to be aligned with our employees and other key stakeholders. We need a growth mindset of both/and – not either/or.

Asking leaders to walk their talk is a tough sell. It is a hard path for anyone – even for those who are completely committed. Many organizations claim innovation as one of their key drivers, and yet, when challenged or viewed closely, only superficial lip service is the result, despite the best intentions. Mere words are easy. Action is much harder. What is needed is courage - courage to make the move from strategy to action – the courage to change – and humans do not like to change! Once a claim for a change is made, it seems as though the universe steps in and tests our resolve. Perhaps that is how we ended up facing a pandemic.

With an emphasis on providing clarity around what is innovation in our current context and its practical application, perhaps a shift in culture would assist us and our people in increasing understanding and capacity for reflexivity and creativity and also provide cultural insight into how best to focus leadership development initiatives to drive and foster social innovation in tough economic times (Robinson & Stern, 1998). So, let us establish some ground rules by which to operate.

We Are All Adults

The good news is that we are all adults and have the capacity to choose to be caring experts and activists for social change, especially in the face of a pandemic. Let us make the assumption that each person approaches his or her work with the desire to do a good job, to make a lasting contribution to the strategic intent of the organization. The challenge will be in the rapid development of skills needed to adapt to this new normal. With the advent of a global economy that is characterized by a rapid pace and scale of change, the accompanying uncertainty and ambiguity that this has and will create is changing the skills needed to thrive. If you are one of lucky few

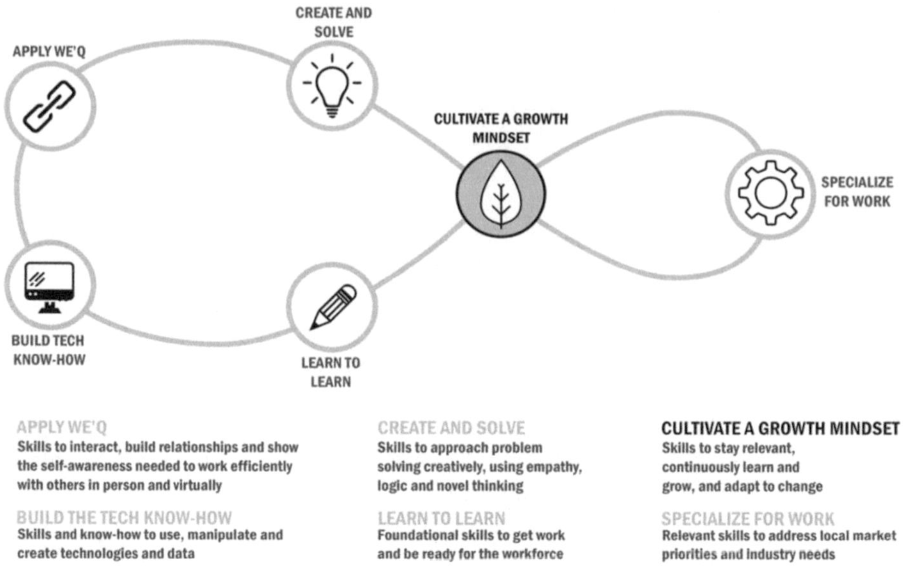

Fig. 19.2 Learning path. (Source: Accenture.com/New Skills Now (2016))

who are able to work from home, then care must be taken to ensure that each person has what they need in order to succeed. A different learning path is needed – one which allows each individual to explore and build strengths and will approximately follow the learning path outlined below and adapted from Accenture.com/New Skills Now (2016) (Fig. 19.2).

Upon a review of the diagram, you may notice that there is great emphasis on what traditionally have been called "soft skills" that are now termed twenty-first century skills (Wagner, 2010, 2012). When the way forward is unclear, these are the most important skills that we need to develop, nurture and maintain. We will be able to move past this current pandemic. But the lessons we learn during this timeframe, we may retain and adopt as core skills as we move forward.

We Need Meaning

Human beings need meaning, especially when facing an uncertain future. This is not the time for micromanagement. It has been my experience that if I trust people to act as adults and choose to believe that they come to work every day with the intent to do a great job, then that is what I will be given. My work has led me to believe that each one of us needs three basic needs to make life worth living. These three needs can also lead to untapped human potential. I need recognition from others for my efforts and of what I bring to the challenges presented to me. I need

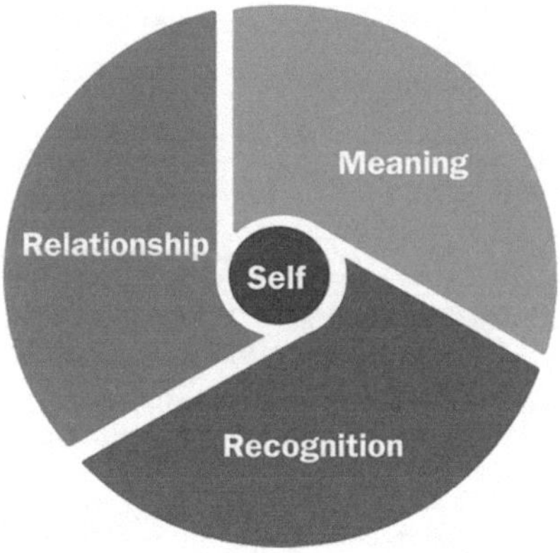

Fig. 19.3 Three basic needs (Grant, 2005)

relationship with others to make my personal journey more interesting. And finally, I need my work and my life to have meaning (Fig. 19.3).

I have heard this over and over again from my colleagues, my friends, and my clients. It resonates with me on a personal level. I believe that this is the secret sauce available to every one of us who works in or with organizations. It is the key to finding and then unlocking hidden potential both in ourselves and in each other. And we need that potential now more than ever.

I think a gift given by this pandemic has forced all of us to slow down and contemplate what really matters. So, perhaps ask yourself these questions (Table 19.1):

Collaboration Is Key

There is a crucial link between employee commitment and emotional engagement and successful implementation of corporate strategy. When you think of it, it makes perfect sense. Every employee, once hired, is 100% committed if not more. So, what happens to them? To honor that foundational link in an organizational setting leads to an alignment of strategic intent, full engagement of the workforce, and integration of the brand, internally and externally (Fig. 19.4).

Again, slow down and contemplate these questions with your team. Are there any surprises in the discussion? If so, where are the gaps between belief and behaviors? (Table 19.2).

Create a Culture of Care

Each member of a team or community has unique and personal knowledge that they contribute to the group. After all, is that not why you hired them? But, how is this knowledge communicated, offered and shared in the group? It is easy to offer

Table 19.1 Reflective questions to self

Theme	Your creative core
Identity	Who am I?
Personality	What kind of person am I? What have I noticed in my behavior because of the pandemic? How do I perceive, learn, and communicate? How do I communicate with others who are different from me?
Strengths and skills	What are my talents and passions? What is my unique contribution?
Purpose and meaning	Why am I here? What is my legacy to my family and/or friends? How do I perceive the world and my role in it? What is my personal sense of purpose?
Values	What is important to me? What worldview governs my priorities?What core values guide my actions in this time of crisis?
Principles and practice	Do I behave in accordance with my values, purpose, and sense of meaning? Do I allocate my resources of time and energy in accordance with my values?
Experience	What stories do I tell about myself and my experience? What values can be derived by others from these stories?
Reputation	How do I project myself to others? How do I think I am perceived? Is my self-image and my public image aligned?

Adapted from Grant (2017)

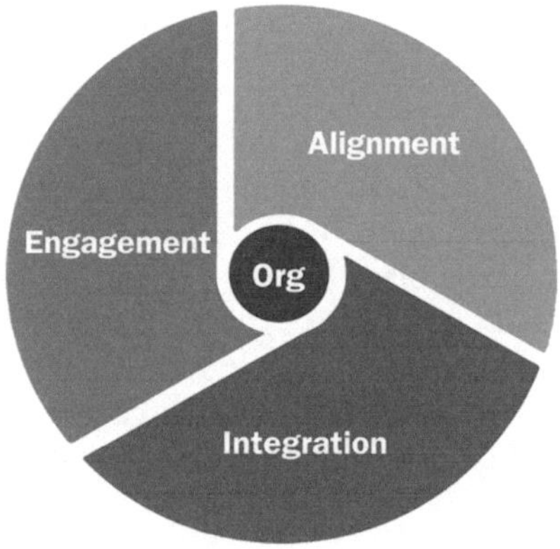

Fig. 19.4 Interrelated performance link (Grant, 2005).

explicit knowledge – processes, procedures, and tools; all of which can be explained. Tacit knowledge is different; it can be much harder to explain and, in some cases, might not be easily translated into words. In order for tacit personal knowledge to be shared, mutual trust is necessary. Let me give you an example so you can see what I mean. In your workplace (current or past), I am sure you would have seen a policy and procedure manual that outlines exactly how you should go about doing

Table 19.2 Gaps between belief and behaviors

Theme	Your creative team
Identity	Who are we?
Personality	What kind of team or group is this? What kind of team do I lead? Is my team diverse in age, gender, and ethnicity? How do we integrate diversity? How do we handle team conflict?
Strengths and skills	What are our core competencies? What is our unique contribution? How will we stand out in this time of crisis?
Purpose and meaning	Why have we come together? Where do we fit? What is our shared worldview? What is our legacy as leaders? What enriches and enlivens us?
Values	How do our personal values align with organizational values? What do we value most as a team? Do these values serve our purpose?
Principles and practice	How do the policies, practices, and performance of our organization reflect our purpose, our values, and our desire for meaning? Do we allocate our resources of time and energy in accordance with our purpose and our values?
Experience	What stories do we tell about our organization? Why are they considered worthy of the tell? What reaction do they elicit? What values can be derived from these stories?
Reputation and brand	What is our brand? Do we "walk our talk"? Do we brand from the inside out?

Adapted from Grant (2017)

the work required. Perhaps when you first started that new job, you might have read the manual. Human Resources usually will provide such documentation. Did you read it? Or did you ask someone in your group questions about the "way things are done around here"? Get the difference? One is a formal structure that may or may not work. That is the explicit version. The tacit version is the one that gives you insider knowledge, who to go to in order to get things done. For you to obtain this insider knowledge, mutual trust is necessary and will need to be maintained if that knowledge transfer is to continue.

I have been thinking about this conundrum for a couple of years now. I follow a brilliant practitioner, Ikujiro Nonaka. He is a master collaborator and strategist, and the reference list at the end of this chapter will give you much of his lifework along with many of his colleagues. I have been fascinated by their collaborations for some time but, for the life of me, could not see how it could be adopted in the cutthroat North American business culture. I did not want to repeat the disaster of the quality circle movement. The Japanese model was copied and inserted into the American car companies with disastrous results. No one thought to account for the cultural

Table 19.3 The context of care

Cultural context	Individual knowledge	Social knowledge
Low care	*Seizing* Everyone is out for themselves	*Transacting* Swapping documents or other forms of explicit knowledge
High care	*Bestowing* Helping each other by sharing insights	*Indwelling* Living with the concept together

Adapted from Von Groh, Ichijo and Nonaka, pg. 55

context of care in the adaptation. And I believe that this context of care is the foundation on which knowledge is built (Table 19.3).

The differences between a low-care culture and a high-care culture are self-evident, and the results in the bottom line of the Japanese companies that adopt these practices speak more loudly than words. So can this unsettling pandemic provide enough disruption that we are willing to try a different focus and make the move to high care? We are living that ancient curse "May you live in interesting times." COVID-19 has disrupted the entire planet – every country has been affected by this virus, and at this point in time, no relief is in sight. So, when we do not know what to do, why repeat what we have done before? The definition of insanity is doing the same thing over and over and expecting a different result. The way we have managed people in the past cannot be the way we manage people in the future. The Corona virus has taught us that much. Consequently, if we adopt a growth mindset, perhaps the time is now right to bring in a value-based approach that puts people before profit.

We need to translate knowledge from our current experience and then transfer that knowledge to our five generations in the workforce. We need not one approach but multiple approaches – a both/and way of adaptive thinking that allows us to use and value both our subjective intuition and our objective knowledge at the same time. We need to adapt and quickly. We need to get the job done – not engage in what Bruch and Ghoshal termed 'busy going nowhere' (2004). I believe we must make the move away from predatory practices to a cultural context of high care. And there is a path that we can choose to make this move a reality. It starts with two people – one learning from the other. Tacit knowledge is shared, and in that sharing, hopefully, a bond of trust will be built. Nonaka et al. termed it SECI (socialization, externalization, combination, and lastly, internalization). The descriptions are adapted from Nonaka et al. (1995, 1998, 2001, 2012, 2019) as follows:

Socialization – one to one Here we see the initial interaction between person to person, whether teacher and student, expert and beginner, or colleague to colleague. For example: take a task or tool to be learned. The expert shows the novice how to do the particular task and sometimes, more importantly, tells stories of how he or she learned the task (and all the mistakes they first made). The beginner can mimic the expert, imitating the aspects of the task at hand (the explicit knowledge). The finer details, those small but oh so important details that are shared in the stories

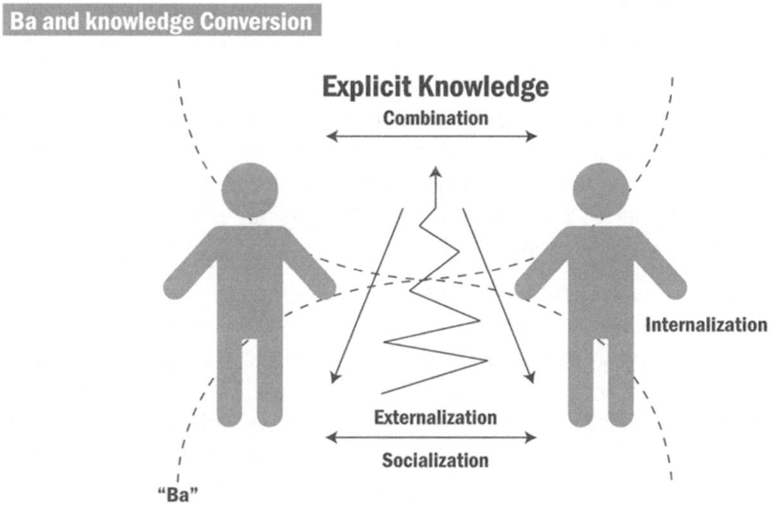

Fig. 19.5 Explicit knowledge (Adapted from Nonaka (2019)

told, are based in years of experience and trial and error (the tacit knowledge). Mistakes are made and corrected. The novice can ask questions and an ongoing discussion can ensue. A bond of trust begins to develop based upon the vulnerability of the teacher (the mistakes made) which permits a level of comfort in the beginner in the realization that we all start as a beginner, not knowing what to do. This initial knowledge is shared through the common experience, joint activities, and being in the same environment as opposed to memorization from a textbook or manual. Socialization in this sense involves the sharing of both the explicit and this tacit knowledge between individuals. The tacit knowledge is the secret sauce that is only given when mutual respect is present. I was taught this way. And it is a teaching I will never forget (Fig. 19.5).

An environment for this transfer is created, one of safety where trust can be built and enhanced. Nonaka called this environment a "Ba" – meaning place. I view this space as a temenos or sacred container where learning takes place experientially and naturally. There are no "lectures" – just caring conversations. It is an active learning space that emphasizes the importance of group exploration, collaborative problem-solving, as well as personal exploration and personal reflection. The leader/learner is focused on creation and development of the learner/leader's experience, providing a framework around which both can explore, discover, and fail or succeed in that process. Underlying this caring approach is the idea of improving each learner's understanding of self and how, by developing a deeper understanding of self, they can improve on the way in which they lead, learn, and interact with others. Essential to this learning process is the importance of experiencing discomfort and uncertainty as a mechanism to provoke that deeper thinking and gain greater insight. The model also challenges us to develop skills in questioning the norm, such that we question routine patterns of personal, family, team, and organizational behavior and open all of our thinking processes to gain greater insight as creative thinkers, problem-solvers, and innovators.

Externalization – shared with a group or team The translation of the tacit knowledge into a form that can be shared with others is the next step. Stories may be told, models or maps made, manuals created, and processes developed. Shared conversations continue in support of the new way of doing things. What was before tacit knowledge is now made explicit.

Combination – shared with an organization Here this new knowledge can be presented or shared within a more formal setting, meetings or presentations or in our current context Teams or Zoom meetings. One benefit of working in a virtual environment is that now this new knowledge can be shared across a much wider audience, not just city to city but even country to country. Perhaps these presentations are recorded so that they can be viewed again and again. The dialogue continues, and the explicit knowledge is refined, adapted, enhanced, and re-presented in new forms or in storytelling. This is explicit to explicit knowledge creation.

Internalization – becomes praxis The last stage is the conversion of this processed explicit knowledge back into tacit knowledge. This internalization relies on two dimensions. First, the explicit has to be embodied into concrete action, such as through group collaborations or training programs. Second, the explicit knowledge is embodied through the doing – experiential learning is key. Think of when you first learned to drive or to play a particular sport. Initially the rules and procedures seem overwhelming. How will you ever remember all the steps necessary? And then such practice becomes your praxis. That knowledge is internalized and no longer is consciously undertaken but unconsciously adopted – the "ways things are done around here." The student now becomes the master, and the cycle continues as that process of knowledge transfer continues (Fig. 19.6).

So, where do we go from here? What we now need is what I will call, Heroes@Work.

1. *All Bets Are Off: We Are the Case Study*

Heroes@Work do not use the old approach that involves traditional "spray and pray" approaches that see a professor or leader as the active donor of knowledge and the student or employee as a passive recipient. If handled well, this SECI process is a highly experiential and practical process of development that uses personal storytelling and visual imagery that translates into an emotional and shared experience that conveys and assimilates fresh concepts and pragmatic practices.

This approach is based on several core beliefs: (1) that existing problems cannot be solved with the same mindset that created them; (2) that within any work group, most of the solutions lie dormant waiting to be discovered; and that (3) both subjective intuition and objective knowledge need to be combined into a both/and approach to problem-solving. Thus, the task of today's leaders is to create the conditions and the environment whereby creativity can emerge and flourish. We need to build our own "Ba."

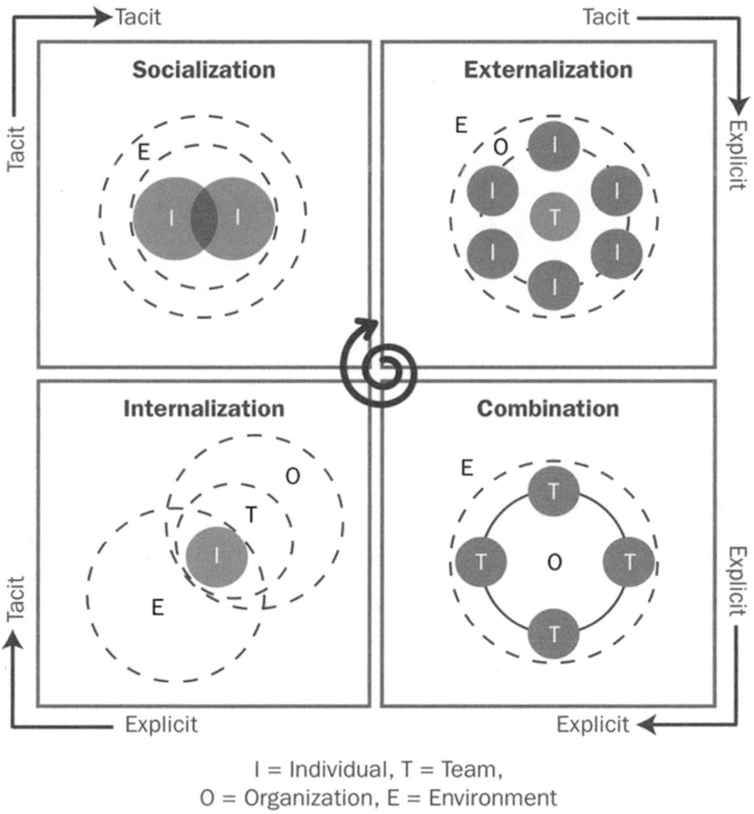

Fig. 19.6 Internalizing knowledge. (Adapted from Nonaka et al (2019))

Why?

Heroes@Work is designed to fill a serious gap uncovered by the pandemic by focusing on the development of capacity rather than the communication of method and the provision of "how to" steps based on a new and often singular theory regarding behavior. The latter suggest that there are quick fixes and best practices that, if followed, will generate success. They encourage a limiting dependency on external cues and ignore the problem-solving capacity within each individual. While I stand by the academic rigor necessary to access and develop these philosophies, my focus instead is on the communication and sharing of insights gained from such a rich palette in colors and shapes that are accessible to those with a limited academic background. Emphasis is placed on developing insights to convert into action (Von Krogh et al, 2000).

The pace, complexity, and depth of change occurring in every facet of human existence requires novel and fresh responses that are inhibited by a focus on doing as opposed to being. Nothing less than a fundamental transformation in the way humans see their role in the world and their ability to co-exist on our fragile, limited resource is required. If our organizations are to thrive, they must be able to attract, retain, nourish, and inspire their most important and now mobile assets – the people who work in and for them. New styles of leadership are required now along with innovative business models, organizational structures, and work processes. It is not sufficient for leaders to simply act differently – they must think, see, and become different from the inside out and have an infinitely higher tolerance for uncertainty, ambiguity, complexity, and paradox.

Thus, the emphasis on capacity. As Gandhi both taught and modeled, today's leaders must "be the change they wish to see" in the world. The time for talk is over. Now is the time to be and behave differently. Our Heroes@Work are true lifelong learners. This is not a "quick fix"; shifting mindsets requires care and time in the process. I see the following benefits:

1. An accurate and ongoing sense of purpose, source of passion, and personal strength.
2. Awareness of the hidden, tacit perceptual filters that limit the ability to approach problems with fresh eyes and to communicate with peers.
3. The capacity to examine an issue from multiple perspectives and communicate complex topics in a language that empowers and inspires purposeful action by others.
4. The ability to create a working environment that fosters innovation and creativity and thereby increases both productivity gains and employee engagement.

Chapter Takeaways

What do we do when we run out of words to describe the invisible culture and forces that shape an organization and determine its effectiveness? We resort to images, stories, and myths that can convey essence and meaning in general terms and that can enable the participant and the observer to apply them to their own specific situation and condition. And why? Because stories can convey so much more information at more levels than intellectual analysis and factual reporting. Mythic stories dig deep into silent, invisible, sometimes forgotten longings and yearnings that demand to be aired. They enable problems to be perceived without attachment to specific events or people and create an imaginary space whereby fresh insights might emerge. They can make complex subject matter accessible and enjoyable to assimilate and stimulate our own inner ability to tell our stories.

The most compelling stories are myths that may be defined as "stories that transcend the limitations of time and space to convey the human condition." While this dry definition may function, it does not match that given by a real, kindergarten budding genius who, when asked to describe a myth, pondered a minute before confidently explaining "a myth is a story that is true on the inside but not on the outside." Out of the mouths of babes.

Myths live in our imagination, can be shared through the collective unconscious, and help us navigate more effectively in and through the real world. They provide a rich palette of color, imagery, and meaning that can be used to better understand an event, a personality, a culture, a set of shared beliefs, and assumptions about how this world works. In this context, the distinction between myths and marketing is less important to us, because the caring capacities of understanding, interpretation, and communication are essentially the story. Myths are particularly helpful communicators of complex, intangible, tacit concepts, and meaning which can be comprehended intuitively but which are difficult to explain in words. They are powerful because they resonate with all four aspects of our being (our physical, mental, emotional, and spiritual selves). Myths are not just told; they are *felt.* When our souls are starving for meaning, they feed us and have the capacity to inspire. And we need that inspiration now.

Perhaps it took a pandemic for us to recognize that we are all together in our determination to conquer this virus for we are all in relationship with this planet. From what wisdom will we make new meaning? That answer lies in front of us and is a story yet to be told.

Reflection Questions

1. How does politics play out for you at work? Can you put aside personal agendas in service to a common goal? Why or, perhaps more importantly if true, why not?
2. Where do you find meaning? Work? Home? Church? Organization? Charity? Can you integrate them so that they all feed your soul?
3. Can you collaborate in order to compete? How will you ensure that your "Ba" space stays safe throughout the process?
4. The true test of authenticity! Can you have tough conversations and yet ensure that all save face?
5. How willing are you to step into the unknown and find your footing? We need new rules for the world yet to come. How will you build the path even as you and yours are walking on it?

References

Alterio, M., & McDrury, J. (2004). *Learning through Storytelling: using reflection and experience in higher education contexts*. E-Book: Kogan Page Limited.

Ayas, K., & Zeniuk, N. (2001). Project-based learning: Building communities of reflective practitioners. *Management Learning, 32*(1), 61–76.

Barell, J. (2010). Problem based learning: The foundation for 21st century skills. In J. Bellanca & R. Brandt (Eds.), *21st century skills: Rethinking how students learn* (pp. 175–200). Solution Tree Press.

Beaumont, C., & Frank, B. (2003). *Enhancing employability through problem-based learning*, Delivering employability conference, UCLAN April 9, 2003.
Brockbank, A., & McGill, I. (2012). *Facilitating reflective learning: Coaching, mentoring and supervision* (2nd ed.). Kogan Page (eBook).
Bruch, H., & Ghoshal, S. (2004). *A Bias for action*. Harvard Business School Press.
Dweck, C. (2006). *Mindset: The new psychology of success*. Ballantine Books.
Grant, G. (2005). *Re-visioning the way we work*. Trafford Publishing.
Grant, G. (2017). The untapped power of imagination in the workplace. In J. Neal (Ed.), *Handbook of personal and organizational transformation* (pp. 1–35). Springer International Publishing AG.
Hyatt, K., & De Ciantis, C. (2015). *What's important: Understanding and working with values perspectives*. Integral Publishing.
Kay, K. (2010). 21st century skills: Why they matter, what they are, and how we get there. In J. Bellanca & R. Brandt (Eds.), *21st century skills: Rethinking how students learn* (pp. xiii–xxxi). Solution Tree Press.
Mishra, P., & Mehta, R. (2017). What we educators get wrong about 21st-century learning: Results of a survey. *Journal of Digital Learning in Teacher Education, 33*(1), 6–19.
Neuberger-Fernandez, L., & Barton, R. (2017). *New skills now: Inclusion in the digital economy*. Accenture LLP.
Nonaka, I., & Konna, N. (1998). The concept of "Ba": Building a Foundation for Knowledge Creation. *California Management Review., 40*(3), 40–54.
Nonaka, I., & Nishiguchi, T. (2001). *Knowledge emergence: Social, technical and evolutionary dimensions of knowledge creation*. Oxford University Press.
Nonaka, I., & Takeuchi, H. (1995). *The knowledge creating company*. Oxford University Press.
Nonaka, I., & Takeuchi, H. (2019). *The wise company: How companies create continuous innovation*. Oxford University Press.
Nonaka, I., & Zhu, Z. (2012). *Pragmatic strategy: Eastern wisdom, global success*. Cambridge University Press.
Robinson, A. G., & Stern, S. (1998). *Corporate creativity*. Berrett-Koehler Publishers.
Robinson, K. (2015). *Creative schools: The grassroots revolution that is transforming education*. Penguin Random House.
Rotherham, A., & Willingham, D. (2010). 21st century Skills: Not new but a worthy challenge. *American Educator, 34*, 17–20.
Simmons, A. (2016). *A safe place for dangerous truths: using dialogue to overcome fear and distrust at work.*
Von Krogh, G., Ichijo, K., & Nonaka, I. (2000). *Enabling knowledge creation: How to unlock the mystery of tacit knowledge and release the power of innovation*. Oxford University Press.
Wagner, T. (2010). *The global achievement gap: Why even our best schools don't teach the new survival skills our children need and why*. Basic Books.
Wagner, T. (2012). *Creating innovators: The making of young people who will change the world*. Scribner.

Chapter 20
Community-Based Responsible Leadership and Social Value Creation in Social Enterprise Context

Susanna L. M. Chui and Nazha Gali

Abstract This chapter proposes a model of community-based responsible leadership which focuses on moral identification at individual and team levels within the context of social entrepreneurship. In this proposal, we first discuss the organizing principles of a community and the relevance of studying responsible leadership within the context of social entrepreneurship. Then the contributions of this chapter are outlined. Integrating theories of social identity model of leadership, collective action, and moral identity, a multi-level model of collective responsible leadership that results in social value creation is conceptualized.

Keywords Responsible leadership · Moral identity · Team leadership identification · Team entrepreneurial orientation · Social value creation

Introduction

This chapter conceptualizes the attribution of social value creation to community-based responsible leadership. Collective moral and leadership identities of communities within social enterprise practices very often are the crucial drivers of social goal accomplishment. Responsible leadership, which is a "socio-relational construct," is set within stakeholder theory due to its ethical focus. It stems from social interactions among networks of stakeholders encompassing multiple markets and cultures (Maak & Pless, 2006). As such, responsible leadership undertakes a

---

S. L. M. Chui (✉)
Hang Seng University of Hong Kong (HSU) School of Business, Department of Management
Hang Shin Link, Siu Lek Yuen, Hong Kong
e-mail: susannachui@hsu.edu.hk

N. Gali
Institute for Research on Innovation and Science (IRIS), University of Michigan,
Ann Arbor, MI, USA
e-mail: ngali@umich.edu

J. Marques (ed.), *Innovative Leadership in Times of Compelling Changes*, Management, Change, Strategy and Positive Leadership, https://doi.org/10.1007/978-3-030-67258-4_20

stakeholder perspective of leadership (Waldman & Galvin, 2008) and centers leadership around ethical principles that drive the relationships between leaders and the stakeholders (Bull & Ridley-Duff, 2019; Pless, 2007). Adopting the principle of organizing of a community, according to Adler and Heckscher (2006), the authors propose that the meaning of community in the social enterprise sector is interpreted as a collaborative community with the merging of professional and local community actors working together to tackle social issues. This form of community-based responsible leadership that exists within the realm of social enterprises very often involves the pursuit of social or environmental goals, for social good and sustainable value creation (Miska & Mendenhall, 2018).

Social entrepreneurship has increasingly gained scholarly attention. Social enterprises or social ventures (Doherty et al., 2014) are commonly considered to be hybrid organizations which explicitly focus on achieving their social mission and striving to create social value while seeking to maintain their viability through profit generation using an entrepreneurial and innovative way (Certo & Miller, 2008). These hybrid organizations are emerging due to governmental voids/failure or the unwillingness of the private sector to address the unmet social challenges (Teasdale, 2011). Hence, they are considered as change agents which use a business logic in an entrepreneurial manner to improve the situation of marginalized or excluded segments of populations (Peredo & McLean, 2006). Social entrepreneurship (SE) has been shown to be a powerful tool to eliminate poverty, empower women, result in institutional change, and catalyze social transformation (Saebi et al., 2019). SE involves "the innovative use of resource combinations to pursue opportunities aiming at the creation of organizations and or practices that yield and sustain social benefits" (Mair & Noboa, 2006, p.122). Most of the definitions of SE refer to the behavioral characteristics of entrepreneurs, dual mission of social enterprises (social purpose attainment and financial viability/sustainability), and the entrepreneurial behaviors or activities that lead to social value creation (i.e., social entrepreneurial orientation). SE challenges the notion of conventional entrepreneurship (purely profit oriented) and aims to address social problems by providing innovative solutions. As such, SE can be considered as an ethical form of entrepreneurial activity pursued by value-based organizations, which focuses on attaining its social agenda (Branzei, 2012).

The social value proposition of SE refers to the ability of SE to "create social value by stimulating social change or meeting a social need" (Mair & Marti, 2006, p.37). Thus, the social value proposition of SE, the "steering axle of SE," represents the intended promise of a venture in providing value for its beneficiaries (Covin et al., 2015). At its essence, it refers to the value that social entrepreneurs aim to provide for a target market (Kraus et al., 2014). The social impact of a social venture relies upon the ability of the venture to provide benefits to its various societal beneficiaries and to adjust its social value proposition to maximize value for its intended targets and the ecosystem. The social aspect within social entrepreneurship refers to benefits that are societal in nature and that transcend the boundaries of the organization itself. The process of social value creation is a complex multi-level and multi-process that involves the interplay of individualistic institutional change agents, meso-level teams, and organizational-level infrastructure, values, and artifacts whose outcomes extend to the global community level (Lepak et al., 2007; Lumpkin et al., 2018). As the proposed paper aims to examine the multi-level leadership process in social entrepreneurship, the contribution presented in this chapter is twofold.

First, we conceptualize a multi-level framework through which responsible leadership with an integrated community and stakeholder perspective can achieve outcomes at the meso and macro levels. We propose how community-based responsible leadership can lead to social value creation specific to the context of social enterprises. Most management phenomena are multi-level (Klein & Kozlowski, 2000), and successful theorizing necessitates the examination of casual mechanisms within and across different analytical levels; a multi-level framework can facilitate such an integration (Saebi et al., 2019). Second, we extend previous moral identity research, mostly discussed at the individual level, by conceptualizing how moral identification at both the individual and team levels can lead to team leadership identity and team entrepreneurial orientation. The team phenomena aggregate to the organizational-level entrepreneurial orientation and attribute to social value creation. This collective moral and leadership identification of multiple stakeholders is underpinned by an unified perspective of prior literature drawn from social psychology, leadership, and entrepreneurship. Therefore, this paper conceptualizes a multi-level view of community-based responsible leadership that involves moral and leadership identifications and entrepreneurial orientation of teams that attribute to the organizational-/community-level entrepreneurial orientation, in which social value creation is resulted.

Theoretical Development

Community-Based Organizing and the Social Enterprise Sector

Collectives very often exemplify different principles of organizing depending on the forms of community. There are three typical forms of community which include *community*, *market,* and *hierarchy*. (Adler & Heckscher, 2006). *Community* as collectives involves interdependent actors who develop strong trust as the core coordinating mechanism. The coordinating mechanism of a *market* is price, while that in a *hierarchy* is authority. Compared to the *market*, which has an independent relational orientation, and *hierarchy*, which has a dependent relational orientation, the *community's* interdependence among its actors offers more potential for collaborative, innovative, and entrepreneurial activities to occur, particularly within a social enterprise context. This is because the purpose-driven context of social enterprises facilitates social interaction for solution seeking that can put right social issues. This sense of common mission produces the drive to create social good. Moreover, Adler and Heckscher (2006) identified the three key features of a *community* which is distinctive from a *market* and a *hierarchy*. *Community* symbolizes a set of shared values. *Community* is also a social structure characterized by interdependent processes and a collaborative orientation. *Community* reconciles the multiple and conflicting identities of its social actors and can build a sense of wholeness and attachment despite human differences in terms of ethnic, social status, and expertise. The potency of a collaborative community allowed social actors to pour in energy beyond individual interests and beyond the rationality of obtaining individual benefits. Hence this kind of community logic is most favorable for social interaction and rapid synergy to work towards innovative solution ideas. It is also this kind of community logic that emerges within the social enterprise sector.

Within the rapidly developing social enterprise sector, there is a gradual growth of its complexity because different groups of communities are at play in the sector. These include local minority or disadvantaged groups who very often serve as the social clients or beneficiaries, the social organizational actors, and the knowledge-based and solution-oriented communities in different professions, including the legal, medical health, business and financial advisory, engineering, or marketing and communication sectors (Bridgstock et al., 2010). The presence of heterogeneity of different players with different backgrounds, roles, and expertise operating for a social mission can help organizational innovation because of *diversity management* (Bridgstock et al., 2010). These players, who are internal and external actors, can form collectives of a social enterprise, creating a collaborative community of stakeholders who pursue the same social goal for addressing a social issue. This kind of collaborative community involving different groups of stakeholders who contribute to social entrepreneuring and innovation want to create shared value and for a common purpose (Adler & Heckscher, 2006).

The social glue of a collaborative community is different from that of a hierarchical community. In a hierarchy, the loyalty ethic permeates its organization to secure commitment. However, the ethic in a collaborative community is based on two elements (Adler & Heckscher, 2006). First, it is the contribution of the social actors towards the group's purpose. That means the problem-solving motivation is based on a sense of purpose rather than a sense of fulfilling the necessary job duties. This sense of voluntary responsibility within individuals legitimizes the taking of risks and the motivation to lead of collectives. Second, it is the contribution to the impact that benefits others. This kind of moral legitimacy commands by social enterprises is not present in either a market or a hierarchy. Inspired by the community-based organizing logic suggested by Adler and Heckscher (2006), this chapter conceptualizes a multi-level model of social value creation. The three dimensions of a community's organizing principle, (i) value rationality, the (ii) interdependent processes of individual players, and (iii) the interdependent self-construals, provide the insights for the model theorization of this chapter. The team-level collective moral and leadership identifications and the entrepreneurial orientation, which are nested within the individual level, will lead to the organizational level of entrepreneurial orientation that eventually drives social value creation.

Moral Identity: A Collective Moral Prototype

Moral identity formation involves a social-cognitive process steered by an individual's cognitive alignment with moral values, goals, traits, and action-related scripts (Aquino et al., 2009). That means when one's moral identity is activated, the more likely would this person commit to perform moral actions because the moral functioning intensifies the defining of one's self as part of the autobiographical memory processing (Hardy & Carlo, 2005). Hence, this can satisfy the self-consistency need and can lead to moral development. Very often, this kind of moral selfhood at the individual level will continue to satisfy the self-consistency need in work or voluntary roles with a larger collective as a kind of moral agency. Life experiences, such as the involvement in volunteering, social campaign, or advocacy, can develop moral knowledge which, over time, shapes one's identity, motivation, and even actions (Aquino et al., 2011). Initial experimental evidence has shown that exemplary moral leaders, through the way they treat, trust, inspire, and interact with others with uncommon goodness, can influence others in driving moral elevation (Aquino et al., 2011). Such prototypical leaders can create a kind of social contagion that leads to prosocial motivation and behavior. Within the social enterprise sector, it is proposed that the moral identity of individuals, though having different background and expertise, can be activated when engaged at the problem-solving processes at social enterprise. Thus the individual-level moral identity can aggregate to the team-level identification making team moral identity salient.

Proposition 1 *Moral identity at the individual level can influence the team moral identity within a social enterprise.*

Responsible Leadership, Group Influence, and Social Identity Theories

Within social enterprises there is an emphasis on the social relationships and the goodwill inherent within social exchange processes, which aim to foster collective action (Adler & Kwon, 2002). Maak and Pless (2006) have emphasized the importance of such social exchanges within their responsible leadership model, since responsible leadership focuses on stakeholder relationships and building a formal stakeholder network. The goodwill inherent within such stakeholder interactions could then be mobilized to create social entrepreneurship (Chung & Gibbons, 1997). Responsible leadership expands the knowledge base within social enterprises by promoting an active stakeholder dialogue, in which different participants engage and contribute their knowledge to solve social problems. Responsible leadership does not only aim at fostering stakeholder dialogue within the organizational boundaries but also extends to external stakeholders, which promotes exchange of information and the birth of innovative ideas (Voegtlin et al., 2012). Thus, responsible leadership within social enterprises facilitates the engagement of the beneficiaries, and they become part of the value creating process (Saebi et al., 2019). The social mission of SE is a key driver for motivating entrepreneurial and prosocial actions, and thus entrepreneurial action would not occur without moral incentives (McMullen, 2011). This kind of motivation at the individual level is proposed to be a fundamental drive which when aggregated as group-level actions can evolve to become strong moral convictions and entrepreneurial momentum that steer the collective action of social value creation.

We propose that responsible leadership is typically formed by collaborative efforts of multiple actors within a social enterprise. Pearce et al. (2014) discussed the interactive and shared influence of actors in exercising leadership in a responsible way as shared leadership. However, their discussion of shared responsible leadership is confined to members of the same organization. Limited literature has covered the underpinning identity dynamics that contribute to the social entrepreneurship of how multiple stakeholders act as a united front for a common goal pursuit.

Proposition 2 *Responsible leadership at the organizational level can influence team moral identity development within a social enterprise context.*

The social identity approach provides a framework that integrates diverse theories in explaining shared leadership. Social-cognitive, motivational, social-interactive, and societal level theories work in conjunction to elucidate the relationships between individual and group phenomena (Abrams & Hogg, 2001). The linkage of individual identity to collective identity and motivation involves three aspects: group influence, social identity salience, and group-oriented motivation.

Group Influence Each actor within a group or community membership can create social influence for others. Some of these actors can be internal members of a social enterprise, while some can be external actors who might offer their pro-bono professional expertise, such as legal or health care advisory. People who are most prototypical that can define the group characteristics become the source of information in influencing or profiling group prototypes and setting group norms. Organizational membership is a typical social schema category that in-group members identify with. Categories are prototypical characteristics in-group members choose to define who they are (Turner, Hogg, Oakes, Reicher, & Wetherell, 1987).

Social Identity Salience "Identity salience is defined as the probability that one will invoke a specific identity across situations" (Stets & Serpe, 2013, p. 36). Salient identities are considered by the self as central social representations. Intergroup relations are a dominant aspect in forming social identity salience (Tajfel & Turner, 1986). Social attraction and relational dynamics work alongside with attribution and information processing to shape group prototypicality into group behaviors and actions, such as team leadership.

Social identification and work motivation are closely related as group members who see themselves as one collective are energized by shared experiences in shared events (Ellemers et al., 2004). Moreover, in-group members are situationally motivated as they are challenged by task goals or a shared purpose. In understanding how group dynamics and social identification can be attributed by the power of group identification in mobilizing individual energy in pursuit of shared purposes, an integrated Social Identity Model of Collective Action (SIMCA) and Social Identity Model of Leadership (SIMOL) perspective is adopted. SIMCA conceptualizes the psychological basis that arrives at the identification of a relevant group rooted "in the experience of group-based anger and group efficacy beliefs that motivate collective action" (Van Zomeren et al., 2011, p. 736). The model was originally conceptualized to characterize the collective action among the disadvantaged (Van Zomeren et al., 2008). The fundamental interests of the disadvantaged were to challenge social inequality. Related studies supported that moral conviction predicted collective action tendencies as SIMCA was examined (Van Zomeren et al., 2010). Moral convictions as a construct fill the missing link in explaining why social actors participate in collective action in a social movement.

Based on the social identity analyses of leadership (van Knippenberg & Hogg, 2003), SIMOL proposes that as group members identify more strongly with their group and group identification is salient, leadership perceptions, evaluations, and effectiveness are increased in strength. The core characteristic of SIMOL lies in followers' identification with the leader who is perceived as a prototypical leader. Cohesion within a group hinges on leadership endorsement based on group prototypicality (Hogg et al., 1998). Social identity studies showed that the more group members identify more with the group's prototype, the more this prototype becomes the determinant of perceived leadership effectiveness (Lord et al., 1984). Using the SIMOL lens, it can explain why collective action is turned into dynamic and proactive leadership processes which yield results and meet superordinate goals.

Therefore, the integrated theorization of social identity theory of leadership and the social contagion of moral identification is considered crucial for understanding responsible leadership. It is because SIMOL suggested that salient group membership creates a self-categorization effect in which individuals conceive themselves in terms of their membership in the group. Therefore, moral identification, when attained by actors who pursue a common goal, can drive shared responsible leadership in goal pursuit. These moral practices in social enterprises connect individual, team, and collective levels of prosocial motivation and actions to achieve social value creation.

Proposition 3 *Moral identity at the team level can lead to team leadership identification within a social enterprise.*

Team Leadership and Entrepreneurial Orientation at Team and Organizational Levels

Teams' attribution to organizational performance has been recognized in corporate entrepreneurship literature. Yet research that targets team-level entrepreneurial actions has been underexamined (e.g., Cardon et al., 2017; Forbes et al., 2006;

Harper, 2008; Santos & Cardon, 2019). The social construction of opportunity as entrepreneurial processes has been discussed (Fletcher, 2006). The joint reasoning and joint action in entrepreneuring very often rely on relational processes in the discovery of solutions and its implementation. Furthermore, a majority of "entrepreneurial firms are founded by teams" (Klotz et al., 2014) and "teams are at the heart of any new venture" (Cooper & Daily, 1997, p. 144). The act of entrepreneurship involves team processes of collectives (Shepherd & Kreuger, 2002).

Team processes become of a higher quality when team members work together, engage in collaborative mutual interactions, and experience good relationships with members of the team (Farmer et al., 2015). Because of the team leader identity, group members become concerned on the welfare of the group rather than pursuing their self-interests and are more loyal and trusting of one another (Earley & Mosakowski, 2000). The group leader identity allows team members to learn from one another and share knowledge structures, which lead to greater team integration and cohesion (Klimoski & Mohammed, 1994). Such intense collaboration and the emphasis on a group culture that is characterized by a focus on close interpersonal relationships elevate the confidence of the organizational members in their organization and increases their risk-taking and fosters their entrepreneurial orientation (EO) (Brettel et al., 2015). Team EO within a SEV refers to the team's propensity to engage in entrepreneurial behaviors (proactiveness, innovativeness, risk-taking) to ultimately support the organization in addressing its mission (Guo & Bielefeld, 2014).

The team leader identity drives commitment to group goals rather than the goals of the individual team members (Earley & Mosakowski, 2000) and results in better team interactions, driving the enterprising members to work together effectively (Van Der Vegt & Bunderson, 2005). The team leader identity prompts the team members to work together more effectively to achieve the collective goals of social enterprises (Powell & Baker, 2017). With team leader identity, the key question becomes "who they are as a team" (Brewer & Gardner, 1996) as members come together aspiring to help the community. Bacharach's (2006) interdependence hypothesis states that if entrepreneurs perceive a strong interdependence and a common interest, they will be primed to identify themselves as a team and frame themselves as "we" when engaging in entrepreneurial discovery and problem-solving.

Proposition 4 *Team leadership identification can lead to team entrepreneurial orientation within a social enterprise.*

EO is the entrepreneurial team style that captures the team's goals, beliefs, logic, and communications revealing the commitment to EO (Wales et al., 2020). Entrepreneurial orientation of the firm arises from the entrepreneurial actions of the members of collectives who seek to identify new opportunities and capitalize on their existing competencies and are highly motivated to pitch in their ideas and to get the work done as they perceive it as "our" work (Fiske & Taylor, 1991). This entails that team entrepreneurial orientation is neither explicitly enforced nor required by the formal job requirements in a SEV (Hui et al., 1999) and aggregates to manifest as entrepreneurial orientation at the organizational level.

There is strong evidence that constructs at the group level of analysis are theoretically distinct from the same constructs at the organizational level (Wallace et al., 2016), and thereby the organizational-level entrepreneurial orientation construct requires consideration.

Essentially EO has emerged from the concept that organizations can be conceived as entrepreneurial actors (Covin & Slevin, 1989; Miller, 1983). The venture team is integral for the attainment of EO in which the conscious influence of the entrepreneurial team on the venture's direction determines the manifestation of organizational entrepreneurial orientation. Without the embrace of the team within the venture on entrepreneurial action, little does EO emerge as an organizational phenomenon.

Proposition 5 *Team entrepreneurial orientation aggregates to organizational entrepreneurial orientation within a social enterprise.*

Social Value Creation at the Organizational/Community Level

Corporate entrepreneurship research has moved beyond the earlier theoretical presumptions that entrepreneurial action is driven primarily by economic goals (Baker & Pollock, 2007). Researchers have acknowledged that there is a wide range of aspiration and motivations for entrepreneurial action (Hmieleski & Baron, 2009; Sapienza et al., 2003). Furthermore, even though a recent review revealed that the dominant dependent variable in corporate entrepreneurship research is financial firm performance (Shepherd et al., 2019), the relative share of research examining the effect of corporate entrepreneurship on economic outcomes is decreasing, and other dependent variables are receiving increased attention such as well-being (Wiklund et al., 2019). Hence, with the double bottom line being pursued by hybrid organizations, social and financial value creation is the dual outcomes born from entrepreneurial pursuit.

The purpose of social enterprises in enhancing social welfare becomes contingent upon the entrepreneurial orientation of the firm, which arises from the entrepreneurial actions of multiple social entrepreneurial actors who engage in knowledge transfer and in which social entrepreneurial actors' tasks and outcomes are highly interdependent (Bridoux et al., 2016), as they leverage and exploit their resources. Social value creation is the result of the decision-making activities and practices of the firm to explore new avenues and to be more innovative and to take risks. We define social value creation as the purpose of social enterprises to "create social value by stimulating social change or meeting a social need" (Mair & Marti, 2006, p. 37). Thus, social value creation entails the explicit creation of benefits beyond those captured by the venture's founder or leadership (Miller et al., 2012; Santos, 2012). Yet, the propensity of the firm to successfully enact innovative solutions to social problems depends upon the social entrepreneurial team members' interactions in innovation and knowledge exchange processes and who frame their

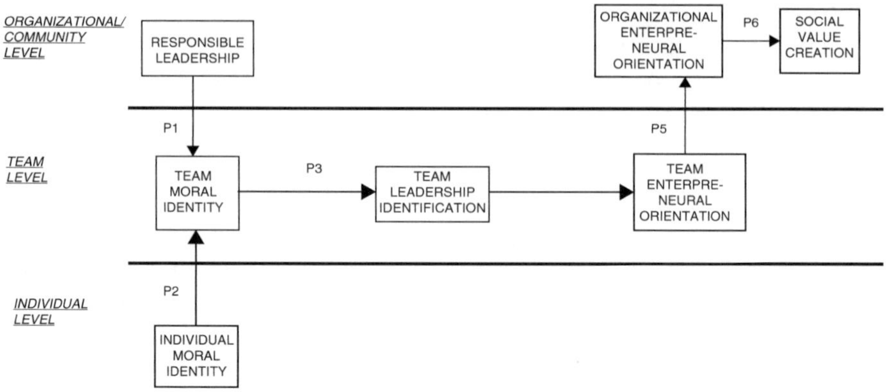

Fig. 20.1 Community-based Responsible Leadership Conceptual Model

relationships as "communal sharing" (a relationship characterized by a collective team leader identity and unity according to relational model theory) (Fiske & Taylor, 1991; Fiske, 2004).

Proposition 6 *Organizational entrepreneurial orientation leads to social value creation at the organizational level within a social enterprise* (Fig. 20.1).

Conclusion

This chapter has advanced a model of community-based responsible leadership that reveals how moral identity across individual and team levels can transcend to the organizational level and lead to social value creation within social enterprises. To help address the gaps in the responsible leadership and SE literature, we have developed a multi-level framework. Yet, this framework also goes a long way to identifying many of the cross-level linkages or temporal effects and contingencies that influence the responsible leadership and SE processes.

Chapter Takeaways

- Moral identity at the individual level can influence the team moral identity within a social enterprise.
- Responsible leadership at the organizational level can influence team moral identity development within a social enterprise context.
- Team leadership identification mediates the relationship between team moral identification and team entrepreneurial orientation within a social enterprise.
- Team entrepreneurial orientation aggregates to organizational entrepreneurial orientation which leads to social value creation within a social enterprise.

Reflective Questions

1. Can social entrepreneurs act as a solo entrepreneur in the process of social value creation?
2. What are the advantages for social enterprises which are driven by community-based leadership?
3. How can community-based social enterprises ensure that their social mission can be attained?
4. How to promote collective moral and leadership identifications in social enterprises?
5. What is the connection of collective (moral and leadership) identities, entrepreneurial orientation, and social value creation?

References

Abrams, D., & Hogg, M. A. (2001). Collective identity: Group membership and self-conception. In M. A. Hogg & R. S. Tindale (Eds.), *Blackwell handbook of social psychology: Group processes*. Blackwell.

Adler, P. S. & Heckscher, C. (2006). Towards collaborative community. In C. Heckscher and P. S. Adler, (Eds.), The Firm as a Collaborative Community: Reconstructing Trust in the Knowledge Economy, pp.11–106. New York: Oxford University Press.

Adler, P. S., & Kwon, S. W. (2002). Social capital: Prospects for a new concept. *Academy of Management Review, 27*(1), 17–40.

Aquino, K., Freeman, D., Reed, A., II, Lim, V. K. G., & Felps, W. (2009). Testing a social-cognitive model of moral behaviour: The interactive influence of situations and moral identity. *Journal of Personality and Social Psychology, 97*(1), 123–141.

Aquino, K., McFerran, B., & Laven, M. (2011). Moral identity and the experience of moral elevation in response to acts of uncommon goodness. *Personality Processes and Individual Differences, 100*(4), 703–718.

Bacharach, M. (2006). Beyond individual choice: Teams and frames in game theory, Princeton University Press. Baker, T., & Pollock, T. G. (2007). Making the marriage work: The benefits of strategy's takeover of entrepreneurship for strategic orientation. *Strategic Organization, 5*(3), 297–312.

Branzei, O. (2012). Social change agency under adversity: How relational processes (re) produce hope in hopeless settings. In *Using a positive lens to explore social change and organizations* (pp. 45–71). Routledge.

Brewer, M. B., & Gardner, W. (1996). Who is this "We"? Levels of collective identity and self representations. *Journal of Personality and Social Psychology, 71*(1), 83–93.

Bridgstock, R., Lettice, F., Ozbilgin, M. F., & Tatli, A. (2010). Diversity management for innovation in social enterprises in the UK. *Entrepreneurship and Regional Development, 22*(6), 557–574.

Bridoux, F., & Stoelhorst, J. W. (2016). Stakeholder relationships and social welfare: A behavioral theory of contributions to joint value creation. *Academy of Management Review, 41*(2), 229–251.

Bull, M., & Ridley-Duff, R. (2019). Towards an appreciation of ethics in social enterprise business models. *Journal of Business Ethics, 159*, 619–634.

Cardon, M. S., Glauser, M. & Murnieks, C. Y. (2017). Passion for what? Expanding the domain of entrepreneurial passion. *Journal of Business Venturing Insights, 8*, 24–32.

Certo, S. T., & Miller, T. (2008). Social entrepreneurship: Key issues and concepts. *Business Horizons, 51*(4), 267–271.
Chung, L. H., & Gibbons, P. T. (1997). Corporate entrepreneurship: The roles of ideology and social capital. *Group & Organization Management, 22*(1), 10–30.
Cooper, A. C., & Daily, C. M. (1997). Entrepreneurial teams. In Sexton, D.L., Smilor, R.W. (Eds.), Entrepreneurship 2000, pp. 127–150. Chicago: Upstart Publishing.
Covin, J. G., & Slevin, D. P. (1989). Strategic management of small firms in hostile and benign environments. *Strategic Management Journal, 10*(1), 75–87.
Covin, J. G., Garrett, R. P., Jr., Kuratko, D. F., & Shepherd, D. A. (2015). Value proposition evolution and the performance of internal corporate ventures. *Journal of Business Venturing, 30*(5), 749–774.
Doherty, B., Haugh, H., & Lyon, F. (2014). Social enterprises as hybrid organizations: A review and research agenda. *International Journal of Management Reviews, 16*(4), 417–436.
Earley, C. P., & Mosakowski, E. (2000). Creating hybrid team cultures: An empirical test of transnational team functioning. *Academy of Management Journal, 43*(1), 26–49.
Ellmers, N., Gilder, D. D., & Haslam, S. A. (2004). Motivating individuals and groups at work: A social identity perspective on leadership and group performance. *Academy of Management Review, 29*(3), 459–479.
Farmer, S. M., Van Dyne, L., & Kamdar, D. (2015). The contextualized self: How team–member exchange leads to coworker identification and helping OCB. *Journal of Applied Psychology, 100*(2), 583–595.
Fiske, A. P. (2004). Relational models theory 2.0. In N. Haslam (Ed.), Relational Models Theory: A Contemporary Overview (pp. 3–25). Mahwah, NJ: Erlbaum.
Fiske, S. T., & Taylor, S. E. (1991). Social Cognition. McGraw-Hill Book Company.
Fletcher, D. E. (2006). Entrepreneurial processes and the social construction of opportunity. *Entrepreneurial & Regional Development, 18*(5), 421–444.
Forbes, D. P., Borchert, P. S., Zellmer-Bruhn, & Sapienza, H. J. (2006). Entrepreneurial team formation: An exploration of new member addition. Entrepreneurship Theory and Practice, March, https://doi.org/10.1111/j.1540-6520.2006.00119.x.
Guo, C. & Bielefeld, W. (2014). Social entrepreneurship: An evidence-based approach to creating social value. San Francisco: Jossey-Bass.
Hardy, S. A. & Carlo, G. (2005). Identity as a source of moral motivation. *Human Development, 48*, 232–256.
Harper, D. A. (2008). Towards a theory of entrepreneurial teams. *Journal of Business Venturing, 23*(6), 613–626..
Hmieleski, K. M., & Baron, R. A. (2009). Entrepreneurs' optimism and new venture performance: A social cognitive perspective. *The Academy of Management Journal, 52*(3), 473–488.
Hogg, M. A., Hain, S. C., & Mason, I. (1998). Identification and leadership in small groups: Salience, frame of reference, and leader stereotypicality effects on leader evaluations. *Journal of Personality and Social Psychology, 75*(5), 1248–1263.
Klein, K. J., & Kozlowski, S. J. W. (2000). *Multi-level theory, research, and methods in organizations*. Wiley.
Klimoski, R., & Mohammed, S. (1994). Team mental model: Construct or metaphor? *Journal of Management, 20*(2), 403–437.
Kraus, S., Filser, M., O'Dwyer, M., & Shaw, E. (2014). Social entrepreneurship: An exploratory citation analysis. *Review of Managerial Science, 8*(2), 275–292.
Lepak, D. P., Smith, K. G., & Taylor, M. S. (2007). Value creation and value capture: a multilevel perspective. *Academy of Management Review, 32*(1), 180–194.
Lord, R. G., Foti, R. J., & De Vader, C. (1984). A test of leadership categorization theory: Internal structure, information processing, and leadership perception. *Organizational Behavior and Human Performance, 34*(3), 343–378.

Lumpkin, G. T., Bacq, S., & Pidduck, R. J. (2018). Where change happens: Community-level phenomena in social entrepreneurship research. *Journal of Small Business Management, 56*(1), 24–50.
Maak, T., & Pless, N. M. (2006). Responsible leadership in a stakeholder society–a relational perspective. *Journal of Business Ethics, 66*(1), 99–115.
Mair, J., & Marti, I. (2006). Social entrepreneurship research: A source of explanation, prediction, and delight. *Journal of World Business, 41*(1), 36–44.
Mair, J., & Noboa, E. (2006). Social entrepreneurship: How intentions to create a social venture are formed. In *Social entrepreneurship* (pp. 121–135). Palgrave Macmillan.
McMullen, J. S. (2011). Delineating the domain of development entrepreneurship: A market–based approach to facilitating inclusive economic growth. *Entrepreneurship Theory and Practice, 35*(1), 185–215.
Miller, T. L., Grimes, M. G., McMullen, J. S., & Vogus, T. J. (2012). Venturing for others with heart and head: How compassion encourages social entrepreneurship. *Academy of Management Review, 37*(4), 616–640.
Miska, C., & Mendenhall, M. E. (2018). Responsible leadership: A mapping of extant research and future directions. *Journal of Business Ethics, 148*(1), 117–134.
Pearce, C. I., Wassenaar, C. L., & Manz, C. C. (2014). Is shared leadership the key to responsible leadership? *The Academy of Management Perspective, 28*(3), 275–288.
Peredo, A. M., & McLean, M. (2006). Social entrepreneurship: A critical review of the concept. *Journal of World Business, 41*(1), 56–65.
Pless, N. M. (2007). Understanding responsible leadership: Role identity and motivational drivers. *Journal of Business Ethics, 74*(4), 437–456.
Powell, E. E., & Baker, T. (2017). In the beginning: Identity processes and organizing in multi-founder nascent ventures. *Academy of Management Journal, 60*(6), 2381–2414.
Saebi, T., Foss, N. J., & Linder, S. (2019). Social entrepreneurship research: Past achievements and future promises. *Journal of Management, 45*(1), 70–95.
Santos, F. M. (2012). A positive theory of social entrepreneurship. *Journal of Business Ethics, 111*(3), 335–351.
Santos, S. C., & Cardon, M. S. (2019). What's love got to do with it? Team entrepreneurial passion and performance in new venture teams. *Entrepreneurship Theory and Practice, 43*(3), 475–504.
Sapienza, H. J., Korsgaard, M A., Forbes, D. P. (2003). The self-determination motive and entrepreneurs' choice of financing. In Cognitive Approaches to Entrepreneurship Research, Volume 6, pp. 105–138. Emerald Group Publishing.
Shepherd, D. A., & Krueger, N. F. (2002). An intention–based model of entrepreneurial teams' social cognition. *Entrepreneurship Theory and Practice, 27*(2), 167–185.
Shepherd, D. A., Williams, T. A., & Zhao, E. Y. (2019). A framework for exploring the degree of hybridity in entrepreneurship. *Academy of Management Perspectives, 33*(4), 491–512.
Stets, J. E., & Serpe, R. T. (2013). Identity theory. In J. DeLamater & A. Ward (Eds.), *Handbook of social psychology* (pp. 31–60). Springer.
Tajfel, H., & Turner, J. C. (1986). The social identity theory of intergroup behaviour. In S. Worchel & W. G. Austin (Eds.), *The psychology of intergroup relations*. Nelson-Hall.
Teasdale, P. (2011). 'What's in a name? Making sense of social enterprise discourses', *Public Policy and Administration, 27*, 2, 99–119.
Turner, J. C., Hogg, M.A., Oakes, P. J., Reicher, S. D., Wetherell, M. S. (1987). Rediscovering the social group: A self-categorization theory. Oxford & NY: Basil Blackwell.
Van Der Vegt, G. S. & Bunderson, J. S. (2005). Learning and performance in multidisciplinary teams: The importance of collective team identification. *Academy of Management Journal, 48*(3), https://doi.org/10.5465/amj.2005.17407918.
Van Knippenberg, D., & Hogg, M. A. (2003). A social identity model of leadership effectiveness in organizations. *Research in Organizational Behavior, 25*, 243–295.

Van Zomeren, M., Postmes, T., & Spears, R. (2008). Toward an integrative social identity model of collective action: A quantitative research synthesis of three socio-psychological perspectives. *Psychological Bulletin, 134*(4), 504–535.

Van Zomeren, M., Postmes, T., & Spears, R. (2010). On conviction's collective consequences: Integrating moral conviction with the social identity model of collective action. *British Journal of Social Psychology, 51*, 52–71.

Van Zomeren, M., Postmes, T., & Spears, R. (2011). Can moral convictions motivate the advantaged to challenge social inequality?: Extending the social identity model of collective action. *Journal of Group Processes & Intergroup Relations.* https://doi.org/10.1177/1368430210395637

Voegtlin, C., Patzer, M., & Scherer, A. G. (2012). Responsible leadership in global business: A new approach to leadership and its multi-level outcomes. *Journal of Business Ethics, 105*(1), 1–16.

Waldman, D. A., & Galvin, B. M. (2008). Alternative perspectives of responsible leadership. *Organizational Dynamics, 37*(4), 327–341.

Wales, W. J., & Covin, J. G., & Monsen, E. (2020). Entrepreneurial orientation: The necessity of a multilevel conceptualization. *Strategic Entrepreneurship Journal, 14*(4), 639–660.

Wallace, J. Craig, Butts, M. M., Johnson, P. D., Stevens, F. G., Smith, M. B. (2016). A multilevel model of employee innovation: Understanding the effects of regulatory focus, thriving, and employee involvement climate. *Journal of Management, 42*(4), 982–1004.

Wiklund, J., Wright, M., & Zahra, S. A. (2019). Conquering relevance: Entrepreneurship research's grand challenge. Entrepreneurship Theory & Practice, October, https://doi.org/10.1177/1042258718807478.

Chapter 21
Design Thinking in Contemporary Political Leadership: Lessons Learned from Angela Merkel

Claude Helene Mayer and James L. Kelley

Abstract Design leadership, a conceptual component in design theory, provides a useful template for leaders in an ever-changing world. Design leadership has gained importance in global leadership and decision-making processes in contemporary politics.

This chapter focuses on the life and work of the famous German political leader, Angela Merkel, who has become one of the most influential, global, woman leaders in world history. A psychobiographical approach to Merkel's life and leadership is taken to explore design leadership. The findings will provide insight into successful global governance in terms of design leadership. This chapter provides an example of future-oriented design leadership by using a single case study approach with a purposeful sampling process within a qualitative hermeneutical and interpretative research paradigm. Findings will provide applied insights into design leadership; recommendations will include guidelines for future research and the presentation of best practices.

Keywords Design thinking · Design leadership · Psychobiography · Woman leaders · Innovation

> The question is not whether we are able to change but whether we are changing fast enough.
>
> —Angela Merkel

C. H. Mayer (✉)
University of Johannesburg, Johannesburg, South Africa

J. L. Kelley
Independent Researcher, Norman, OK, USA

J. Marques (ed.), *Innovative Leadership in Times of Compelling Changes*, Management, Change, Strategy and Positive Leadership, https://doi.org/10.1007/978-3-030-67258-4_21

Introduction

Design thinking has gained in popularity during the past two decades (Friedman, 2003; Dunne & Martin, 2006). Not only has it been described as one of the surest routes to creativity and innovation (Johansson-Sköldberg et al., 2013), design thinking has also been identified as a new transdisciplinary paradigm for finding solutions in various professions (e.g., Martin, 2009). This is particularly the case today, where an ever-changing sociopolitical climate calls for solutions based upon a broad repertoire of design practices (Lawson & Dorst, 2009). Design leadership elevates design thinking to a strategic level and is "related to the vision for how design could be used within an organization to achieve corporate goals" (Gloppen, 2009, p. 35). Further, this new type of leader links innovation, creativity, and strategy through an overarching set of design motifs. Thus, the success of design thinking underscores the importance of both creativity (Gloppen, 2009) and imagination (Manu, 2007) to any contemporary problem-solving strategy.

This chapter follows the assumption of Meinel and Leifer (2011) that "great innovators and leaders need to be great design thinkers." Such a design-guided perspective is "social in nature"; it "preserv[es] ambiguity," it "re-design[s]" or adapts previous solutions to novel situations, and it "mak[es] ideas tangible" while facilitating communication (Meinel & Leifer, 2011). However, design leadership still remains little known, and thus there is a void in research which needs to be addressed (Jozaisse, 2011). Accordingly, the present chapter addresses design leadership from a psychobiographical perspective, taking Angela Merkel as a sample.

Psychobiography uses psychological theories to analyze the lives of extraordinary individuals (Schultz, 2005). This chapter is a psychobiography of one of today's most prominent political leaders, German chancellor Angela Merkel (Koelbl, 1998). It builds on a previous psychobiographical analysis of Merkel's creativity (Mayer & van Niekerk, 2020), her wellness (Mayer et al., 2020), and her faith (Mayer, 2021), with a view to providing insights into possible resonances with design thinking.

Methodologically, Merkel was chosen based on a purposeful sampling process, the selection criteria being her unique position as a global leader who is also a woman, as well as her unheralded political longevity, as evinced in her having been elected German chancellor four times in a row.

This chapter's first aim is to explore the life of Angela Merkel by using selected aspects of design leadership models to analyze specific life events across her life and career span. The authors' application of design thinking to Angela Merkel's life provides indicators for fostering creativity and innovation that could contribute to political progress and world betterment. The second aim of this chapter is to present Angela Merkel's life story as a lens through which to explore design leadership as exercised in the global political arena.

Design Thinking and Design Leadership

According to *Forbes*, "Design thinking should serve as a leadership philosophy" (Himsworth, 2018). Thus, leadership skills such as critical thinking and problem-solving are numbered among design thinking's core values (Himsworth, 2018). For Meinel and Leifer (2011), design thinking is a user-focused approach which, through multidisciplinary collaboration and iterative improvements, produces innovative products, organizations, and services. An array of approaches to design thinking has been developed in design schools (Stanford University, 2016; Singapore Polytechnic, 2016) but also in unaffiliated enterprises and organizations (Design Council, 2021).

All versions of design theory, despite their many differences, emphasize (1) the power of the collective brain and (2) human-centeredness. That is, (1) leadership, according to design theory, can only be effective when it forges links with the collective experiences, attitudes, and worldviews of the group of belonging, and also, (2) design thinking integrates humanness with technology while striving for innovation and creativity (Himsworth, 2018). The approach in design thinking and design leadership is systemic, in that it commences from the philosophical bases of expansion and indeterminism (Pourdehnad et al., 2011) in an attempt to address complex problems in the context of meso- and macro-level strategic, economic, social, environmental, and political projects and questions (Irbite & Strode, 2016). According to Brown (2016), design leadership should address complex global problems, such as the need for new health concepts, healthy food systems, technological opportunities and challenges, future-oriented work designs and cooperation, as well as government services which are citizen-oriented and decisions which serve the global poor. Thereby, sociocultural, conceptual, political, and governmental boundaries can be overcome (Friedman, 2011) in the service of higher goals of complex decision-making processes which take effective ways of changing mindsets, global focus, personal development, and improved business and leadership skills into account (Cacioppe, 1998).

According to one writer, design leadership has five aspects: (1) problem-solving, (2) creativity, (3) systemic thinking, (4) coordination, and (5) cultural and artistic activity (Borja de Mozota, 2003). The aesthetic and collaborative emphases in this list imply that design leadership is, above all, an integration of "design processes" (Hargadon, 2005) and "design attitude[s]" (Boland & Collopy, 2004), the whole approach being geared more to an open-ended exploration than to a preordained goal (Lawson, 2006). Some leadership skills particularly relevant to design thought include knowledge about how to (1) discover and learn and foster insight in others, (2) identify and validate ideas and transform them into growth, and (3) nourish and trigger the imaginations of individuals and groups (Gloppen, 2009).

The d.school (Hasso-Plattner Institute of Design at Stanford) has developed a five-part executive model of a design thinking process which can be applied in design leadership (Balcaitis, 2019):

1. Empathize: Understand people within the context of the design challenge by viewing their behavior, understanding their actions, asking questions about why they behave as they do, and using the environment to ask deeper questions.
2. Define: Craft a meaningful and actionable problem statement, synthesize findings into insights, and create a point of view.
3. Ideate: Transition from problems to solutions, creating unconventional, unfiltered ideas. Forward the best ideas into prototyping.
4. Prototype: A series of artifacts are produced which get you progressively closer to your final solution. A prototype can be anything that facilitates individuals to conceptualize and reflect on their ideas. To be workable, a prototype must be created with the user in mind.
5. Test: Solicit feedback about the prototype from its users in a manner that bespeaks empathy for the intended users of the product, policy, or idea. Create a test in a real-world context and note user feedback.

These stages are not intended to be a fixed sequence; rather, pivoting and otherwise zig-zagging between stages often is necessary in creating solutions using the d.school model.

Section "Findings and Discussion: A Case Illustration of Innovative Political Leadership" of this chapter contends that Angela Merkel uses some of the design leadership and design thinking processes discussed in this section in her politics.

Psychobiography

Psychobiography, which focuses on specific events across the life span of extraordinary individuals and explores and interprets these events based on psychological theory (Fouché & Van Niekerk, 2010), has gained currency in recent psychological research (Schultz, 2005; Ponterotto, 2014; Mayer & Kovary, 2019). It has been argued recently, along psychobiographical lines, that the analysis of the lives of notable people can provide indicators that assist individuals, groups, and societies across cultural divides in coping with contemporary challenges (Kelley, 2021; Mayer & Fouché, 2021). In short, psychobiographies shed new light onto unexplored aspects of extraordinary peoples' lives and might thereby also contribute to further articulations of developmental, meaning-in-life theory (Kelley, 2019, pp. 367–368; Mayer, 2017).

Research Methodology

This chapter uses a single case study design to explore the life and political leadership of Angela Merkel. The research paradigm is qualitative in nature and uses a hermeneutical-interpretative research approach (Creswell & Piano Clark 2011;

Hassan & Ghauri, 2014). The sample has been purposefully selected (Shaheen & Pradhan, 2019). Primary and secondary data were collected, and all were analyzed through the five-step process of content analysis referred to by Terre Blanche et al. (2006), according to which the information was examined through familiarization and immersion, inducing themes, coding, elaboration, interpretation, and checking. In the following sections, the authors will present three selected and extraordinary aspects and political events, namely: "becoming a chancellor of all Germans," "transforming the refugee crisis," and Merkel's approach regarding "surviving COVID-19."

The ethical considerations for psychobiographical research recommended by Ponterotto et al. (2017) were followed: data were accessed from the public domain (journals, newspapers, video clips, etc.), and rigor was applied throughout the research process. Data were chosen and interpreted in a respectful way. It needs to be pointed out that the study comes with limitations since it is strongly qualitative in nature and focuses on one single, elite, extraordinary individual. Generations cannot be drawn from this data set.

> Germany has become a country that many people abroad associate with hope. — Angela Merkel

Findings and Discussion: A Case Illustration of Innovative Political Leadership

In the following, Angela Merkel will be introduced with regard to her life and political career. Three selected events in her life will be presented and analyzed with regard to her design leadership approach.

Angela Merkel, born Kastner, has risen to become one of the most influential female global leaders in the world (Moore, 2017). Born in Hamburg, West Germany, in 1954, Merkel's childhood was marked by her family crossing the Berlin Wall to live in a small East German town. An exemplary student with strong intellectual abilities, Angela adapted to new situations easily. She became proficient in Russian and excelled in the natural sciences, eventually earning a doctorate in quantum chemistry (Kottasová, 2020). In 1989, at age 35, she joined the party Demokratischer Aufbruch (DA) (Klormann & Udelhoven, 2008). After the fall of the Berlin Wall in 1989, Merkel's political career gained steam: she occupied several posts in the regional centers of the CDU (Christian Democratic Union), moved into positions on the national level as Minister of Women and Youth (Schley, 2005), Minister of Protection of Nature and Reactor Security (Klormann & Udelhoven, 2008), General Secretary of the CDU in 1998, the leader of the CDU in 2000, and chancellor in 2005. She stepped down as head of the CDU in 2018 and has been German chancellor since 2005.

In the following, three outstanding political events in Merkel's career will be analyzed with regard to design leadership.

Being the "Chancellor of All Germans" Through Design Leadership

One of the challenges in Merkel's early career was to overcome the political, cultural, social, and economic split of the two parts of Germany and support the reunification process which was implemented by her mentor and previous chancellor, Helmut Kohl.

Empathize

Merkel's rise to the chancellorship began in 2000, when she wrote an open letter to her party denouncing party leader Helmut Kohl's part in a recently revealed financial scandal. She thereby established her image as an honest leader and empathized with the German people who felt betrayed by Kohl. Her election as chancellor 5 years later fulfilled every German citizen's wish to "feel reunited and complete" as a German nation. Indeed, Merkel managed to establish herself as an honest and trustworthy "chancellor for all Germans" (Spiegel, 2005). Merkel's actions exhibited her ability to respond to the German people's dual desire for an end to government corruption and an initiation of a feeling of national unity after the divisions of the post WWII era. Her ability to bridge chasms did not end here: Merkel also overcame gender divisions by becoming the first woman to ever be elected German chancellor (Langguth, 2005).

Define

Merkel broke with traditional gender stereotypes, defined Germany as a pillar in the fight for a strong EU, worked herself through the different viewpoints of leaders within the EU, synthesized her findings and observations, and created new viewpoints throughout her early years in politics. She impressed many as an unassuming woman who rose to the occasion only when necessary, as when she exposed the weaknesses and dishonesty Helmut Kohl and other prominent men.

Ideate

Merkel managed the phase of ideation very well and established herself thereby as an honest female leader who had always been viewed as an outsider (the daughter of a West German pastor in East Germany, a protestant in a catholic party, a woman in physical chemistry, a woman leader in a male-dominated world of German politics) (Stock, 2000; Klormann & Udelhoven, 2008; Mayer, 2021). Thus, she creatively synthesized sociopolitical disparities along her journey to become "chancellor for all Germans" (Spiegel, 2005), all the while stressing her inclusive, "all-German" identity (Stock, 2000; Mayer & van Niekerk, 2020).

Prototype

Merkel managed to become a German for all Germans, not only by integrating different aspects of ingroup and outgroup members of subgroups within the German society but also by representing important values, such as being level-headed, business-like, realistic, economical, and reserved (Bollmann, 2013). Bollmann (2013) points out that Merkel is rare in her ability to internalize so completely the standpoints and emotions of the average German and to create legislation that speaks thereto.

Test

Merkel's ability to be a German for all Germans was primarily tested by time and by her four re-elections. It was also reflected in her wise decision to step down as a party leader in 2018, a move that was expected from her but at the same time dignified her in the eyes of the citizens (Goldhammer, 2018).

Transforming the Refugee Crisis in Europe Through Design Leadership

In 2015, Merkel's response to the European refugee crisis was supported by German elites, though her policy in this area was severely criticized within the European Union (Karnitschnig, 2018).

Empathize

When Merkel opened Germany in 2015 to refugees coming into Europe, she justified her policy by highlighting the "welcoming culture" of Germany and focusing on the need to undo Germany's history of separation and discrimination (Mushaben, 2017). By framing the issue in terms of Germany as a whole, Merkel managed to empathize both with German elites and with the average German. During this crisis,

Merkel always highlighted tolerance and freedom (Clemens, 2006), as well as religious values of self-sacrifice and communal responsibility (Carrel, 2017) that are deeply embedded in her personally. Thus, her decisions during this crisis were highly influenced by her Christian worldview of compassionate love (Mayer et al., 2020).

Define

For Merkel, the issues of human rights and human dignity can never be compromised and thus must be dealt with effectively (Dempsey, 2011). Accordingly, the refugee issue was tackled by considering various points of view and creating a synthesis translatable into immediate and clear government action (Macias, 2017). Most surprising of all, the language Merkel used in the public addresses she gave during the refugee crisis found her uncharacteristically emotional (Mück, 2017), a tendency encapsulated by her catchphrase: "Wir schaffen das!" ("We can make it!") (Mück, 2017; Mushaben, 2017).

Ideate

Though Merkel is often perceived to be irresolute, she has always insisted that she needs to take ample time to arrive at creative solutions (Mayer et al., 2020). Most important for her is that her policies are both actionable and grounded in humanitarian values, ethical commitment, and passionate emotions (Helms et al., 2018). Merkel exhibits her problem-solving skills through her agile diplomacy (Armitstead & Govan, 2012; Klormann & Udelhoven, 2008), which strikes a balance between upholding the interests of her constituency and insisting on human dignity, human rights, and equality for all people (Muller, 2017).

Prototype

Merkel's catchphrase "Wir schaffen das!" (Mück, 2017; Mushaben, 2017), uttered on 31 August, 2015, was her clarion call for national and international cooperation based upon each person's unique abilities. Admittedly, her presentation on that day did not include a full-fledged strategy of sociopolitical integration of refugees into society; nevertheless, her lapidary slogan encapsulates her aim to create a German "Willkommenskultur" ("a welcoming culture") (Hildebrandt & Ulrich, 2015). And, undoubtedly, her words had a positive effect on the influx of 400,000 or more refugees, many of whom were integrated into German society through training, vocational programs, and language courses within a year of their arrival (Spiegel, 2018). It can be assumed that Merkel's "We can make it!" was formulated with German society in mind, anticipating the need for self-direction and self-determination within a given scenario. Her rhetorical style also displayed her intuition that constituents have a capacity and a desire to regulate their own lives and that this self-organizing ability can be co-opted by government representatives, the resultant synergy being the representational force that integrates a people into a state.

Test

Merkel's approach was empathetic in that she understood her hearers' need for a positive and affirmative message. Nonetheless, she was strongly criticized by many politicians who felt that "We can make it!" did nothing to answer *how* we can make it or *who* can make it (Osnabrücker Zeitung, 2016). To judge by surveys from 2017 and 2018 (e.g., Die Welt, 2017; Süddeutsche Zeitung, 2018), Merkel's statement was mainly supported by her own party, while members of all the other parties felt that her "We can make it!" refugee policy was ineffectual (Die Welt, 2017). Merkel, far from appearing defensive, rather listened and acknowledged her critics and thus presented herself as forbearing and self-reflective in the post-2015 years in terms of her famous catchphrase and the refugee policy that accompanied it (Vorreiter, 2018).

Surviving COVID-19 Through Design Leadership

The COVID-19 crisis has evoked various responses in international leaders. According to Friedman (2020), Merkel's strategy is in the main scientific, while New Zealand's Prime Minister's approach, which is influenced by design leadership, is more empathetic. Merkel has been criticized continuously for not having a compassionate approach in communicating with the public about the COVID-19 restrictions (Oltermann, 2020). In terms of the d.school design thinking model, Merkel's scientific plan of action lacks the very first step, according to which it is necessary to *empathize* with the persons who will use or be otherwise effected by the proposed policy or action.

In March 2020, Merkel and the German health minister Spahn designed what they hoped was the best possible strategy for answering the pandemic. They sought to strike a balance between three related goals: (1) eliminating the COVID-19 virus, (2) caring for the health of each and every German, and (3) preventing German hospitals from becoming overburdened. She was criticized strongly for her pessimistic prediction that 70% of Germans would become infected by the virus. Thus, her formulation of the problem and its possible solution was couched in abstract, scientific terms (Martin, 2020). Her critics, consequently, might object that Merkel failed to synthesize findings into insights accessible to the average citizen, but rather catered more to the intelligentsia, a group to which Merkel herself belongs.

However, her televised speech to the German people on March 18 is evidence that Merkel has been effective in her response to the COVID-19 scare ("Germany excels," 2020; Miller, 2020; Thurau, 2020) and thus can stand as a counterweight to the naysaying she has endured. The remainder of this section will analyze this speech as a discourse specimen that fits well with the d.school model of design thinking's five stages:

Empathize

As we have said, the "empathize" aspect of d.school design theory has to do with open-ended dialogue that "can surprise both the designer and the subject by the unanticipated insights that are revealed" (Balcaitis, 2019). While Angela Merkel's televised COVID-19 speech was not interactive or dialogic in any obvious sense, her words did convey a strong sense that she had already conferred not only with scientific experts such as the RKI researchers but also with a number of ordinary citizens, as when she stated that the COVID-19 death toll and related statistics "are not just abstract numbers…but a father or grandfather, a mother or grandmother, a partner…" (Merkel, 2020).

Define

The "define" aspect of d.school design theory overlaps with the concept, common to many branches of the social sciences, of framing (Goffman, 1974; Weaver, 2007). Specifically, Merkel's televised speech places the COVID-19 crisis in the larger context of the global challenges Germany had faced during and after World War II. Besides her controversial reference to the Nazi era's historic challenges (Miller, 2020), Merkel also alludes to her experience as a young girl in East Germany ruled by the Stasi: "Let me assure you: For someone like me, for whom freedom of travel and movement was a hard-won right, such restrictions can only be justified as an absolute necessity" (Merkel, 2020). By casting a backward glance at the postwar era, Merkel makes a successful linkage between the fall of the Berlin Wall, which many have perceived to be more of an accomplishment of the German people than of government actors (Mills, 2008, p. 17), and the present viral foe, victory against which Merkel knows "takes all our efforts" (Merkel, 2020).

Ideate

The "ideate" piece of d.school design thought is reflected in Merkel's use of the theme of "democracy" in her COVID-19 speech. In the d.school model, to ideate is to make to leap from "identifying problems to creating solutions" (Balcaitis, 2019) by casting a wide net and calling for a wide participation in the solution-generating process. In Merkel's speech, she makes the lapidary statement: "We are a democracy" (Merkel, 2020), after which she stresses that individual German citizens will need to apply governmental recommendations about COVID-19 to their particular situation, thus bridging the gap between generalized directives and specific applications. In other words, Merkel's use of language makes tangible the need for collaboration and "filling in the blanks" in response to the virus specifically while also implying that this interactive style of problem-solving is the heart and soul of democracy in general.

Prototype

Design thinking theorists aver that trial-and-error efforts are often needed to reach a viable solution to any complex problem (Pressman, 2019, p. 33). Merkel's COVID-19 speech makes mention of "many creative forms" of safe interaction that the German people have developed more or less spontaneously, such as "grandchildren who are recording a podcast for their grandparents so they won't be lonely" or assistance "for the elderly who cannot go shopping for themselves" (Merkel, 2020). Here the German chancellor both acknowledges the self-generated, improvisational strategizing of her citizens and encourages more of the same going forward.

Test

Merkel ends her groundbreaking speech by framing the present moment in German history as a test case that depends upon each person's effort: "...[I]t will all depend...on how disciplined everyone [is]" (Merkel, 2020). Here Merkel ties together the disparate thematic strands of her discourse – dependence upon reason-driven experimentation, reliance on the historic strengths of the German people, and emphasis on the need for individual application of policies – in a manner that can be seen to reflect design thinking, since she follows the design thought plot in attempting to achieve a desired transformation by integrating interests in a transparent, collaborative process (Borja de Mozota, 2002, 2003).

Conclusion

This chapter interlinked design leadership and psychobiographical perspectives while expanding on previous research in both areas. It demonstrated how design leadership can contribute to political success through the power of the collective brain and human-centeredness.

The authors aimed at exploring Angela Merkel's life with regard to three selected events which were markers of her leadership decisions during her political career. These three markers provide insight into Merkel's design leadership approaches and show that Merkel follows a process of design leadership that generates innovation, creativity, and strategy while being social and solution focused. It provides evidence that Merkel's strength lies in following the processes of design thinking and applied design leadership particularly with regard to defining, analyzing, and ideating.

Future research should further explore design thinking and design leadership models in the context of the lives and careers of extraordinary individuals to substantiate the success of applying the processes in political contexts but also in other careers, such as business and entertainment.

Psychobiographical research should also open up towards theories in other fields than psychology and explore design and/or leadership theories to contribute also to disciplines other than psychology.

On a practical note, design thinking and leadership courses, consultants, trainers, and even organizations could use psychobiographical accounts of extraordinary leaders in their fields to present well-researched examples of how design leadership is being applied successfully on individual, organizational, and even global levels of problem-solving.

Finally, future research and practice also needs to explore the limitations of design thinking and leadership processes further to develop the theory, deepen its theoretical roots, and present refined and contextualized applied approaches.

Chapter Takeaways

- Design leadership is a strategic approach which supports solution-finding through a combined effort of creativity, innovation, and systemic thinking.
- An in-depth view into an extraordinary person's life can provide in-depth and detailed information on how to address complex challenges.
- The complex approaches of design thinking and design leadership can lead to complex solution-finding, tackling challenges across disciplines, cultures, and levels of society.

Reflection Questions

1. What are the underlying principles and values in design thinking and design leadership approaches?
2. How does the design leadership process through design thinking work? Explain the steps.
3. What is psychobiography, and how does it contribute to design thinking and design leadership research and practice?
4. How did design thinking and design leadership inform Merkel's bid to "become a chancellor of all Germans," to tackle the European refugee crisis, and to address the COVID-19 pandemic?
5. What are the best practices and lessons learned from this chapter?

References

Armitstead, L. & Govan, F. (2012). Europe needs creativity not billions of euros, says German Chancellor Angela Merkel. The telegraph, 12. November 2018. https://www.telegraph.co.uk/finance/financialcrisis/9239450/Europe-needs-creativity-not-billions-of-euros-says-German-Chancellor-Angela-Merkel.html

Balcaitis, R. (2019). *Design thinking models*. Stanford d.school. https://empathizeit.com/design-thinking-models-stanford-d-school/

Boland, R. J., & Collopy, F. L. (2004). Managing as designing. OAI.

Bollmann, R. (2013). *Die Deutsche. Angela Merkel und wir*. Klett-Cotta.

Borja de Mozota, B. (2002). Design and competitive edge: A model for design management excellence in European SMEs. *Design Management Journal Academic Review, 2*(1), 88–103.

Borja de Mozota, B. (2003). *Design management: Using design to build brand value and corporate innovation*. Allworth.

Brown, T. (2016). *The next big thing in design*. Retrieved 21 January 2016 from https://medium.com/ideo-stories/the-next-big-thing-in-design-513522543a6f#.h2lu74oan. Accessed April 24, 2020.

Cacioppe, R. (1998). An integrated model and approach for the design of effective leadership development programs. *Leadership & Organization Development Journal, 19*(1), 44–53.

Carrel, P. (2017). Burdened but unbowed, Merkel faces biggest test in tilt at fourth term. https://www.reuters.com/article/us-germany-merkel-test-analysisidUSKBN13F0YT

Clemens, C. (2006). From the outside in: Angela Merkel as opposition leader 2000-2005. *German Politics and Society, 24*(3), 41–81.

Creswell, J. W., & Plano Clark, V. L. (2011). *Designing and conducting mixed methods research* (2nd ed.). Sage Publications London.

Dempsey, J. (2011, February 6). Looking to Egypt's future, Merkel recalls her past. *New York Times*. https://www.nytimes.com/2011/02/06/world/europe/06merkel.html

Design Council (2021). Beyond Net Zero. A systemic design approach. London: Design Council.

Die Welt. (2017, September 1). Mehrheit der Deutschen sieht "Wir schaffen das" nicht erfüllt. *Die Welt*. https://www.welt.de/politik/deutschland/article168201110/Mehrheit-der-Deutschen-sieht-Merkels-Wir-schaffen-das-nicht-erfuellt.html

Dunne, D., & Martin, R. (2006). Design thinking and how it will change management education: An interview and discussion. *Academy of Management Learning & Education, 5*(4), 512–523.

Fouché, J. P., & Van Niekerk, R. (2010). Academic psycho-biography in South Africa: Past, present and future. *South Africa Journal of Psychology, 40*(4), 495–507. https://doi.org/10.1177/008124631004000410

Friedman, K. (2003). Theory construction in design research: Criteria, approaches, and methods. *Design Studies, 24*(6), 500–519.

Friedman, K. (2011). *Interdisciplinary research: The challenge*. https://www.academia.edu/3727725/Friedman._2013._The_Challenge_of_Interdisciplinary_Research. Accessed April 24, 2020.

Friedman, U. (2020, April 21). New Zealand's Prime Minister may be the most effective leader on the planat. *The Atlantic*. https://medium.com/the-atlantic/new-zealands-prime-minister-may-be-the-most-effective-leader-on-the-planet-b944c6403e01

"Germany excels". (2020, April 25). Germany excels among its European peers. *The Economist*. Retrieved from https://www.economist.com/europe/2020/04/25/germany-excels-among-its-european-peers

Gloppen, J. (2009). Perspectives on Design Leadership and Design Thinking and How They Relate to European Service Industries. dmi Design Management Journal. https://doi.org/10.1111/j.1942-5074.2009.00005.x. https://onlinelibrary.wiley.com/doi/epdf/10.1111/j.1942-5074.2009.00005.x

Goffman, E. (1974). *Frame analysis: An essay on the organization of experience*. Harvard University Press.

Goldhammer, A. (2018, November 2). The permanent becomes the ephemeral: Merkel steps back. *The American Prospect*. https://prospect.org/world/permanent-becomes-ephemeral-merkel-steps-back/

Hargadon, A. (2005). Leading with vision: The design of new Ventures. *Design Management Review*. Winter 2005.

Hassan, I., & Ghauri, P. N. (2014). *Evaluating companies for mergers and acquisitions. International Business and Management* (Vol. 40, pp. 75–89). Emerald Group Publishing Limited.

Helms, L., Van Esch, F., & Crawford, B. (2018). Merkel III: From committed pragmatist to "conviction leader"? *German Politics, 28*(3), 350–370.

Hildebrandt, T., & Ulrich, B. (2015, September 17). Im Auge des Orkans. *Die Zeit*, 38/2015. https://www.zeit.de/2015/38/angela-merkel-fluechtlinge-krisenkanzlerin

Himsworth, J. (2018). Why Design Thinking Should Also Serve As A Leadership Philosophy. Forbes, 19 July 2018. https://www.forbes.com/sites/forbesagencycouncil/2018/07/19/why-design-thinking-should-also-serve-as-a-leadership-philosophy/?sh=e77c8fd5a90f

Irbite, A., & Strode, A. (2016). Design thinking models in design research and education. *Society. Integration. Education. Proceedings of the International Scientific Conference*, IV, May 27th – 28th, 2016, 488–500.

Johansson-Sköldberg, U., Woodilla, J., & Cetinkaya, M. (2013). Design thinking: Past, present and possible futures. *Creativity and Innovation Management, 22*(2), 121–146.

Jozaisse, F. (2011). Design leadership: Current limits and future opportunities. In R. Cooper, S. Junginger, & T. Lockwood (Eds.), *The handbook of design management* (pp. 398–413). Berg.

Karnitschnig, M. (2018, June 28). How Merkel broke the EU. *Politico*. https://www.politico.eu/article/germany-broke-the-eu-migration-crisis-refugees/

Kelley, J. L. (2019). "I have to be all things to all people": Jim Jones, nurture failure, and apocalypticism. In C.-H. Mayer & Z. Kovary (Eds.), *New trends in psychobiography* (pp. 363–379). Springer. https://doi.org/10.1007/978-3-030-16953-4_20

Kelley, J. L. (2021). "If any man loveth not his father": Søren Kierkegaard's psychology of love. In C.-H. Mayer & E. Vanherheiden (Eds.), *International handbook of love: Transcultural and transdisciplinary perspectives*. Springer. 1047–1062.

Klormann, S., & Udelhoven, B. (2008). Der Imagewandel von Helmut Kohl, Gerhard Schröder und Angela Merkel. Vom Kanzlerkandidaten zum Kanzler – Ein Schauspiel in zwei Akten.

Inszenierung und Management von Machtwechseln in Deutschland 02/2008. *CAP Working Paper.* http://www.cap.lmu.de/download/2008/CAP-WP-2008-02.pdf
Koelbl, H. (1998). *Spuren der Macht. Die Verwandlung des Menschen durch das Amt. Eine Langzeitstudie*. Knesebeck.
Kottasová, I. (2020). How Angela Merkel went from lame duck to global leader on coronavirus. *CNN World.* https://www.cnn.com/2020/05/07/europe/angela-merkel-coronavirus-legacy-grm-intl/index.html
Langguth, G. (2005). *Angela Merkel: Aufstieg zur Macht.* DtV.
Lawson, B. (2006). *How designers think.* Architectural Press.
Lawson, B., & Dorst, K. (2009). *Design expertise*. Architectural Press.
Macias, A. (2017). *Angela Merkel's incredible rise from quantum chemist to the world's most powerful woman.* https://www.businessinsider.com/angela-merkel-biography?IR=T#e-brokered-a-massive-bailout-for-19-nations-12
Manu, A. (2007). *The imagination challenge. Strategic foresight and innovation in the global economy*. New Riders.
Martin, R. (2009). *The design of business*. Harvard Business Press.
Martin, G. (2020, March 12). Angela Merkel's Covid-19 plan: What travelers should know about coronavirus in Germany. *Forbes Life*. https://www.forbes.com/sites/guymartin/2020/03/12/germanys-chancellor-angela-merkel-lays-out-the-covid-19-plan-what-travelers-must-know-as-germanys-cases-spike/#3bddf821219d
Mayer, C.-H. (2017). *The life and creative works of Paulo Coelho: A psychobiography from a positive psychology perspective*. Springer.
Mayer, C.-H. (2021). Leading with faith: Angela Merkel in psychobiographical perspective. In: Po, E., Klipatrick, R., & Pratt, T. (eds.). Reimagining Faith and Management: The Impact of Faith in the Workplace (pp. 32–46). New York: Routledge.
Mayer, C.-H., & Fouché, J. P. (2021). Lessons Learned From Baruch Spinoza: Shame And Faith Development In The Light Of Challenges In Contemporary Society. In C.-H. Mayer & E. Vanderheiden (Eds.), Shame 4.0 (xx–xx). Cham: Springer.
Mayer, C.-H., & Kovary, Z. (2019). *New trends in psychobiography*. Springer.
Mayer, C.-H., & van Niekerk, R. (2020). Creative minds of leaders in psychobiographical perspectives: Exploring the life and work of Christian Barnard and Angela Merkel. In S. Dhiman & J. Marquis (Eds.), *New horizons in positive leadership and change* (pp. 189–205). Springer.
Mayer, C.-H., van Niekerk, R., & Fouché, P. J. P. (2020). Holistic wellness in the life of Angela Merkel: A call to revise the wheel of wellness in the light of new positive psychology movements and socio-cultural changes. *International Review of Psychiatry, 32*(7–8), 625–637.
Meinel, C., & Leifer, L. (2011). Design thinking research. In J. Plattner, C. Meinel, & L. Leifer (Eds.), *Design thinking. Understand – improve – apply* (pp. xiii–xxi). Berlin: Spring.
Merkel, A. (2020). Germany excels among its European peers. https://www.economist.com/europe/2020/04/25/germany-excels-among-its-european-peers
Miller, S. (2020, April 20). The secret to Germany's COVID-19 success: Angela Merkel is a scientist. *The Atlantic*. https://www.theatlantic.com/international/archive/2020/04/angela-merkel-germany-coronavirus-pandemic/610225/
Mills, C. W. (2008). *Angela Merkel.* Chelsea House.
Moore, S. (2017, May 29). Angela Merkel shows how the leader of the free world should act. *The Guardian.* https://www.theguardian.com/commentisfree/2017/may/29/angela-merkel-leader-free-world-donald-trump
Mück, K. (2017). "Wir schaffen das!" Hat die Persönlichkeit Angela Merkels Einfluss auf ihre Flüchtlingspolitik? In X. Gu & H. Ohnesorge (Eds.), *Politische Persönlichkeiten und ihre weltpolitische Gestaltung* (pp. 245–273). Springer VS.
Muller, N. (2017). *Angela Merkel wins Finland gender equality prize.* https://www.dw.com/en/angela-merkel-wins-finland-gender-equality-prize/a-41804063
Mushaben, J. M. (2017). Wir schaffen das! Angela Merkel and the European refugee crisis. *German Politics, 26*(4), 516–533.

Oltermann, P. (2020, April 16). *Angela Merkel draws on science background in Covid-19 explainer*. https://www.theguardian.com/world/2020/apr/16/angela-merkel-draws-on-science-background-in-covid-19-explainer-lockdown-exit

Osnabrücker Zeitung. (2016, August 28). *Integration der Flüchtlinge: Gabriel schlägt Krach*. https://www.noz.de/deutschland-welt/politik/artikel/765872/integration-der-fluechtlinge-gabriel-schlaegt-krach-1

Ponterotto, J. G. (2014). Best practices in psychobiographical research. *Qualitative Psychology, 1*(1), 77–90. https://doi.org/10.1037/qup0000005

Ponterotto, J. G., Reynolds, T., & Choi, J. D. (2017). Ethical and legal considerations in psychobiography. *American Psychologist, 72*(5), 446–458. https://doi.org/10.1037/amp0000047

Pourdehnad, J., Wexler, E. R., & Wilson, D. V. (2011). *Systems and design thinking: A conceptual framework for their integration*. http://repository.upenn.edu/cgi/viewcontent.cgi?article=1009&context=od_working_papers. Accessed April 24, 2020.

Pressman, A. (2019). *Design thinking: A guide to creative problem solving for everyone*. Routledge.

Schley, N. (2005). *Angela Merkel – Deutschlands Zukunft ist weiblich*. Knaur Taschenbuch Verlag.

Schultz, W. T. (Ed.). (2005). *Handbook of psychobiography*. Oxford: Oxford University Press.

Shaheen, M., & Pradhan, S. (2019). Sampling in qualitative research. In *Qualitative techniques for workplace data analysis* (pp. 25–51). IGI Global.

Singapore Polytechnic. (2016). *SP's design thinking framework*. http://ejuz.lv/7f3. Accessed April 24, 2020.

Spiegel. (2005). Ich will Kanzlerin aller Deutschen werden. *Der Spiegel, 30*(4). https://www.spiegel.de/politik/ich-will-kanzlerin-aller-deutschen-werden-a-5312ede2-0002-0001-0000-000041179077?context=issue

Spiegel. (2018, December 14). *Die Integration der Flüchtlinge läuft besser als erwartet*. https://www.spiegel.de/wirtschaft/unternehmen/fluechtlinge-die-integration-laeuft-besser-als-erwartet-a-1243659.html

Stanford University, Design Institute. (2016). *The design thinking process*. http://dschool.stanford.edu/our-point-of-view/#design-thinking. Accessed April 24, 2020.

Stock, W. (2000). *Angela Merkel – Eine politische Biographie*. Olzog.

Süddeutsche Zeitung. (2018, August 31). *Ihr Fazit zu drei Jahren "Wir schaffen das"*. https://www.sueddeutsche.de/politik/leserdiskussion-ihr-fazit-zu-drei-jahren-wir-schaffen-das-1.4111684

Terre Blanche, M., Durrheim, K., & Kelly, K. (2006). First steps in qualitative data analysis. In M. Terre Blanche, K. Durrheim, & D. Painter (Eds.), *Research in practice applied methods for the social sciences* (pp. 321–344). University of Cape Town Press.

Thurau, J. (2020, April 4). Opinion: Germans rally behind Merkel amid coronavirus crisis. *DW*. https://www.dw.com/en/opinion-germans-rally-behind-merkel-amid-coronavirus-crisis/a-53014974

Vorreiter, P. (2018, March 21). *Deutschland kann es schaffen*. https://www.deutschlandfunk.de/merkels-regierungserklaerung-deutschland-kann-es-schaffen.1783.de.html?dram:article_id=413650

Weaver, D. H. (2007). Thoughts on agenda setting, framing, and priming. *Journal of Communication, 57*, 142–147. https://doi.org/10.1111/j.1460-2466.2006.00333.x

Chapter 22
The FuturePerfect Organization: *Driven by Quantum-Thinking*

William Guillory

Abstract A FuturePerfect organization is comprised of leadership that anticipates to future business paradigms with a high degree of accuracy. The ability to accurately anticipate future business paradigms is called quantum-thinking. We are in initial stage of transitioning from the paradigm of human potential to technology integration. This ability applies equally to predicting future shifts in cultural and societal paradigms. At present, the possibility is a societal/global transformation from a survival-driven consciousness to compatibility. In this chapter, we discuss the model of a FuturePerfect organization for the twenty-first century, including the steps required to successfully implement this transition.

Keywords A FuturePerfect organization · Quantum-thinking · Technology integration · Cultural compatibility · Sleep-state consciousness exploration

Introduction

A FuturePerfect Organization is comprised of leadership that anticipates future business paradigms with a high degree of accuracy. The ability to accurately anticipate future business paradigms is called quantum-thinking. For example, it is clear to everyone, at this point, that we are in the stage of transitioning from the paradigm of human potential to technology integration. This ability applies equally to predicting future shifts in cultural and societal paradigms. At present, the possibility is a societal/global transformation from a survival-driven consciousness to compatibility. As a species, we have not yet decided to proactively engage such a transformation, although it is the natural evolution of a human species corresponding to a FuturePerfect global society. The model which illustrates these futuristic transitions, in practice, is shown by Fig. 22.1.

W. Guillory (✉)
Innovations International, Salt Lake City, UT, USA
e-mail: bill.guillory@innovint.com

J. Marques (ed.), *Innovative Leadership in Times of Compelling Changes*, Management, Change, Strategy and Positive Leadership, https://doi.org/10.1007/978-3-030-67258-4_22

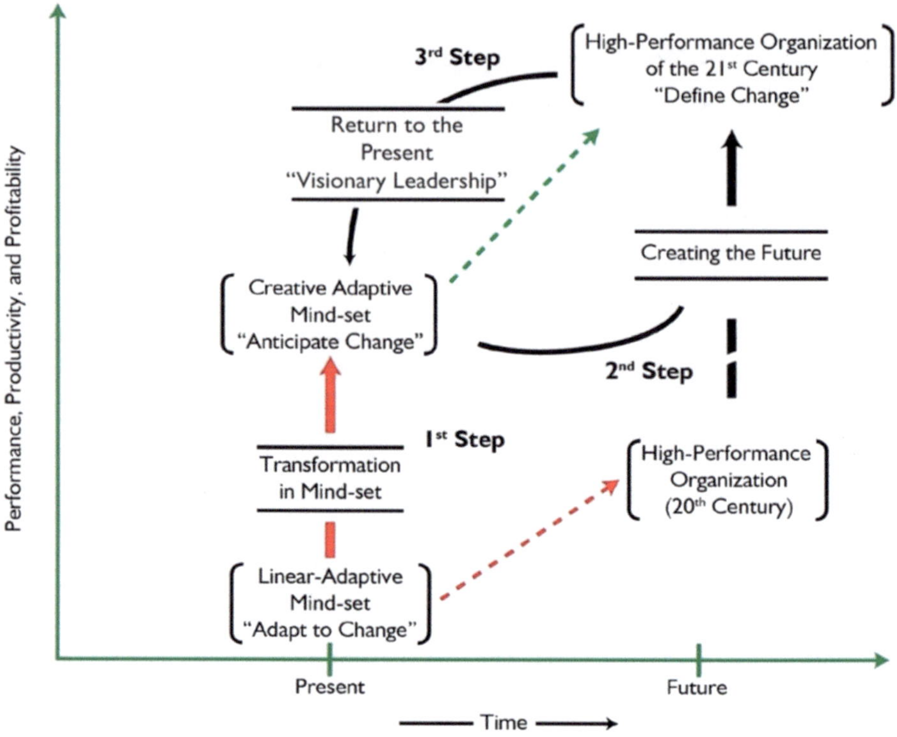

Fig. 22.1 Model of a FuturePerfect organization for the twenty-first century

This model has three steps in terms of implementation:

Step 1 The first step involves *personal transformation* from a *linear-adaptive* to a *creative-adaptive* mindset (or way of thinking). Creative adaptation is the ability to proactively embrace an expansion in consciousness in *anticipation* of change, irrespective of rate, dimension, or form. It is a response that molds change, rather than react to it.

Step 2 The second step is creating the *FuturePerfect* way of operating: principles, practices, and behaviors corresponding to the next high-performance organization of the early twenty-first century. High performance is used in a generic sense and "organically" changes with continuous technology integration and enhancement of human potential – both naturally and artificially. This step defines the future mode of operation – both human and machine. In essence, it is inclusive of the contribution of human cyborgs, through artificial enhancement and androids, through artificial intelligence (AI).

Step 3 The third step is returning to the present and mentally projecting one's self into that future way of functioning as though the future existed today. This step is represented by the dotted line from the present creative adaptative state to the futuristic high-performance state. In essence, FuturePerfect leaders literally "pull" their workforce into the future, rather than sequentially "pushing" them forward in a stepwise fashion. The essence of such leadership is leading by example and inspiring others to follow.

Let us begin our journey by an in-depth understanding of each of these steps and explore the role of quantum-thinking as a driving force.

Step One: Transformation in Mindset

Know thyself. – Temple of Apollo at Delphi

As stated above, transitioning from a linear-adaptative to a creative-adaptative mindset provides a greater potential of achieving quantum-thinking or paradigm creation. In essence it creates a "more flexible platform" in consciousness to explore one's expanded creative consciousness. A metaphoric example would be using the moon as a launching platform for interstellar exploration instead of planet Earth, since Earth is six times greater in gravitational attraction and therefore more "restraining" in terms of escape for exploration. This factor is indicative of how much easier it is to launch larger payloads from the moon and, by comparison, human exploration of expanded states of consciousness.

In a similar manner, the process of acquiring the five cognitive skills listed below dramatically increases the potential of an individual to explore and perform at an extraordinary level of creativity, innovation, and imagination. The process is the essence of transformation from a linear-adaptative mindset to creative-adaptative, resulting in an expanded consciousness of potential.

The question which naturally follows is, "what are the five skills necessary for being creative-adaptive?"

Individual/Team Exercise

Let us take a moment to determine how creative-adaptive you are using the self-evaluation shown below. Select and enter your score on a scale of 0–10 for each statement. (Please select only even numbers in your self-evaluation.)

Creative Adaptation: A Self Evaluation

1. ***Visionary/insightful*** – the ability to envision futuristic ways of thinking, organizing, and operating. Least (0) 2 4 6 8 Highly (10) Score______.
2. ***Risk-taking*** – the ability to take measured and challenging "*risks*" where there is a significant degree of uncertainty of success. Least (0) 2 4 6 8 Highly (10) Score______.
3. ***Open-mindedness*** – the ability to be open and receptive to "divergently different" ideas, opinions, and radically different ways of operating that challenge one's way of thinking. Least (0) 2 4 6 8 Highly (10) Score_______.
4. ***Creative*** – the ability to explore possibilities beyond one's present reality. Least (0) 2 4 6 8 Highly (10) Score______.
5. ***Wisdom*** – a *state of being* highly receptive to insights through personal transformation and consciousness exploration. Least (0) 2 4 6 8 Highly (10) Score______.

Total score (X 2) ________.

Sum your scores and multiply by two to convert to a 100% scale.
Evaluate yourself as follows:

Excellent (A role model for creative adaptation)

Average (Open to master the skills of creative adaptation)

Fair (Reluctant to change your way of thinking, particularly, if the present works)

Quick Debrief: Reflect on the three questions below, and revisit this self-evaluation when you complete the reading of this publication and others, similar in content.

1. How would you evaluate yourself according the descriptions of creative adaptation above? Why?
2. What skill challenged you most in terms of your self-evaluation? Why?
3. What skill do you find most personally necessary for adapting to the future? Why?

State of Mind of a Creative-Adaptive

Given the characteristics proposed above for a creative-adaptive individual, let us explore their way of thinking as applied to working situations. The natural assumption is that one's programmed way of thinking – both conscious and unconscious – is the direct determinant of one's behavior. However, it is, more importantly, the determinant of the results produced, *as a pattern*, in one's life. These statements are captured by the Innovations' state of mind diagram shown as Fig. 22.2.

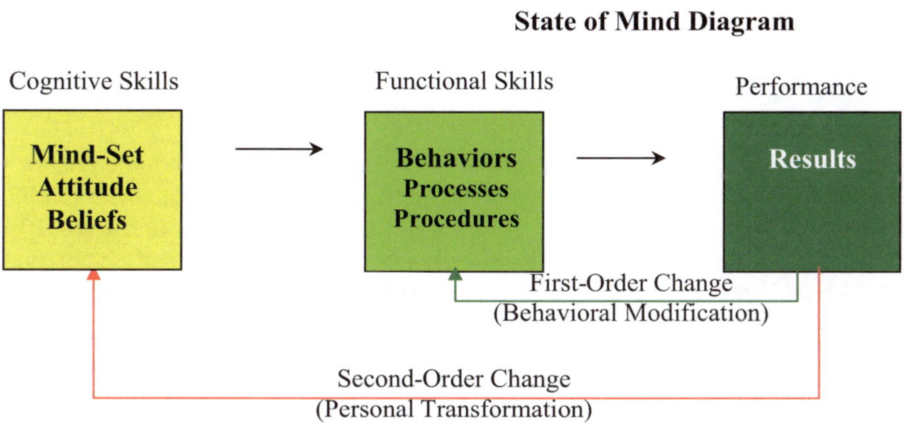

Fig. 22.2 The sequential process and skills of the state of mind diagram

State of Mind Diagram

Collectively, they reflect the practiced behaviors and results of an organization's internal operations. They are the culture, in practice. Let us take a look at a few examples and notice whether we experience them as realistic, effective, and/or "capable of serving as our launching pad from the moon."

1. "Pursuit of perfection"; "zero-defect thinking." Therefore, our products and services are synonymous with this mindset of quality. "We rarely make mistakes; and correct them ourselves."
2. How we function internally is a direct measure (reflection) of how we interact externally with customers, clients, and those we serve. "Honesty, openness, and authenticity prevail in our working relationships."
3. We have an expectation of self-motivated, continuous learning which creates an employee-engaged culture that, in turn, creates customer engagement. *Therefore, our customers become an extension of our sales force (through word of mouth and referrals)!*
4. Every customer we serve is a "moment of truth," those moments in disguise that provide the opportunity to exceed a customer's expectation (Jan Carlzon, former CEO of SAS). *Every employee* ***touches*** *the customer and/or our product/service in some way and is therefore a member of our sales and marketing team.*
5. Branding is based upon living true to practicing what we preach, in terms of our core values: the quality of our products and services and delivery modes. *Confirmed by new and return customers.*

The *interpersonal glue* which holds these principles together to create the reality of the branding advertised is 100% personal responsibility and accountability, continuously improved open and honest relationship and communication, and creative exploration of new products and services and delivery systems.

Step Two: Creating the FuturePerfect Organization

Technology Integration

We are about to launch from the moon into interstellar space – from the creative-adaptive platform into the "Blue Nowhere" (Jeffrey Deaver's concept of the infinite, unexplored dark web). However, we do have, as objectives, two destinations in mind. One is to gain insight into the next business paradigm in the early 2020s and possibly beyond. Two is insight into the corresponding principles, practices, and culture of high performance corresponding to that paradigm.

At Innovations, we began this voyage several years ago. In step one, personal transformation was required to become creative-adaptive. In this stage of the voyage into one's creative consciousness, we require preparation in terms of *quantum-thinking*. In the most general sense, *quantum-thinking is simply the ability to explore consciousness. Consciousness is the potential for discovery and expression – as defined by the explorer.* For our present exploration, we define quantum-thinking as the ability to *envision* future business paradigms[1] and their corresponding business form of operation. As a result of our exploration, we, among others, defined the next business paradigm as technology integration – which began on the leading tail during 2019, as shown in Fig. 22.3.

Technology integration is the comprehensive application of information technology to enhance the acquisition of learning in terms of:

- Knowledge (the experiential synthesis of information)
- Wisdom (an expanded way of being and including)
- Performance as creating futuristic vistas between man and machine

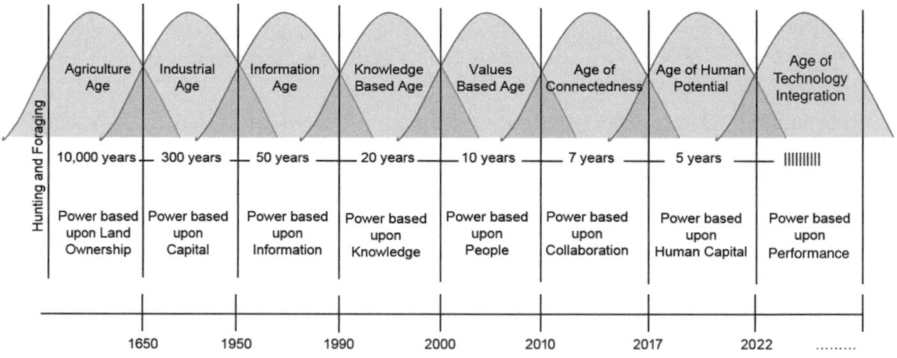

Fig. 22.3 The succession of societal and business paradigms

[1] *A paradigm* is a system of principles (mostly unspoken and unwritten) which govern the thinking, practices, and behaviors of a group or society.

as well as the simultaneous creation of new products and services which measurably improve efficiency of operations and quality of life. The succession of business paradigms subsequent to hunting and foraging is shown as Fig. 22.3.

Global Societal and Business Paradigms

The Requirements for Quantum-Thinking

The six competencies that must be learned in order to fully practice quantum-thinking are the following:

1. *Personal mastery* – the ability to freely explore higher-order (expanded) possibilities (futuristic concepts) beyond one's present reality
2. *Mastery of context* – the ability to envision a future context from the least amount of data and information (fragment parts)
3. *Context integration* – the ability to integrate information (content) of different contexts into one higher-order (expanded) context
4. *Creative synthesis* – the ability to transform information (fragments parts) into new knowledge
5. *Intuition* – the ability to receive "out-of-context" insights without rational thinking
6. *Hyper-accelerated information processing* – the ability of the mind to acquire, process, and integrate information at hyper-accelerated speeds

In general, it is unusual for a single individual to have mastery of all six skills. Therefore, future-paradigm exploration is most commonly implemented as a team exercise, with each member having mastery of one or more of the above competencies.

For example, if an individual has acquired *personal mastery*, *mastery of context*, and *creative synthesis*, she, he, or they is a valued member of such a team and is probably a polymath, a multitalented individual who is highly skilled in several disciplines – for example, art, science, and music. This is the process employed by the Innovations Exploratory Team in defining the principles, competencies, and corresponding behaviors for the engagement initiative – as described below.

Sleep-State Programming and Consciousness Exploration

One of the most effective means of exploring future-state paradigms is sleep-state programming. An individual who is adept at lucid dreaming and sleep-state exploration can also program the direction such an exploration might take, simply by requesting an objective or a goal of the exploration. The request may require several sleep-state attempts before a *connection* is made and a transmission is received. Since such transmissions are not communicated in words or language, a response is commonly symbolic, like a dream. The symbology must be translated into a meaningful response by the individual making the sleep-state request.

This was the process our team at Innovations used in suggesting the last and presently emerging paradigms as shown in Fig. 22.3: the age of human potential, driven by human capital and the age of technology integration, driven by performance, in accordance with the predictions of others. For example, when a previous sleep-state request for the "next-generation exceptional performance system" was made prior to 2017, the sleep-state response was a series of dreams of holograms with elementary symbology attached. The translated messages were as follows:

- Provide greater freedom.
- Enhanced performance.
- Transformation in thinking.
- Assistance from technology and learning.
- Open system of relationships and communication.
- Become an astronaut of inner space.
- *Create your reality. Create your reality. Create.*

Using these phrases as guidelines along with a series of intense brainstorming sessions involving millennial feedback data from Innovations surveys, we eventually created our high-performance program with the following engagement principles.

1. *Empowerment* – the capacity to perform, inclusive of one's present and potential capability
2. *Democracy* – the proactive involvement of employees in the organization's operation
3. *Transparency* – an open, honest, and shared system of communication
4. *Innovation* – the creation of cutting-edge processes, products, and services that *anticipate* the expectations of customers
5. *Inclusion* – an employee-supportive workplace environment where equitable opportunity exists for everyone's success

The Emerging High-Performance Paradigm: Engagement in a Virtual World

Using the engagement principles and a series of sleep-state transmissions as a base for projection, we recently repeated the process for the emerging age of technology integration – aided by the impact of the COVID-19 pandemic. The descriptions we derived are the following, corresponding to *engagement in a virtual world*:

1. *Polymath* – Multiskilled and talented, high-performing individual
2. *IT proficient* – Technology integration, as a natural way of life
3. *Self-management* – Self-directed learning, growing, and organizing
4. *Mastery of cognitive and functional skills* – Relate and communicate with sensitivity, understanding, and respect
5. *Creativity, innovation, and exploration* – The courage to live on the edge of your full potential.
6. *Compatibility* – To live in harmony and respect with other human beings, animals and plants, and the environment which supports our existence.

These competencies of the emerging engagement in a virtual world performance paradigm will be discussed below.

Polymath

The technical definition of a polymath is a person of wide-ranging knowledge or learning, an individual who has great depth of knowledge in one or more areas and a broad range of expertise in other disciplines that can be used in making enlightened decisions – similar to our quantum-thinkers. The most critical characteristic is an individual who strives to acquire greater knowledge and wisdom. A key function is *critical thinking* which draws upon a variety of information and knowledge to think holistically.

IT Proficient

This description is fairly obvious. But again, the objective here is to view their talents holistically, particularly where applications are concerned, rather than mechanically. Associated with this proficiency, there are competencies that are absolute necessities. However, more often than not, a project may involve a variety of IT steps, some of which we are proficient and some we are not, but the basic IT skills are always second nature.

Self-Management

A decided shift has already begun in terms of the role of an employee (or individual) in acquiring self-management skills. These skills are comprised of both personal and professional necessities for successfully operating independently. Regardless of what the future holds in terms of populous and independent workspaces, there is an increasing necessity for greater personal responsibility and accountability. These self-management skills begin with self-reliance in terms of resiliency, self-discipline, and self-directed organization, growth, and planning.

Mastery of Cognitive and Functional Skills

Although we are never formally taught these skills as a requirement in our educational systems, how to compatibility get along with others will also be a requirement – without the ready assistance of a manager. Cognitive skills are the mindset we consciously and unconsciously *bring* to every interpersonal transaction we have – as a predisposition – whether the transaction is personal or digital. Cognitive skills include awareness, sensitivity, understanding, respect, dedication, commitment, and responsibility and accountability. These predispositions are *communicated* to others, no matter the form of a transaction. They also include the full range of prejudices, biases, and ethnocentric attitudes we possess.

Functional skills include a full range of behaviors, processes, procedures, and practices consistent with our cognitive mindset. These include skills related to diversity, inclusion, teaming, coaching and mentoring, and managing. I describe them as functional because they go beyond behaviors and involve the ways we uniquely organize, plan, design, coach, and manage others.

Creativity, Innovation, and Exploration

Creativity and innovation refer to the creativity and innovation processes we use on a daily basis. They also extend to extraordinary problem-solving on an occasional basis such as the invention of the transistor. Even more occasional is the expansion to include vision and imagination. At this point, a decided shift occurs in expanded exploration to quantum-thinking and paradigm exploration. The extent to which these skills are used is a function of one's job responsibilities. They also involve Pablo Picasso's famous quote in terms of the consequences of unlimited exploration:

> The act of creation is simultaneously the act of destruction.

I interpret this quote to mean, as we explore, fearlessly, beyond our present reality, we naturally encounter a self-imposed limitation based upon a self-limiting belief about ourselves. The willingness to persevere beyond this limitation results in a significantly expanded sphere of consciousness. The individual who achieves this "rite of passage" is now free to explore his, her, or their creative-consciousness, limited only by exploration *beyond* that achieved!

Compatibility: The Next Cultural Paradigm

Compatibility is a workplace environment where:

- Differences in ideas are viewed as the *creative tension* necessary to achieve exceptional performance
- Employees *experience* a culture of human equality
- The focus is on *customer success* and *exceptional performance*
- The culture is *organically flexible* to integrate both rapidly evolving technology and the values of younger generations.

Creative tension is defined as situations where differences in ideas are viewed as opportunities for new, breakthrough possibilities in *synergism*, *synchronicity*, and *quantum-thinking*. It is most important to emphasize that compatibility evolves from and builds upon inclusion. Therefore, it must be comprehensively *embedded* into every aspect of organizational functioning: such as recruitment, development, succession planning, visible opportunities, leadership, mission, vision, and the well-being and success of all employees.

In order to maximize performance, it is necessary to ensure a *culture of equality* by comprehensive measurements of numerical placements *and* a serious cultural survey. Human equality (mindset) is very different from equitable opportunity or equity (procedure), as shown in the state of mind diagram on page 4. The former is a *way of being* and the latter is a *way of doing*. Therefore, simply changing policy and procedure will not necessarily "transform a culture" at any credible rate, except *possibly* in an inevitable evolutionary way, over time.

Human equality is a state of being equal in terms of one's personhood. It begins with a personal realization, by an individual, that equality cannot be:

- Realized through a written document
- Made reality through the acknowledgement of others
- Earned through opportunity, accomplishments, awards, etc.

That human equality is a birthright.

The realization of one's equality, from within, is made a functional reality through a "rite of passage," from a state of believing to a state of being. This rite of passage involves a non-victimized state of mind and corresponding behaviors which are constructive and empowering in one's behalf.

The other two factors, discussed above, critical to exceptional performance, are *synergism* and *synchronicity*. Synergism is the interaction among two or more individuals or situations which produces a combined effect greater than the sum of their individual contributions. Examples include the influence a charismatic leader and leadership team can have on an organization's performance and how the resolution of racial inequality can positively influence the elimination of other forms in inequality, such as sexism and ethnocentrism. In essence, the result of creative tension situation is an example of 1 + 1 = 3 or more.

Synchronicity is the simultaneous occurrence of events which appear to be significantly related, often after the fact, but have no discernable causal relationship. Carl Jung coined this concept and stated, "Everything that irritates and excites us about someone else reveals a greater understanding about ourselves." Additional examples include meeting someone for the first time, having a conversation, experiencing a spiritual connection, and concluding the meeting was not an accident. A final example is the fact that the theory of evolution was simultaneously and separately published by Charles Darwin *and* Alfred Russel Wallace.

These phenomena as well as higher-order thinking become commonplace when compatibility is embedded into an organization's culture.

The transformation from inclusion to compatibility involves the integration of the following principles of operation into the organizational culture: collaboration, reconciliation, receptiveness, resilience, and cohesiveness. As outlined above, it is based upon the three-step process for achieving compatibility: education and training, measurement and planning, and implementation and cultural transformation.

A culture of compatibility is characterized by the following principles:

1. *Collaboration* – working with others in a mutually respectful, trusting, open, and supportive way
2. *Reconciliation* – working with others to amicably resolve and synergize differences
3. *Receptiveness* – working with others with openness, transparency, and the creative exchange of ideas.
4. *Resilience* – working with others to proactively respond to conflict, adversity, and change as learning experiences
5. *Cohesiveness* – working with others as a connected, united, whole of one.

The overall intention of this initiative is to create an interactive employee collaborative learning environment designed to improve morale, learning, customer service, and organizational success.

Step Three: Leading from the Future

Let us refine our focus even further, by exploring, *in practice*, what is meant by *leading from the future*. This step is straightforward, yet initially most challenging – returning to the present and "skillfully" organizing, managing, and behaving as though the future state exists *in the present*. Specifically, projecting our mindset into the future state according the dotted trajectory from the creative-adaptive to the twenty-first century high performance, FuturePerfect state – *engagement in a virtual world* (Fig. 22.1).

The principles and skills of leadership corresponding to the *FuturePerfect state* have been summarized in the previous section (pages 8 through 12). Challenges which may be encountered when "leading from the future" are summarized below.

Polymath

Challenged by operating at the edge of one's capability requires *invalidating long-standing, self-imposed limitations* – reasons, excuses, and a lack of responsibility – through personal transformation.

IT Proficient

Challenged by *discomfort with new technology and software* advances accelerating and becoming more complex leads to increased anxiety, stress, and loss of productivity, if not confronted and resolved.

Self-Management

Challenged by the necessity of *mastering self-directed organizational skills* previously overseen and coached by an in-house manager. Critical skills include resiliency, self-discipline, and self-motivated learning.

Mastery of Cognitive and Functional Skills

Challenged by the continuous *personal growth* necessary to master those skills which are critical to amicably working with others – whether in person or digitally. No choice!

Creativity, Innovation, and Exploration

Challenged by how an individual's *reality will be changed, transformed, and more inclusive* as a result of in-depth personal exploration.

Compatibility

Challenged by the necessity to *disengage the superior/inferior dyad illusion* and transform to a consciousness (mindset) of human equality – for both individuals.

Quick Exercise: Take a moment to consider which of these six principles and skills you would have the greatest difficulty adopting, mastering, and managing in yourself and others. Why?

The final piece of the puzzle is the leadership context I propose which encompasses the principles and corresponding skills for *engagement in a virtual world.*

The FuturePerfect Leadership Paradigm of the 2020s

1. ***Leadership*** is the *earned privilege* of executing the guidelines for the achievement of a challenging mission, vision, or goal.
2. ***Leadership*** is the *willingness* to establish a bond of respect and trust with those who have granted permission to be led.
3. ***Leadership*** is *ensuring* that your goal or objective is compelling, challenging, and capable of overcoming any inevitable crisis of greatest difficulty.
4. ***Leadership*** is establishing and ensuring the practice of a *code of ethics and conduct* based upon human dignity, respect, and equality.
5. ***Leadership*** is establishing "holistic learning and development of people and performance" – within the *infrastructure* of the organization.
6. ***Leadership*** is establishing and ensuring a *culture of exceptional performance* based upon 100% responsibility and 100% accountability, by example.
7. ***Leadership*** is feeding your troops first and then eating what is left.

Chapter Takeaways

Step one is really a "rite of passage." It is initiated by the question:

> With respect to change, what unique barrier would I have to personally master to become (exceptionally) creative-adaptive?

Step two calls upon our creative and intuitive abilities of quantum and insight thinking. It raises the .question:

> What are the major elements of the future business system corresponding to high-performance in the 2020s?

Step three challenges our courage to "boldly go into that future state in the present."

> Mentally and behaviorally, project ourselves into the future designed by step two and lead as though the future existed today.

These three steps provide a powerful prescription for "effectively implementing" a FuturePerfect organization and society.

Reflection Questions

1. Do you feel our present system of democracy, driven by capitalism, *in practice*, serves the best interest of *all* Americans? Think of yourself and others.
2. Do you feel that everyone *deserves* food, shelter, and clothing by virtue of being human? Think of your personal and religious morals.
3. Do you believe that a continued focus technology development will solve most, if not all, of our major problems? Consider whether humans are expendable.
4. Do you believe that we should rethink how we presently function? If so, what is the major condition you feel needs to be addressed? Beyond your personal interests.
5. Do you feel we need a global crisis (exceeding COVID-19), as humans, to seriously alter our course? What is the one condition that would make us pay attention during a global crisis?

Index

J. Marques (ed.), *Innovative Leadership in Times of Compelling Changes*, Management, Change, Strategy and Positive Leadership, https://doi.org/10.1007/978-3-030-67258-4

K

L

GPSR Compliance

The European Union's (EU) General Product Safety Regulation (GPSR) is a set of rules that requires consumer products to be safe and our obligations to ensure this.

If you have any concerns about our products, you can contact us on ProductSafety@springernature.com

In case Publisher is established outside the EU, the EU authorized representative is:

Springer Nature Customer Service Center GmbH
Europaplatz 3
69115 Heidelberg, Germany

Batch number: 10777424

Printed by Printforce, the Netherlands